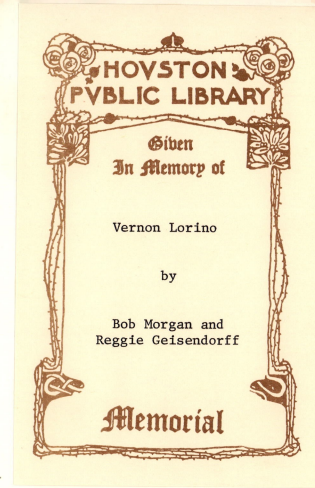

CERVANTES, ARISTOTLE, AND THE *PERSILES*

Cervantes Aristotle and the *Persiles*

ALBAN K. FORCIONE

PRINCETON, NEW JERSEY

PRINCETON UNIVERSITY PRESS

1970

Publication of this book has been aided by
The Research Committee of Princeton University

This book has been set in Linotype Granjon
Printed in the United States of America
by Princeton University Press, Princeton, New Jersey

For my mother and father

Preface

This book is a revised version of my doctoral dissertation. I have provided English translations for all quotations in foreign languages (except those in the footnotes). I have used the Ormsby and the Cohen translations of the *Quixote*, N. Macoll's translation of the *Exemplary Novels*, H. Oelsner and A. B. Wellford's translation of the *Galatea*, and L. D. Stanley's translation of the *Persiles*, modifying occasionally in order to bring out the sense of the Spanish necessary to my argument. Translations of all other works cited are my own unless otherwise indicated.

I wish to express my thanks to Professor Vicente Llorens and to Professor Raymond S. Willis, both of whom offered me guidance, criticism, and encouragement, and generously shared their broad knowledge of Cervantes studies with me; both have profoundly influenced my ideas.

I am grateful to those who have read the completed manuscript and offered helpful criticisms and valuable suggestions for revisions: Professors Juan Bautista Avalle-Arce, Robert Hollander, Elias L. Rivers, and Ira Wade.

I am also grateful to my teachers and colleagues at Princeton University who followed my work with interest and were always willing to help me with particular problems: the late Professor E.B.O. Borgerhoff and Professors Blanchard Bates, Claudio Guillén, A. Bartlett Giamatti, John Hughes, James Irby, Enrique Tierno Galván, and Karl Uitti.

Professors Pietro Aragno, John Cameron, Paolo Cucchi, and Helmut Dreitzel kindly offered me advice and assistance in the translation of Renaissance texts. Polly Hanford has been a resourceful and helpful editor. Evan Kimble has been a stimulating critic. My wife has been a charming assistant. To each of them go my thanks.

My greatest debt of all is to Professor Edmund L. King, who introduced me to Spanish culture several years ago and has accompanied me as teacher and friend through my undergraduate and graduate studies. He has helped me with this book in every possible way—with advice concerning editorial difficulties and problems of translation, with illuminating criticisms of its major argument, and with constant encouragement.

Finally, I wish to thank the Research Committee of Princeton University for a grant which made possible the publication of this book.

A. K. F.

Princeton, New Jersey

Contents

Contents

CERVANTES, ARISTOTLE, AND THE *PERSILES*

Introduction

A NY STUDENT of Cervantes' literary production must at some point take into account the theories which inspired the plan and creation of *Los Trabajos de Persiles y Sigismunda*, for of all Cervantes' works, the *Persiles* is the one most directly related to the author's awareness of literary theory. In conceiving his epic in prose, Cervantes was attempting to solve the basic aesthetic problems preoccupying contemporary theorists and to create a masterpiece according to their envisioned ideal of the highest literary genre, the epic. William Atkinson has written that Cervantes' "discovery of Aristotle, even at second or third hand, with the revelation that literature had its own body of precept, its rules, was the great aesthetic experience of his life."[1] Whatever the artistic merits of the *Persiles* may be, the work represents Cervantes' tribute to the classical aesthetic which his age had erected on the double foundation of Horace's *Ars Poetica* and Aristotle's *Poetics*.

I propose to trace the evolution of the literary problems associated with the romances of chivalry, the emergence of the theoretical pressures centering on the re-creation of the classical epic, and the development of the critical evaluation of Heliodorus' *Ethiopian History* in the sixteenth century. In doing so, I hope both to situate the *Persiles* in its historical literary circumstances and to reply to the surviving judgment of Menéndez Pelayo, who, subordinating historical understanding to personal taste, wrote that "there could be little glory for Cervantes in the attempt to surpass Heliodorus, Achilles Tatius, and all their imitators together, and it is a pity that he should have undertaken such a sterile task."[2] At the same time I shall attempt to clarify a much more difficult and fundamental problem—namely, Cervantes' relationship to the great crit-

[1] "Miguel de Cervantes," *Fortnightly Review* (November 1947), p. 375.

[2] "Cultura literaria de Miguel de Cervantes y elaboración del 'Quijote,' " *Discursos* (Madrid, 1956), p. 132. It is worth recalling F. Baldensperger's words on the importance of an objective foundation for literary historiography. Observing the limitations of Brunetière's method of literary study in its emphasis on "*les oeuvres maîtresses* et les grands courants *actuellement mémorables*," he asks: "A ne prendre, en effet, que les résultats filtrés aujourd'hui, et d'ailleurs toujours provisoires, de la notoriété et de la réputation, comment savoir . . . qu'Héliodore importe autant peut-être qu'Eschyle dans le legs de l'Antiquité?" ("Littérature comparée: le mot et la chose," *Revue de Littérature Comparée*, I [1921], 24).

ical movement which affected in one way or another all the writers, theorists, and academic circles of his time.

Since Giuseppe Toffanin's discovery of the importance of Aristotelian literary theories in the genesis of the *Quixote*, various studies have dealt with this subject, from De Lollis' *Cervantes reazionario* (1924) to Riley's *Cervantes's Theory of the Novel* (1962). As valuable as these contributions have been, I believe that there is still more to say on the matter. For nearly all these studies have yielded to the temptation to extract Cervantes' various discursive statements on literary matters from their surrounding contexts and present them as an abstract system or a corpus of literary ideas. The general result has been the portrayal of Cervantes as a mediocre theorist, who was more or less classical and conservative in literary tastes and who had no real theory of what he was doing in creating the modern novel. The studies deal excellently with the classical tendency in Cervantes but neglect his "anticlassical" tendency, or, put another way, his critical response to Aristotle.

While it is undeniably true that Cervantes had no novelistic theories such as those which three hundred years later Ortega y Gasset and Américo Castro were to formulate on the basis of his work, his position on literary theorizing is far more complex and sophisticated than the designations "conservative" or "classical" would suggest. Indeed, it can be properly evaluated only by returning to Toffanin's method of analyzing the context which always frames the appearance of a literary idea. By examining the commonplace ideas as they *function* within the *Quixote*, Toffanin concluded that Cervantes' great achievement in discovering the poetic possibilities of historical reality—which, in deference to Aristotle's distinction between poetic and historical truth and the general idealizing tendency of the Horatian-Aristotelian dogma, the classicists had excluded from serious literary treatment—resulted precisely from his simultaneous interest in and independence of the Aristotelian position.[3]

[3] *La fine dell'umanesimo* (Turin, 1920), Chap. XV. My study represents in part an exploration and amplification of Toffanin's conclusion that the *Quixote* is "la risposta più profonda data da un poeta, ed in poesia, al questionario aristotelico" (p. 218). Moreover, as the following pages make clear, I have found it fruitful to push to the limit of its implications Toffanin's suggestive antithesis: "Le fonti

Introduction

The major part of my study, then, concerns Cervantes' engagement with Aristotle. I prefer to see this engagement as a dialogue rather than as a conflict because Cervantes' relationship to the classical dogma remains in the last analysis ambivalent. Two opposed tendencies were alive in his creative and theoretical endeavors. The first drew him toward the normative world represented by the classical ideal in literature, responsible on the one hand for the Canon of Toledo's judicious critique of the romances and the theater of Lope, on the other for Cervantes' literary plan and his aspirations in the conception of the *Persiles*. The second tendency drew him toward both the world of free fantasy and that of historical reality, the former responsible for his recurrent burlesque of the hallowed concept of mimesis in its empirically oriented interpretation characteristic of Renaissance Aristotelians, the latter responsible for his creation of the *Quixote*. Except in the early works, the dialogue with Aristotle is one of the most recurrent features of Cervantes' writing, from its most complete and discursive formulation in the literary debate between Don Quixote and the Canon of Toledo to its most dramatic and complex expression in Periandro's long recital at the court of King Policarpo in the *Persiles*.

My method is to subject to close analysis the texts of Cervantes' dialogue with Aristotle, considering especially the way in which action, character, setting, language, and style reflect upon literary ideas and the reliability of their spokesmen in Cervantes' works. This type of analysis of course presupposes an awareness of the literary issues raised and alluded to in all Cervantes' literary interludes. The introductory part of my study, which deals with the theoretical grounds underlying Cervantes' conception of the *Persiles*, has the additional function of establishing a frame of reference for the analysis that follows. For in it I trace historically the development of certain aesthetic problems fundamental to all of Cervantes' critical examinations of Aristotelian dogma. In effect, I am attempting to do what Wayne Booth claims Riley's *Cervantes's Theory of the Novel* has left undone—the analytical examination of

---

teoriche di lui [Cervantes] furon proprio le medesime che tormentarono il Tasso. . . . Fra il Tasso e il Cervantes ci fu questa sola differenza: che dove l'uno pianse e si disperò, l'altro, genio sublime, sorrise" (p. 213).

Introduction

the function of literary ideas in Cervantes' fiction. And I begin my analysis by attempting to clarify the point which Booth correctly believes to be essential to an understanding of Cervantes' ideas about fiction—namely, the critical reliability of the Canon of Toledo.[4]

The examination of the general problem of Cervantes' dialogue with Aristotle is relevant to an understanding of the *Persiles* in several respects. Cervantes' epic in prose indeed reflects the fundamental view of the general literary aims and specific principles of narrative fiction derived by the sixteenth-century theorists in their exegesis of the *Poetics*. At the same time, however, some of Cervantes' most important dialogues with Aristotle and assertions of an anticlassical aesthetic position appear in it. Moreover, the *Persiles* occasionally breaks down in terms of the theories which nourished its conception, and its breakdown is closely related to the rejection of literary classicism in favor of historical realism, that rejection which made possible the creation of the *Quixote*. And finally, the common body of structures and themes revealed by the analysis of literary interludes in the *Quixote* and the *Persiles* leads one to question the widely accepted notion that the two works have nothing in common. The most vigorous statement of this misconception, which usually measures the *Persiles* unfavorably by the outstanding features of the *Quixote* (e.g., "novelisticness," character, history, actuality) is to be found in Mack Singleton's view that there are in the *Persiles* "practically none of the mature Cervantes' preoccupations" and that "*Persiles* is so terribly alien to *Don Quixote* that, if someone else had signed his name to it, I could not imagine a more arduous critical task than that of attributing it to Cervantes."[5]

In a sense my close analysis of the numerous literary interludes in Cervantes' works amounts to the process of decoding, of discovering in statements made by narrators and characters their allusiveness to ideas which have long ago ceased to be the property of the educated reading public. It is not surprising that Cervantes' most complex treatment of these ideas, the extended narration of Periandro, has been called by a modern commentator on the *Persiles*

[4] Review of *Cervantes's Theory of the Novel* in *Modern Philology*, LXII (1964), 163-165.
[5] "El misterio del *Persiles*," *Realidad*, II (1947), 240.

6

Introduction

one of the strangest mysteries of a strange work and has been consistently either overlooked or misinterpreted by critical treatment of the work.[6] In decoding these scenes, I hope not only to clarify Cervantes' position on aesthetic matters and the creation of the *Persiles*, but also to enrich the text of the *Quixote* by illuminating an area which has been obscured by the changing tastes of the succeeding epochs.

As is well known, humor is one of the phenomena of human experience that is most dependent on the circumstances of the particular historical moment. We need no further proof of this than to recall how eighteenth-century France laughed over *Don Quixote* as a satire directed against the benighted civilization of the Middle Ages while England laughed heartily over the comedy of situation in its numerous scenes of farce.[7] Since the early nineteenth century mankind's laughter over *Don Quixote* has been subdued somewhat, and the work has ceased to be primarily a funny book. It could be said that the tears of sympathy shed by birds, brooks, and flowers in Heinrich Heine's garden as the young poet sat reading *Don Quixote* aloud symbolize a new epoch for Cervantes' masterpiece, an epoch in which the reader's reaction to the work has been conditioned by his own awareness that he, just like the demented knight-errant, is a homeless wanderer, lost somewhere between the world as he would like it to be and the world as he knows it to be.[8] Without having to impose upon ourselves the metaphysical probings of Friedrich Schlegel, we nevertheless bear within ourselves, as does our entire culture, the feeling of tension between the ideal and the real, infinity and finitude (*Unendlichkeit* and *Endlichkeit*), which are reconcilable only in their opposition. Though seldom reaching the extremes of Unamuno's somber reading, we nevertheless tend to read the *Quixote* in terms of our own preoccupations and concentrate on the tragic, or at best the tragicomic implications of the protagonist's losing struggle. The rich humor of the work, which Cervantes' contemporaries undoubtedly enjoyed in their readings,

---

[6] Pedro de Novo y F. Chicarro, *Bosquejo para una edición crítica de "Los trabajos de Persiles y Sigismunda"* (Madrid, 1928), p. 99.

[7] See Werner Brüggemann, *Cervantes und die Figur des Don Quijote in Kunstanschauung und Dichtung der Deutschen Romantik* (Münster, 1958), pp. 31-41.

[8] See *Sämtliche Werke*, ed. E. Elster (Leipzig, n.d.), III, 422-424.

is somewhat out of place in our anxious age. The elements of literary parody which we can understand because they are self-explanatory, i.e., the ridicule of the romances of chivalry, bore us as they go on and on. The scenes of farce may occasionally amuse us. Other elements of humor escape us entirely.

While it would be just as meaningless to criticize the present age for its tastes as it would be to expect it to respond to the *Quixote* as did Cervantes' contemporaries, it remains, nevertheless, one of the obligations of literary history to preserve those dimensions of the great works of art forgotten by the casual reader. I shall consider my study successful if it contributes in any way to an appreciation of the rich layer of refined, academic humor of the *Persiles* and the *Quixote*, a humor which is highly topical in its dependence on the preoccupations of Renaissance literary theorists and which, precisely through its topicality, caused some amusement to seventeenth-century readers.

PART ONE: THE GENESIS OF THE *PERSILES*

Romances of Chivalry and the Classical Aesthetic

CHAPTER I

The Critique and Purification of
the Romance of Chivalry

> If I were permitted now, and my hearers desired it, I would say
> something about the qualities that books of chivalry require in
> order to be good.
>
> Pero Pérez, the curate[1]

I F IT COULD ever be said that a work of literature is almost exclusively a product of literature and literary theory, it could be said
of Cervantes' final work *Los Trabajos de Persiles y Sigismunda*.
Everywhere the eclectic character of the work is visible: in its undisguised appropriation of scenes and passages from Virgil's *Aeneid*
and Heliodorus' *Ethiopian History*, in its inclusion of an Italian
novella and many brief reminiscences from biblical tradition,
medieval romance, and other works of classical antiquity, and in
its presentation of various recurrent topics of imaginative literature
which are as old as literature itself. Moreover, the specific literary
theories which inspired the fusion of so many widely disparate elements into a coherent whole are everywhere apparent in its texture.
They are revealed in occasional authorial digressions about aesthetic
problems and in brief remarks of the self-conscious narrator drawing
attention to the criteria governing his selective processes in the
inclusion of a specific element. But more basically they become
deeply imbedded in the action of the work itself, informing an
extended dramatic situation and its development in the second book.

Considered from any point of view, e.g., Cervantes' orthodoxy,
Cervantes' idealism, Cervantes' supposed senility, the *Persiles* is undeniably both literary and literarily self-conscious. In this respect it
can be said of Cervantes' final work that it was a product of his
epoch, an age that has been called by one of its recent analysts the
"age of criticism."[2] With the rediscovery of Aristotle's *Poetics*

---

[1] "Y si me fuera lícito agora, y el auditorio lo requiriera, yo dijera cosas acerca
de lo que han de tener los libros de caballerías para ser buenos" (Miguel de Cervantes Saavedra, *Don Quijote de la Mancha*, ed. M. de Riquer, 2 vols. [Barcelona,
1958], I, 325; all subsequent volume and page references are to this edition).

[2] "Sixteenth-century Italy was the time and place in which philosophers turned
their full attention to the nature of creative activity, in contradistinction to the

11

shortly before the middle of the sixteenth century, the appearance of the numerous commentaries on Horace and Aristotle that immediately followed, the rising influence of the literary academies in Italy in the second half of the century, and the literary polemics associated with these academies, the artist of the time could hardly escape the heavy burden of a critical self-consciousness and its inevitable effect on his creative powers. It was in this "age of criticism" that Cervantes' sensibilities were molded, and his creative production can be understood properly only against the background of critical ferment that surrounded the solidification of the Aristotelian canon of criticism.

In order to discover the way in which literary theory was the generating force in the conception and creation of the *Persiles*, it is necessary to trace briefly the fortunes of the romance of chivalry in critical thinking of the sixteenth century. It is my belief that both Cervantes' aesthetic orientation and literary aspirations were analogous to those of his Italian contemporary, Torquato Tasso, whose theories and example dominated literary thinking in both Italy and Spain of the period. Like Tasso, Cervantes was deeply attracted to the free fantasies of the medieval romance, which he knew to be an outmoded literary genre. At the same time he conceived of the possibility of a new genre which would retain the appeal of the romances and, by its observance of Aristotelian rules, meet the demands of contemporary literary tastes. Fortunately Greek antiquity, though not precisely the classical period, offered a model for the endeavor in the prose romance of Heliodorus. Just as Tasso had the examples of Virgil and Homer to guide him in his task, Cervantes had in the *Aethiopica*, the rediscovery of which coincided roughly with that of Aristotle's *Poetics*, a model which in academic circles was regarded as an epic in prose, a model, along with the works of Virgil and Homer, for the aspiring epic poet of the period.

---

fifteenth century when the Humanists were filled with passion for the study of the poetry of Greece and Rome, supposing it to be more important than philosophy, and to the following epochs beginning with Bacon, Descartes, Pascal, and Locke when philosophy meant something more like interest in scientific method, mathematics, and the life of reason" (Baxter Hathaway, *The Age of Criticism: the Late Renaissance in Italy* [Ithaca, 1962], pp. 5-6).

Romances of Chivalry & the Classical Aesthetic

THE MORALISTIC CRITIQUE OF THE ROMANCE OF CHIVALRY

The age which witnessed the discovery of Heliodorus' *Ethiopian History* and the emergence of the *Poetics* of Aristotle as the theoretical basis of literary tastes was also the age in which the romance of chivalry reached its apogee. The years between 1510 and 1550 produced a vast proliferation of Spanish works dealing with the exploits of such figures as Amadís, Esplandián, and Palmerín, and their translation and diffusion all over Europe was immediate. These were the years when Saint Teresa indulged her fantasy with the heroics of the knights-errant and King Francis I of France is said to have demanded personally a French translation of *Amadís de Gaula*. The romances of chivalry were the first "best-sellers" of the age of printing, and their influence was felt in all stations of society.

It is not strange that the extraordinary popularity and diffusion of these final offspring of a genre which had originated centuries before should provoke a strong reaction in various circles, some of which had been traditionally hostile to imaginative literature. The documents and substance of the sixteenth-century critique of the romances of chivalry have been treated in various contexts,[3] and it

[3] See Marcelino Menéndez y Pelayo, *Orígenes de la novela, Obras completas* (Santander, 1943), XIII, 440-447, 463-465; Américo Castro, *El pensamiento de Cervantes* (Madrid, 1925), pp. 25-27; Henry Thomas, *Spanish and Portuguese Romances of Chivalry* (Cambridge, 1920), Chap. V and pp. 195-199, 216-221, 227-234, 238-241. Marcel Bataillon (*Erasmo y España*, tr. A. Alatorre [Mexico, 1950], II, 225) has supplemented the stock of documents used in the previous discussions of the matter and has examined the controversy in relation to the movement of Christian humanism and its orientation toward the ethical, the informative, and the practical in literature. He concludes: "Esta crítica de las novelas, y particularmente de la literatura caballeresca, es un rasgo fundamental del erasmismo español" (p. 217). Werner Krauss ("Die Kritik des Siglo de Oro am Ritter- und Schäferroman," *Gesammelte Aufsätze zur Literatur- und Sprachwissenschaft* [Frankfurt, 1949], pp. 152-176) offers the fruitful approach of differentiating a moralistic from an aesthetic tendency within the critical literature on the romances and relating the latter to the emergence of the Aristotelian critical canon. As the following pages will make clear, I pursue this approach, for I feel that particular aesthetic problems formed an important part of Cervantes' complex attitude toward the romances and were to a large extent responsible for his conception of the *Persiles*. Unlike Krauss, who limits his study primarily to Spanish documents and considers Arias Montano's *Rhetoricorum libri III* (1569) the first appearance of a primarily aesthetic evaluation of the Spanish romances (see p. 162), I prefer to view the evolution of the aesthetic problems concerning the romances against the background of the solidification of the Aristotelian critical doctrine in Italy and the theorizing surrounding the *romanzi* which accompanied that process.

is unnecessary to deal with them at length here. However, not enough attention has been given the varying perspectives which lay behind the criticism and which must be borne in mind when we deal with the complexity and ambivalence that mark the attitudes of such figures as Tasso and Cervantes toward this type of fiction.

The criticism can be broken down conveniently into two types, that which is based on criteria which we regard today as nonliterary and that which results from a basically aesthetic point of view toward the work of art. The former was in no way a revolution in critical tastes and is far older than the romances themselves. It focuses on two aspects of imaginative literature, its untruth and its powers to arouse the passions of the reader. Both objections are of remote and illustrious origins. The contrast between fiction and truth is at least as old as Hesiod's "we know how to utter many false things which are like the truth."[4] Coupled with the removal of fictional imitation from the realm of the true, criticism of the harmful effect that literature has in exciting passions regarded as undesirable in real life forms the basis of Plato's influential banishment of all poets from his ideal state.[5] Both of these arguments were applied to the romances of chivalry at an early date and were repeated with renewed vigor by Renaissance moralists in response to the enormous popularity of the old genre in the age. In Petrarch's phrase "dream of sick minds and foolishness of romances" (*sogno d'infermi e fola di romanzi*), which was to become a commonplace of Renaissance criticism of the romances, we discern the Horatian censure of an art which deviates from nature as well as an echo of the more ancient critique of the lie in literature.[6] A century later

---

[4] Cited by G.M.A. Grube, *The Greek and Roman Critics* (Toronto, 1965), p. 5. For bibliography on classical censures of the "lies" of poetry, see A. Gudemann, *Aristoteles peri poietikes* (Berlin, 1934), pp. 411-412. On the survival of the Platonic tradition of literature as lie in the Middle Ages, see E. R. Curtius, "Zur Literaturästhetik des Mittelalters I," *Zeitschrift für Romanische Philologie*, LVIII (1938), 44ff.

[5] *Republic*, X; see F. M. Cornford, ed. (New York, 1956), pp. 321-340.

[6] *Trionfo d'amore*, IV, l. 66; see *I trionfi*, ed. E. Chiorboli (Bari, 1930), p. 321. The Horatian comparison of the monstrous products of the undisciplined poet with the dreams of a sick mind ("velut aegri somnia, vanae fingentur species" [*Epistola ad Pisones*, ll. 7-8; see *The Works of Horace*, ed. A. J. MacLeane (Cambridge, Mass., 1856), p. 223]) may lie behind the association of the dream and the nonsense of the romances.

Alfonso Martínez de Toledo's defense of the truth of the examples which he presents for moral edification is coupled with a disparaging remark about the fictitious character of both contemporary historiography and the romances of chivalry: "This is neither a chronicle nor a history of deeds of chivalry, in which they occasionally put B for C, for you are to know that what I have said is truth."[7]

In humanist Luis Vives' *De institutione feminae christianae* traditional criticism of mendacity fuses with the Platonic-Christian suspicion of the effect of literature of the imagination on ethical behavior to form one of the most typical documents of the purely moralistic attacks on the romances in the Renaissance. Vives' discussion of the literature that young ladies should read is informed by a puritanical attitude toward the corruptibility of human nature and a belief that only through surveillance, strict education, and constant activity can the young lady resist the temptations of the flesh. These temptations are strongest in moments of idleness, and it is in such moments that man turns to literature for pleasure. Vives sadly notes that the most popular books among his contemporaries are those written in "romance" on arms and love. The humanist has no sympathy for these works, which he calls "pestiferous books," claiming that they are "composed by writers who are idle, lazy, and ignorant, men much given to vices and impurity."[8] He offers a long list of examples, including many of the most famous Spanish and French romances of chivalry as well as the *Celestina*, the *Decameron*, and *Cárcel de amor*, and proposes that there be a law prohibiting the appearance of such books. Although at one point Vives voices his distaste for the glorification of deeds of war in the romances, the recurrent theme of his attack is the danger they represent to the morals of young ladies. Referring to the poisonous effect of reading of "other people's love affairs" and the fires of hell which will punish a woman following her surrender to vice, Vives asserts that the plot of such books has no

[7] "Non es esto coronica nin ystoria de caualleria, en las quales a las veses ponen c por b; que esto que dicho he, sabe que es verdad" (*El Arcipreste de Talavera* [1438], ed. L. B. Simpson [Berkeley, 1939], p. 114).

[8] ". . . quos omnes libros conscripserunt homines otiosi, male feriati, imperiti, vitiis ac spurcitiae dediti" (*Opera omnia* [Valencia, 1783], IV, 87).

other rationale than to demonstrate the arts of seduction. He then
suggests that their authors would do better to write manuals of
pandering (*libros de arte lenonia*). What we observe in Vives' argument is essentially the same indictment of the romances that two
hundred years earlier Dante had presented in the fifth canto of his
Inferno. For it was an old French romance that Paolo and Francesca were reading when their fatal passion erupted, and in the
words of Francesca the book itself was the pander ("Galeotto fu il
libro e chi lo scrisse") of their liaison. It was an old argument but
one which would be repeated with minor variation often through
the sixteenth and seventeenth centuries all over Europe. For example, in 1605 François de la Noue would attack the *Amadís* books,
suggesting that they were to be recommended for those men who
would like to grow horns.[9]

To this traditional argument, which ultimately derives from Plato,
Vives adds the other Platonic criticism of imaginative literature,
which, as we have already seen, had similarly been directed against
the romances during the Middle Ages. Such literature, it is charged,
is fictitious and as such consists of lies. Vives denies that there can
be any pleasure in "things which they feign so foolishly and openly"
(. . . *in rebus quas tam apertè et stultè confingunt*). As examples
he offers the case of one man's killing thirty opponents and two
giants, and his miraculously fast recovery from wounds sustained
in battle, concluding: "Is it not madness to be carried away by such
idiocies and to be held by them?" (*Quae insania est, iis duci, aut*

---

[9] *Discours politiques, et militaires* (n.p., 1612), pp. 142-143. In his *Poetica* (1596)
Tommaso Campanella, in condemning *Amadís de Gaula*, recalls that Dante "in-
segna che il libro dell'amore di Lancellotto fusse stato ruffiano" and cites the
famous passage from the *Inferno* (ed. Luigi Firpo [Rome, 1944], pp. 118-119).
The recurrent identification of the reading of romances with exposing oneself to
temptation of the flesh was the result not only of the notorious promiscuity of their
heroes but also of the system of values countenancing extramarital, physical love,
which underlies the literary genre. Perión de Gaula was an illustrious example of
Andreas Capellanus' doctrine of courtly love and its precept that "love cannot exert
its powers between two people who are married to each other" (*The Art of Courtly
Love*, tr. J. J. Parry [New York, 1941], p. 106) as he traveled around the country-
side of northern Europe fathering Amadís by the maiden Elisena and Florestán
by the daughter of the Count of Selandia. Dante's relegation of Paolo and Francesca to the second circle of hell is a condemnation of both the ideal of courtly
love and the fictional genre which gave it its broadest expression, the romance
of chivalry.

teneri?)[10] It is important to observe here Vives' distaste for such impossible occurrences in the romances, for it is characteristic of a general attitude of the humanists toward the fantastic elements in literature which had formed *before* the popularization of Aristotle's *Poetics* and which would have an influence on the way in which the humanists would interpret Aristotle's concepts of mimesis and verisimilitude in the following decades.

In its austerity Vives' critique marked one extreme in the attacks on the romances, an extreme which was well represented throughout the century.[11] There was, however, particularly among Vives' fellow humanists, a more benign critique of the genre. In its orien-

[10] Curiously Vives' attitude toward the implausible is formally the same as that of the Aristotelians, Tasso and Cervantes' Canon of Toledo. However, the correspondence is purely fortuitous. While the latter refuse to allow an aesthetic pleasure that is aroused by the inverisimilar, their interest is in defining the boundaries of the permissible, i.e., plausible lie and the creation of literature within these boundaries. Vives' entire orientation is nonliterary; moral and practical concerns dominate his view of literature to the extent that it is probable that he would classify and condemn as a lie any fictitious work, whether plausible or not. His recommendations of books are all inspired by his belief that the aim of all reading is moral edification (*vt rectius viuat*). Thus we find the Gospels and the Acts of the Apostles as well as Cicero and Seneca.

[11] If we are to believe the theories of the writers who pursued this extreme line of criticism, the devil had quite a hand in the corruption of literary tastes in the age. Vives' association of the creators of the romances with the diabolic lingered throughout the century, e.g., "sermonarios de Sathanas" (Vanegas de Busto, 1546, and Juan Sánchez Valdés de la Plata, 1598 [see Thomas, pp. 167-168]), "quien la [mentira, e.g., libros de Amadís] escribe hijo suyo [del diablo] será" (G. Fernández de Oviedo y Valdés, *Historia general y natural de las Indias*, ed. J. Amador de los Ríos [Asunción del Paraguay, 1944], IV, 74), "sopra la falsità nessuna arte, se non diabolica, si fonda, sendo il Diavolo padre del mendacio, come dice Cristo" (T. Campanella, *Poetica*, p. 119). Carvallo (1602) attributes the "vanidades" of classical literature as well as the enthusiasm of his age for them to the devil's successful effort to be "mona de dios" and to receive through poetry the veneration that God receives in the Bible and in the music of the spheres (*Cisne de Apolo*, ed. A. Porqueras Mayo [Madrid, 1958], I, 126-128). A curious aspect of the association was the linkage of the devil to the particular aesthetic category on which the romance of chivalry depended for its success, the marvelous. Well known are Mariana's discovery of the work of the devil in the excesses of the Spanish theater and his lament: ". . . es propio de nuestra naturaleza maravillarnos de cosas extraordinarias, menospreciar lo que pasa cada día" (cited by Américo Castro, "La comedia clásica," in A. Del Río and M. J. Benardete, *El concepto contemporáneo de España* [New York, 1962], p. 595). This unbroken tradition, associating the marvelous and the imaginary in literature with the diabolic, which coexisted with the Aristotelian theorists' suspicion of the same elements in their opposition to verisimilitude, nourishes the imaginative implications of the bonfire that awaits the unfortunate victims of the curate's judgment in Don Quixote's library.

17

tation toward the practical problems of life, Christian humanism
simply objected to the lack of doctrine in the romances and their
nonutility, failing to associate them necessarily with the temptations
of the flesh and the instruments of the devil. What annoyed the
spokesmen of this tendency in romance criticism was not the loss
of the reader's soul, but rather his loss of hours which could be put
to more profitable use. The recurrent motifs of their attacks were
the observance of the unreality of the fictions in the works and
the characterization of the reading of the romances as a waste of
time. Again this criticism represented nothing new, for in the early
fifteenth century Pero López de Ayala had complained:

> Plógome otrosi oyr muchas vegadas,
> Libros de deuaneos e mentiras probadas,
> Amadis, Lanzalote e burlas asacadas,
> En que perdi mi tiempo a muy malas jornadas.[12]

In the writings of Spanish humanists we observe the frequent
resumption of López de Ayala's criticism, which, like Petrarch's
"sogno d'infermi e fola di romanzi," may be said to be a topic of
sixteenth-century criticism of the romances. In 1529 Antonio de
Guevara laments his contemporaries' love of the books of chivalry:
"They waste time, for in such works one does not learn how vices
must be shunned."[13] In the prologue of his translation, *Las obras de
Xenophonte* (1552), Diego Gracián de Alderete complains that the
romances "serve no purpose other than to waste time and to dis-
credit other books which are good, truthful, and full of good doctrine and profit. For the monstrous and disorderly fables which are
read of in these mendacious books destroy the credit of the true
deeds which are read of in true histories."[14] We observe the same

[12] "Moreover, many times I enjoyed listening to books full of nonsense and
proven lies, of Amadis, Lancelot, and invented jests; in them I wasted my time
and was poorly rewarded" (*Rimado de palacio*, ed. B.A.E., LVII, 430; cited by
Thomas, p. 54).

[13] ". . . pierden el tiempo, porque alli no deprendẽ como se han de apartar
delos vicios" (cited by Thomas, p. 170).

[14] ". . . no siruen de otra cosa, sino de perder el tiempo y desautorizar los otros
buenos libros verdaderos de buena doctrina y prouecho. Porque las patrañas
disformes y desconcertadas que en estos libros de mentiras se leen, derogan el
credito a las verdaderas hazañas que se leen en las historias de verdad" (cited by
Thomas, p. 160). A similar charge had been leveled at the romances by another

attitude in Juan de Valdés' benign criticism of the nonutility and lies of the romances and his admission that during the ten best years of his life his literary tastes were so corrupted that he devoted his hours of reading almost exclusively to "these lies."[15]

It is significant that the first translators of Greek romances into Spanish echo this attitude toward the romances of chivalry, revealing how omnipresent the suspicion of imaginative literature of any type was among the humanists. In justifying his labors in translating Ludovico Dolce's *Ragionamenti amorosi*, itself an Italian translation of the last four books of Achilles Tatius' *Clitophon and Leucippe*, Alonso Núñez de Reinoso claims that he undertook the enterprise to "instruct in how to live well" (*avisar a bien vivir*), that there is an allegorical significance in each character, and that the work is in no way to be identified with the "vanities" of the romances of chivalry. In concluding, he emphasizes that he did not waste (*malgastar*) his time, but rather: "I consider well employed all the time which I have spent in this."[16] In a similar vein J. Amyot, whose prologue to his French translation of Heliodorus' *Ethiopian History* will be the subject of closer examination below, justifies his efforts only after acknowledging that man should be very careful when reading fiction, "fabulous books, lest his mind become accustomed gradually to loving lies and vanities; besides his time is ill-spent."[17] He admits that these dangers lend validity to the argument that "all fabulous writings, those in which the subject is not

---

historian, Pedro Mexía. They present their subject matter under the title of *historia*, and in so doing offend the serious historian, who regards historiography as the presentation of truth: "Abuso es muy grande y dañoso, que entre otros incõuiniẽtes, se sigue de grande ignominia y afrẽta alas chronicas & hystorias verdaderas, permitir que anden cosas tan nefandas, a lapar con ellas" (Thomas, p. 158). It is important to note the flexibility with which the term *historia* was used in the sixteenth century, a flexibility which it retained despite the complaints of the humanist historians and the subsequent popularization of Aristotle's distinction between history and poetry. As will be pointed out below, Cervantes exploits this flexibility for humorous equivocation on many occasions.

[15] Juan de Valdés, *Diálogo de la lengua*, ed. J. Montesinos (Madrid, 1964), p. 174.

[16] ". . . doy por bien empleado todo el tiempo que eñ esto he gastado" (*Historia de los amores de Clareo y Florisea*, ed. B.A.E., III, 431-432).

[17] ". . . libros fabulosos, de miedo que sus entendimientos no se acostumbren poco a poco a amar mentiras y vanidades, demás que el tiempo es mal empleado."

true,"[18] be condemned. He proceeds, however, to justify imaginative literature, asserting that in its weakness human nature demands the pleasure it affords and offering in Heliodorus' work a form of fiction which, in its lofty moral tone, the plausibility of its lies, and its wealth of erudition, is to be preferred to the useless romances of chivalry.[19]

THE AESTHETIC CRITIQUE OF THE ROMANCE OF CHIVALRY

It is indeed the generous attitude toward imaginative literature of such humanists as Valdés and Amyot that paved the way for the recognition both that the fictitious element is essential to literature and that literature exists in an autonomous province and is not to be measured by the standards of historiography.[20] Like Amyot, Valdés cannot escape the prejudice against the lie which marks theoretical writings on literature since Plato; yet like Amyot he can prefer a lie that is plausible to a lie that is implausible. Echoing the Horatian precept, "Let what is feigned for the sake of pleasure be

[18] ". . . todos escritos fabulosos, y de los cuales el subjecto no es verdadero."

[19] Amyot's prologue appeared in 1547. I cite the Spanish translation of this document, which accompanied the first Spanish version of the *Aethiopica* (1554). Francisco López Estrada includes Amyot's prologue in his edition of Fernando de Mena's translation (1587) of Heliodorus' romance: *Historia etiópica* (Madrid, 1954). See pp. lxxvii-lxxviii.

[20] Werner Krauss observes that the major step toward an aesthetically oriented critique of the romances was the dissociation of the genre from the tradition of historical, i.e., chronicle, writing to which the writer of romance adhered not only in such techniques as offering "historical sources" and employing the archaisms familiar in the chronicles but also in the direct assertion that his matter is historical. He suggests that the essential factor in the process was the objection of the serious humanist historiographers of the Renaissance, e.g., Pedro Mexía (see above) to the consideration of such works as histories, an objection which automatically forced these works to be considered in the category of literature: "Wenn daher die humanistische Kritik den Ritterroman aus dem Bereich der Geschichte verwies, so lag gerade darin der Hinweis auf ein eigenes Stoffgebiet der Dichtung, dessen Gesetzlichkeit von den Aristotelikern der Spätrenaissance erarbeitet wurde. Durch diese Wendung wird eine ästhetische Kritik an den Ritterromanen angebahnt" ("Die Kritik des Siglo de Oro am Ritter- und Schäferroman," *Gesammelte Aufsätze*, p. 162). Krauss is correct in observing the formation of a new perspective on the romances, but it seems to me that he focuses on the secondary factor in explaining the process. It is precisely the acceptance of the fact that poetry had "ein eigenes Stoffgebiet," which before the discovery of Aristotle was at the most an unformulated predisposition of various humanists, which allowed for this development, to which the criticism of the historians no doubt then did contribute secondarily.

very close to truth" ("Ficta voluptatis causa sint proxima veris"),[21] Valdés criticizes the inverisimilitude of the romances:

> Since those who write lies should write them in such a way that they approximate truth as much as possible, so that they can sell their lies for truths, our author of the *Amadís*, sometimes in carelessness and sometimes I do not know for what reason, says things that are so clearly mendacious, that in no way can you accept them as true.[22]

The samples of the implausibilities in the *Amadís* which Valdés proceeds to offer are interesting, for they reveal the intensity of the humanist's preoccupation with the necessary illusion of empirical truth in a work of art. The writer errs in allowing Perión de Gaula to cast his sword and shield to the floor in his nocturnal encounter with Elisena, for it is inconceivable that the noise of such an act would not attract the attention of the others in the castle. Valdés finds a breach of decorum, i.e., an implausibility in character, in Elisena's decision to receive Perión as her lover on the first night of their acquaintance. In a king's daughter such conduct is beyond the limits of the credible.[23]

Such concern that the falsehood of literature be close to truth, conjoined with the lingering suspicion of the fictitious (i.e., the lie as a defect), was to have important effects on literary theorizing and production as the century wore on. The rediscovery of Aristotle's *Poetics* came at the right moment if we judge by the general hostile tendency of the moralists' and humanists' writings about imaginative literature. For the *Poetics* offered the first authoritative recognition that the very element in literature which was the target of all attacks on the genre of the romance, its departure from truth, was its essential element. Aristotle's various statements on the subject: his influential distinctions between poetic and historical truth, the universal and the individual, the verisimilar and the true,

---

[21] *Epistola ad Pisones*, l. 338, ed. cit., p. 231.

[22] ". . . siendo esto assí que los que scriven mentiras las deven escrivir de suerte que se lleguen, quanto fuere possible, a la verdad, de tal manera que puedan vender sus mentiras por verdades, nuestro autor de *Amadís* unas vezes por descuido y otras no sé por qué, dize cosas tan a la clara mentirosas, que de ninguna manera las podéis tener por verdaderas" (*Diálogo de la lengua*, p. 177).

[23] Ibid., pp. 176-177.

his recognition that in a sense the poet's task consists of lying, that lies have a natural pleasure for man, that poetry presents man as more perfect than he is in reality, and his affirmation that the marvelous, the aesthetic category with which the fantastic has always been associated, is essential both to epic and tragedy, all appeared in time to offer imaginative literature a much-needed support. And in spite of the humanists' interpretation of these statements in accord with their own primarily didactic and truth-oriented views of literature, their tendency to accept grudgingly the lie in literature if it is plausible was strengthened immeasurably by the new doctrines. Moreover, an apparatus for considering works of literature in terms of their aesthetic qualities or internal reality was available, and a wholly new type of critical writing, focusing on these qualities, followed.

With the discovery and diffusion of Aristotle's *Poetics* in critical circles it is only natural that a more aesthetically oriented critique of the romance of chivalry should emerge to accompany the continuing moralizing attacks on the genre which moralists and humanists of the early part of the sixteenth century had inherited from the Middle Ages. It was in Italy that such criticism originated and developed in full force, and only toward the end of the century in the critical writings of the Aristotelians El Pinciano and Cascales and in the work of Cervantes was its full impact felt in Spain. The classical revival of the Renaissance had always been strongest in Italy, and it was here that the rediscovery of Aristotle occurred and the commentaries on both the *Poetics* and Horace's *Ars Poetica* first appeared. It was in Italy that humanists conceived of the possibility of the re-created classical epic according to the models of Virgil and Homer and the Horatian-Aristotelian rules. Moreover, in Italy the romance of chivalry had attained a perfection and a spectacular success in the *Orlando Furioso* of Ariosto, a success which the classicists could not deny in spite of its only too apparent differences from the venerated classical epic.

It is not surprising that Giangiorgio Trissino should introduce the product of his efforts to revive the classical epic, *L'Italia liberata dai goti* (1547-1548), with an implied criticism of the work which had enthralled Italian audiences since its publication in 1516.[24] In his theoretical work, *Le sei divisioni della poetica* (published posthumously in 1563), which has been called by Spingarn the first application of Aristotelian principles to epic poetry in the Renaissance,[25] Trissino offers a direct aesthetic criticism of the romances. In defending the Aristotelian principle of a single action of a single hero and acclaiming Homer and Virgil for observing it, Trissino offers three examples of works of poetry which violate the principle: Statius' *Achilleid*, Boccaccio's *Filocolo*, and *Amadís de Gaula*. He adds that the latter two "are poems although they are not in verse; and many others are to be found which place in a single plot several actions of a character, actions of different types, which by no means can constitute a single action but are many actions of a single character."[26] It should be noted that what is perhaps the first evaluation of the Spanish romance of chivalry from the vantage point provided by the Aristotelian theoretical apparatus not only censures the lack of unity of the work but also fails to observe any essential difference between the prose romance and classical epic poetry, remaining consistent with Aristotle's theory that poetry is dependent on imitation and not meter. The classification of both verse and prose romances of chivalry as heroic poetry will continue through the age.[27]

Shortly before the midpoint of the century literary theorists in Italy were beginning to use the Aristotelian critical canon for a more thoroughgoing attack on the romances of chivalry. Their efforts were directed almost exclusively at one work, Ariosto's *Orlando*

[24] "Avendo io adunque . . . co i precetti di Aristotele, come ho detto, e con la idea di Omero, composto questo mio Eroico Poema, cosa che non si è fatta più ne la nostra lingua Italiana" (*Tutte le opere* [Verona, 1729], I, n.p.).

[25] Joel E. Spingarn, *Literary Criticism in the Renaissance*, Harbinger Paperback (New York, 1963), p. 68. Parts of Trissino's work were written as early as 1529.

[26] ". . . sono Poemi, avvegna che non siano in versi; e molto altri si truovano, che pongono in una favola diverse azioni di alcuno, e di genere differenti, le quali per niun modo non possono essere una, ma sono molte azioni di uno" (*Tutte le opere*, II, 97).

[27] It is perhaps well to point out that Renaissance critics not only failed to observe any *essential* difference between romances of chivalry and classical epic poetry and between the verse narrative and the prose narrative, but also failed to consider the great differences between Ariosto's work and what we understand today to be medieval romance. As far as critical awareness of the time was concerned, the *Furioso* represented the perfection of the older French and Spanish prose romances.

Furioso. As Weinberg has pointed out, Simone Fornari's defense of the *Furioso*'s unity of plot and verisimilitude clearly indicates that an attack on the work by the Aristotelians had already begun by 1549.[28] The details of the discussion of the work that followed for the next thirty years as well as the outbreak of the polemic over Tasso and Ariosto that succeeded the publication of the *Gerusalemme liberata* in 1581 have been thoroughly treated by Weinberg.[29] In the present context it is sufficient for our purposes to note that both critics and defenders of Ariosto used moral and aesthetic criteria in their judgments. Charges concerning the didactic uselessness of Ariosto's erotic scenes were countered by affirmations of the exemplary qualities of the characters and allegorical readings of the controversial scenes. Aesthetic judgments focused on problems presented by implausibilities in Ariosto's poem as well as its flaws in unity: its bulk, its lack of a beginning, its great number of heroes, and the episodic construction of its plot. Each side used Aristotle to support its conclusions, citing and interpreting the relevant passages of the *Poetics* according to its interest. This controversy is extremely important in Tasso's attempts to reconcile the qualities of romance and epic, and, as I shall point out below, had a great effect on Cervantes' theoretical and creative literary endeavors. The literary dialogue between the Canon of Toledo and Don Quixote, as well as the conception of the *Persiles*, has its roots in these discussions.

It is useful to examine one of the early documents of the Ariosto controversy, for it illustrates how the Spanish romances had been drawn into the orbit of aesthetic theorizing in Italian academic circles. In 1554 Giovanni Battista Pigna published a treatise *I romanzi*, in which he offered a systematic defense of Ariosto as well as a presentation of the *romanzo* as a new genre based on Aristotelian theory. Pigna asserts that the romance has developed from its origins in France and Spain as an independent literary form, which in part follows the Aristotelian laws of epic poetry and in part observes certain laws of its own. Insofar as it is an imitation

---

[28] Bernard Weinberg, *A History of Literary Criticism in the Italian Renaissance* (Chicago, 1961), pp. 954-957.
[29] Weinberg, pp. 954-1073.

of heroic actions in which the verisimilar marvelous, the exemplary, and the informative all have an important place, it is like the classical epic. However, whereas epic poetry founds its imitation on truth, by which Pigna means occurrences which are historical or accepted as historical, the romance generally creates a verisimilar imitation from entirely fictitious matter. Pigna likens the modern genre in this respect to comedy, in which, as Aristotle had suggested, "every falsehood is accepted" (". . . ogni cosa falsa si piglia")[30] but hastens to add that unlike comedy, its fabrications are made of lofty subject matter. Pigna states categorically that Ariosto's poem offers a perfect example of a fiction that is both plausible and lofty.[31] In discussing the controversial disposition of the romances, Pigna acknowledges that unlike classical epic the romance has developed as an "errant form" and tends toward a multiplicity of actions.[32] While suggesting that this characteristic allows for greater variety and pleasure, as the poet can leap from one action to another, Pigna succumbs to the

[30] I romanzi (Venice, 1554), p. 21. Like all his contemporaries Pigna stresses the importance of the plausible lie (bugia) in poetry: ". . . se bene in sul vero non saremo fondati, in sul verisimile almeno staremo talmente, che egli mai trapposto non sarà" (p. 22). Actually most Aristotelians admitted the possibility that the epic itself could conceivably be created out of purely fictitious matter, following Aristotle's remark on Agathon's tragedy. Tasso denies that Pigna's argument is valid for establishing an essential difference between epic and romance and offers recommendations (admittedly without enthusiasm) for the entirely fictitious plot (see Del poema eroico, ed. L. Poma [Bari, 1964], pp. 131-132, 109). These are the recommendations which Cervantes was following in the composition of the Persiles. El Pinciano points to Heliodorus' Ethiopian History as proof of the possibility of an epic based on fictitious matter (see below).

[31] In defense of his venerated masterpiece, Pigna simply rejects the classicists' repeated criticisms of Ariosto's implausibilities. That he was aware that such phenomena as flying horses and magical rings and shields could not be accepted as plausible is evident in his justification of them by an allegorical reading in the close examination of Ariosto's work in the second book of his treatise (see pp. 85-90). The curious coexistence of the traditional allegorizing tendency and the Aristotelian tendency in Pigna's literary theories is most obvious in his insistence that literary lies be plausible and his claim that it is a function of the lie in literature to make a "higher truth" obscure (". . . vna bugia d'un buon poeta ogni verità sepellisce" [p. 22]), offering as an example the false attribution of human sentiments to God in the Psalms of David. It is worth noting that Pigna approaches but does not embrace the theory of the verisimilitude of the Christian marvelous, which Tasso elaborates and Cervantes' employs in the Persiles (see below).

[32] Pigna offers a fallacious historical explanation, evidently allowing the Spanish use of the word "romance" to influence his interpretation: the romanzi originated in fragmentary poems describing wars in Spain; such poems were gradually linked together and expanded (p. 44).

prestige of the Aristotelian concept of unity and claims that the romance observes unity, "which is the perfection of any material," by subordinating its various actions to a central one and its various heroes to "a perfect knight."[33]

What is particularly interesting in this forced reconciliation of Ariosto and Aristotle is Pigna's evaluation of the Spanish prose romances. Here he apparently diverts all the arguments which other classicists were aiming at Ariosto's implausibilies and allows them to fall on his Spanish predecessors and contemporaries. Just as a bee seeks the sweetest flowers to gather its pollen, Ariosto carefully selected only the best in the older Spanish and French books, which are immeasurably inferior to their descendant. Pigna affirms that the only good romances are Italian, adding that "foreign romances have been condemned" and that Petrarch's famous comment "sogni d'infermi & fole di Romanzi" [sic] was indeed justified because it referred to them. What Pigna censures in this literature is most evident in the Spanish romances, its failure to observe verisimilitude and to distinguish between a *legitimate* and an *illegitimate* marvelous. His criticism is remarkably similar in detail to that which Cervantes' Canon of Toledo will pronounce fifty years later:

> Nearly all the Spanish romances are full of worthless follies, being founded, as they are, solely on miraculous occurrences and with their supernatural spirits of one sort or another always bringing about things far removed from the natural world and from *true pleasure, which is generally produced by legitimate marvels.* . . . [The Spanish romances] have the custom of presenting journeys by horse without taking into account the sea which lies between rider and destination, and they present journeys by ship although there is land there to oppose such passage; they make the short roads long and the long ones short, and they include places which are not in the world; moreover, they lose themselves continually in vain love affairs and empty reasonings. There are nearly always in the battles

---

[33] Ibid., pp. 25-26. Pigna's argument on the problem of unity, which reappears in Tasso's *Del poema eroico*, informs one of Cervantes' various dramatizations of sixteenth-century literary theories and problems in the *Quixote* and the *Persiles*. See below, Part Three, Chap. VI.

described by the Spanish romances the most impossible things accepted as the most true.[34]

Thus in addition to noting the low moral tone and uselessness of their subject matter, Pigna focuses his attack on the lack of verisimilitude in the plots of the romances: their violations of the most fundamental laws of human experience (the empirical laws of nature, specifically those of time and space), their fantastic geographies, and their exaggeration of the heroic exploits of their protagonists. Underlying the criticism is the assumption that aesthetic pleasure in plausible or legitimate marvels is valid and is recognized by the *dotti*, for such works as Spanish romances are only for "fools, children, and the scum of the mob" (*li sciocchi, per li fanciulli, & per la feccia del volgo*). Pigna finds in their worthlessness a justification for his failure to cite any of them as examples of his theories of the new genre.

In the writings of Pigna and Trissino we observe how by the mid-fifties the Spanish romance had been measured unfavorably by the two essential aesthetic standards of the Aristotelians, unity and verisimilitude, and had become associated with those controversies which were to dominate much of Italian literary theorizing throughout the remainder of the century, the re-creation of the classical epic, the popularity of the romances, and the envisagement of the possibility of fusing the two genres without departing from the classical rules.

TASSO AND THE AESTHETIC PURIFICATION OF THE ROMANCE

A Unified Variety

At the center of these controversies was the figure of Torquato Tasso, who in both theoretical and practical writings attempted to

[34] "Le Spagnole Romanzerie quasi tutte di uanità son piene: stando elle solo in su i miracoli: & con li spiriti ò dell'una sorte ò dell'altra facendo sempre nascere cose dal naturale lontane, & dal *diletto, che per le leggitime marauiglie suol nascere.* . . . [The Spanish Romances] hanno in vsanza di far viaggi à cauallo, senza riguardare il mare che vi è tra mezzo & in naue passano; se ben vi è la terra ch'al passo s'oppone & lunghe fanno le strade corte & corte le lunghe & luoghi pongono ch'al mondo non sono & in vani amori del continuo si perdono & in vani ragionamenti. Nelle battaglie poi sonui quasi sempre cose impossibile accettate per verissime" (ibid., pp. 40-41; the italics are mine).

achieve the reconciliation which the literary and ideological pressures of the age demanded. Behind his creative trajectory from the early *Rinaldo* (1562) to the *Mondo creato* (posthumous, 1607) and his endless theoretical struggles with the restrictions imposed on poetic freedom by the Aristotelian canon lie not only his religious orthodoxy and his veneration of Aristotle, Homer, and Virgil, but also his awareness of the failure of Trissino's attempt to resurrect the classical epic and his genuine love of the genre of romance and its most sophisticated poet, Ariosto. In the prologue of his early poem, the *Rinaldo*, Tasso expresses his desire to reconcile the divergent tastes of the "moderns" and the "ancients": "But I would wish that my work be judged neither by the strict philosophers, the adherents of Aristotle, who have before their eyes the perfect example of Virgil and Homer and who never consider the importance of pleasure and what is required by the customs of today, nor by those who are most devoted to Ariosto."[35] What Tasso objects to in the classicists is their rigid application of the Aristotelian principle of unity (*le più severe leggi d'Aristotile*), limiting the poet's use of the episode to that on which the central plot is absolutely dependent.[36] Episodic variety was widely recognized as a source of delight in the romances. Tasso's solution is a liberal interpretation of the Aristotelian principle, as he allows the inclusion of some episodes which are clearly subordinate to the main plot and could be excluded without damaging its coherence. He rejects, however, the liberties of construction allowed the poet by Ariosto's freely intervening narrator, who offers explanations, reminders, and summaries to tie his varied matter together.

In the early tract, *Dell'arte poetica* (1564?), in defending unity of action against the principal arguments which the moderns use in order to defend the properties of the romances, Tasso admits the failure of Trissino and acknowledges the greatness of Ariosto. But

---

[35] "Ma io desidererei, che le mie cose né da' severi filosofi seguaci d'Aristotile, che hanno innanzi gli occhi il perfetto esempio di Virgilio e d'Omero, né riguardano mai al diletto ed a quel che richieggiono i costumi d'oggidí né da i troppo affezionati de l'Ariosto fossero giudicate" (*Rinaldo*, ed. L. Bonfigli [Bari, 1936], p. 5).

[36] Below, in my treatment of Cervantes' critical examination of contemporary theories of artistic unity, I deal with the more specific arguments concerning the use of the episode advanced by the neo-Aristotelians (see Chap. VI).

he adds that the latter should not be followed in his incorporation of multiple actions, since unity of plot is one of those eternal rules of nature which remain unchanged in spite of the vicissitudes of custom and fashion. At the same time Tasso admits that the defenders of the modern genre have a valid argument in observing the importance of pleasure in the apprehension of a work of art and recognizes the superior pleasure that is to be derived from the reading of the romances:

> I grant what I deem to be the truth and what many would deny, that is, that pleasure is the end of poetry; I grant likewise what experience proves to us, that is, that the *Furioso* furnishes men of our time with a greater pleasure than the *Italia liberata* or even the *Iliad* or the *Odyssey*.[37]

Tasso attributes this pleasure to the marvelous fictions of the romances and to the appropriateness of their heroes' customs and activities according to modern sensibilities. He agrees with his adversaries that variety in subject matter is an undeniable source of aesthetic pleasure, that indeed "things which yet in themselves are disagreeable, nonetheless become pleasant to us in variety, and that the sight of deserts and the awesome severity of the Alps delight us after the amenity of lakes and gardens."[38] However, observing that "variety is praiseworthy up to that point beyond which it turns into confusion" ("la varietà è lodevole sino a quel termine che non passi in confusione"), he maintains that the creation of such variety is not incompatible with the observance of unity of plot and adds

[37] "Concedo io quel che vero stimo, e che molti negarebbono, cioè che 'l diletto sia il fine della poesia; concedo parimente quel che l'esperienza ci dimostra, cioè che maggior diletto rechi a' nostri uomini il *Furioso* che l'*Italia liberata* o pur l'*Iliada* o l'*Odissea*" (*Discorsi dell' arte poetica e del poema eroico*, ed. L. Poma [Bari, 1964], p. 34). The reconciliatory tone of Tasso's theoretical writings can be heard most clearly here as he recommends that the poet combine the best qualities of the romances with the best qualities of the classical epic to please both learned and ignorant readers: ". . . che con diletto non meno de gli uomini vulgari che de gli intelligenti i precetti dell'arte siano osservati, prendendosi dall'un lato, con quella vaghezza d'invenzioni che ci rendono sì grati i romanzi, il decoro de'costumi, dall'altro, con l'unità della favola, la saldezza e 'l verisimile che ne' poemi d'Omero e di Virgilio si vede" (p. 34).

[38] ". . . cose ancora che per se stesse sono spiacevoli, per la varietà nondimeno care ci divengono, e che la vista de' deserti e l'orrore e la rigidezza delle alpi ci piace doppo l'amenità de' laghi e de' giardini" (ibid., p. 35).

29

that the difficulty which a poet overcomes in achieving such unity in variety is the source of greater wonder for the reader than that aroused by the haphazard combination of actions and phenomena in the romances. It is here that Tasso has recourse to the famous analogy drawn by the neo-Platonists between the unified variety of the poem and that of the universe and between the divine creator and the poet.

The Legitimation of the Marvelous

In his defense of a unified variety and acknowledgment that the reader experiences more pleasure in reading Ariosto than the classics, Tasso is actually dealing with both of the aesthetic problems central to the critique of the romances: unity–variety and verisimilitude–the marvelous. Indeed as soon as the discussion of unity turns to the subject of delight, it passes over by its own logic into the aesthetic province of the marvelous. For Tasso's analysis of the delight that the variety of the universe produces in the beholder and his emphasis on the reader's pleasure in witnessing the poet's feat in overcoming structural difficulties[39] illustrate two aspects of his complex theories of *admiratio* deriving from the attempt to reconcile the two qualities which Aristotle had demanded in the work of art, the verisimilar and the marvelous. As these theories, which were really the logical development of the predisposition of the early interpreters of Aristotle, were to play an important part in the creative writings of both Tasso and Cervantes and in the subsequent reaction against the verisimilar that marks much of baroque literature, it is necessary to examine briefly the basic lines of their development.

It is important to recognize that the type of reasoning which we observed above in Valdés' interpretation of the implausibilities in the plot of *Amadís de Gaula*, a reasoning colored by the lingering Platonic-Christian suspicion of falsehood in literature, continued to

---

[39] "Questa varietà sì fatta tanto sarà più lodevole quanto recarà seco più di difficultà, peroché è assai agevol cosa e di nissuna industria il far che 'n molte e separate azioni nasca gran varietà d'accidenti; ma che la stessa varietà in una sola azione si trovi, *hoc opus, hic labor est.* . . . questa [varietà] per l'ordine e per la legatura delle sue parti non solo sarà più chiara e più distinta, ma molto più portarà di novità e di meraviglia" (ibid., p. 36).

survive unshaken as sixteenth-century theorists engaged in the task of interpreting and applying Aristotelian critical apparatus. The most notable effect of this predisposition of the Renaissance reader of the *Poetics* was the tortuous reasoning that surrounded the touchstone of the Aristotelian theory of literature, the concept of mimesis.

To suggest that the Aristotelians of the Renaissance understood the doctrine of poetic imitation as we interpret it today is to ignore the dominant preoccupation with truth and falsehood in literature which they inherited from centuries of literary theorizing marked by a mistrust of the fictitious. Interpreters of the *Poetics* tended to focus on Aristotle's various statements supporting a literal interpretation of his concepts of mimesis and verisimilitude—his preference for the probable though it be untrue over the true that is improbable, his allowance of the historical event only when it is probable, and his reiterated disapproval of the poet who resorts to miracle in composing his plot. But when Aristotle himself acknowledged that poetry presents "ideal types" and "higher realities," when he distinguished between essential and accidental errors in a literary context, the neo-Aristotelians turned a deaf ear. Their repetition of the familiar phrases on the universal truth of poetry and its presentation of ideal figures was in reality mere lip service to their mentor. They were basically more interested in the problems of the plausibility of the particulars of which the soul of poetry, its plot, is composed than in the problem of how the universal is manifest in those particulars, both of which are encompassed in the Aristotelian concept as we understand it today.[40]

The process of imitation was identified with "invention," the creation of the poetic illusion, but the repeated description of this process as "deception," "lying," "feigning" (*engañar con la verdad*) betrayed the surviving misgivings that it aroused in the theorists' minds. Hence these misgivings had to be allayed by the insistence

[40] For a clear discussion of the problems raised by Aristotle's various statements on the "verisimilar," the "true," "historical truth," and "poetic truth," as well as an intelligent attempt to find consistency in his sketchy treatment of such matters, see Kurt von Fritz, "Entstehung und Inhalt des Neunten Kapitels von Aristoteles 'Poetik,'" *Antike und Moderne Tragödie* (Berlin, 1962), pp. 430-457. At the end of this chapter I include a note in which I discuss various interpretations of mimesis in Renaissance literary theory which have been advanced by recent scholarship.

that the creation of the poetic illusion be carefully restricted by a narrow concept of the verisimilar or credibility. Audience belief in the possibility of the literal level of the plot became the definition of the credible.[41] Nothing is to be taken for granted by an author in estimating the willingness of his audience to believe in its apprehension of a work of art. Consequently the artist's major responsibility is that the things and actions which compose the fabric of his plot conform to the possibilities of empirical reality, that his characters' actions and customs correspond to what was commonly regarded as typical of characters of their station in real life, and that if, as Aristotle recommends, the author uses historical matter in the service of both grandeur and plausibility, his details not contradict the historical facts insofar as they are known by his audience. Perhaps the best indication of the preoccupation with the literal level of the mimesis concept was the recurrent discussions, incriminations, and rationalizing defenses which surrounded Virgil's free manipulation of historical epochs and events and his other violations of plausibility, all of which are amply documented in theoretical writings of the age.

An important consequence of the emphasis on credibility was the peculiar theorizing that surrounded the marvelous, the aesthetic category which had always been central to imaginative literature and which had been regarded with suspicion by moralists and humanists alike. One of the most important features of Aristotle's *Poetics* for the salvation and continued development of imaginative literature lay in his recognition that lies are a legitimate source of pleasure and that the marvelous is necessary in tragedy and even more so in epic poetry. From the middle of the century on we observe in theoretical writing a consciousness of the problem presented by the coupling of the marvelous with the verisimilar and a tendency to devise ways of reconciling the two. This thinking led to a distinction between a *legitimate* and an *illegitimate* marvelous,

---

[41] Tasso's definitions: "l'imitare non è altro che il *rassomigliare*" (*Del poema eroico*, p. 96) and "tanto significa imitare, quanto *far simile*" (*Dell' arte poetica*, p. 7), suggest the "mirroring" implications of mimesis in Renaissance literary theories. Castelvetro too uses *rassomigliare* interchangeably with *imitare*, e.g., ". . . poesia è rassomiglianza, & la sua maniera generale è rassomiglianza" (*Poetica d'Aristotele vulgarizzata* [Basel, 1576], p. 12).

a distinction which is difficult for us to appreciate properly today, as we judge poetic truth in terms of a truth residing within a work of art or within its creator and not in terms of external reality. Nevertheless, the distinction was enormously significant in the age, particularly in the theoretical and creative writing of Torquato Tasso.[42]

One tendency of theoretical endeavors to reconcile the marvelous and the verisimilar avoided the major difficulties which the concepts presented by attaching the marvelous to the normal structural workings of the Aristotelian verisimilar plot. Minturno finds the chief source of the marvelous in the unexpected turn of events (peripeteia) in the development of the plot: "We marvel at those things which occur contrary to our expectation, particularly when they are so aptly joined that the one seems to follow the other by reason."[43] Similarly the unexpected recognition is a source of *admiratio*, particularly if it is of Aristotle's artificial type and proceeds from the events of the plot itself: "Of recognitions . . . of those which are artificial, the most praiseworthy are the ones which, born from the plot itself, with the resemblance to truth engender more of the marvelous."[44] Like Minturno, Pigna observes in structural aspects of the perfectly executed plot a source of the marvelous. In the complex entanglement of dramatic threads and the unexpected unraveling, which Aristotle recommends for the tragic plot, the reader is caught and held in suspense and experiences the necessary *admiratio*.[45]

Closely related to these structural bases for the arousal of *admiratio* in the reader were the association of the aesthetic pleasure with the audience's delight in ornamental language and in the artist's virtuosity as revealed in the *difficulté vaincue*. Thus Pigna could defend

---

[42] As I shall point out below, both the Canon of Toledo and the Cervantes of the *Persiles* accept this distinction. Over and over again in the *Persiles* Cervantes calls the reader's attention to the fact that his techniques of arousing *admiratio* are *legitimate*. At the same time Cervantes was well aware, as Tasso was not, of the dangerous consequence to which the legitimation of the marvelous would lead—the needless impoverishment of the creative imagination.

[43] "Merauiglianoci di quelle cose, che oltre alla nostra openione accadeno, massimamente doue elle sì attamente sien congiunte, che l'una paia dopo l'altra ragioneuolmente seguire" (Antonio Sebastiano Minturno, *L'arte poetica* [Venice, 1564], p. 40).

[44] "De' riconoscimenti . . . degli artificiosi quelli sono i più lodati, che nati dalla istessa fauola con la somiglianza del uero generano più di merauiglia" (ibid., p. 44).

[45] *I romanzi*, p. 38.

the "*in-medias-res* structural technique"[46] for the great demands it places on a poet's talents of gathering and interweaving narrative strands into a coherent whole and for the effect the reader experiences on beholding such a feat: "For the tighter the space in which our intellect is confined, and the greater the difficulty in which it finds itself (difficult things occurring seldom and being therefore more beautiful) . . . all the more ingenious will our intellective power show us to be."[47] As for the marvelous in poetic language, the association of *admiratio* with stylistic qualities such as *energia* or visual vividness was repeated everywhere in Renaissance theoretical writings, from Trissino's remarks on elocution[48] to Tasso's complete formulation of the grand style.

Nevertheless, the legitimations of the marvelous by associating it with structural and linguistic procedures were basically ways by which most theorists avoided the central problem raised by the Aristotelian demands of verisimilitude and the marvelous. The domain of the marvelous in literature has always been new and unusual subject matter, the novelty of which may depend on its violation of the laws of empirical reality,[49] and the popularity of the romances of chivalry was a confirmation of this fact which the classicists could not fail to overlook. Such flagrant incursions into the realm of the fantastic as Ariosto's hippogryph and magic ring and shield became topics of discussion which appeared commonly

[46] The quotation marks, which will hereafter be omitted, are meant to acknowledge the obvious clumsiness of the nonetheless indispensable term.

[47] ". . . che quanto piu stretto è il campo, in che l'ingegno nostro è ridotto, che tanta piu difficoltà ui si vede; & che le cose difficili di rado avengono; & sono perciò piu belle . . . cosi l'intellettiua virtù assai ingegnosi ci mostrerà" (*I romanzi*, pp. 36-37).

[48] ". . . tutti quelli che narranno, o che riferiscono alcuna cosa, sempre vi aggiungono del suo, per fare più meraviglia a chi lo ascolta; et a fare questo ammirabile ancora giovano le comparazioni . . . le comparazioni poi si fanno per tre effetti, o per augumentazione, o per chiarezza, o per enargia, che è un ponere la cosa quasi avanti gli occhi" (*Le sei divisioni della poetica*, in *Tutte le opere*, II, 115).

[49] Thus Giovambattista Giraldi Cintio writes (1554) of the dependence of the marvelous on the irrational and hence the lie: "Laonde [Aristotle] c'insegnò, come si deve essa bugia fingere, perchè ne nasca questo maraviglioso. Perocchè può egli mal nascere dalle cose vere e conosciute per tali dagli uomini, che non è maraviglia in quello, che o spesso o naturalmente occorre, ma ella è bene in quello che pare impossibile e pur si piglia per avvenuto, se non per lo vero, almeno per la finzione: come le mutazioni degli uomini in arbori, di navi in Ninfe" (*De' romanzi*, ed. G. Antimaco [Milan, 1864], p. 62).

alongside of Virgil's transformation of ships into nymphs and the miraculous intervention of the ancient deities in the world of mortals in the classical epic. It was customary to condone such offenses to modern sensibilities in ancient literature by admitting a different capacity for belief in the ancient audience, but the offenses of Ariosto remained unpardonable.

Minturno recognized the importance of the marvelous in subject matter in the epic poem in addition to the marvelous in structure and language. However, he insists that the poet exercise extreme prudence in exploiting its possibilities and restates the assumption underlying the legitimation of the marvelous which we observe in classical literary theories of the second half of the sixteenth century and which will be maintained by Cervantes' Canon of Toledo. It is admitted that novelty in subject matter and unusual occurrence delight the reader, but his pleasure will endure only so long as he accepts the plausibility of what he observes. The poet must be sensitive to the limits of credibility of his audience and deceive it by lying skillfully.[50]

It remained, however, for Tasso to confront the problem squarely and develop the implications of the necessary reconciliation of the Aristotelian demands of verisimilitude and the marvelous. The love of the marvelous was probably the dominant characteristic of Tasso's artistic sensibilities,[51] and in his work we observe the completion of that process of the legitimation of the marvelous which seemed to

[50] "Ma, perche e delle cose, e delle parole nasce la merauiglia; quelle cose mirabili riputiamo, che non uanamente son finte, ma prudentemente . . . E benche sogliano mentire i Poeti per merauiglia negli animi altrui generare; nondimeno fingono, e trouano quelle cose, le quali s'approuino; *chi mai si merauiglierà di quel, ch' egli non approua?*" (*L'arte poetica*, p. 41). The italics are mine.

[51] Ulrich Leo writes: ". . . dass die Wurzel des Tassoschen Dichtertums im 'Erschüttertwerden' lag" (*Torquato Tasso: Studien zur Vorgeschichte des Secentismo* [Bern, 1951], p. 102). He observes that the word *maraviglioso* appears hundreds of times in Tasso's theoretical writings and letters and proceeds to show how his preoccupation with the marvelous completely permeates his theorizing on other specific aesthetic problems, e.g., unity and poetic language (see pp. 102-109). Throughout the *Persiles* one is struck by the recurrence of the words *maravilloso-maravilla-maravillado* and *admiración-admirado*. The frequency of such terms increases in the third and fourth books as the characters often form an audience which comments on the events of the narration. Schevill is correct in stating that Cervantes "quiso maravillar a toda costa" in the *Persiles* (Introduction to his edition of *Persiles y Sigismunda* [Madrid, 1914], p. lxiv).

be the natural consequence of the Renaissance failure to abandon the ancient preoccupation with truth in literature in its interpretation of Aristotle's concept of mimesis. On the one hand Tasso adopted the theories of the marvelous in structural elements and language which we have observed in his predecessors. His association of *admiratio* with the fragmentary exposition of the *in-medias-res* technique and the unexpected recognition and reversals in the well-constructed plot is stated often in his critical writings.[52] As for Tasso's recognition of a marvelous in the ornaments of the lofty style of epic, it need only be said that after struggling for years with the problems involved in adapting marvelous subject matter to a verisimilar context, Tasso came to rely chiefly on the grand style

[52] Thus his rejection of Robortello's allowances for falsehoods in poetry becomes implicitly a recognition of the preferability of the marvelous in structure to that of subject matter: ". . . che la novità del poema non consista principalmente nella falsità del suggetto non udito, ma nel bel nodo e nello scioglimento della favola" (*Del poema eroico*, p. 86). For Tasso "novelty" is used almost synonymously with the marvelous, e.g., "la maraviglia è delle cose nuove" (p. 72). Again in distinguishing the art of the sophist, who deals in such falsehoods as those which fill the romances, from that of the poet, Tasso writes: ". . . il poeta in qualche parte è amico della verità, la quale illustra e abbellisce di nuovi colori . . . e nuovo sarà il poema in cui nuova sarà la testura de' nodi, nuove le soluzioni, nuovi gli episodii che per entro vi sono traposti . . . perché la novità del poema si considera più tosto alla forma che alla materia" (p. 92). In recommending the artificial or *in-medias-res* technique as opposed to the chronological technique of exposition exemplified by Lucan's *Pharsalia*, Tasso observes that the poet must offer his reader suggestive fragments of information, which will arouse in him the desire to discover what remains obscure. "Prima deono esser dette quelle senza le quali non s'avrebbe alcuna cognizione dello stato delle cose presenti; ma se ne posson tacer molte, le quali scemano l'espettazione e la meraviglia, avenga che il poeta debba tenere sempre l'auditore sospeso e desideroso di legger più oltre" (p. 121). In a letter Tasso offers Heliodorus' work as well as the *Aeneid* as an example of the perfectibility of this technique of the structural marvelous (see below).

The following passage from a letter of Camillo Pellegrino to Tasso (November 1587) is interesting in indicating the emphasis on a legitimate marvelous as opposed to an illegitimate marvelous, as well as the systematic cast of the theorizing of the Renaissance Aristotelians in these matters: "Per cosa maravigliosa in epico poema intesi, non i cavalli alati, non la nave convertita in ninfa, non i miracoli e non gl'incanti; ma appunto quel ch'ella [V.S. i.e., Tasso] dice nella Risposta al Lombardelli, la maraviglia che porta la favola della mutazion della forma e dal riconoscimento: quella maraviglia, dico, dalla quale, secondo Aristotile, nasce lo spavento e la confusione, della quale maraviglia, tuttochè sia ricca la Gerusalemme di Vostra Signoria sopra ogni altra" (see A. Solerti, *Vita di Torquato Tasso* [Rome, 1895], II, 278).

as his source of the marvelous, devoting the greater part of the expansion of his early *Dell'arte poetica* to matters of elocution.[53]

Nevertheless, as Leo has demonstrated, Tasso's theoretical reliance on structural and stylistic solutions to the problem presented by the marvelous should not obscure his persistent devotion to marvelous subject matter and his untiring efforts to deal theoretically with the problem of reconciling it with the demand of verisimilitude. It is in the ticklish area of the marvelous in subject matter that the theories of Tasso are most original and important. On the one hand Tasso recommends the use of extraordinary events of history as a basis for a plot, for both the grandeur of the events and their plausibility are attested by their survival in legend and historical chronicle. At the same time their temporal removal veils the events in an atmosphere of imprecision which the poet can exploit to add and modify details without destroying the overall plausibility of his subject. Moreover, Tasso recommends variety in description as a source of *admiratio*. Above we noted his celebration of the unified variety in the poetic microcosm and exaltation of the poet in accordance with the neo-Platonic notion of the poet as creator of a new cosmos. However, in his preoccupation with the problem of a plausible variety and his intense desire for novelty Tasso is not content with the stock of commonplace pieces of marvelous descriptive

[53] Three of the six books of the late *Discorsi del poema eroico* deal exclusively with problems of style. In his lengthy and highly systematic discussion of verse, poetic language, the traditional rhetorical figures, and the necessity of *energia* in style, Tasso repeatedly couples his specific recommendations with the epic poet's overall aim of arousing wonder in his audience. For example foreign words are to be employed in the poetic context because "sono come forestieri tra cittadine; laonde paiono peregrine e producono meraviglia" (p. 185). Homer is acclaimed for his extensive vocabulary, which ranges widely, including archaism and foreign words in order to fill his audience with "stupore" and "l' incanti con la meraviglia" (pp. 245-246). Ulrich Leo has traced clearly Tasso's long and difficult confrontation of the problem of the marvelous and his turn from an emphasis on the marvelous in subject matter to the marvelous in style, noting how in such a transformation the focal point of the aesthetic phenomenon shifts away from the work itself to the reaction of the beholder of the work. Leo explains this shift, which from the point of view of literary history is a significant marker in the gradual formation of the tastes that will dominate baroque literature, against the background both of the Aristotelian critical movement and Tasso's individual psychological peculiarities (see *Torquato Tasso*, pp. 101-118).

matter recommended by his predecessors[54] and proceeds to offer new possibilities in subject matter to supplement that which for centuries had captured the fantasies of literary audiences but was at present losing its imaginative appeal. Herein resides the importance in Tasso's theories of the bizarre and exotic in natural phenomena which contemporary exploration and science were discovering. The poet should incorporate into his work the geography and natural wonders of distant lands and the strange customs of their inhabitants. In the incompleteness of its knowledge of them, the audience will be attracted by their novelty, accept their plausibility, and not question the modifications of truth that the poet may care to make in his transmutation of them into elements of his imitation or plot. Here spatial distance serves the same purpose as does temporal distance in the recommended use of history.[55]

It is in the midst of his extensive listings of the traditional topics for description by the heroic poet, e.g., palaces, ships, battles, weapons, games, and tourneys, places, storms, et cetera, that we discover Tasso's marvelous in variety verging on the miraculous, the traditional major source of the marvelous in literature, and his careful attempt to preserve a legitimate miraculous within well-defined limits. He cautions the poet who would enter this realm:

[54] For example, Giraldi Cintio suggests "tempeste, battaglie, abbattimenti, espugnazioni di terre, fatti d'arme, legazioni, ragionamenti, contese, descrizioni di paesi, di tempi, d'ufficj e di persone . . . perchè ciò arreca maraviglioso piacere a chi legge" (*De' romanzi*, pp. 62-63). In Tasso the conventional list is expanded greatly (see *Del poema eroico*, pp. 109-112, 140).

[55] In praising Homer's use of a very simple plot which "variò con molti episodi e con la narrazione di molte cose meravigliose" (*Del poema eroico*, p. 147), Tasso concludes that "la diversità de' paesi descritti" and "la moltitudine e novità delle cose vedute" are excellent vehicles of the marvelous in variety. In discussing the licenses of the contemporary poet in composing a verisimilar plot based on purely fictitious matter, Tasso warns the poet to avoid employing well-known lands as a setting and suggests that "di Gotia e di Norveggia e di Suevia e d'Islanda o dell' Indie Orientali o di paesi di nuovo ritrovati nel vastissimo Oceano oltre le Colonne d'Ercole se dee prender la materia de sì fatti poemi" (p. 109). As I shall observe below, the Aristotelian El Pinciano will categorize the *Ethiopian History* as such a poem, i.e., one based entirely on fictitious matter, and will commend Heliodorus' observance of verisimilitude by choosing distant, unknown lands as his setting. It is probable that Tasso's words were influential in Cervantes' original conception of the *Persiles*, where both the northern landscape and customs of "paesi di nuovo ritrovati" beyond the Pillars of Hercules appear in the service of a verisimilar, i.e., legitimate marvelous (see below, Part III, Chap. VIII).

He should not be too unrestrained in feigning things that are impossible, monstrous, prodigious, and unbecoming . . . but *he should consider the power of the art of magic and that of nature itself as if enclosed within certain limits and restricted by certain laws,* and he should consider the ancient and old wonders, and the occasions of the marvelous occurrences, the miracles, and the prodigies, as well as the diversity of religions and the seriousness of the persons involved; and *he should try to increase as much as he can our faith in the marvelous phenomenon* without diminishing our pleasure in it.[56]

It is important to note that the prodigious, a major source of the marvelous since Homer and an inseparable element of the romance of chivalry, is allowed *if* it conforms to the laws of magic and nature and does not offend against the religious views and standards of propriety of the particular audience of the poet. This pairing of the laws of nature and magic may be incomprehensible to the modern audience, and indeed since the mid-seventeenth century the notion that Tasso was a poet of wild fantasies has been repeated often by critics. Such a judgment, however, fails to do justice to Tasso's ceaseless preoccupation with truth and verisimilitude, and ignores the significance of a development which would inevitably have an important effect on that area of aesthetic problems which preoccupied Tasso most, that of the verisimilar and the marvelous. This development was man's discovery and acceptance of experimental science as a method of dealing with the problem of truth, a development which separates modern sensibilities from those of the Renaissance by an unbridgeable chasm.[57]

[56] ". . . non sia troppo licenzioso nel fingere le cose impossibili, le mostruose, le prodigiose, le sconvenevoli . . . ma *consideri il poter dell'arte maga e della natura istessa quasi rinchiuso dentro a certi confini e ristretto sotto alcune leggi,* e gli antichi e i vecchi prodigi, e l'occasioni delle meraviglie e de' miracoli e de' mostri, e la diversità delle religioni, e la gravità delle persone; e *cerchi di accrescere quanto egli può fede alla meraviglia* senza diminuire il diletto" (*Del poema eroico*, pp. 110-111). The italics are mine.

[57] In order to understand Tasso's theories of the marvelous and the sincerity of his belief that he is reconciling the miraculous and the plausible, it is well to remember that in the sixteenth century modern experimental science was barely in its formative stages and that man had not yet solved the problem of the knowledge of the external world. Tasso's theories of the marvelous were nourished by such disciplines as magic, astrology, teratology, and demonology, the findings of which

The Genesis of the *Persiles*

The closest approximation to the traditional elements of the miraculous in literature in Tasso's legitimized marvelous lies in his theory of the Christian marvelous. Herein the modern poet enjoys the license of presenting actions and things which violate all natural laws and incorporating into his work those miraculous elements which were so important in ancient literature and romance. Indeed in introducing his theory, Tasso asserts that there is a marvelous in subject matter that is independent of the marvelous produced by verse and would not lose its effect in a prose context. He offers as examples, taken for the most part from the romances of chivalry,

---

for the Renaissance mind possessed all the empirical validity which we attribute to the findings of natural science. "So long as definite *criteria* of experience were not created through the medium of mathematics and through the other new intellectual means furnished by it, the empiricism of the Renaissance lacked objective standards of value and any principle of selection among the teeming phenomena. . . . The theory of nature of the fifteenth and sixteenth centuries laid the first foundation for exact description and exact experimentation; but closely connected with this, we find also the attempts at the foundation of an 'empirical magic.' . . . Thus, the world of experience here borders on the world of miracles, and both constantly overlap and merge with each other. The whole atmosphere of this 'science' of nature is filled to the brim with miracles" (Ernst Cassirer, *The Individual and The Cosmos in Renaissance Philosophy*, tr. M. Domandi, Harper Torchbook [New York, 1964], pp. 151-152).

A good example of the coexistence of the genuine desire to ascertain the truth and the capability of embracing the most fantastic phenomena as scientifically authorized was a work which offered Cervantes much of the legitimately marvelous subject matter of the *Persiles*, Antonio de Torquemada's *Jardín de flores curiosas* (1570). Here we observe over and over again the subjection of apparently incredible phenomena from the inexhaustible province of nature to tests of credibility. However, the orientation is toward the validation of unusual phenomena rather than the establishment of general laws of nature. Indeed the greater part of the dialogues seem to be intended to confirm the assumption that nature, the creation of God, is ultimately unknowable in its teeming variety. Hearsay reports on phenomena are measured by such authorities as Galen, Aristotle, and Pliny, and syllogistic reasoning is the method of the measurement. The work admits the validity of both demonic and the "empirical" magic which Cassirer mentions as well as such prodigies as sea monsters, sheep with eight horns, and the extraordinary birth of 366 children in one delivery of a Princess Margarita of Ireland. Any problems that arise as reports of witnesses occasionally strain the capacity for belief of the participants in Torquemada's dialogue are resolved by the reminder of the infinite variety of God's universe, the workings of which obey the logic of God's will, which in last analysis is unfathomable for the human mind. It could be recalled that Montaigne too accepted the existence of "incredible" monsters and cited the will of God as a "natural law" which the human mind can never fathom: "Ce que nous appelons monstres, ne le sont pas à Dieu . . . cette raison universelle et naturelle chasse de nous l'erreur et l'estonnement que la nouvelleté nous apporte" (*Essais*, II, xxx).

"the enchanted rings, the flying horses, the ships transformed into nymphs, and those spirits which intervene in the battle, the flaming sword, the wreath of flowers, the well-guarded chamber, the arch of true lovers, and the other inventions."[58] Tasso proceeds to recognize the problem of coupling the marvelous and verisimilitude, but denies that the two categories are contradictory: "I judge that one and the same action may be both marvelous and verisimilar."[59] He maintains that such phenomena as those listed above will capture the belief of the audience if they are given an acceptable supernatural cause. The wonders of Christian mythology are universally accepted, and consequently, so long as such servants of God and Satan as angels and witches are involved in violations of the laws of empirical reality, the audience will readily accept suspension of the workings of natural law and the most prodigious feats imaginable:

The poet should ascribe to God, his angels, the devils, or those to whom power is granted by God or the devils—saints, sorcerers, and fairies—actions which far exceed the power of men. If such actions are considered in themselves, they appear marvelous, indeed they are called miracles in common parlance. If the power of him who has performed these same acts is considered, they will be judged verisimilar, because, as people of our time have been nursed in the very cradle on the belief in such powers, and, as it has been confirmed in them by the teachings of the holy faith, . . . they will not judge implausible what they believe not only to be possible but indeed to have occurred many times and apt to occur again many times in the future. . . . Thus one and the same action may be both marvelous and verisimilar, marvelous considering it in itself and circumscribed within natural limits, verisimilar considering it removed from these limits in its cause, which is a supernatural force powerful and accustomed to produce such marvels.[60]

[58] ". . . parlo de gli anelli incantati, de' corsieri volanti, delle navi converse in ninfe e di quelle larve che s'interpongono nella battaglia, dell'ardente spada, della ghirlanda de' fiori, della camera difesa, dell'arco de' leali amanti e d'altre invenzioni" (*Del poema eroico*, p. 93).

[59] ". . . giudico che un'azione medesima possa essere e meravigliosa e verisimile" (ibid., p. 96).

[60] "Attribuisca il poeta alcune operazioni, che di gran lunga eccedono il poter de gli uomini, a Dio, a gli angioli suoi, a' demoni o a coloro a' quali da Dio o da'

The Genesis of the *Persiles*

As much of what follows in my study centers on Cervantes' criticism of the neo-Aristotelians' doctrine of verisimilitude, it is perhaps fitting to conclude the presentation of Tasso's theories of the marvelous by pointing to their effect on his creative activity. For nothing demonstrates more aptly the inhibiting power which the Renaissance view of mimetic art could exercise over the poet. In spite of the subtle distinctions between an illegitimate and a legitimate marvelous in Tasso's theories, the problem of verisimilitude became an obsessive preoccupation which haunted him throughout his creative endeavors. It caused him, on the one hand, to expurgate his masterpiece, the *Gerusalemme liberata*, of any subject matter which

---

demoni è conceduta potestà, quali sono i santi, i magi e le fate. Queste opere, se per se stesse saranno considerate, meravigliose parranno, anzi miracoli sono chiamati nel commune uso di parlare. Queste medesime, se si averà riguardo alla virtù e alla potenza di chi l'ha operate, verisimili saranno giudicate, perché, avendo gli uomini nostri bevuta nelle fasce insieme col latte questa opinione, ed essendo poi in loro confermata da i maestri della nostra santa fede . . . non parrà loro fuori del verisimile quello che credono non solo esser possibile, ma stimano spesse fiate esser avvenuto e poter di nuovo molte volte avvenire. . . . Può esser dunque una medesima azione e meravigliosa e verisimile: meravigliosa riguardandola in se stessa e circonscritta dentro a i termini naturali, verisimile considerandola divisa da questi termini, nella sua cagione, la quale è una virtù sopranaturale, possente e usata a far simili meraviglie" (ibid., pp. 96-97). Like most of Tasso's theories, that of the Christian marvelous had been anticipated by his predecessors, who, nevertheless, did not present it in relation with the acute problem of the fusion of the plausible and the miraculous which preoccupied Tasso. In defense of poetry against criticisms of its departure from the possible Trissino condones the use of such apparent impossibilities as *gli Angeli, i Demonj, la Necromanzia*, and *incanti*, because the contemporary audience accepts their existence (*Le sei divisioni della poetica, Tutte le opere*, II, 118). Geraldi Cintio draws the parallel between the romancer's introduction of fairies and infernal spirits and the ancient poets' introduction of the pagan gods to unravel a complicated plot, but associates the practice with neither the marvelous nor the verisimilar (see *De' romanzi*, pp. 80-82). Similarly Pigna allows the use of saints, hermits, angels, demons, magicians, and witches, which he compares to the ancient nymphs, e.g., Circe and Calypso, in a role parallel to that of the ancient *deus ex machina*. However, unlike Tasso his attitude is hostile to the resort to the miraculous, be it Christian or pagan, and he recommends that the poet avoid it if at all possible (see *I romanzi*, p. 38). Closer to Tasso's theories was Minturno's reasoning concerning the Christian supernatural, which accompanies his defense of the relevance of the classical rules for heroic poetry in the modern epoch and in the Italian language. He claims that God, the angels, and the saints parallel the pagan deities, that the necromancers and magicians parallel the old oracles and sibyls, and that the angels parallel Hermes and Jove's other messengers (see *L'arte poetica*, p. 31). Minturno's arguments are repeated by the Spanish theorist Francisco Cascales in his *Tablas poéticas* (1617) (see ed. A. de Sancha [Madrid, 1779], p. 132).

offended against the narrow mimesis concept. On the other hand it led him to turn half-heartedly to a non-Aristotelian justification of implausibilities by allegorical readings. And finally he resorted to a source of epic composition which, in his early theoretical writings he had rejected as imposing too many restrictions on the poet's inventive powers, the Bible, where the marvelous and the absolutely true are unquestionably conjoined.

CONCLUSION

Tasso's critical and creative effort was in large part an attempt to purify the genre of romance, eliminating its major flaws and reconciling its positive qualities with the Aristotelian-Horatian rules for epic poetry. The attempt focused on the two aesthetic shortcomings of the genre which had been recognized by the classicists since the initial popularization of Aristotle's *Poetics* shortly before the middle of the century, its violation of the principles of unity and verisimilitude. In his attempted reconciliation Tasso upholds the classicists' demands concerning unity and structural arrangement while liberalizing somewhat their strict interpretation of Aristotle's allowances for the episode in the epic context. Regarding verisimilitude and the all-important matter of the pleasure associated with the marvelous in literature, Tasso accepted the classicists' notion that the *dotti* can experience such pleasure only if the poet does not overstride the limits of the plausible. He therefore devised an elaborate system of distinguishing a legitimate marvelous from an illegitimate marvelous. The former is based on language, structural elements, variety in description and subject matter, great historical occurrence, and the Christian supernatural.[61] The latter arises from un-

---

[61] In the *Persiles* Cervantes employs all the techniques of the legitimized marvelous which appear in the writings of the sixteenth-century Aristotelians and find fullest expression in the theories of Tasso. To do justice to the ambivalence that marks Cervantes' attitudes toward them, I have chosen to introduce them as I deal with Cervantes' various dramatizations of literary problems rather than to list them systematically with examples. (Such a presentation can be found in E. C. Riley's valuable study *Cervantes's Theory of the Novel* [Oxford, 1962], pp. 178-199.) An understanding of the *Persiles*, in which Cervantes generally submits to the aesthetic currents of the age, his humorous allusions to the process of the legitimization of the marvelous, and such fundamental issues as the romances of chivalry and belief in the *Quixote*, presupposes an awareness of the theoretical development which I have traced in the preceding pages.

controlled multiplicity in subject matter and violations of the laws of empirical reality which have no causes in the Christian supernatural. Only the uneducated mind can experience pleasure in the illegitimate marvelous, and it is to such a mind that the absurdities of the romances appeal.

That Tasso's reconciliation provoked attacks from both sides, the defenders of Ariosto and the strict classicists, and that late in life he tended to sway from his established position and move in the direction of the latter need not concern us here.[62] What is significant is Tasso's position in the development of literary taste concerning the romances of chivalry in the sixteenth century. We have observed a steadily increasing complexity in the factors contributing to the formation of this taste, which evolved from the complete negativism that marked medieval critical evaluation of the genre and continued in the writings of Renaissance moralists (Vives), through the tolerant disdain generally characteristic of the judgments of Renaissance humanism in its orientation toward the practical, the informative, and the edifying in literature (Juan de Valdés), toward a negative aesthetic evaluation of the genre by the early Aristotelians (Trissino and those whom Fornari rebuts in his defense of Ariosto). The shift in critical orientation toward an examination from a purely aesthetic point of view led to the recognition that the romances offer the modern reader a pleasure that is unobtainable in the classics and the consequent attempt to accommodate the genre to the classical aesthetic principles.

Of the various factors contributing to this evolution in critical taste two were most important. One was the discovery of Aristotle's *Poetics* and the popularization of Horatian-Aristotelian literary theory, which recognized the importance of pleasure, the marvelous, and the fictitious in literature. The other was the enormous popularity of the romances, particularly of Ariosto's *Orlando Furioso* in Italy, where the arbiters of literary tastes of the age could not fail to discover both the appeal and the challenge represented by his work.

It was precisely this evolution in critical taste which lay behind

---

[62] See Weinberg, pp. 1054ff. More will be said of the reaction of the defenders of Ariosto below in the analysis of Don Quixote's rejoinder to the Canon of Toledo.

both Cervantes' articulate engagement with classical literary theory and his attitudes toward the romance of chivalry. As we shall see, the complexity that marks Cervantes' attitudes goes beyond that of any other figure of the age. Nevertheless, of the two basic tendencies marking his position, one must be understood firmly within the tradition which we have examined, for it is nearly identical with that represented by Torquato Tasso. This position is embodied in Cervantes' Canon of Toledo, and it is to it that the genesis of the *Persiles* can be attributed. However, before passing to Cervantes, it is necessary to complete the picture of the literary theory which lies behind the *Persiles*. An undercurrent of the critique of the romances of chivalry and the movement toward an accommodation of the romance to classical literary theory was the discussion and evaluation of a Greek work, the discovery of which by happy coincidence was almost simultaneous with the "rediscovery" of Aristotle in the Pazzi translation.[63] The *Ethiopian History* of Heliodorus appeared at an opportune moment, and its immediate entry into the province of theorizing surrounding the problems discussed above was inevitable.

A NOTE ON RENAISSANCE INTERPRETATIONS OF MIMESIS

Cervantes' recurrent critical dialogue with the neo-Aristotelians is meaningful only if the force of the "empirical" or "mirroring" orientation in their interpretations of mimesis is recognized. In view of this orientation I find misleading Spingarn's suggestion that the Aristotelian theory of imitation was understood by Renaissance literary theorists as it is understood today and that it offered an answer to the Platonic and medieval objections to imaginative literature.[64] Just as misleading are M. Herrick's words: "Butcher's elaborate analysis of Aristotle's theory of artistic imitation may not be a thoroughly accurate picture of what Aristotle himself believed, but his summary of poetic imitation will stand as an excellent statement of what the sixteenth-century commentators on Horace evolved from

---

[63] Giorgio Valla's Latin translation of the *Poetics* was published in 1498. However, the work did not have a significant effect on literary activity until the publication of the Greek text and Alessandro de' Pazzi's Latin translation in 1536 (see Weinberg, pp. 361ff.).

[64] *Literary Criticism in the Renaissance*, p. 12.

The Genesis of the *Persiles*

their study of Horace, Plato, Aristotle and Cicero. Butcher says: ' "Imitation," in the sense in which Aristotle applies the word to poetry, is thus seen to be equivalent to "producing" or "creating according to a true idea" '."[65]

It is more accurate to recognize that the Platonic and medieval objection to the fictitious aspect of literature prevailed in the interpretations of the Renaissance theorists to the extent that they could *not* understand Aristotle as did Butcher. With more discernment Guerrieri Crocetti interprets the numerous references to the function of ideal truth in poetry in documents of the age: "The words with which Aristotle distinguished poetry and history, with their respective attributes of particularity and universality, frequently reappear in these treatises, but without really grasping the thought which informed them in any but a superficial way and without enlivening that thought or developing it. They represent neither a point of departure toward new paths of inquiry nor a point of arrival, where the restless movements of thought are quieted; nor do they represent a point for discussion, which might yield new truths and energies; they are rather abstracted quotations and contribute nothing to the definition of mimesis." For most Renaissance theorists "the particular was not felt to be transcended in the concept of the universal."[66] Their preoccupation was with truth and falsehood in literature, and their interpretation of mimesis could not overcome a realist or naturalist tendency and an orientation toward external or objective truth rather than a more abstract truth.[67] The result was, to use M. H. Abrams' terminology, that Renaissance mimetic theories succumbed to one of the "troublesome implications of the mirror," its function as a literal reflector.[68]

Observing the vacillation in Aristotle's *Poetics* between "a concept of art as form, which aspires to the transfiguration of reality, and a concept of art as subject matter, which qualifies and controls the

[65] *The Fusion of Horatian and Aristotelian Literary Criticism, 1531-1555, Illinois Studies in Language and Literature*, XXXII (Urbana, 1946), p. 38; the passage which Herrick cites is from *Aristotle's Theory of Poetry and Fine Arts* (London, 1895), p. 153.
[66] *G. B. Giraldi ed il pensiero critico del sec. XVI* (Milan, 1932), p. 273.
[67] Ibid., pp. 264-265.
[68] See *The Mirror and the Lamp*, Norton Library Paperback (New York, 1958), pp. 34-35.

46

veracity or the mendacity of the artist," Luigi Russo points out that the Renaissance consistently interpreted the concept as *la mimesi tutta materia* and not as *la mimesi tutta forma*. Imitation, as theorists of the age conceived it, was a reproduction of an external reality on which the work of art is then dependent. "Once the principle of art as verisimilar, of art as adjusted to phenomenal reality, is accepted, this verisimilitude must be absolute."[69]

One of the most important results of this interpretation was a repeated insistence on historical subject matter in poetry and a preoccupation with the fear that the historian would discover falsehoods in the poet's adaptation of historical matter. At the same time there was the subordination of the historical to the verisimilar that Aristotle demanded and an interpretation of the verisimilar to allow the poet's inventive powers to work in his creation. However, the interpretation was oriented toward the objects of imitation and was dominated entirely by the issue of audience credibilty in the empirical reality or possibility of the things and actions of the plot. For example, a poet could fabricate some details of an historical occurrence *if* the historical knowledge of the occurrence of his audience was not sufficient to prove that the fabricated events do not conform to history and *if* the fabricated events conform to the laws of probability.[70]

Giuseppe Zonta has correctly observed this historical-empirical tendency in the sixteenth-century readings of Aristotle's theory of imitation, offering an explanation that is, in my opinion, too simple. He conveniently isolates the two aspects of mimesis, the particular and the universal, and associates them respectively with two currents in Renaissance literary theorizings, the didactic (the *pedagogica*) and the pleasurist (the *edonistica*). The former assumed that the edifying function of art is dependent on an historical plot or one which corresponds closely to empirical reality and emphasized the

[69] "La poetica di Aristotile e la coerenza degli interpreti del Rinascimento," *Problemi di metodo critico* (Bari, 1929), pp. 100-101. See also Weinberg, p. 802: "the theorists were really concerned with nature rather than with poetry . . . they were neglecting, for the nonce, those conditions—both of the poem and of its audience—which make a poem different from its object in nature."

[70] Rather than list examples here, I will use theorists' judgments of Heliodorus as well as various statements of Tasso on problems of artistic selectivity to demonstrate this point more clearly in the following chapters.

47

"particular"; the latter employed the "universal" as a justification for the fantastic.[71] Zonta sees the pleasurists, among them Tasso, as triumphing in the emergence of the literary taste which historiography calls *secentismo*. The scheme is neat for the purposes of literary historiography but fails to deal adequately with the real problems. For example the assumption that the historical-empirical tendency in the mimesis interpretation is the result purely of the didactic current is not sound. Moreover, Zonta overlooks the fact that the *fictio fabulosa* cannot be so conveniently dissociated from the didactic and completely fails to do justice to Tasso's attempt to fuse the fantastic and the empirical-historical by carefully delineating the limits of the marvelous in accordance with the intermediary concept of the verisimilar. Zonta indeed fails to analyze the range of implications encompassed by the "verisimilar" and in the interests of his scheme does no more than to point out the way in which the concept could be used to buttress a defense of the fantastic.[72] The important Renaissance differentiation between the verisimilar fiction and the nonverisimilar fiction, i.e., the "illegitimate" fantastic, is ignored. A much more accurate picture of the theoretical pressures of the age which centered on the mimesis-verisimilitude concept and the opposing tendencies toward the extremes of the empirical and the fantastic, can be obtained in Ulrich Leo's study, *Torquato Tasso*.[73]

[71] "Rinascimento aristotelismo e barocco," *Giornale Storico della Letteratura Italiana*, CIV (1934), 1-63, 185-240, esp. pp. 21-27.

[72] Ibid., p. 37.

[73] See Part II, Chaps. 3-6, where, to be sure, Leo emphasizes the importance of the individual psychological predisposition of Tasso in his relationship to the movement of literary theorizing of the century.

CHAPTER II

Heliodorus and Literary Theory

Not everyone can be a Theagenes or an Aristotle.
                                        Cristóbal Suárez de Figueroa

I offer you the *Trabajos de Persiles*, a book which dares to compete with Heliodorus.

                                        Cervantes

IN 1526, one year before Alessandro de' Pazzi wrote the dedication to the translation of Aristotle's *Poetics* which would lead to the reorientation of Renaissance literary theory, an event occurred which was to have far-reaching consequences in the development of the European prose narrative. During the sack of Buda by the Turks, a soldier discovered the richly bound manuscript of Heliodorus' *Aethiopica* in the library of King Matthias Corvinus of Hungary. Shortly thereafter this postclassical Greek romance[1] came into the possession of Vincentius Obsopoeus, who published it in Greek in Basel in 1534. In 1547 Amyot's French translation appeared, to be followed shortly by Warschewicski's Latin (1552) and Ghini's Italian (1556) versions. The Spanish humanists were quick to turn their attention to the newly discovered classical work, and the celebrated Hellenist, Francisco de Vergara undertook the task of translating it. Unfortunately his translation has not survived; and so credit for the first Spanish rendering of the *Ethiopian History* must go to an unknown translator, whose version, based on Amyot's French, appeared in Antwerp in 1554. In 1587 Fernando de Mena, claiming to offer a

---

[1] Throughout my study I refer to the prose works of Heliodorus, Achilles Tatius, and Longus as "Greek romances." I regard the designation *novela bizantina*, commonly used by Spanish literary historiography to refer to these works and medieval and Renaissance imitations of them, inappropriate and misleading. I prefer to follow Erwin Rohde, who makes a distinction between Greek and Byzantine works (see *Der Griechische Roman und seine Vorläufer* [Leipzig, 1900], pp. 554ff.), using "Byzantine" as a chronological-geographical (i.e., not a stylistic) term to refer to the civilization which flourished in Constantinople from around the fifth century to the fall of the city to the Turks in 1453 and to the cultural production of this civilization. As for the term "novel," if it is to mean anything more specific than "long prose fiction," I prefer that it be used to refer to fiction in which actuality and character are dominant elements. "Romance" is a convenient term in English (although not in Spanish) for referring to fiction in which plot or action (as opposed to character) and the wish-fulfillment dream (as opposed to actuality) are dominant.

more faithful translation by working from the original Greek text, published a new edition in Alcalá de Henares.[2]

In this chapter I am not concerned with the many cases of specific influence which Heliodorus' work had on all forms of literature of the sixteenth and seventeenth centuries.[3] As I am seeking to clarify Cervantes' artistic intentions and aspirations in the plan of the work which he regarded as his masterpiece, I have found it more fruitful to situate the Greek work within the climate of literary tastes and problems which I have attempted to describe above in Chapter I. Various critical documents indicate beyond all doubt, first, that the *Ethiopian History* was a frequent topic of discussion among the Renaissance classicists and was measured favorably by all the aesthetic categories which they had derived in their rigorous exegesis of the poetics of Horace and Aristotle, and, second, that the Greek work in its relation to the old prose romances of chivalry came to occupy a place in literary theorizing analogous to that of the classical epic in its relation to the verse romances.

By close examination of the major theoretical writings concerning the subject, I hope to reveal how the *Ethiopian History* was drawn into the orbit of contemporary literary theorizing and to shed more light on those fundamental aesthetic preoccupations—the legitimation of the marvelous and the matter of unity—which we must understand if we wish to understand the *Persiles* and numerous scenes in the *Quixote*. I find it convenient to begin with two documents which chronologically frame the development of the prose narrative from which Heliodorus' work cannot be dissociated. The one points toward all the major lines of development that the ensuing decades would witness, the other recapitulates the entire development within a fully formulated, classical theory of literature. I begin with the latter, reversing the order followed in the first chapter, for in its application of the Horatian-Aristotelian canon to the prose narrative, the stance represented by the document is analogous to that of Tasso's discourses in relation to the verse epic.

[2] See Michael Oeftering, *Heliodor und seine Bedeutung für die Literatur, Litterarhistorische Forschungen*, Vol. XVIII (Berlin, 1901), pp. 44-57; F. López Estrada, prologue to his edition of *Historia etiópica de los amores de Teágenes y Cariclea*, tr. F. de Mena (Madrid, 1954), pp. vii-xviii.

[3] A study of specific influence can be found in Oeftering's *Heliodor und seine Bedeutung für die Litteratur*, pp. 57-168.

Romances of Chivalry & the Classical Aesthetic

PIERRE-DANIEL HUET

Huet's *Traité de l'origine des romans* (1670) is the first systematic historical and critical treatment of the prose narrative in the history of criticism.[4] In tracing the development of the genre from its origins in the Milesian fables to the state of perfection which it reaches in the heroic *roman* of his contemporary, Mademoiselle de Scudéry, Huet accords to Heliodorus a most important role. The *Ethiopian History* represents for him a perfected form which the genre had achieved only after centuries and which was completely lost during the period of barbarism following the collapse of ancient civilization. However, at the moment when the medieval *roman* (i.e., the romance of chivalry) had fallen from its modest peak of aesthetic refinement in the late verse romances of the Italians (i.e., Ariosto and Boiardo) and found itself in a state of complete decay, Heliodorus' masterpiece was discovered. With the example of this "Homer of the *roman*" before them, writers undertook the process of purification which led to the perfection of the seventeenth-century French works.

In his analysis Huet establishes a division between *roman regulier* and *roman irregulier*, or, works which conform to high standards of art and those which do not. Huet's criteria of excellence include both didactic and aesthetic values. The major purpose of the *roman* is educational; hence both natural and moral wisdom are necessities in its composition ("The principal aim of *romans* . . . is the instruction of their readers, who must always be shown virtue rewarded and vice punished").[5] Of equal significance, however, are its observance of verisimilitude in its subject matter and plot ("verisimilitude, which is not always to be found in history, is essential to the *roman*";[6] *romanciers* must know how to "tell lies resembling the truth" [*conter des mensonges semblables à la verité*]) and its artistically coherent structure, which excludes any unessential elements

---

[4] See Max Ludwig Wolff, *Geschichte der Romantheorie* (Nuremberg, 1915), pp. 43-51.

[5] "La fin principale des Romans . . . est l'instruction des lecteurs, à qui il faut toûjours faire voir la vertu couronnée, & le vice puni" (Pierre-Daniel Huet, *Traité de l'origine des romans*, ed. A. Kok [Amsterdam, 1942], p. 115). Huet's definition of the *roman*: "Des histoires feintes d'aventures amoureuses, ecrites en prose avec art, pour le plaisir & l'instruction des lecteurs" (p. 114). The page references which follow are to this edition.

[6] ". . . la vray-semblance qui ne se trouve pas toûjours dans l'Histoire est essentielle au Roman" (p. 118).

and achieves a natural integration of episode and main plot.[7] These standards are obviously derived from the classical movement in criticism, and in effect Huet's theoretical effort was little more than an application to the *roman* of the theories on epic poetry which had been developed in the sixteenth century by the various theorists associated with the exegesis of Aristotle's *Poetics*. In fact at one point in his tract, he admits: "I call regular those [*romans*] which conform to the rules of the heroic poem."[8]

Like nearly all theorists of the Renaissance Huet follows Aristotle in regarding imitation and not verse as distinguishing poetry from nonpoetry; *romans* are poems, and he goes so far as to say that a metrical work can be a *roman*, offering Theodorus Podromus' *History of Rhodantes and Dosikles* as an example (p. 178).[9] In his occasional attempts to make distinctions between *roman* and epic, Huet succeeds merely in bringing into the foreground certain secondary possibilities for epic composition encompassed in the literary theorizing of the preceding century. Epic, in this theory, deals primarily with matters of war and politics and only occasionally with love, whereas *romans* "have love as their principal subject and treat politics and war only incidentally."[10] As for the fusion of the marvelous and the verisimilar, which the classicists had demanded in the epic, Huet claims that the *romancier* must pay more attention to the latter, and the epic poet more to the former, although he can never sacrifice verisimilitude. Moreover, although both *romancier* and epic poet must observe unity of plot, the former enjoys a greater license in the introduction of varied subject matter. Like the epic and tragic

[7] Huet's preference for the *in-medias-res* structural technique is evident in his censure of Longus (p. 179) and Iamblique's *Babyloniques*: ". . . l'ordonnance de son dessein manque d'art. Il a suivi grossierement l'ordre des temps, & n'a pas jetté d'abord le Lecteur dans le milieu du sujet, suivant l'example d'Homere" (p. 156). In criticizing the irrelevance of Achilles Tatius' digressions, Huet writes that the episodes "devroient estre ajustez si proprement avec la piece, qu'ils ne parussent qu'un mesme tissu" (p. 161).

[8] "J'appelle reguliers, ceux [les romans] qui sont dans les regles du Poëme Heroïque" (p. 182).

[9] Rohde describes the metrical work of this twelfth-century Byzantine monk as an unbearably decadent imitation of the *Aethiopica* (see *Der Griechische Roman und seine Vorläufer*, pp. 562-565).

[10] ". . . ont l'amour pour sujet principal, & ne traitent la politique & la guerre que par incident" (p. 116).

poets, the writer of *romans* must mingle the true, or the historical, and the false to construct a plausible plot. However, recalling Aristotle's recommendations of the historical plot for tragedy as well as his allowance for the possibility of an entirely fictitious plot, Huet adds that in the *roman* the entirely feigned plot is particularly successful ("la fiction totale de l'argument est plus recevable dans les Romans" [p. 118]).[11] In the judgment of Huet, Heliodorus is the writer who perfected the artistic possibilities of the genre and whose work has stood as a model for succeeding *romanciers*; he is indeed the Homer of the *roman*.

> Until then nothing more artfully contrived had been seen, nothing more finished in the art of writing *romans*, than the adventures of Theagenes and Chariklea. Nothing is more chaste than their amours . . . in them are seen much fertility and inventiveness. Events are frequent therein, new, verisimilar, well arranged, and well worked out. The *denouement* is admirable; it is natural; it arises naturally out of the subject; and nothing is more touching or more pathetic. The horror of the sacrifices, in which Theagenes and Chariklea are to be offered up and in which the heroine's beauty and admirable qualities inspired compassion in everyone, is followed by the joy of seeing this young woman emerge from this danger through the recognition of her parents and put an end to her lengthy misfortunes by a happy marriage to her lover, to whom she brings for a dowry the crown of Ethiopia. . . . *it served as a model to all writers of* romans *who followed it, and it may be said just as*

[11] As in all the other distinctions which mark his attempt to define *roman* vis-à-vis epic, Huet does not succeed in getting away from the theories of epic poetry formulated in the preceding century. He immediately qualifies his assertion by limiting it to plots involving characters of low condition, for example those of comic *romans*, suggesting the laws of comedy recognized by classicists on the basis of the ninth book of Aristotle's *Poetics*. For "dans les grands Romans, dont les Princes & les Conquerans sont les acteurs, & dont les aventures sont illustres & memorables . . . il ne seroit pas vray-semblable que des grands évenemens fussent demeurez cachez au monde, & neglegez par les Historiens" (p. 118). The same assumptions (the necessity of grandeur and verisimilitude) lie behind Tasso's recommendation of historical matter for the epic and cause El Pinciano some difficulty in dealing with the verisimilitude of the *Ethiopian History* (see below).

truthfully that they have all drawn upon it, as it is said that all *poets have drawn upon the model of Homer.*[12]

Significant for our purposes is Huet's analysis of the epoch succeeding the invasions of the barbarians as a period of decadence in the history of the *roman*, in which the perfection of the Greek *roman regulier* was forgotten and a new, inferior type emerged in France, of which the Spanish *romans* (i.e., the *libros de caballerías*) and Italian *romanzi* are the most modern descendants. Huet theorizes that the old French romances were the developments of earlier attempts to write historical chronicles by men who were incapable of distinguishing between the true and the false, e.g., Turpin, Hunibaldus Francus, Teilessen, and Melkinus. The fantasies of these attempts at historiography were so appealing to the audience of the Middle Ages that they soon disengaged completely from the bonds linking them to reality, and a new literary genre was born (see pp. 192-195). Huet has little respect for this degeneration in the fortunes of the *roman*: "Thus Spain and Italy received from us an art which was the fruit of our ignorance and of our rudeness."[13] The pleasure offered by the medieval works is based on the attraction which the uncultivated mind feels for the purely fantastic; edifying and instructive matter is wanting in them; and in their composition they fail to follow the rules of the *romans reguliers* (218-219). In contrast to the tightly coherent structure achieved by Heliodorus the "old French had multiplied the actions without any kind of order, without proper connections, and without art. It is they whom the

---

[12] "Jusqu'alors on n'avoit rien veu de mieux entendu, ni de plus achevé dans l'art Romanesque, que les aventures de Theagene & de Chariclée. Rien n'est plus chaste que leurs amours . . . on y remarque beaucoup de fertilité & d'invention. Les évenemens y sont fréquens, nouveaux, vray-semblables, bien arrangez, bien débroüillez. Le denoüëment en est admirable; il est naturel, il naist de sujet, & rien n'est plus touchant, ni plus pathetique. A l'horreur du sacrifice, où l'on devoit immoler Theagene & Chariclée, dont la beauté & le merite touchoit tout le monde de compassion, succede la joye de voir cette jeune fille sortir de ce danger par la reconnoissance de ses parens, & finir enfin ses longues miseres par un heureux mariage avec son amant, à qui elle porte pour dot la couronne d'Ethiopie. . . . *il a servi de modele à tous les faiseurs de Romans, qui l'ont suivi, & on peut dire aussi veritablement qu'ils ont tous puisé à sa source, que l'on a dit tous les Poëtes ont puisé à celle d'Homere*" (157-158). The italics are mine.

[13] "Ainsi l'Espagne & l'Italie receurent de nous un art, qui estoit le fruit de nostre ignorance & de nostre grossiereté" (p. 211); see also p. 219.

Italians have imitated. In taking the *romans* from them, they have taken their defects."[14]

Huet concludes his study on the optimistic note that the long period of decadence, in which the romance of chivalry flourished, has finally ended, and that through the efforts of d'Urfé ("the first to rescue our *romans* from barbarism and to subject them to the rules")[15] and Mademoiselle de Scudéry the genre has rediscovered the perfection which it had once known with Heliodorus' work.[16]

In summary, Huet's treatise presents a theory of prose fiction based entirely on Aristotelian-Horatian poetic doctrines. It applies to the prose narrative the theory of epic poetry developed by classicists of the preceding century (i.e., heroism, love, unity, verisimilitude, the exemplary, the encyclopedic). It celebrates Heliodorus as the example of the perfection achieved by the Greeks in the cultivation of the *roman regulier* and therefore as a model for subsequent *romanciers*. And finally, it clearly formulates a distinction between the *roman regulier* of Heliodorus and Huet's contemporaries and the primitive romance of chivalry.

AMYOT

From Huet's vantage point the process which brought the end of the romance of chivalry and the triumph of the "purified" *roman*

[14] ". . . les vieux François les [actions] avoient multipliées sans ordonnance, sans liaison, & sans art. Ce sont eux que les Italiens ont imitez. En prenant d'eux les Romans, ils en ont pris les défauts" (p. 168); see also p. 170. Huet proceeds to reject Giraldi's defense of the multiplicity of actions of the *romanzi*, affirming the Aristotelian principle of a single action, to which all others are subordinate, and drawing the analogy which nearly all of the classicists, including Cervantes' Canon of Toledo, use to describe the well-made plot: ". . . le Roman doit ressembler à un corps parfait, & estre composé de plusieurs parties differentes & proportionnées sous un seul chef, il s'ensuit que l'action principale, qui est comme le chef du Roman, doit estre unique & illustre en comparaison des autres; & que les actions subordonnées, qui sont comme les membres, doivent se rapporter à ce chef, luy ceder en beauté & en dignité, l'orner, le soustenir, & l'accompagner avec dépendance: autrement ce sera un corps à plusieurs testes, monstrueux & difforme" (p. 169).

[15] ". . . le premier qui tira nos Romans de la barbarie, & les assujettit aux regles" (p. 228).

[16] Huet points out that Heliodorus' final scene of reversal and recognition inspired a similar scene in *L'Astrée* (p. 158). Mademoiselle de Scudéry herself writes in her prologue to *Le Grand Cyrus*: "Je vous diray donc que j'ay pris et je prendrai tousjours pour mes uniques Modelles l'immortel Héliodore et le Grand Urfé" (cited by Oeftering, *Heliodor und seine Bedeutung für die Literatur*, p. 77).

of his epoch is complete and clear. For our purposes it is necessary
to direct our attention to the incipient stages of the process, following the steps which led to Cervantes' attempt to realize aesthetically
all the goals which Huet's discursive formulation would set for the
prose narrative fifty years later. Appearing in 1617, the *Persiles*
stands on the threshold of the movement in prose fiction which
Huet was to applaud. However, in reality the roots of the *Persiles*
reach back through three quarters of a century of literary theorizing
to those basic aesthetic problems raised by the early critics of the
romance of chivalry. It is significant that perhaps the first broadly
aesthetic evaluation of the romances of chivalry which appeared in
Spain was the preface by which J. Amyot introduced his 1547
French translation of Heliodorus' *Ethiopian History*. The 1554
Spanish version is accompanied by this document, included by "a
secret friend of his country" (*un secreto amigo de su patria*), who
redirects Amyot's criticism of the old French romances against their
Spanish counterparts.[17]

Amyot's standards of aesthetic evaluation are by his own admission derived from Horace's *Ars Poetica* and Strabo's discussion of
poetry in the first two parts of Book I of the *Geography*. In the last
analysis, poetry is to be judged for its utility and is subordinate to
historical writing. It is justified insofar as delight and relaxation
from the serious side of life are demanded by humanity in its weakness.[18] Nevertheless, its instructive value is of primary importance,
and by no means is a poet to rely solely on delight through the

---

[17] *Historia etiópica de los amores de Teágenes y Cariclea*, tr. F. de Mena, ed. F.
López Estrada (Madrid, 1954), pp. lxxvii-lxxxiii. The following page references are
to this edition.

[18] ". . . la imbecilidad de nuestra natura no puede sufrir que el entendimiento
esté siempre ocupado a leer materias graves y verdaderas" (lxxvii). Amyot, who
regarded his most serious enterprise to be the translation of Plutarch, is typical of
Renaissance historians in his theory of the utility of historiography: ". . . ella [la
historia] haya de ser escrita o leída, antes para por ejemplos de lo pasado instruirse
en los negocios de lo venidero . . ." (lxxviii-lxxix). Literature of entertainment has
its justification because historical writing is "un poco austera" and lacks the delightful rhetorical embellishments which human nature in its "imbecilidad" demands.
Cervantes' curate and canon, whose theories on the purification of the romance of
chivalry recall many of Amyot's judgments, have the same skeptical attitude toward
the function of literature. The best of literature is to be allowed only because "no
es posible que esté continuo el arco armado, ni la condición y flaqueza humana se
pueda sustentar sin alguna lícita recreación" (*Don Quijote*, I, 488).

presentation of pleasing fictions. By synthesizing passages of Horace and Strabo, Amyot derives a theory of verisimilitude which is essentially the same as that by which the Renaissance interpreters of Aristotle's *Poetics* would repeatedly judge the romances. Invoking Horace, he claims that "it is necessary that things which are feigned for entertainment be close to the truth."[19] He retreats, however, from the possible implication that poetry could conceivably be entirely based on "untruth" by adding "it is not necessary that everything be feigned, for, as we know, this is not even permitted to the poets themselves"[20] and interpreting Strabo's formula for poetic creation:

Because, as Strabo writes so learnedly, the art of poetic invention consists of three things: first, of history, the aim of which is truth. Consequently it is not permitted that poets, when speaking of natural things, should write as they please, contradicting truth, because this would be attributed not to their license or art, but rather to their ignorance. Secondly, of order and disposition, the aim of which is to present the subject matter and to hold the reader's attention. Thirdly, of fiction, the aim of which is to inspire wonder and to arouse that delectation which proceeds from the experience of the novelty of things which are strange and wonderful. Accordingly, unrestricted license in the inclusion of things should be all the more prohibited in fictions which we wish to disguise with the name of true history. It is necessary to mix intelligently truth and falsehood, maintaining always the appearance of truth and relating the one to the other, so that there is no discord between the beginning and the middle, and between the middle and the end.[21]

[19] ". . . es menester que las cosas fingidas para delectación sean cercanas de las verdaderas" (lxxix). The allusion is to Horace, *Epistola ad Pisones*, l. 338.

[20] ". . . no es menester que todas las cosas sean fingidas, sabiendo que aun a los poetas mismos no es permitido" (lxxix).

[21] "Porque el artificio de la invención poética, como doctamente escribe Strabón, consiste en tres cosas: primeramente en la Historia, de la que el fin es verdadero. Por lo cual no es lícito a los poetas, cuando hablan de las cosas de natura, escrebir a su voluntad de otra suerte que la verdad, porque esto les sería imputado no a licencia o artificio, mas a ignorancia. Segundamente, en orden y disposición, de lo cual el fin es la declaración y fuerza de atraer al lector. Terceramente, la ficción, de la cual el fin es admiración, y la delectación que procede de la novedad de las cosas extrañas y llenas de admiración. Por lo cual, mucho menos se deben permitir todas cosas en las ficciones que queremos disfrazar con el nombre de Historia

The passage is characteristic of the dominant tendencies of Renaissance criticism. It reveals both the theorists' inability to divorce the poetic process from standards of informative or historical writing, standards which we no longer regard as relevant to the literary work, and their distrust of the purely fantastic, which is, as it were, almost grudgingly recognized as necessary but which is carefully restricted so as to exclude the implausible. Writing in the epoch in which Aristotle's doctrine containing a defense of the marvelous was just beginning to affect critical circles in Italy, Amyot in effect is acknowledging the necessary role of a marvelous which may be based on fiction, as Strabo had done in discussing the Homeric poems, and offering a compromise solution to the problem raised by the suspicious aesthetic category. His compromise is essentially the same as that which all commentators of the *Poetics* will make as they attempt to reconcile Aristotle's acknowledgment of the necessity of the marvelous with his demand for verisimilitude.

It is significant that in his discussion of verisimilitude Amyot refers to the type of literature represented by Heliodorus' work and by the older romances of chivalry as fictions written in the form of histories and disguised "with the name of true history." For at this moment the traditional, uncritical use of the word *historia* to refer to both works of historiography and works of imaginative fiction, specifically the romances of chivalry, was coming into sharp criticism by the emerging historiography of Renaissance humanists,[22] a criticism that would be reinforced by the influential Aristotelian differentiation of the provinces of the poet and the historian. Indeed Amyot's use of the term suggests that its long-established literary usage is still unshaken by the new critical forces. To him "disguised history" (*historia disfrazada*) remains a valid genre of prose literature, and Heliodorus' work in contrast to the old romances is an example of the perfectibility of the genre. Unlike its predecessors it

---

verdadera, antes es menester mezclar tan doctamente lo verdadero con lo falso, guardando siempre aparencia de verdad, y refiriendo lo uno a lo otro, de suerte que no haya discordancia del principio al medio ni del medio al fin" (lxxix-lxxx). The passage is based on Strabo, I, 2, 17 (see *Geography of Strabo*, tr. H. L. Jones, Loeb Classical Library [London, 1917], I, 90-93), and Horace, *Epistola ad Pisones*, ll. 150-152.

[22] See above, Chap. I, pp. 18-20.

combines the true and the false ideally to present an illusion of reality (*aparencia de verdad*). This flexibility within the range of uses of the term "history" is important to note at this point. As we shall see, Cervantes will exploit it for a humorous equivocation throughout his literary production, most notably in his creation of the Arab historian Cide Hamete Benengeli.

The statement of the aesthetic necessity of verisimilitude in the "disguised history" or "book of entertainment" (*libro de entretenimiento*) is the point of departure for a full-scale attack on the romances of chivalry, "books of this type which in the past have been written in our Spanish tongue."[23] Amyot's critique demonstrates well the degree to which didactic and aesthetic criteria were intertwined in the Renaissance humanist's view of art. Recalling the Horatian judgment of grotesque art which combines haphazardly various parts into unnatural wholes, a judgment which since Petrarch's "dream of sick minds and foolishness of romances" had become a topic of criticism of the romances, Amyot writes of the older works: "They are usually so dissonant and so removed from any resemblance to truth that they are more similar to the dreams of a sick man who raves in his fits of fever than to the inventions of a man of acumen and sound judgment." Moreover, in these works there is "no erudition, no knowledge of antiquity, nor a single thing, in truth, from which one may profit."[24] Amyot concludes that, lacking verisimilitude, erudition, and edification, the works cannot please a "good intellect," which does not recognize the appeal of "coarse and rude things." Here we observe another characteristic feature of the Renaissance critical movement, which will become a significant factor in the polemic over Ariosto and Tasso and in Cervantes' various examinations of the problems underlying the aims and functions of literature. Like nearly all Renaissance theorists Amyot stresses the importance of reason and education in the creation and

[23] ". . . los libros de esta suerte que han sido antiguamente escritos en nuestra lengua española" (lxxx). The Spanish translator here modifies Amyot's "escritz en nostre langue" (*L'Histoire aethiopique de Heliodorus*, n.p.).

[24] ". . . están las más veces tan disonantes y tan fuera de verdadera similitud, que paresce que sean antes sueños de algún enfermo que desvaría con la calentura, que invenciones de algún hombre de espíritu y sano juicio"; ". . . no hay ninguna erudición, ningún conocimiento de antigüedad ni cosa alguna, por decir verdad, de la cual se pueda sacar algún provecho."

apprehension of a work of art and treats the lower faculties of perception, i.e., the senses and the imagination, with contempt. The romances are the products of a sick mind rather than a healthy one (*sano juicio*). The pleasure that they afford is idle (*ocioso*), for it is not directed at the intellect (*juicio*). Underlying Amyot's demand for plausibility is an assumption which Tasso and his fellow neo-Aristotelians will develop further in their theories of verisimilitude and which Cervantes' Canon of Toledo will unquestioningly accept. An aesthetic pleasure which is based on reason is allegedly impossible if the object of apprehension clashes with the laws of empirical reality or, viewed in terms of a work of literature, if the things and actions which form the plot do not faithfully reflect the external world. "But just as among paintings the ones *which represent the truth of the natural world* are judged to be best *by those who know*, so among fictions the ones which are *closer to nature* and in which there is more *verisimilitude* please *those who measure their enjoyment with their rational faculties and take their pleasure wisely*."[25]

The educated reader will find all that is wanting in the old Spanish romances in Heliodorus' *Ethiopian History*. It is an "ingenious fiction" (*ingeniosa ficción*), by which Amyot apparently, in accordance with Strabo's counsel on the legitimate marvelous, means a plausible plot, or what most Renaissance neo-Aristotelians, including Cervantes' Canon of Toledo, will refer to as a "verisimilar fiction." In the work there are "beautiful discourses taken from natural and moral philosophy, many notable sayings and pithy maxims, and many orations and colloquies, in which the art of eloquence is employed very well."[26] Amyot's enthusiasm for such qualities is illustrative of the rhetorical emphasis of the Horatian critical tradition which will survive in the Renaissance commentaries of Aristotle's *Poetics*. As we shall see, rhetoric remains an important part of the Aristotelian-Horatian Canon of Toledo's formula for the

[25] "Mas ni más ni menos como entre las pinturas las tablas son estimadas por las mejores de *los que algo conoscen porque representan mejor la verdad del natural*, así entre las ficciones aquellas que están más *cerca de natura* y en las cuales hay más de *verisimilitud* son las que agradan más a *los que miden su placer con la razón y que se deleitan con juicio*" (lxxix). The italics are mine.

[26] ". . . hermosos discursos sacados de la filosofía natural y moral, muchos dichos notables y palabras sentenciosas, muchas oraciones y pláticas, en las cuales el artificio de elocuencia está muy bien empleado" (lxxx).

perfect book of chivalry. And finally the reader of the *Ethiopian History* will observe "human passions and inclinations painted so true to life and with such propriety that no one will be able to find in it any inspiration for wrong-doing. For the author shows all illicit and dishonorable inclinations leading to unhappiness and all good and honorable ones leading to happiness."[27] Behind these words of praise lie the Horatian precepts on the importance of pathos in poetry, the necessity that emotions be presented plausibly, and the civilizing and moral mission that poetry undertakes.[28]

At this point in his evaluation of Heliodorus' work Amyot turns his attention from all that concerns the subject matter and invention to the second traditional category governing rhetorical writing, *dispositio*, and voices a judgment which is to remain central to all succeeding commentaries on the *Ethiopian History*:

> And certainly the disposition is extraordinary, because he begins in the middle of the history, *just as heroic poets do*; and this immediately causes the readers to marvel and arouses in them the passionate desire to hear and understand the beginning; and moreover the author maintains their attention through the ingenious relating of his story, for they do not understand what they have read at the beginning of the first book until they see the end of the fifth; and when they have arrived at that point, they find themselves even more eager to see the end than they have been to see the beginning. Thus the *reader's mind remains constantly in suspense* until he comes to the conclusion, which then leaves him satisfied in the way in which people are satisfied when they finally possess and enjoy a thing which they have long hoped for and desired.[29]

[27] ". . . las pasiones y afecciones humanas, pintadas tan al verdadero y con tan gran honestidad, que no se podrá sacar ocasión de malhacer. Porque de todas aficiones ilícitas y deshonestas, él hace el fin desdichado; y, al contrario, de las buenas y honestas, dischoso" (lxxx).

[28] Horace, *Epistola ad Pisones*, ll. 99-113, 196-201, 309-316, 334-346, 391-407.

[29] "Y cierto la disposición es singular, porque comienza en la mitad de la Historia, *como hacen los poetas heroicos*, lo cual causa, de *prima facie*, una grande admiración a los lectores y les engendra un apasionado deseo de oír y entender el comienzo, y todavía los atrae también con la ingeniosa lección de su cuento, que no entienden lo que han leído en el comienzo del primer libro, hasta que veen el fin del quinto; y cuando allí han llegado, aún les queda mayor deseo de ver el fin,

The Genesis of the *Persiles*

Amyot's praise of Heliodorus' disposition and by implication his criticism of that of the older "disguised histories" rests on a veneration of the classical epics of Homer and Virgil and once again on the authority of his master in aesthetic matters, Horace. Horace's praise of Homer's narrative economy and swiftness based on the *in-medias-res* beginning was well-known to the Renaissance, and there were few pieces of literary theory dealing with the epic or the *romanzi* which failed to mention the "egg of Leda." Amyot's understanding of the *in-medias-res* structural technique, however, goes beyond that of Horace and is undoubtedly the product of his correct interpretation of Heliodorus' peculiar technique. It is not artistic selectivity and economy that he applauds but rather the *admiratio* occasioned by the suspense that the structure of the work arouses. Horace judges the basis of Homer's technique to be the general knowledge that his audience shares with the poet about the events that precede the opening moment of the narrative.[30] Amyot correctly interprets Heliodorus' structure as based on the reader's total ignorance of the occurrences surrounding the origins of the wanderings of his heroes and his desire to discover them. Amyot's association of suspense and *admiratio* with the *in-medias-res* technique was generally accepted by Renaissance theorists in the many discussions of the subject produced in the polemic surrounding heroic literature, both epic and romance.

After having praised the work of Heliodorus on the grounds discussed above, Amyot abruptly turns about-face and retracts his praise: "Still I do not wish to waste much time recommending it,

---

que antes tenían de ver el principio. De suerte que siempre *el entendimiento queda suspenso* hasta que viene a la conclusión, la cual deja al lector satisfecho, como lo son aquellos que al fin vienen a gozar de una cosa muy deseada y de mucho tiempo esperada" (lxxx-lxxxi). The italics are mine. As has been pointed out in Chapter I, one of the principal concerns of the controversy over the *romanzi*, which was just emerging in Italy at this time, was the loose structure of the modern works. Minturno claimed that the frequent fragmentation in their plot development and their sudden shifts from one action to another have the effect not of heightening suspense in the reader but rather of exhausting his patience (see *L'arte poetica*, pp. 34-35). Moreover, theorists noted that the romances frequently failed to observe the *in-medias-res* structural principle of classical epic, adhering to the principle of chronology, which most classicists thought appropriate only to historical writing (see Giraldi Cintio, *De' romanzi*, pp. 18-26).

[30] Horace, *Epistola ad Pisones*, ll. 148-149.

62

for in the final analysis it is merely a work of fiction."[31] Again we observe the ambiguous attitude toward literature of entertainment characteristic of the Renaissance humanist, who could judge the products of the creative imagination only in reference to the practical needs of life. He proceeds to ask forgiveness of the educated for having devoted his energies to such an insignificant task, to request that they accept his work as a means of relaxation from more serious readings, and to remind them that he translated the *Ethiopian History* in spare moments to relax from his work on "other better and more fruitful translations," referring undoubtedly to his long labors on the works of Plutarch. In the midst of this apology he inserts a criticism not of imaginative literature in general but of the *Ethiopian History* in particular, a criticism that will be repeated by subsequent judgments of the work and may suggest that Cervantes did indeed think that he could surpass his model. In the *Ethiopian History* one fails to find grandeur, for its hero Theagenes does not perform "any memorable feat of arms."

In conclusion Amyot's translation of Heliodorus appears at a moment of crisis in the history of the genre of medieval romance both in its verse form in Italy and its prose form in France and Spain. His prologue is of particular significance in Spain, for it offers one of the earliest documents containing an attack on the romances of chivalry from a fully formulated aesthetic view of literature. As such it can be compared with the roughly contemporaneous attacks on the Spanish romances of the Aristotelians Trissino and Pigna in Italy and stands as an example of the aesthetic criteria associated with Renaissance humanism in its orientation toward the informative and edifying possibilities of literature[32] and in its derivation from the classical theories of poetry of Horace and Strabo. However, Amyot's prologue is most important in its introduction of Heliodorus' work as a new, purified form of the "disguised history," acceptable to the prevailing tastes in literature, which had already judged the older form to be unsatisfactory.

[31] "Todavía no me quiero detener mucho a la encomendar, porque en fin es una fábula."

[32] Bataillon has discussed this document as an example of the literary tastes of the Christian humanist movement (see *Erasmo y España*, II, 222-225).

The Genesis of the *Persiles*

In his celebration of the Greek romance Amyot employs critical standards which will be taken over with minor modification in the emerging Aristotelianism that will dominate the academic movements of the second half of the century and lead to the influential theories of Tasso. In comparing the disposition of the *Ethiopian History* to that of the heroic poems and acclaiming the erudition, eloquence, and moral and natural philosophy which the work offers—qualities traditionally celebrated in Homer and Virgil— Amyot prepares the way for the theoretical acceptance of the possibility of the epic in prose. It will in fact become a frequent topic of literary discussion with the popularization of Aristotle's *Poetics* and its affirmation that imitation and not meter is the factor differentiating poetry from nonpoetry.

SCALIGER

In 1561, seven years after Amyot's prologue appeared in Spain, Julius Caesar Scaliger's *Poetices libri septem* was published posthumously in Lyon. This voluminous and influential treatise offered a synthesis of Horatian and Aristotelian literary theory, a critical-historical discussion of all categories of literature, a manual of instruction for those who would undertake the profession of poet, and an encyclopedic presentation of critical evaluations of works of literature written in the classical tongues. As we have seen, Amyot observes an analogy between the *Ethiopian History* and the works of the heroic poets in narrative structure. However, far from proceeding from analogy to identification, he not only fails to classify Heliodorus' work as epic but also censures it for its lack of epic subject matter, evidently adhering strictly to Horace's "Res gestae regumque ducumque et tristia bella" as the formula for epic poetry. Scaliger goes further than Amyot in his estimation of Heliodorus. While refusing to admit the possibility of an epic in prose,[33] he offers the Greek work as a model for the disposition of an epic and, more significantly, places its author in the company of the "greatest of all poets," Virgil.

[33] Unlike the majority of Renaissance Aristotelians, Scaliger maintains that meter is an essential element of poetry and rejects the widely repeated judgment that Lucan's *Pharsalia* is history and not poetry. See Spingarn, *Literary Criticism in the Renaissance*, p. 24.

For Scaliger, the epic is the highest form of poetry, that which is "most noble of all, because it contains all possible subject matter" ("omnium est princeps: quia continet materias universas") and sets the standards for all other forms.[34] Deriving his formula for epic composition from Aristotle and Horace, he maintains that the poet must draw his subject matter from the "birth, life, and deeds of heroes" (*heroum genus, vita, gesta*).[35] In matters of disposition he proclaims two basic laws. The poet shall not begin his work *ab ovo* but shall seize an important event from which all else of necessity follows. Thus the *in-medias-res* technique is not associated with suspense as it had been in Amyot's prologue, but with unity of action. The second law, however, emphasizes the importance of suspense in the narrative structure of epic. Aristotle would give the epic poet license to incorporate into his work varying but relevant episodes to relieve the hearer of the boredom that the poet would inevitably arouse if he limited himself to the narration of the main plot. Basing his argument on Aristotle's discussion of this point, Scaliger recommends interruptions and fragmentations of the major narrative thread both for the sake of holding the hearer in suspense and arousing in him *admiratio* through the variety which episodes afford.[36] In words which recall those which Amyot used in discussing the effect of Heliodorus' *in-medias-res* structure, Scaliger writes: "Accordingly you should not set forth at the beginning what you select for the beginning, so that the mind of the listener is held in suspense, for he seeks something that does not yet exist. This, to be sure, is the unique or outstanding virtue, to hold the listener as if

[34] Julius Caesar Scaliger, *Poetices libri septem*, facsimile of the 1561 edition of Lyon by August Buck (Stuttgart-Bad Cannstatt, 1964), p. 6. For a treatment of Scaliger's sources, see Eduard Brinkschulte, *Julius Caesar Scaligers Kunsttheoretische Anschauungen und deren Hauptquellen, Renaissance und Philosophie*, No. 10 (Bonn, 1914); for the epic, see pp. 78-81.

[35] *Poetices libri septem*, p. 144.

[36] "Altera lex: Non recto tramite ducendam narrationem, ne taedium pariatur" (*Poetices libri septem*, p. 144). The possibility of a contradiction between these two rules of disposition and the difficulty which they might present for a poet who would put them into practice, a possibility which was to become a major preoccupation in the theoretical writings of Tasso and a basis for literary humor in Cervantes' works, is neatly avoided by Scaliger's casual insistence on the relevance of the episodes. The same is true of the original passage in Aristotle, where both unity of action and a variety of "varying episodes" are judged to be fundamental to epic. The episodes must of course be "relevant" (see *Poetics*, xxiii-xxiv).

he were a captive." In illustration of the perfectibility of this technique he adduces the example of the *summus poeta* Virgil, whose history of Camilla represents the way in which the poet should combine relevant episode and main plot for suspense and variety. Following his praise of Virgil, he adds: "You observe this most splendid manner of constructing a work in Heliodorus' *Ethiopian History*, a book which I think should be read with great attention by the epic poet and which should be proposed to him as the best model possible."[37]

The recognition of the *Ethiopian History* as an example of the perfect execution of the classical precepts of Horace and Aristotle, the elevation of it to the rank of model for contemporary poets who would attempt to re-create the classical epic, and the association of Heliodorus with Virgil mark a high point in the literary fortunes of the Greek romance in the Renaissance, a point from which it will not descend for over a century.

TASSO

Torquato Tasso's unending literary preoccupation was with the re-creation of the classical epic, and, as we would expect, he devotes little attention in his writings to the prose narrative and the work of Heliodorus. In the Italian literary tradition the prose romances were thoroughly eclipsed by the dazzling creations of Ariosto and Boiardo,[38] and it was with these that Tasso had to reckon in his struggle to press their undeniable qualities into the classical mold of epic poetry. His attempt was analogous to that which Cervantes' canon proposes for the epic in prose, but the question of prose narrative did not concern him. Nevertheless, there are several indications that he held Heliodorus' work in high esteem and like Scaliger looked upon it as a model for epic composition. It is well

---

[37] "Hoc ipsum igitur quod pro principio sumes, ne statuas in principio, ita enim auditoris animus est suspensus: querit enim quod nondum extat. Ea sanè vel unica vel praecipua virtus, auditorem quasi captiuum detinere. . . . Hanc disponendi rationem splendidissimam habes in Aethiopica historia Heliodori. Quem librum epico Poetae censeo accuratissimè legendum, ac quasi pro optimo exemplari sibi proponendum" (ibid., p. 144).

[38] This is not to say that they were unpopular. The Spanish prose romances were widely translated and widely read in Italy (see Thomas, *Spanish and Portuguese Romances of Chivalry*, pp. 180-199).

known that the history of the warrior maiden Clorinda of the *Gerusalemme liberata* (Canto XII) is modeled closely on that of Chariklea, the heroine of the *Aethiopica*.[39] More important for us are the few theoretical observations about Heliodorus' work scattered through his critical writings.

In his early *Dell'arte poetica* (written between 1561 and 1566, published in 1587), Tasso broadens the range of epic subject matter from the traditional *res gestae regumque*, which we have observed in Amyot and Scaliger's theories, to include love. It should be recalled that Amyot had censured the *Ethiopian History* for the lack of grandeur in its passive hero. Tasso admits that love is not so lofty a subject as heroic deeds and that a poem based on it cannot equal the perfection of the *Aeneid*, but maintains that the cases of Florio and Biancofiore and Theagenes and Chariklea prove the suitability of the theme in epic.

> Although I do not deny that a heroic poem can be made about less magnificent events, such as the amours of Florio and those of Theagenes and Chariklea, nevertheless, in the most perfect poem, the formula for which we are now seeking, it is necessary that the subject matter be in itself of the highest quality in nobility and excellence.[40]

What is interesting in this passage is the underlying assumption that the prose narrative of Heliodorus is categorized as epic poetry as

[39] See M. Oeftering, *Heliodor und seine Bedeutung für die Literatur*, pp. 114-115.

[40] "... bench'io non nieghi che poema eroico non si potesse formare di accidenti meno magnifici, quali sono gli amori di Florio, e quelli di Teagene e di Cariclea, in questa idea nondimeno, che ora andiamo cercando, del perfettissimo poema, fa mestieri che la materia sia in se stessa nel primo grado di nobiltà e di eccellenza" (p. 13). The passage is greatly expanded in the *Del poema eroico*, written nearly thirty years later (see pp. 103-108). Many examples are added to the list: "... l'amor di Leandro e d'Ero, de' quali cantò Museo, antichissimo poeta greco; e quel di Giasone e di Medea, dal qual prese il soggetto Apollonio fra' Greci e Valerio Flacco tra' Latini ... o quelli di Teagene e di Cariclea, e di Leucippe e di Clitofonte, che nella medesima lingua furono scritti per Eliodoro e per Achille Tazio" (p. 108). Curiously in defending love as a justifiable theme of epic poetry, Tasso uses the occasion to praise *Amadís de Gaula*, *Amadís de Grecia*, and *Primaleón*, written by "quegli scrittori spagnuoli i quali favoleggiarono nella loro lingua materna senza obligo alcuno di rime" (p. 106), for the noble conception of love which they present.

well as the absence of any speculation as to the validity of this assumption. Here Tasso remains consistent with his acceptance of Aristotle's principle that imitation and not meter is the distinguishing feature between poetry and nonpoetry, e.g., historical writing.

In a letter to Scipione Gonzaga, May 20, 1575, Tasso echoes the familiar evaluation of Heliodorus' work as a model for disposition in epic. In discussing the critical problem of incorporating episodes into a unified plot, Tasso uses words which recall Amyot's praise of Heliodorus' technique of capturing the reader's interest by offering him an action at its midpoint and arousing in him the desire to discover its origins: "Holding the listener in suspense as he proceeds from confusion to clarity, from the universal to the particular, is the enduring art of Virgil; and this is one of the reasons why Heliodorus is so enjoyable." Claiming to have employed this technique of fragmentary clarification many times in his work, Tasso points to the history of Erminia in the *Liberata*. In the third canto of his poem the reader discovers "a shadowy fragment of confused information" about the maiden; "his knowledge of her becomes more distinct in the sixth canto; and in the penultimate canto it is rounded out with most specific detail revealed through her own words."[41] Here we observe again the association of Heliodorus with Virgil and the recommendation of his work as a model for the epic poet which first appeared in Scaliger's poetics. It is well to note how Tasso's words on his development of the Erminia narrative thread could be applied to Cervantes' exposition of the history of Persiles and Sigismunda, which is offered the reader in shadowy fragments and is fully illuminated only in the final chapter of the work.

EL PINCIANO

The Epic in Prose

The influence of Aristotle's *Poetics* was slow in spreading to Spain. The first full exposition in Spanish of the doctrines and critical prob-

[41] "Il lasciar l'auditor sospeso, procedendo dal confuso al distinto, da l'universale a'particolare, è arte perpetua di Virgilio; e questa è una de le cagioni che fa piacer tanto Eliodoro"; ". . . alcuna ombra di confusa notizia; più distinta cognizione se n'ha nel sesto; particolarissima se n'avrà per sue parole nel penultimo canto" (*Le lettere di Torquato Tasso*, ed. C. Guasti [Florence, 1853-1855], I, 77-78).

lems which had been dominating Italian academic circles since the middle of the sixteenth century was the *Philosophía antigua poética* of López Pinciano, published in 1596, two years after the death of Tasso. It is not surprising that we discover in this work more attention devoted to Heliodorus than in any of the Italian tracts on poetry and a more thorough confrontation of his work in terms of the major aesthetic preoccupations of the Aristotelian movement. The indigenous literary tradition which the Spanish classicists had to confront was not that of Ariosto and the verse romance but rather that of the *Amadís de Gaula* and the prose romance. It was this tradition to which the "friend of his country" referred in offering his translation of Heliodorus as an alternative to the older works in Spanish.[42] Perhaps because there was already a tradition of prose which a new genre could supplant, the work of Heliodorus not only aroused the interest of Spanish theorists and translators, but also inspired imitation, while in Italy the interest of educated circles in the Greek work remained always secondary to its interest in the recreation of the classical epic vis-à-vis the verse romances.[43]

[42] Similarly in France, where the indigenous literary tradition of prose romance was strong, we observe theorists suggesting a purification of the genre in accordance with the model of Heliodorus. In addition to Amyot's criticism of the old books written in French and praise of Heliodorus, we observe in Jean Vauquelin de la Fresnaye's *L'Art poétique* (1605) the following: "En Prose tu pourras poëtiser aussi:/ Le grand Stagiritain te le permet ainsi./ Si tu veux voir en Prose vn oeuure Poëtique,/ D'Heliodore voy l'histoire Ethiopique" (ed. G. Pellissier [Paris, 1885], pp. 78-79). Referring to the old French books, he adds: "Nos Romans seroient tels, si leur longue matiere/ Ils n'alloient deduisant, comme vne histoire entiere." Gomberville, the founder of the French heroic-gallant romance, is very explicit in distinguishing the new genre from the old in its observance of the Aristotelian dictate of verisimilitude. In introducing *La Carithee* (1620), he writes: "Il y a deux especes toutes contraires en ce genre d'escrire; la plus estimable & la plus difficile est celle où l'on obserue vne si exacte vraysemblance que souuent on se laisse emporter à croire que c'est vne verité: de ceste sorte sont tous les Amours faits à l'imitation de Theagene & de Cariclee. L'autre est plus prodigieuse & plus espouuentable, mais comme elle ne fait point d'impression sur l'ame de ceux que ne s'esmeuuent que pour les choses ou vrayes ou vraysemblables: de ceste qualité sont tous les Poetes Anciens, l'Amadis . . . & vn nombre infiny d'autres semblables" (cited by Werner Krauss, "Die Kritik des Siglo de Oro am Ritter- und Schäfer- roman," pp. 170-171).

[43] Considering the bulk of Italian theoretical writings, the attention which they devote to Heliodorus' work is very slight. I have found nothing comparable to El Pinciano's discussion of the work in terms of every major aesthetic category of the classical dogma. The best indication of the secondary importance of the Greek work in Italy, however, is the absence of a tradition of prose literature correspond-

On many occasions in El Pinciano's dialogues the principal interlocutors, Ugo, Fadrique, and El Pinciano, refer to Heliodorus' *Ethiopian History* as an epic in prose. The first reference is in the third epistle "De la essencia y causas de la poetica," in a discussion of Aristotle's dictum that imitation and not meter determines whether a piece of writing is poetry or history. All enthusiastically accept the doctrine and invoke the example which appears in nearly all documents of Renaissance criticism—Lucan's *Pharsalia* is history although it is written in meter. At this point the conversation takes a humorous turn as Ugo and El Pinciano make an unconventional application of the principles of imitation and verisimilitude to verse to claim that, since nobody speaks in meter, meter is entirely inimical to imitation and hence to poetic composition. This piece of sophistry is made for the sake of humor, and Fadrique, who usually speaks for *el Philósopho*, corrects his ingenuous colleagues, coming to the defense of meter ("'Not so harsh,' said Fadrique at this point. 'Do not inflict so many injuries upon meter'")[44] and suggesting that "the imitation in meter be called a perfect poem, and the imitation without meter and the metrical composition without imitation should be called imperfect poems."[45] Nevertheless, in his sophistical rejection of meter the speaker El Pinciano presents an opinion which the author El Pinciano undoubtedly shares: "I understand that the *Ethiopian History* is a highly praised poem, although it is written in prose."[46] In the sixth epistle, "Lenguaje," we discover a similar context of humor involving the speaker El Pinciano's misunderstandings, in which attention again is drawn to the fact that Heliodorus' work is a poem in prose: "In poems without meter, lofty and

---

ing to the seventeenth-century prose romances of Spain and France. Oeftering writes of Italian literature: ". . . eine eigene litterarische Geschmacksrichtung wie in Frankreich, als deren Meister Heliodor förmlich gegolten hätte, lässt sich aber nicht auffinden" (*Heliodor und seine Bedeutung für die Literatur*, p. 113). It is interesting that one of the three sixteenth-century translations of the *Aethiopica* in Italy should attempt to recast the work in the meter of heroic poetry (ibid., p. 50).

[44] "Passo, dixo aquí Fadrique; no tantas injurias a los metros" (López Pinciano, *Philosophía antigua poética*, ed. A. Carballo Picazo [Madrid, 1953], I, 207; page references which follow are to this edition).

[45] ". . . la imitación con metro llamassen poesía perfecta, y, a la imitación sin metro y al metro sin imitación, poesías imperfectas" (I, 208).

[46] ". . . he caydo en la cuenta que la Historia de Ethiopía es vn poema muy loado, mas en prosa" (I, 206).

perfect language is not so necessary, as is demonstrated by Heliodorus and others."[47]

The Structural Excellence of the Ethiopian History

In the fifth epistle "Fábula," in which the speakers discuss the
manner of composing a perfect plot, El Pinciano turns his attention
to the techniques of disposition which Amyot, Scaliger, and Tasso
had praised in the Greek romance. However, in his interpretation of
the qualities and effect of Heliodorus' disposition, El Pinciano varies
somewhat the traditional approach. Whereas Amyot's intelligent explanation of the suspense which the *Ethiopian History* arouses is
based on an original interpretation of Horace's recommendation of
beginning *in-medias-res* (i.e., the reader's desire to discover the unknown origins of the plot), and Scaliger's analysis of the same effect
is founded on an original application of Aristotle's statement on dis-
similar threads (i.e., the reader is kept in the dark by retarding interruptions in the development of the principal plot), El Pinciano's
interpretation is a complete application of Aristotle's criteria on
tragedy to epic. It is based on Aristotle's discussion of the two parts
of the plot of tragedy, complication and unraveling. The properly
constructed plot "is considered to be like a thread, which has a knot
and an unraveling."[48] The knot of complication in the threads of
dramatic action must be tightened until there seems to be no way of
unraveling it. However, the poet must always leave free "a bit of
thread which he can catch hold of" and must avoid an entanglement that can be resolved only by the introduction of a miraculous
element, which in its implausibility destroys the effect of the peripeteia. At the moment of highest tension the unexpected way out or
unraveling is found, and the catastrophe or peripeteia occurs, bringing a relaxation of tension. Ugo humorously compares the process

[47] ". . . en los poemas sin metro, no es tan necessario el alto lenguaje y peregrino,
como lo vemos en Heliodoro y otros" (II, 184).
[48] ". . . se considera como cuerda y tiene ñudo y soltura" (II, 83). "Every tragedy
falls into two parts—Complication and Unravelling (or *Denouement*). . . . By the
Complication I mean all that comes between the beginning of the action and the
part which marks the turning-point to good or bad fortune. The Unravelling is
that which comes between the beginning of the change and the end. . . . Many
poets tie the knot well, but unravel it ill" (*Poetics*, xviii). I cite S. H. Butcher's
translation, *Aristotle's Theory of Poetry and Fine Art* (London, 1898), pp. 65-67.

71

to that of garroting, the confession or death of the tortured man forming the "unraveling." The best plot moves with increasing tension toward one catastrophe and denouement, but because of its length the epic must usually present a series of tightenings and loosenings of the knot of complication. One observes such a process in the fourth book of the *Aeneid* when Juno apparently relents in her persecution of Aeneas. In the process of "tying and untying" (*atar y desatar*) Heliodorus surpasses Virgil, for in spite of the epic length of his work, it presses toward the final peripeteia with ever increasing tension.

Then El Pinciano said: "Heliodorus' history is epic, but, if one examines it carefully, one discovers that it continuously ties the knot of complication and never unravels it until the end. I say this because there is no contradiction between being epic and tying a single knot tighter and tighter throughout the work."

Fadrique said: "Gift of the sun is Heliodorus, and in this matter of tying and untying knots, he is unsurpassed, and in the other techniques of composition, he is excelled by but a few."[49]

---

[49] "El Pinciano dixo luego: 'La historia de Heliodoro épica es, mas, si bien se mira, atando va siempre, y nunca jamás desata hasta el fin. Dígolo, porque no contradize ser épica y ir atando siempre más y más.' Fadrique dixo: 'Don del sol es Heliodoro, y en esso del ñudo y soltar nadie le hizo ventaja, y, en lo demás, casi nadie'" (II, 85-86). In his *Agudeza y arte de ingenio*, written over fifty years later, Baltasar Gracián chooses the same phenomenon in acclaiming the high artistry of Heliodorus' work. Characteristic of the new orientation of his baroque poetics is the association of the technique of plot development not with the sixteenth-century critical preoccupation with overall unity in plot and implications of the principle of verisimilitude, i.e., qualities within the work of art itself, but rather with that peculiar effect of amazement which resides in the reader and which a properly constructed work of art must arouse and that admiration which the reader feels for the virtuosity (*agudeza*) of the artist who has succeeded in startling him. The artist's ability to unravel suddenly a complicated entanglement is categorized as "la agudeza por desempeño en el hecho." Drawing analogies to the literary act in the dilemmas and solutions of Alexander before the Gordian knot, Theseus in the labyrinth, and Solomon before the mothers, Gracián claims that the technique of complication "es el principal artificio, que hace tan gustosas y entretenidas las épicas, ficciones, novelas, comedias y tragedias: vanse empeñando los sucesos y apretando los lances, de tal suerte que parecen a veces no poder tener salida . . . Mas aquí está el primor del arte, y la valentía de la inventiva, en hallar medio extravagante, pero verisímil, con que salir del enredado laberinto con gran gusto y fruición del que lee y del que oye" (*Obras completas*, ed. A. del Hoyo [Madrid, 1960], p. 439). Horace is cited for the exclusion of the miraculous solution, and among the many examples of this *agudeza* adduced is that of Heliodorus (p. 440).

Romances of Chivalry & the Classical Aesthetic

Like Huet, El Pinciano lavishes praise on Heliodorus' final peripeteia and recognition scene, apparently failing to share the modern reader's reservations about the author's sacrifice of narrative logic in favor of a maximum prolongation of the reader's suspense. In the same epistle El Pinciano introduces the climactic scene in Meroe in a discussion of the Aristotelian formula for recognition scenes. The speakers end their discussion of the four types of recognition outlined in the *Poetics*, concluding that it is impossible to determine which is to be most recommended, for each can serve very well the purpose of the "unraveling" of the plot. Fadrique recalls Aristotle's final words on the matter, that the "best [recognition] is that which arises from the incidents themselves, where the startling discovery is made by natural means."[50] Ugo apparently forgets Aristotle's explicit exclusion of recognitions based on tokens from this category and proceeds to offer Heliodorus' conclusion as an illustration of this most effective type of recognition scene.

> I have nothing more to say than to verify and illustrate your axiom with Heliodorus' *Ethiopian History*, which in my opinion is a fine tale [*fábula*]; throughout it the poet sowed the seeds for the recognition of Chariklea, first with writings, then, with gems, and after that, with bodily marks; from all of these proceeded the final recognition and the unraveling of a knot so graceful and pleasing that there is none other to rival it. And although in its form the recognition belongs to the category of the least artistic recognitions, which is that of *will* [El Pinciano reinterprets Aristotle's discussion of recognition to fit into the three categories of *intellect*, *will*, and *memory*; his recognition by will is a modification of Aristotle's second category and includes all those recognitions in which a character deliberately reveals his identity], nevertheless, the poet was so skillful, and he designed the recognition so artfully, that it equals those of higher categories, because he did not make Chariklea the revealer of herself but rather Sisimithres, who was the man who

---

[50] *Poetics*, xvi. See ed. cit., p. 61. El Pinciano writes: ". . . los buenos reconocimientos, de qualquier especie que sean, deuen estar sembrados por la misma fábula, para que sin máchina ni milagro sea desatada; sino que ella, de suyo, sin violencia ni fuerça alguna, se desmarañe y manifieste al pueblo" (II, 38).

raised her. [In other words, unlike Ulysses, who informs his shepherds that he is Ulysses and then shows them signs in proof (sic), Chariklea, much to the discomfort of Theagenes and the modern reader, refuses to inform her parents of her identity and thereby end the danger of sacrifice which menaces her and her lover. When, after considerable delay, she decides to reveal herself, she chooses to allow the priest Sisimithres to make the discovery by interpreting the writing on her garment.][51]

Regardless of what we may think of El Pinciano's interpretation of Aristotle on this matter, we nevertheless observe in the passage his admiration for Heliodorus' work and his interpretation of it as a perfect execution of Aristotelian theories on tragedy.

In the long eleventh epistle "La Heroyca," the speakers discuss epic composition and freely draw examples to support their precepts from the practices of Homer, Virgil, and Heliodorus, treating the works of each as belonging to the same species of poetry.[52] Resuming his praise of the high qualities of disposition observable in the Greek romance and applauding its effects of suspense, El Pinciano now invokes not Aristotle's analysis of the tragic plot but rather the Horatian precept on the *in-medias-res* beginning, interpreting its workings as Amyot had done. The reader must be seized by the desire to discover the origins of the action. Hence the epic poem "should begin in the middle of the action, and Homer proceeded thus in his *Odyssey*, and Heliodorus in his *Ethiopian History*; and the reason is that, as the heroic work is long, it needs a trick in order to make the reader read more attentively; and thus it is that, as the poet begins in the middle of the action, the listener proceeds desirous of discovering the beginning, which he comes upon in the middle of

[51] ". . . no tengo que dezir más que aprouar y prouar vuestra sentencia con la *Historia de Heliodoro*, la qual para mí es vna galana fábula, y en quien el poeta sembró por toda ella la simiente del reconocimiento de Cariclea, primero, con las escrituras, después, con las joyas, y, después, con las señales del cuerpo; de todas las quales vino vltimamente el reconocimiento y soltura de ñudo tan gracioso y agradable, que ninguno más. Y, aunque la forma del reconocimiento toca al menos artificioso, que es al de la voluntad, mas el poeta fué tan agudo, y le hizo tan artificioso, que iguala a los demás, porque no hizo a Cariclea manifestadora de sí misma, sino a Sisimithres, que era el que la auía criado" (II, 38-39).

[52] For example, Fadrique observes that epics generally have happy endings, alluding to the *Iliad*, the *Odyssey*, the *Ethiopian History*, and the *Aeneid* (III, 155).

the book, and having passed the mid-point of the volume, he finds little annoyance in reading the remainder."[53] In the execution of this technique Heliodorus surpasses Homer and Virgil: "Heliodorus observed this technique with more exactitude than any other poet, because Homer did not observe it with such rigor . . . and if we examine Virgil, we discover that he too did not begin in the middle, because, of his twelve books, he devotes slightly more than two, the second and the third, to the action that has already occurred."[54]

In the discussion of the quantitative divisions of the epic plot, the work of Heliodorus appears once again as a subject of examination, and a principle for the composition of prose epic is formulated. Whereas the classical epics consist of a prologue or proposition, an invocation, and a narration, the *Ethiopian History* begins with the narration. Acknowledging that epic perfection demands the former procedure, Fadrique suggests that it is a convention of the prose epic to dispense with proposition and invocation: ". . . it is a great perfection of heroic poetry to begin with a proposition and an invocation, which are generally lacking in heroic poems which are not in meter; such poems begin with a dissimulated prologue and the narration."[55] Fadrique's claim that there is such a thing as a *prólogo dissimulado* is simply a convenient way of preserving venerated terminology and avoiding the admission that in Heliodorus' work a prologue is lacking.

The association of Heliodorus with the models of classical epic continues as El Pinciano proceeds to point out the parallel function of the accounts of Ulysses at the court of Alcinous, Aeneas at the court of Dido, and Calasiris in the presence of Gnemón in their

[53] ". . . deue començar del medio de la acción, y que ansí lo hizo Homero en su Vlysea, y ansí Heliodoro en su Historia de Ethiopía; y es la razón porque, como la obra heroyca es larga, tiene necessidad de ardid para que sea mejor leyda; y es assí que començando el poeta del medio de la acción, va el oyente desseosso de encontrar con el principio, en el qual se halla al medio libro, y que, auiendo passado la mitad del volumen, el resto se acaba de leer sin mucho enfado" (III, 206-207).

[54] "Heliodoro guardó esso más que ningún otro poeta, porque Homero no lo guardó con esse rigor . . . y si miramos a Virgilio, tampoco començó del medio, porque él tiene doze libros, y poco más que dos, que son segundo y tercero, gasta en la acción ya passada" (III, 207).

[55] ". . . gran perfección es de la heroyca començar por proposición y inuocación, de quienes suelen carecer los poemas heroycos que no son en metro, los quales entran con su prólogo dissimulado y narración" (III, 193).

respective works, claiming that each is like a necessary prologue on which the narrations of the final events of the poems are dependent. His statement provokes an objection on the part of Ugo that the poet could have presented the events which they contain in a normal prologue and followed the chronological order of events in his narration. This objection becomes a point of departure for an introduction of Aristotle's precept that the heroic poet "should speak as little as possible" (*deue hablar lo menos que el pueda* [III, 208]) and a recollection of his praise of Homer for observing this precept.[56] The implication is that had Heliodorus, Homer, and Virgil begun by narrating the events which in fact their characters relate, they would have violated the rule.

Subject Matter and Verisimilitude

If in matters of structure Heliodorus is adjudged superior to Virgil and Homer on the basis of two of the Aristotelian-Horatian principles of disposition, in the all-important matter of epic subject matter, El Pinciano is in accord with Tasso in characterizing the work as belonging to a secondary type of epic poetry. Once again the issues are the suitability of love as a subject and the absence of the traditional heroic deeds of arms in the Greek romance. El Pinciano allows three types of subject matter in epic poetry: "Some poets treat religious subject matter, as did Marco Girolamo Vida . . . others sing of cases of love, as did Musaeus, Heliodorus, and Achilles Tatius; others sing of battles and victories, as did Homer and Virgil, and this type of poetry has been distinguished with the name "heroic."[57] El Pinciano, however, immediately qualifies his admission of the first two: "Religious subjects, by their very nature, are not well suited to imitation;[58] and it would seem that amatory subject matter is like-

---

[56] *Poetics*, xxiv. This question does not produce much discussion and elaboration in El Pinciano's dialogues. On the other hand, in Italian critical circles it was one of the most acute problems of theoretical writings. Again it is important to recall the formidable opponent who confronted Italian classicists, Ariosto, whose garrulous narrator used the prologue freely to introduce his cantos.

[57] ". . . vnos poetas tratan materia de religión, como lo hizo Marco Ierónimo Vida . . . cantan otros casos amorosos, como Museo; Heliodoro, y Achiles Tacio; otros, batallas y victorias, como Homero y Virgilio, y esta especie se ha alçado con el nombre de heroyca" (III, 180).

[58] Marco Girolamo Vida wrote an epic in Latin hexameters, the *Christias* (1535),

wise unsuitable. But, when writers of such subject matter are as serious as the three mentioned above, one can well allow it, because below that apparently insubstantial chaff there is very solid grain; thus I praise them; I do not condemn them."[59] In other words El Pinciano is much more skeptical than Tasso about the suitability of love, and will allow it only because of his great admiration for Heliodorus, Achilles Tatius, and Musaeus. At the conclusion of the epistle on heroic poetry El Pinciano is more explicit in judging Heliodorus' work to be a secondary type of epic. Following a list of the great virtues of the work, his sudden retraction recalls that of Amyot.

> As for the *Ethiopian History*, I must confess that Heliodorus, its author, was a very serious man and an excellent poet, particularly in the art of tying and unraveling; he pleases with his skillfully contrived tale and even with the solid doctrine which he has sown within it. But, if we are seeking epic perfection, it does not seem to me that the *Ethiopian History* has the necessary grandeur. I am not referring to its language, which, as it is not in meter, is pardoned, but rather to its very subject and plot, be-

---

about the life of Christ. Earlier El Pinciano writes: ". . . cae mucho mejor la imitación y ficción sobre materia que no sea religiosa, porque el poeta se puede mucho mejor ensanchar y aun traer episodios mucho más deleytosos y sabrosos a las orejas de los oyentes" (III, 168). El Pinciano is echoing Tasso's opinion on the difficulty which scriptural matter presents the epic poet. Because of the exalted character of sacred history, and the detailed knowledge of it which the poet's audience has, the poet dare not employ it as a basis for an epic poem, the aim of which is never the recording of history but the imitation of an action. Imitation demands artistic arrangement of the subject matter, additions based on the poet's inventive powers, and, as may be necessary, a "manipulation" of historical event, which the poet uses in last analysis not in the interest of historiography but in that of giving grandeur and verisimilitude to his imitation. The history of the Middle Ages offers the epic poet an ideal source; for in it he finds events of grandeur, which are neither as exalted as those of the Bible nor as well known in detail as those of recent and contemporary history. Consequently his inventive powers can freely mold them into an imitation (see Tasso, *Del poema eroico*, pp. 98-99).

[59] ". . . la materia de religión, por ser della, no parece tan bien en imitación; y la materia de amores solamente no es razón que lo parezca, mas, quando fuessen tan graues los escriptores de la amorosa materia como los tres sobredichos, bien se pueden admitir, porque, debaxo de aquella paja floxa, ay grano de mucha sustancia; ansí los alabo; no condeno" (III, 180-181). Just what El Pinciano means by *mucha sustancia* is not clear. It is probable that he is referring to the erudition and the natural and moral philosophy which these works contain.

cause its ordinary characters have a greater role in the action than its lofty characters.[60]

Most of El Pinciano's remaining comments on the high qualities of Heliodorus' narrative are in connection with the widely discussed problem of verisimilitude. As they are all informed by a preoccupation with the empirical-historical implications of the concept of mimesis, they are illustrative of the tendencies in Renaissance criticism which I have emphasized in Chapter I. It should be recalled that already in 1547 Amyot had praised the Greek romance for its plausibility, basing his criterion on Strabo's skeptical attitude toward the value of the purely imaginary in fiction. The half century following his preface witnessed the emergence of Aristotle as the authority dominating literary taste and an intense critical ferment surrounding the exegesis of the *Poetics*. As I have pointed out in the preceding chapter, the development was not nearly so revolutionary as the sudden proliferation and wide diffusion of commentaries on the Greek text might suggest, for the theorists approached the *Poetics* with the same attitudes toward literature which marked the writings of the earlier humanists such as Amyot. The same suspicion as to the autonomous value of literature, the distrust of the purely imaginary, and the belief that literature had its justification only in the instructive and the edifying were the dominant preconceptions which in general the humanists could not escape in their readings of the *Poetics*, and these preoccupations produced such distortions as the Christian-ethical interpretation of catharsis[61] and a historically-

[60] ". . . a la Historia de Ethiopía digo y confieso que Heliodoro, su autor, fué vn varón muy graue y gentil poeta en el ñudo y soltura, traça y deleyte de su ficción, y aun en mucha doctrina que tiene sembrada, mas, si se atiende a la perfección épica, no me parece que tiene la grandeza necessaria; no digo en el lenguaje, que por no ser metro está desculpado, sino en la cosa misma, porque las principales personas son menos en su acción, y las comunes son más" (III, 224).

[61] Toffanin refers to the moment of this misinterpretation of catharsis in Vincenzo Maggi's commentary on the *Poetics* (1550) as "la fine del humanesimo," the moment when a disinterested respect for an examination of all documents from antiquity gave way to a reinterpretive or falsifying impulse based on contemporary preconceptions and expediency. To Toffanin the force of the Counterreformation is responsible (*La fine dell' umanesimo*, Chap. VI, esp. pp. 89-92). As Bataillon has shown, the difference between the attitudes which mark Christian humanism and the Counterreformation is not so great as has been commonly supposed (see *Erasmo y España*, II, 432). It is perhaps well at this point to emphasize that such Renaissance "distortions" of Aristotle as the ethical interpretation of cartharsis and the

empirically oriented interpretation of the related concepts of mimesis, verisimilitude, and poetic truth–historical truth.

El Pinciano's theories of imitation are essentially the same as those of Tasso, although to be sure the exploration of the problematic aspects of these theories vis-à-vis the marvelous which fills Tasso's writings and underlies a series of dramatizations of literary problems in Cervantes' works is absent in the work of the Spanish theorist. His first reflection on the verisimilitude of Heliodorus' work in relation to these theories occurs in the discussion of tragedy in Epistle Eight. Ugo has repeated Aristotle's recommendation of historical personages for tragedy, for, since their grandeur is universally acknowledged, they will be ideal for evoking compassion in the audience, and, with the authority which historical acceptance and documentation provide, their actions will be accepted as plausible. However, he proceeds to fall into the error of assuming that subject matter from history is absolutely essential in the verisimilar plot and admits his bewilderment before the dilemma which Heliodorus' work then presents: ". . . Heliodorus' *History*, which is feigned in its entirety, even in the names of its characters, and is one of the best poems ever written."[62] Fadrique's answer illustrates well the difference between the verisimilar and the historical and the subordination of the latter to the former in the Renaissance Aristotelian's conception of the properly constructed plot:

> This difficulty is not so great, for Theagenes was not so great a prince that his name should have been preserved in memory and fame (although he was the descendant of Pyrrhus), and Chariklea, heiress to the kingdom of Ethiopia, was *a figure who would be unknown here and in Greece*; and, by inventing her as a queen and princess of unknown lands, the poet obeyed the mandate of verisimilitude, because *nobody could say that there was*

---

empirical-instructive interpretation of mimesis, although alien to the modern critical temper, cannot be dismissed as negative forces in the history of literature. Dilthey asserts that the flowering of the French classical theater presupposed the close relationship between literature and man's ethical life proclaimed in Scaliger's "Aristotelian" poetics. See *Weltanschauung und Analyse des Menschen seit Renaissance und Reformation, Gesammelte Schriften* (Leipzig, 1914), II, 432-433.

[62] ". . . la Historia de Heliodoro, la qual es fingida toda hasta los nombres y es de los poemas mejores que ha auido en el mundo" (II, 331).

not such a king as Hydaspes nor a queen such as Persina in Ethiopia.[63]

In other words the *Ethiopian History* is a legitimate *historia fingida* or *disfrazada*, to recall Amyot's terms, because it is plausible and because our familiarity and that of Heliodorus' immediate audience, the Greeks, with the history of Ethiopia is limited by spatial distance and the absence of documentation. Thus the poet is protected from a fear which, to judge by theoretical writings of the epoch, must have been an obsession, the fear of contradiction by the pedantic historian and the consequent charge of lying implausibly.[64] This fear lay behind Tasso's recommendation of subject matter from medieval history for the epic poem. Not only do the events from this period have the grandeur which history has bestowed upon them and occur in an age in which customs and beliefs are not so different from those of the present as to strike the modern audience as implausible (as would the customs of antiquity); but, moreover, they are surrounded by a veil of incomplete historical knowledge, which will shield the poet from the cavilings of pedants and allow him ample sweep for his inventive talents as he transforms history into an imitation.[65] A corollary of this approach and solution to the problem of verisimilitude is the recommendation of the history of distant lands as a source of epic subject matter. Knowledge of the existence of these lands coupled with an ignorance as to details concerning

[63] "No es grande essa dificultad; que Theágenes no era tan gran príncipe que se deuiera tener el nombre suyo en memoria y fama (bien que decendiente de Pirrho); y Chariclea, heredera del reyno de Ethiopía era *de quien acá y en la Grecia auía poca noticia*, y, con fingir Reyna y Princesa de tierras ignotas, cumplió con la verisimilitud el poeta, *porque nadie podría dezir que en Ethiopía no huuo rey Hydaspes, ni reyna Persina*" (II, 331-332). The italics are mine.

[64] See Amyot's invocation of Strabo's words on the poet's risks of being called ignorant (above). This was the age in which all theorists felt obligated to deal with Virgil's well-known alterations of history and Tasso would spend twenty years studying the historical sources of his masterpiece, seeking possible errors of fact, the age in which Tasso could write: ". . . fra le mutate [cose] io ho peggiorati i versi onde ho tolta la parola *mori*; ma così bisognava, perchè gli arabi non son mori nè tartari" (letter to Scipione Gonzaga, April 15, 1575, *Le lettere*, I, 66), and literary theorists were troubled by the problem of the historicity of Turpin's chronicle.

[65] In El Pinciano's recommendation of the history of Pelayo we observe by implication the theories of Tasso: ". . . la historia es admirable, y ni tan antigua que esté oluidada, ni tan moderna que pueda dezir nadie 'esso no passó ansí'" (III, 169).

them on the part of the audience is the basis for the recommendation.[66] El Pinciano's praise of Heliodorus for selecting "unknown lands" is based on this doctrine. The historicity of his subject is not important. The important thing is that neither we nor the Greeks can know whether it is historical or not, and, since in other respects the actions of the work are plausible, the poet "obeyed the mandate of verisimilitude."[67]

El Pinciano's comment on the fame of Theagenes, which begins his judgment of the verisimilitude of Heliodorus' work, dramatically reveals the extremes of tortuous thought which the Renaissance notion of mimesis could produce about matters which today we consider irrelevant to poetic creation. Here there is indeed a problem, which remains in spite of the Ethiopian setting, for (a) the hero is Greek, the land of the audience, and (b) he is presented as a descendant of a famous historical figure Pyrrhus (the son of Achilles). The problem arises not because the Theagenes of the literary context does not conform to his historical model, but because there is no historical model widely known or recorded for a man who by virtue of his ancestry alone must be illustrious; and it is implausible that the name of a figure of grandeur not be recorded in history.[68]

---

[66] "L'istoria *di secolo o di nazione lontanissima* pare . . . soggetto assai conveniente al poema eroico, peroché, essendo quelle cose in guisa sepolte nell'antichità ch'a pena ne rimane debole e oscura memoria, può il poeta mutarle e rimutarle e narrarle come gli piace" (Tasso, *Del poema eroico*, pp. 98-99). The italics are mine.

[67] The point is made more forcefully in the subsequent discussion of heroic poetry. El Pinciano criticizes the absence of a historical foundation in Heliodorus' epic. Fadrique replies: "¿Y cómo sabéys vos esso? ¿Por ventura ay alguna historia antigua de Grecia que os diga que Theágenes no fué de la sangre de Pyrrho, y alguna de Ethiopía que Cariclea no fué hija de Hidaspes y Persina, reyes de Ethiopía? Yo quiero que sea ficción, como dezís, y yo creo; mas como no se puede aueriguar, no ay por que condenar al tal fundamento como fingido; y en esto, como en lo demás, fué prudentíssimo Heliodoro que puso reyes de tierra incógnita, y de quienes se puede mal aueriguar la verdad o falsedad, como antes está dicho, de su argumento" (III, 194-195). The fear of contradiction by the historian as well as the primacy of verisimilitude over historical accuracy which characterize Renaissance literary theory is clearly revealed in El Pinciano's example of the improper use of history by poets. If a poet were to compose a plot about the court of Spain, in which the Goth Oronte had the main part, "los hombres que de Historia saben, se reyrían, porque nunca tal rey ha auido en España" (II, 332). On the other hand an Ethiopian or Persian poet could allow himself this license, for in his country his audience knows very little about Spanish history.

[68] ". . . non è verisimile che un'azione illustre . . . non sia scritta e passata alla memoria de' posteri con la penna d'alcuno istorico . . . e ove non siano recati in

An audience may be troubled by this and begin to doubt the plausibility of the entire work.

Acknowledging the validity both of his implied criticism of Heliodorus' allusion to Theagenes' ancestry and of the assumption on which the criticism is based, El Pinciano overcomes the difficulty by casually asserting that the Greek audience would think that Theagenes must not have been such a great prince that his name and deeds would be preserved by history and fame, despite his illustrious ancestry. It never occurs to him to infer from his own apparent lack of concern that perhaps an audience never is troubled by such preoccupations with credibility in its apprehension of a work of art. As we shall see, it remained for Cervantes to ridicule the way in which the Renaissance critical movement dealt with the questions of imitation and belief in literature.

In his discussion of the epic in Epistle Eleven El Pinciano returns to the problem of verisimilitude, and once again Heliodorus' work appears as an example of the correct way to "deceive with the appearance of truth." The occasion is of particular significance in our study, for it is the only allusion in the poetics of El Pinciano to the controversy which had dominated Italian critical writings during the preceding decades, the polemic over Ariosto and Tasso. The speaker El Pinciano admits that he is baffled by the problem of what subject matter is suitable in epic poetry. Fadrique recognizes that there is currently a variety of theories concerning the subject, many contradictory, and claims that the source of the difficulty is "the poems which are now very fashionable, the so-called *romanzi* of the Italians, which lack any foundation in truth."[69] Here we observe once again that recurrent problem of sixteenth-century classicists as they confronted the enormously popular nonclassical genre. Fadrique's solution follows the pattern of the "ancients" in Italy, as he refuses to admit that the romances constitute a new genre and insists on measuring them by Aristotle's principles. Like most of his contemporaries he asserts that there is no essential difference between

scrittura, da questo solo argumentano gli uomini la loro falsità" (Tasso, *Del poema eroico*, p. 84).

[69] ". . . los poemas que agora son muy vsados, dichos romances de los italianos, los quales carecen de fundamento verdadero" (III, 164-165).

fictitious romance and historical epic. The essence of poetry is imitation and not truth, and—as Aristotle had pointed out, citing the example of Agathon's *Antheus*—a mimetic work could conceivably be based entirely on fictitious elements.[70] However, the measure of the perfection of a work is its grandeur coupled with its maintenance of verisimilitude. In general, historical subjects are to be preferred to fictitious ones, for they offer subject matter which meets these two requirements. Nevertheless, it is possible that an entirely fictional work can have the grandeur and verisimilitude demanded by the heroic genre. The works of the Greek romancers provide examples.

> The loves of Theagenes and Chariklea, by Heliodorus, and those of Leucippe and Clitophon, by Achilles Tatius, are as epic as the *Iliad* and the *Aeneid* . . . the heroic poem which lacks a foundation in truth can have much beauty and perfection in its composition, and in some respects it may surpass those works which are founded in truth; I, for one, would rather have been the author of Heliodorus' *Ethiopian History* than the author of Lucan's *Pharsalia*.[71]

On the other hand, in their lack of verisimilitude and edifying doctrine, the romances of chivalry are to be judged as inferior to these lofty works (see III, 178).[72]

The discussion of the verisimilitude of the *Ethiopian History* concludes with a full summary of the qualities which the Aristotelians found in the Greek romance. It is occasioned by the speaker El Pinciano's suggestion that the fact that Heliodorus wrote a *historia*

[70] On another occasion Aristotle's "Flor de Agathon" and Heliodorus' *Ethiopian History* are adduced as examples that a verisimilar plot of tragedy can be constructed on an imaginary, i.e., nonhistorical, foundation (III, 28).

[71] ". . . los amores de Theágenes y Cariclea, de Heliodoro, y los de Leucipo y Clitofonte, de Achiles Tacio, son tan épica como la Ilíada y la Eneyda . . . la [heroica] que carece de verdadero fundamento, puede tener mucho primor y perfección en su obra, y que en otras cosas aventaje a las que en verdad se fundamentan; yo, a lo menos, más quisiera auer sido autor de la Historia de Heliodoro que no de la Farsalia de Lucano" (III, 165-166).

[72] Like Tasso (*Del poema eroico*, p. 107), El Pinciano excepts *Amadís de Gaula* and *Amadís de Grecia* from any censure (III, 178); Cervantes saves *Amadís de Gaula*, but allows *Amadís de Grecia* to perish in the flames of the curate's bonfire (*Don Quijote*, I, vi).

and chose prose as his medium proves that he is not a poet. Fadrique comes to the defense of Heliodorus:

> There is no doubt that Heliodorus is a poet, and one of the finest epic poets who have ever written. At least there is none in the world who produces more tragic delight or ties and unravels better than he. His language is very fine, and his *sententiae* are very lofty. And, if one wanted to squeeze out some allegory, he could easily extract it from this work, and it would not be bad.[73]

Literary Theory in a Humorous Context

Throughout El Pinciano's dialogues, the character El Pinciano often assumes the role of the novice, misunderstanding the arguments of his more learned colleagues or drawing ridiculous conclusions on the basis of naive interpretations of the Aristotelian terminology. For example, he occasionally interprets imitation and verisimilitude in a more literal way than even the most unimaginative of the Renaissance neo-Aristotelians. He can argue that, since nobody speaks in meter, literary imitation should not employ meter. He objects to a poem describing a garden paradise, asserting that it could not be an imitation because real gardens are never so perfect (I, 263). One of his arguments is particularly interesting, for it points toward one of Cervantes' favorite equivocations. Following Fadrique's reference to Heliodorus' *History* and the *Pharsalia*, Ugo recalls the well-known judgment of Lucan: "The latter is not held to be a poet." El Pinciano makes the blunder of assuming that Ugo's "the latter" refers to Heliodorus, and readily offers some support

---

[73] ". . . que de Heliodoro no ay duda que sea poeta, y de los más finos épicos que han hasta agora escripto; a lo menos, ninguno tiene más deleyte trágico y ninguno en el mundo añuda y suelta mejor que él; tiene muy buen lenguaje y muy altas sentencias; y si quisiessen exprimir alegoría, la sacarían dél no mala" (III, 167). The way in which allegory is introduced here betrays El Pinciano's characteristically Aristotelian lack of interest in allegory. Indeed when it becomes a topic of conversation, Ugo claims: "No tengo doctrina de Aristóteles en esta materia poética" (III, 174). The conception of allegory which Fadrique presents is simple. The term refers generally to all that is instructive or edifying in a work and particularly to the fragments of natural and moral philosophy, the *sententiae* (see III, 175-176).

for his opinion: "He is right . . . because, in addition to the fact that the work is not in meter, its title says *History* of Ethiopia, and not *poem*."[74] Fadrique and Ugo smile at each other and proceed to enlighten their ingenuous friend concerning his unfortunate, literal interpretation of the term *historia* and his ignorance both of the irrelevance of versification in the determination of poetry and of the contemporary judgment that Lucan's epic is history rather than poetry. In all these cases humor arises in a dramatic context and works against the ignorance of the Philistine, who is reprimanded by the man of unquestioned superior knowledge.

As will be pointed out in the following chapters, Cervantes continually exploits the possibilities for equivocation in the aesthetic terminology of the contemporary Aristotelians. For example, the double implication in the term *historia*, i.e., the validity of El Pinciano's naive interpretation of the term,[75] is the basis for a recurrent literary joke in the *Quixote* and the *Persiles*. Cervantes' humor is much more complex than that of El Pinciano and generally moves in the opposite direction, striking at the "man of unquestioned superior knowledge" and the entire Aristotelian poetic canon. Nevertheless, to the extent that such possibilities are exploited for humorous dialogue by the theorist El Pinciano, the *Philosophia antigua poética* can be seen as an important forerunner of Cervantes' literary scenes.[76]

CONCLUSION

The detailed examination of various documents of literary theory, from Amyot's prologue to his translation of Heliodorus' *Ethiopian History* to Huet's *Traité de l'origine des romans*, has revealed that educated circles, from the early sixteenth century on, universally

[74] "Tiene razón . . . porque, allende que no tiene metro, el título de la obra dize *Historia* de Ethiopía, y no *poema*" (III, 166-167). The italics are mine.

[75] In a context concerning the duplicity of the poetic act, Fadrique alludes to the flexibility of the term: ". . . tampoco la Historia de Ethiopía es historia, sino que los autores, para autorizar sus escritos, les dan el nombre que se les antoja y mejor les viene a cuento" (I, 214).

[76] For a thorough presentation of the Aristotelian commonplaces which El Pinciano and Cervantes share, see Jean-François Canavaggio, "Alonso López Pinciano y la estética literaria de Cervantes en el 'Quijote,'" *Anales Cervantinos*, VII (1958), 13-107. See also, William C. Atkinson, "Cervantes, El Pinciano and the 'Novelas ejemplares,'" *Hispanic Review*, XVI (1948), 189-208.

condemned the popular romances of chivalry, measuring them by
the resurgent classical literary doctrines of Horace and Aristotle, and
seized upon the newly discovered *Aethiopica* of Heliodorus as an
alternative form of prose fiction which satisfied the most rigid
standards set for acceptable literature by the classicists. The process
inevitably led to the application of Aristotelian-Horatian criteria for
tragedy and epic to the prose narrative, and with the diffusion and
acceptance of the Aristotelian distinction between historical writing
and poetry, the possibility that the work might receive special consideration as a composition in prose vanished. In the writings of
Tasso and El Pinciano, the *Ethiopian History* is considered to belong
to the genre of epic poetry, and, when nearly a century later Huet
did formulate a theory of prose fiction, he readily admitted that he
was merely applying the rules of epic poetry to the prose narrative.

In accordance with the strongly ethical orientation of the Renaissance classical aesthetic, theorists praised the exemplary value of
Heliodorus' work: the purity of the love of the protagonists, the
moral wisdom contained in its *sententiae*, and the fact that in it
virtue is rewarded and vice is punished. In accordance with the Renaissance's revival of the Horatian celebration of the high civilizing
mission of poetry and application of the Ciceronian ideal of the
orator's encyclopedic knowledge to the poet, theorists acclaimed
Heliodorus' work for its wealth of erudition. Of more interest to us,
the classicists discovered in the Greek work two aesthetic qualities
which were absent in the romance of chivalry and formed the basis
of nearly all aesthetically oriented attacks on the popular genre:
unity and verisimilitude. In its singleness of action, proper subordination and integration of episode, and *in-medias-res* beginning, the
Ethiopian History was offered by Scaliger beside the work of the
"greatest poet," Virgil, as a model for all aspiring epic poets. Similarly Tasso, whose struggle with the problems involved in the disposition of epic subject matter was long and arduous, acknowledged
that Virgil and Heliodorus are the masters of the elusive technique
of fragmentary exposition. In the poetics of El Pinciano the critical
discussion of the Greek romancer broadens to encompass not only
his structural techniques, which indeed are declared superior to those
of Virgil and Homer, but also his successful observation of the prin-

ciple of verisimilitude as it had been interpreted by the Aristotelian theorists of the age. In this context the *Ethiopian History* appears as an example of Aristotle's allowance for the possibility of a purely fictitious, yet completely verisimilar, plot for tragedy and epic and is contrasted with the romances of chivalry, which, although belonging to the same species of poetry, are immeasurably inferior in their failure to observe verisimilitude. Moreover, the possibility of the epic in prose is often discussed by El Pinciano, and Heliodorus' work is repeatedly offered as the example of its perfectibility. As the *Ethiopian History* was completely drawn into the orbit of the theorizing surrounding the re-creation of the classical epic, which dominated the influential academic movement of the second half of the sixteenth century, it is easy to see that the Greek work stood in relation to the romances of chivalry as in Italy the *Aeneid* and the Homeric poems stood in relation to Ariosto's *Orlando Furioso* and the other *romanzi*.

It is only against this background of literary theorizing that we can properly understand Cervantes' undeniably high literary aspirations in the conception of the *Persiles*, his desire to rival Heliodorus, his theorizing concerning the possibility of the purification of the romance of chivalry and the creation of the epic in prose, the important thematic role that contemporary literary theory—particularly those problems surrounding the polemic over Ariosto and Tasso—has both in the *Quixote* and the *Persiles*, the creation of the *Persiles*, and finally the literary humor which functions so successfully in the context of the *Quixote* but gives the *Persiles* a puzzling ambivalence. Cervantes' most important discussion of literary theory and all the problems which we have discussed up to this point occurs in the debate between Don Quixote and the Canon of Toledo. It is here that the study of Cervantes' relationship to the classical aesthetic must begin.

87

PART TWO:

CERVANTES AND THE CLASSICAL AESTHETIC

Don Quixote

CHAPTER III

The Dialogue Between the Canon and Don Quixote

THE dialogue between Don Quixote and the Canon of Toledo is, as all critics have agreed, Cervantes' most complete and profound statement of a theory of literature. As the practical focus of this dialogue is the *libro de caballerías*, it becomes fully meaningful only when examined against the background of the literary polemic surrounding the *romanzi* in Italy and the romances of chivalry in Spain. For basically the discussion is a reasoned debate between the apologists for a type of artistry best exemplified by the chaotic fantasies of the *romanzi* and the advocates of a type of artistry which encompassed both certain aesthetic values of the *romanzi* and a classicist theory of poetry. It is important to note at the outset that the Canon of Toledo, who speaks for the latter group, is deeply sympathetic to the pleasurable appeal of the romances. His attitudes toward literature are in no way to be identified with the rigidly puritanical school of critics exemplified by Luis Vives. As we shall see, his evaluation of the chivalric romance is marked by the same spirit of reconciliation which informs Torquato Tasso's critical engagement with the works of Ariosto, Boiardo, and the other writers of the *romanzi*. Although his attack on the medieval genre utilizes all the traditional weapons, his intention is not destruction but rather purification. He envisions a new type of prose fiction, which, while eliminating the flaws which moralists and classicists attacked in the romances and adhering to the dominant Aristotelian aesthetic criteria, would continue to produce the pleasure of variety on which its chivalric ancestor was based. Indeed his position contains in concentrated form the entire evolution in critical tastes which we have followed in the preceding two chapters, from the negative moralizing that marked early Renaissance evaluations of the romances, through the new aesthetic orientation that accompanied the emergence of the Aristotelian critical dogma, to the constructive attempt of Tasso to reconcile the new and the old in the perfect heroic poem and the gradual recognition of Heliodorus' *Ethiopian History* as a prose epic which solved all the aesthetic problems raised by the romances.

Cervantes & the Classical Aesthetic

The canon begins his remarks on the romances of chivalry with the traditional moralistic censure of their harmful effects on readers. Recalling the Platonic condemnation of poetry, he refers to the romances and their authors as *perjudiciales en la república*. The notion that literature is subordinate to the aims of the state was popular in the period, and it appears more than once in Cervantes' numerous discussions of poetry. Its most important evocation occurs later in the present context when the curate suggests that playwrights and romancers should submit their works to a learned representative of the court who would evaluate their aesthetic and didactic qualities and then decide to prohibit or approve their representation or publication. Continuing the moralistic attack on the genre, he likens the romances to the Milesian fable, which contemporary criticism regarded as the most decadent type of fiction in its lack of truth and its erotic subject matter.[1]

At this point the canon abandons the moralistic line of argument and proceeds to the common negative evaluation of the romances on aesthetic grounds. Granting that the genre by its very nature leans more heavily on the *delectare* than the *prodesse* for its justification, he maintains that legitimate pleasure can be aroused by a work of literature only if it observes certain rules which the romances constantly violate. His two points of attack put the dialogue squarely within the tradition of the polemic which had dominated much of Italian critical writing of the second half of the sixteenth century—the controversy over Ariosto and Tasso. As has been pointed out above, the attacks of the "ancients" on the *romanzi* had been

---

[1] Both Clemencín and Rodríguez Marín attribute this comparison to Vanegas de Busto's prefatory remarks to a work of Cervantes de Salazar in 1546. It is well to observe that by Cervantes' time the association of the chivalric romance with the Milesian fable was so widespread that the author could have found it in almost any one of the theoretical works which he knew. Actually, the present context, in which it is juxtaposed to the Aesopian fable, suggests not the unsophisticated moralizing context of Vanegas de Busto, but rather that of the Aristotelians, who viewed both Aesop's and Apuleius' works as examples of a low order of fiction, one which fails to observe verisimilitude in its invented matter, the former justifiable for its exemplary value, the latter totally reprehensible. See Tasso, *Del poema eroico*, pp. 83-84; El Pinciano, *Philosophía antigua poética*, II, 8, 12-13, III, 153-154, 177; Carvallo, *Cisne de Apolo*, I, 81-82.

based on two aesthetic principles, unity and verisimilitude, each of which was in part derived from, in part strengthened by, the discovery and exegesis of Aristotle's *Poetics*. Judged by Aristotle's formula that an epic poem should have for its subject "a single action, whole and complete, with a beginning, a middle, and an end,"[2] the romances, which in the sixteenth century were consistently classified as heroic or epic poems, were found to be at best many actions of one man, at worst many actions of many. One of the canon's aesthetic criticisms of the romances of chivalry centers on their structural disorder. In words recalling the Horatian monstrosity and Aristotle's unified, living organism which must be entirely visible to the glance of the beholder, the canon employs an analogy which was used by nearly every theorist of the century who chose to attack the multiplicity of plot and protagonist in the romances:

> I have never seen a book of chivalry with a whole body for a plot, with all its limbs complete, so that the middle corresponds to the beginning, and the end to the beginning and middle, for they are generally made up of so many limbs that they seem intended rather to form a chimaera or a monster than a well-proportioned figure.[3]

The canon introduces his criticism of the other major artistic flaw in the romances in words which suggest that he views it as simply another manifestation of their faulty disposition. In reality his disparaging query: "What beauty can there be, or what harmony between the parts and the whole, or between the whole and its parts, in a book or story in which a sixteen-year-old lad deals a giant as tall as a tower one blow with his sword . . . ?"[4] brings up an entirely different aesthetic principle, which like that of unity had been in-

---

[2] *Poetics*, xxiii; ed. cit., p. 89.

[3] "No he visto ningún libro de caballerías que haga un cuerpo de fábula entero con todos sus miembros, de manera que el medio corresponda al principio, y el fin al principio y al medio; sino que los componen con tantos miembros, que más parece que llevan intención a formar una quimera o un monstruo que a hacer una figura proporcionada" (I, 482).

[4] "Pues ¿qué hermosura puede haber, o qué proporción de partes con el todo, y del todo con las partes, en un libro o fábula donde un mozo de diez y seis años da una cuchillada a un gigante como una torre . . . ?" (I, 481).

voked by nearly all critics of the genre, namely the principle of verisimilitude.[5] The canon's criticisms of the implausibilities of the romances indicate that his concept of verisimilitude was oriented toward the empirical possibility of the fictions, that like Tasso and so

[5] The subordination of the two notions derived from Aristotle's *Poetics* (i.e., unity and verisimilitude) to a more general concept of proportion is not at all surprising, if we recall the wide diffusion in the age of neo-Platonic theories of beauty, which many of the Aristotelian literary theorists shared, and that within these theories the body analogy appeared not in the context of problems of rhetorical and literary disposition, but rather in a context concerning a more general aesthetic category—that of beauty. Here the *locus classicus* is neither Horace nor Aristotle, but rather the *Symposium* in the resurrected form which it took in the commentaries of such theorists as Ficino and León Hebreo. In their dialogues the notion of beauty as proportion, which had descended from Aristotle's *Metaphysics* through Thomas Aquinas' *Summa* to contemporary aestheticians, was modified to include sensuous effects of light, color, and sound. (See León Hebreo, *Diálogos de amor*, tr. Garcilaso Inga de la Vega, ed. E. J. Martínez [Madrid, 1949], II, 261-270; also Leo Spitzer, *Classical and Christian Ideas of World Harmony* [Baltimore, 1963], pp. 126-127.) Cervantes expresses the neo-Platonist concept of beauty as proportion and color in the body analogy in the *Galatea*: ". . . todas las partes del cuerpo sean de por sí buenas, y que todas juntas hagan un todo perfecto y formen un cuerpo proporcionado de miembros y suavidad de colores" (ed. J. B. Avalle-Arce [Madrid, 1961], II, 44). Although Geoffrey Stagg ("Plagiarism in 'La Galatea,'" *Filologia Romanza*, VI [1959], 255-276) has revealed close correspondences to this passage in Mario Equicola's *Libro de natura d'amore* and Herrera's "Anotaciones" on Garcilaso's works, it is worth pointing out the following lines of a literary theorist who like the canon was both a rigid Aristotelian and a neo-Platonist—Torquato Tasso: "Opera della natura è la bellezza, la qual consistendo in certa proporzion di membra con grandezza convenevole e con vaga soavità di colori" (*Dell' arte poetica*, p. 32). In the most elaborately developed analogy between the Aristotelian *favola* and the human body which I have come across in the theoretical writings of the age, Geraldi Cintio invokes the same formula, justifying his bold use of the simile by claiming to be following Plato and Cicero (*De' romanzi*, pp. 20-21).

Actually we are dealing with an ancient formula (i.e., corporeal beauty as proportion and color), which Renaissance neo-Platonism reinvigorated by placing it in a new philosophical context. It had already assumed its Renaissance wording in Cicero's *Disputationes Tusculanae* (see Loeb Classical Library, *Cicero* [Cambridge, Mass., 1950], pp. 358-360) and Augustine's *De Civitate Dei*: "Omnis enim corporis pulchritudo est partium congruentia cum quadam coloris suavitate" (ed. J.E.C. Welldon [London, 1924], II, 616). Given this more general notion of proportion (i.e., not in relation to Horatian-Aristotelian techniques of disposition), a flaw in verisimilitude could be viewed as a flaw in proportion. Another specific equation of verisimilitude and the neo-Platonic notions of proportion and harmony appears in the *Persiles* (III, x). For an illuminating discussion of the importance of proportion and harmony in the Renaissance philosopher's vision of the external world and the way in which they were related to his notions on verisimilitude in art, see Ernst Cassirer, *The Individual and the Cosmos in Renaissance Philosophy*, pp. 162-165.

many others he interpreted *imitare* literally to mean *fare simile*. They include breaches of both *decoro de las cosas* and *decoro de las personas*.[6] The canon refers to the presentation of realities that simply do not exist in the natural world, e.g., giants as big as towers, imaginary geographical settings ("lands of Prester John of the Indies," "other [lands] which Ptolemy never knew nor Marco Polo visited"). He refers to actions that offend our awareness of the physical limitations imposed on man by the natural world, e.g., the rapid movement of knights around the world in spite of the realities of time and space and a boy's defeating a huge giant in battle. Moreover, he alludes to the improbabilities of the characters' actions which offend our sense of how people of specific stations, sexes, nationalities, ages, religions, et cetera normally act in a given situation ("Then what are we to say of the ease with which a hereditary queen or empress throws herself into the arms of an unknown and wandering knight?").[7]

THE LEGITIMATE MARVELOUS AND THE IDEAL ROMANCE

At this point the canon's argument takes an important turn from the negativism that marks his initial statements on the romances. He speaks with enthusiasm about the aesthetic criterion on which all contemporary defenses of the romances were based, that of pure pleasure. If properly constructed, the works, "keeping the mind in suspense, may so astonish, hold, excite, and entertain, that wonder and pleasure go hand in hand."[8] His statements of sympathy for the value of the pleasurable aspects of reading, which seem to contra-

[6] Carvallo uses these terms in referring to the two areas in which plausibility is most important (*Cisne de Apolo*, II, 117, 125). This Spanish contemporary of Cervantes offers a good statement of the empirically oriented interpretation of imitation discussed above (Chap. I) in relation to Italian literary circles: "Las [fictiones] verisimiles son las que cuentan algo, que sino fue, pudo ser, ò podra succeder, y estas han de ser muy apparentes, y semejantes a verdad, sin que se cuente en ellas cosas imposibles, que repugnen el entendimiento, y orden, ordinario de successos, ni a la naturaleza" (I, 80-81).

[7] "Pues ¿qué diremos de la facilidad con que una reina o emperatriz heredera se conduce en los brazos de un andante y no conocido caballero?" (I, 481). The similarity between the details of these criticisms and those of Valdés, Vives, and Pigna (see Chap. I) is obvious.

[8] ". . . suspendiendo los ánimos, admiren, suspendan, alborocen, y entretengan, de modo que anden a un mismo paso la admiración y la alegría juntas" (I, 482).

dict his initial condemnation of works "whose purpose is only to delight, and not to instruct," recall the ambivalence of Tasso, who was keenly aware that the fantasies of the *romanzi* are more delightful than the subject matter of ancient epics[9] and yet found himself compelled by his hostility to mendacity and any art which is essentially nondidactic to censure the romances over and over again in his writings.

If the canon is like Tasso in his sympathy for pleasure in literature, he is, moreover, like him in his refusal to admit that aesthetic pleasure may be independent of literal belief in its object in literature, or, seen another way, that aesthetic belief may be a phenomenon fundamentally distinct from literal belief. Tasso asserts dogmatically that the capacity of a literary audience to experience *admiratio* presupposes its capacity to believe that what it is reading is in fact truth.[10] If the readers question the veracity of the events of the narration,

> they do not readily consent to the things written, by which they now are moved to anger, now to pity, now to fear, now made sad, now full of vain joy, now in suspense, now carried away . . . for, where belief is lacking, the emotion or pleasure of what is being read or heard cannot abound.[11]

The canon makes the same assumption, for, after claiming that works must be composed so that "they astonish, hold, excite, and

---

[9] *Dell'arte poetica*, p. 34.

[10] Tasso's entire effort to legitimize the marvelous was based on this assumption, which he shared with nearly all other theorists of the age (see Minturno's words, cited above, Chap. I, n. 50). Cervantes examines it critically over and over again in his works.

[11] ". . . non consentono di leggieri alle cose scritte, per le quali o sono mossi ad ira, ora a pietà, ora a timore, or constristati, or pieni di vana allegrezza, or sospesi, or rapiti . . . perché, dove manca la fede, non può abbondare l'affetto o il piacere di quel che si legge o s'ascolta" (*Del poema eroico*, p. 84). See Robert M. Durling's discussion of Tasso's ideas concerning audience belief (*The Figure of the Poet in Renaissance Epic* [Cambridge (Mass.), 1965], pp. 192ff.). It should be recalled that one year before the *Quixote* appeared Lope de Vega had published the *Peregrino en su patria*, a work inspired by literary theories similar to those formulated by the canon. For our purposes it is significant that Lope introduces the fourth book of the work by stressing its verisimilitude and alluding to Tasso's theory: "Las [cosas] que no tienen apariencia de verdad no mueven, porque como dice en su *Poetica* Torquato Tasso, donde falta la fe, falta el afecto o el gusto de lo que se lee" (*Obras sueltas* [Madrid, 1776], V, 298).

entertain," he adds that "none of this can be achieved by anyone departing from verisimilitude or from that imitation of nature in which lies the perfection of all that is written."[12] Since verisimilitude depends ultimately on the capacity or willingness of the reader to believe, the poet's task is to choose and to construct his inventions or "lies" carefully, giving them enough semblance of truth so that the reader's willingness to believe is strained but not destroyed ("The more the lie resembles the truth, the better it is, and the more of the doubtful and the possible there is about it, the more pleasure it gives. The mendacious plots of fiction should be wedded to the understanding of the readers, and be constructed in such a way that reconciling impossibilities, smoothing over excesses . . .").[13]

After recommending these restrictions on the poet's inventive powers, the canon looks forward to the creation of a new type of romance, which, by meeting the aesthetic and didactic requirements of the classical literary doctrine, will thoroughly eclipse its inadequate ancestor. He emphasizes the rhetorical possibilities which the new genre will offer. Here the poet can display "all those qualities which the most sweet and pleasing sciences of poetry and rhetoric contain."[14] He can exhibit the universality of his knowledge ("Sometimes he may show himself to be an astronomer, or an excellent cosmographer, or a musician, or one versed in affairs of state")[15]

[12] ". . . todas estas cosas no podrá hacer el que huyere de la verisimilitud y de la imitación, en quien consiste la perfección de lo que se escribe" (I, 482). For other statements of the classicist position on verisimilitude in Cervantes' writings, see *Don Quijote*, II, 1000, and *Viage del Parnaso, Obras completas*, ed. R. Schevill and A. Bonilla (Madrid, 1922), p. 85.

[13] ". . . que tanto la mentira es mejor cuanto más parece verdadera, y tanto más agrada cuanto tiene más de lo dudoso y posible. Hanse de casar las fábulas mentirosas con el entendimiento de los que las leyeren, escribiéndose de suerte que, facilitando los imposibles, allanando las grandezas . . ." (I, 482). Here, in the phrases *lo dudoso y posible* and *facilitando imposibles* we discover Cervantes' most direct statement of the theory of the legitimate marvelous. The canon does not explore the implications of these phrases, but the many vehicles of the marvelous in the *Persiles*, all of which appear in Tasso's theories, indicate that he understood them as did his Italian counterpart.

[14] ". . . todas aquellas partes que encierran en sí las dulcísimas y agradables ciencias de la poesía y de la oratoria."

[15] "Ya puede mostrarse astrólogo, ya cosmógrafo excelente, ya músico, ya inteligente en las materias de estado" (I, 483). The belief that poetry was a science which included all knowledge was widely accepted by Renaissance criticism, which derived the notion from Horace's attribution of a high civilizing mission to poetry

and reveal his virtuosity in the description of a wide variety of events (storms, shipwrecks, battles, orations, et cetera) and in the depiction of all types of characters. Later in the discussion the curate asserts that the new romance will enrich the Spanish language with "the precious treasure of eloquence." Turning to another common topic of Renaissance literary theorizing—the nature of the epic hero—the canon maintains that in his envisioned work the poet can present an ideal hero, combining the virtues of all the traditional heroes of historical and epic literature.

The canon's concluding remarks round out his discourse perfectly in that they are addressed to the specific issues which he has raised at the beginning of his evaluation of books of chivalry. The old books "are intended only to delight, and not instruct"; the new books will "instruct and delight at the same time." The old books are marred by structural disorder and inverisimilitude; their descendants will observe the "science of poetry" both in disposition (the "web woven of beautiful and varied threads"—*tela de varios y hermosos lazos tejida*) and subject matter, i.e., the verisimilar or legitimate marvelous ("ingenious invention, aiming at truth as much as possible"). Moreover, the new genre will allow for a variety in form and tonality unknown in the verse epic since, being in prose—*la escritura desatada*—it is not restricted to a particular metrical pattern.[16] The appended statement "for the epic may be written in

and Cicero's conception of the ideal orator. In Cervantes' *Viage del Parnaso* poetry appears as a beautiful and richly adorned woman attended by various nymphs representing the liberal arts and all sciences. Poetry "todo lo sabe, todo lo dispone" (p. 58), is the "ciencia universal" (p. 62). See also *Don Quijote*, II, 649. El Pinciano writes: "la poesía comprehende . . . todas las sciencias especulatiuas, prácticas, actiuas, y effectiuas." The epic is the most universal, including politics, astrology, economics, medicine, and navigation (see I, 216-219). For the importance of the rhetorical tradition in Renaissance literary theorizing, see Spingarn, p. 34; Weinberg, pp. 805-806; Herrick, pp. 41-42, 106.

[16] I believe that Cervantes refers in this phrase to the medium, prose, and not to the lack of restrictions on the variety in subject matter characteristic of the romances of chivalry, nor to the poet's independence of the fundamental compositional technique of *atar* and *desatar*, derived from Aristotle's theory on tragedy, i.e., his freedom to create a "loosely" constructed or episodic plot. The following references to the variety in styles as well as to the epic in prose suggest that, far from upholding chaotic disorder in plot, he simply means that, free from the restrictions demanded by the single, continuous scheme of meter of the verse epic, the poet can use in his work a variety of lyric forms as well as prose, the conventional medium of comedy. I find a support for my interpretation in El Pinciano's discus-

prose just as well as in verse," while stating a commonplace of Renaissance critical thought, is particularly significant in the context in which it appears. Curiously enough it follows closely on the statement that the writer of the ideal romance can "show his talent for the epic, the lyric, the tragic, and the comic." Cervantes' lack of concern about the ambiguity which surrounds the juxtaposition of the two statements[17] indicates that the final comment occurred to

sion of Aristotle's words "la épica haze su imitación con solo lenguaje o metro" (whether this is or is not a mistranslation of the *Poetics*, xxiii, need not concern us here) to suggest that the prince of philosophers may have allowed an epic in prose. He interprets the phrase as meaning "agora sea lenguaje suelto, agora atado, es suficiente para la épica" [*Philosophía antigua poética*, III, 192-193]). This juxtaposition of "lenguaje atado" as meter to "lenguaje suelto" as prose suggests that Cervantes' "escritura desatada" did in fact mean merely what the surrounding context suggests: a work in prose. Similarly his phrase "largo y espacioso campo por donde sin empacho alguno pudiese correr la pluma" should not be interpreted as a recommendation of the uncontrolled variety characteristic of the old romance of chivalry. Upholding the Aristotelian idea of a single action with properly subordinated episodes (". . . la trama ha de ser del hilo de la vrdiembre, para que no se hagan las fábulas y marañas dichas episódicas, las quales Aristóteles condena"), El Pinciano suggests the history of Pelayo as a subject for an epic and asserts that "dará al poeta *ancho campo para sus episodios*" (III, 170-173).

[17] The proposition of an "epic" that may be epic, lyric, and tragic may seem ambiguous, but it is explicable in terms of Tasso's theories on the heroic poem, which allowed the epic poet to incorporate into his work occasionally the subject matter and styles of the lyric poet and the writer of tragedy: "Non è disconvenevole nondimeno al poeta epico ch'uscendo alquanto da' termini di quella sua illustre magnificenza, alcuna volta pieghi lo stile alla gravità del tragico, il che fa più spesso, alcun' altra al fiorito ornamento del lirico, il che fa più di rado" (*Del poema eroico*, p. 198). For example, in certain passages of the *Aeneid* Virgil shows himself to be an inimitable lyric poet (p. 226). Cervantes does in fact introduce lyric poems occasionally in his prose epic. The real ambiguity, or perhaps novelty, of this theory of the prose epic is Cervantes' allowance for its use of comedy. Tasso admitted that laughter, which he associated with the contemplation of an ugly object, is a source of *admiratio*, but its *admiratio* is of an order inferior to that aroused in the contemplation of a beautiful object. Hence both epic and tragedy are "enemies of laughter" (pp. 229-230). After abandoning the seriousness of the first book of the *Persiles*, Cervantes occasionally introduces comic elements into his work, particularly in the southern adventures of this "Arctic" romance, in which a tone of festivity emerges. One passage, the grotesque description of the old woman whom the wanderers encounter on the road to Toledo (III, vi), in detail so reminiscent of those of Maritornes and Clara Perlerina in the *Quixote*, is a good example of Tasso's theories of *admiratio* through ugliness. The prototype for such descriptions was Ariosto's hideous Gabrina: ". . . ci maravigliamo de' nani e delle brutte vecchie c'hanno volto di bertuccia, come avea Gabrina" (p. 229). It should be pointed out that one of El Pinciano's speakers claims that the epic poet can employ comic elements; he acknowledges, however, that many of his contemporaries feel that the resulting poem would be a monstrosity (*Philosophía antigua poética*, III, 219-220).

him as an important afterthought which could serve as a recapitulation of his entire discourse. In effect the remark crystalizes what was already implicit in the canon's general observations about the possibilities of the romance of chivalry. He is in reality suggesting a purification of the genre in accordance with the dictates of the Aristotelian-Horatian aesthetic criteria for the ideal epic. The idea is taken up immediately by the curate at the opening of the following chapter in a statement which shows that Cervantes was aware, just as Amyot had been a half century earlier and Huet would be a half century later, that the historical moment was ripe for the development of the "epic-romance":

> For that reason the writers of such books are most blameworthy, since *up to now* they have paid no attention to good sense or *to the art and rules. For if they had been guided by them, they might have become as famous in prose as the two princes of poetry, Greek and Latin, are in verse.*[18]

The concluding statements of the canon's discourse are all the more meaningful if we take into account some of the reminiscences of Tasso's influential theories on epic poetry observable in his formula for the ideal romance and recall that Tasso's theories represent in general the same reconciliation between the classical epic and medieval and Renaissance romance which the canon is proposing. The canon's description of the variety of events and characters which the romance can describe is very similar in structure and detail to a passage in Tasso's *Discorsi dell'arte poetica* and his *Discorsi del poema eroico*. Both include standard "epic" events— *Cervantes*: "shipwrecks, tempests, skirmishes, battles" (*Tasso*: "dispositions of armies," "battles by land and sea," "stormings of cities," "skirmishes and duels," "tempests"); actions and descrip-

---

[18] ". . . por esta causa son más dignos de reprehensión los que *hasta aquí* han compuesto semejantes libros sin tener advertencia a ningún buen discurso, ni al *arte y reglas por donde pudieran guiarse y hacerse famosos en prosa, como lo son en verso los dos príncipes de la poesía griega y latina*" (I, 484). The italics are mine. In the sonnets introducing the *Peregrino en su patria* Lope's work is compared to Virgil's *Aeneid* and Homer's *Odyssey* (see pp. vii-viii). Lope writes that his hero wanders "en una pequeña parte de su patria España con mas diversidad de sucessos, que Eneas hasta Italia, y Ulysses hasta Grecia, con mas fortunas de mar, persecuciones de Juno, engaños de Circe y peligros de Lotophagos y Polyphemos" (p. 335).

tions of character in which moral aspects are emphasized—*Cervantes*: "portraying a valiant captain . . . showing his wisdom in forseeing the wiles of the enemy, showing himself an eloquent orator . . . ripe in counsel" (*Tasso*: "acts of cruelty, of audacity, of courtesy, of generosity"); and general types of moving occurrences—*Cervantes*: "now depicting a tragic and lamentable incident, now a joyful and unexpected event" (*Tasso*: "events of love, now happy, now unhappy, now gay, now piteous").[19] In the canon's words proposing the creation of an ideal hero, who would combine the best qualities of all traditional heroes, an echo of Tasso's theories is more audible:

> He can portray the cunning of Ulysses, the piety of Aeneas, the valour of Achilles, the misfortunes of Hector, the treachery of Sinon, the friendship of Euryalus, the generosity of Alexander, the courage of Caesar, the clemency and truthfulness of Trajan, the fidelity of Zopyrus, the prudence of Cato, and, in fact, all those attributes which constitute the perfect hero, sometimes placing them in one single man, at other times dividing them amongst many.[20]

> One finds the excellence of piety in Aeneas, of military fortitude in Achilles, of prudence in Ulysses, and, to come down to our [heroes] of loyalty in Amadís and constancy in Bradamante.[21]

[19] ". . . naufragios, tormentas, rencuentros y batallas" ("ordinanze d'esserciti," "battaglie terrestri e navali," "espugnazioni di città, scaramucce e duelli," "tempeste"); "pintando un capitán valeroso . . . mostrándose prudente previniendo las astucias de sus enemigos, y elocuente orador . . . maduro en el consejo" ("opere di crudelità, di audacia, di cortesia, di generosità"); ". . . pintando ora un lamentable y trágico suceso, ahora un alegre y no pesado acontecimiento" ("avvenimenti d'amore, or felici, or infelici, or lieti or compassionevoli") (*Don Quijote*, I, 482-483; *Discorsi*, pp. 36, 140).

[20] "Puede mostrar las astucias de Ulixes, la piedad de Eneas, la valentía de Aquiles, las desgracias de Héctor, las traiciones de Sinón, la amistad de Eurialio, la liberalidad de Alejandro, el valor de César, la clemencia y verdad de Trajano, la fidelidad de Zopiro, la prudencia de Catón, y, finalmente, todas aquellas acciones que pueden hacer perfecto a un varón ilustre, ahora poniéndolas en uno solo, ahora dividiéndolas en muchos" (I, 483).

[21] "Si ritrova in Enea l'eccellenza della pietà, della fortezza militare in Achille, della prudenza in Ulisse, e, per venire a i nostri, della lealtà in Amadigi, della constanza in Bradamante" (*Discorsi*, pp. 12, 103). Riley points out that it is very probable that Cervantes was influenced by Tasso's *Discorsi*, but he adds that establishing proof of direct influence is complicated by the extremely topical character

Cervantes & the Classical Aesthetic

At this point in the discussion the curate and the canon turn their attention to the Spanish theater and offer a systematic criticism of its shortcomings. For our purposes this phase of the dialogue is significant in its introduction of another important aspect of con-

---

of the Aristotelian literary theories of the epoch. In spite of Riley's cautious conclusion that direct literary influence "can be no more than a suspicion where such general matters are concerned" (p. 8), I am convinced that we are dealing with a case of direct influence. My conviction is based on a variety of considerations: the unparalleled prestige which Tasso enjoyed in the age as poet and theoretician; his central position in the controversy about the romances of chivalry (El Pinciano devotes very little attention to the romances); Cervantes' literary aspirations in the plan of the *Persiles*, the epic in prose; the obsessive preoccupation with the problem of reconciling the marvelous and verisimilitude, which distinguished Tasso from all other theorists of the time and which underlies numerous dramatizations of literary principles in Cervantes' works; Tasso's specific recommendations of thematic matter and techniques of the marvelous which Cervantes uses in the *Persiles* (e.g., the northern geographical setting and the marvels of the new world); the direct introduction of his doctrines on verisimilitude into Lope's *Peregrino en su patria* (see above), a generic predecessor of the *Persiles*; and finally that one missing link which is responsible for Riley's caution, a case of direct borrowing. In accordance with Tasso's recommendations for the lofty style of heroic poetry, Cervantes occasionally employs the extended epic simile in the *Persiles*. Thus he describes the wanderers as they must wade across a river: ". . . bien assi como quando al repressado rebaño de mansas ouejas, puestas en lugar estrecho, haze camino la vna, a quien las demas al momento siguen, Belarminia se arrojò al agua, a quien todos siguieron" (*Los trabajos de Persiles y Sigismunda, Historia septentrional*, ed. R. Schevill and A. Bonilla [Madrid, 1914], II, 152; all subsequent references to the *Persiles* are to this edition). The simile is clearly modeled on Dante's

> Come le pecorelle escon del chiuso
> a una, a due, a tre, e l'altre stanno
> timidette atterrando l'occhio e 'l muso;
> e ciò che fa la prima, e l'altre fanno,
> addossandosi a lei, s'ella s'arresta,
> semplici e quete, e lo 'mperchè non sanno.
> (*Purgatorio*, III, 79-84)

Given the other factors suggesting the influence of Tasso in the work, we can be almost certain that Cervantes' source was not Dante, but rather Tasso's two major *Discorsi* on poetry, in each of which the simile is given as an example of the necessary *energia* or visual power in epic style (pp. 47, 244). Although this is one of the few literary examples of the expanded *Del poema eroico* which did appear also in the earlier *Dell'arte poetica* (written around 1564, published in 1587), I agree with Riley that the absence of any of the Aristotelian literary concerns in the *Galatea* suggests that Cervantes' first contact with the work of Tasso occurred subsequent to 1587. In any event his extreme interest in these matters probably began at about this time. El Pinciano's work, the other Aristotelian tract greatly influencing Cervantes, appeared in 1596. In the following chapters I will point out many of the cases in which the influence of Tasso is present but less specific in character, as I have done in the passage discussed above.

temporary literary doctrine and the controversy surrounding the romances. As Renaissance theorists explored the problems of truth and verisimilitude in literature, they came to the realization that a solution to such problems presupposes a thorough understanding of the reader's capacity to believe. Hence they devoted much attention both to the question of what constitutes an audience and to the distinctions between different types of audiences. As El Pinciano pointed out, a poet writing an epic about Spanish history for a Persian audience could make the Goth Oronte the King of Spain without violating the principle of verisimilitude.[22] These theoretical problems became issues of much greater urgency in the practical context of the Ariosto controversy, for the defenders of the romances did not deny themselves the argument of the genre's appeal to an audience traditionally despised by the learned men of the Renaissance—the masses.[23]

Cervantes' canon acknowledges that it is the "foolish crowd who are generally the most given to reading such books." Although he and the curate are harsh in their judgment of the *vulgo* and the Spanish theater for bowing to its tastes, they nevertheless maintain that this vast audience has the capacity for appreciating both the ideal romance and the ideal drama which they would substitute for the present decadent form. Both *discretos* and *ignorantes* have read with pleasure the first pages of the canon's new romance, and the new, classical drama will move "the listener's mind, however boorish and dull he may be." Their ambivalent attitude is similar to that of Tasso, who criticizes the tastes of the *vulgo* yet insists that the poet write for both *giudiziosi* and *ignoranti* and even allows him to present as verisimilar beliefs of the *vulgo* which he himself does not share.[24] It is well to note here that Cervantes was very

[22] See above, Chap. II, n. 67.

[23] See Weinberg, pp. 805-806, 989-990, 1073, 1108-1112.

[24] See *Dell'arte poetica*, pp. 8, 34; *Del poema eroico*, p. 93. As will be made clear in the following chapters, Cervantes' attitude on this matter is even more complex. In theory he follows the humanist tradition of disdain for the *vulgo* audience, e.g., "el vulgo mal limado y bronco" (*Viage del Parnaso*, p. 16). However, like Tasso and the canon he grants that this audience can appreciate good art. In offering a definition of the "legitimate marvelous," he states that it appeals to both audiences: "Que entonces la mentira satisfaze,/ quando verdad parece, y está escrita/ con gracia, que al discreto y simple aplaze" (*Viage del Parnaso*, p. 85).

conscious of the existence of the two audiences and their different standards of judgment and capacities for belief. In nearly all the critical examinations of literary principles in his works, the points of view of the respective audiences are present as dramatic participants.

A COMIC INTERLUDE: THE CRITICAL RESPONSE TO CLASSICISM

Don Quixote's rebuttal to the canon's discourse on literary principles and the romances of chivalry is preceded by a short argument between the knight and Sancho as to whether the two masked figures guiding Don Quixote's cage are in reality the curate and the barber and whether Don Quixote is in reality enchanted. Serving primarily to recall our attention to the movement of the novel, which has been interrupted by the long digression, the dialogue has, moreover, a significance in relation to the discussion which we have just heard and sets the tone that will mark Don Quixote's methods of dealing with the classical literary doctrines.

The argument starts when Sancho observes that the masked figures are the curate and the barber and attempts to convince his master that he is not an enchanted knight on his way to more adventures but in reality a victim of deception. Don Quixote persists in his belief, and Sancho has recourse to an argument based on a commonly held notion ("what is commonly said around us"): an enchanted person neither eats nor sleeps nor does "what cannot be avoided," a premise which Don Quixote readily accepts. The comedy of situation springing from the exchange and the condition of the cage ("things are none too clean") does not conceal an oblique allusion to the foregoing literary discussion. Sancho is attempting to reveal the absurdity of his master's belief by subjecting it to the scrutiny demanded by the canon's principle of verisimilitude. In doing so, he employs the syllogistic reasoning characteristic of the neo-Aristotelian theorists. Don Quixote's response is an ingenious burlesque of that principle and the mode of thinking which it represents:

On the other hand his sympathy for the pleasure which the *vulgo* experiences in fantastic literature, which the classicists condemned, is evident on many occasions (see, for example, *Don Quijote*, I, xxxii; *Persiles*, II, xiv).

Don Quixote

"You are right, Sancho," replied Don Quixote; "but I have told you already that there are many kinds of enchantments; and *time may have changed the fashion from one kind to another. It may be usual now for people under a spell to do all that I do, although they did not before; so that there is no arguing or drawing conclusions against the usage of the times.* I most certainly know that I am enchanted, and that is sufficient to ease my conscience."[25]

In its intricacy the parody bears close examination. Don Quixote's assertion of the possibility that new methods of enchantment have been developed and that one must realize that customs change with the times is clearly an evocation of the literary principle which the "moderns" had always used against the rigid classicism of the "ancients" and which both the most enthusiastic defenders of the romances and those classicists who recognized the appeal of the modern genre accepted as valid.[26] However, through intentional misapplication of the valid aesthetic principle which it introduces, Don Quixote's statement represents a parody of that very principle. The argument to which he alludes would criticize an insistent conservatism in art, which refuses to dispense with elements offensive to modern sensibilities or changing demands of verisimilitude—the examples of the failures of Boccaccio's *Teseida* and Trissino's *L'Italia liberata dai goti* in their adherence to a rigid classicism were frequently cited in sixteenth-century discussions of literature. Tasso went to the extreme of defining the range of subject matter in which the poet should bow to changing customs—e.g., new types of armor,

[25] "—Verdad dices, Sancho—respondió don Quijote—; pero ya te he dicho que hay muchas maneras de encantamentos, y podría ser que *con el tiempo se hubiesen mudado de unos en otros, y que agora se use que los encantados hagan todo lo que yo hago, aunque antes no lo hacían. De manera, que contra el uso de los tiempos no hay que argüir ni de qué hacer consecuencias.* Yo sé y tengo para mí que voy encantado, y esto me basta para la seguridad de mi conciencia" (I, 491-492). The italics are mine.

[26] Cervantes' famous defense of his departure from the rules in his late comedy is based on the argument: "Los tiempos mudan las cosas/ y perfeccionan las artes,/ . . . He dejado parte de ellos [the 'preceptos graves'],/ y he también guardado parte,/ porque lo quiere así el uso,/ que no se sujeta al arte" (*El rufián dichoso, Obras completas,* ed. A. Valbuena Prat [Madrid, 1956], p. 343). For an example of the use of the argument that customs and times change in a defense of the romances, see Giuseppe Malatesta's *Della poesia romanzesca* (1596), cited by Weinberg, pp. 1061-1062.

banquets and ceremonies, the horror of sacrifices, and modern notions of decorum of character (princesses of Nausicaa's rank no
longer do their own laundry). He failed, of course, to mention new
modes of enchantment which permit the basic bodily functions to
continue, and distinguished all of this from the eternal precepts
which are independent of the particular ages (e.g., unity of plot).[27]
However, in Cervantes' context the patent absurdity of the "new
customs" which the argument is invoked to justify not only undercuts the serious value of Sancho's mode of approaching the problem
of belief, but also renders the very serious principle and the whole
canon of critical thought which stands behind it ridiculous. Don
Quixote's emphatic statement: "I most certainly know that I am
enchanted," in spite of its absurdity, is the logical conclusion in the
literary frame of the discussion. Belief depends ultimately on the
will of the individual reader, and attempts to define sharply the
limits of the truth which he will tolerate are idle.

What we observe in this small scene of low comedy, which structurally provides a transition from the long digression of the canon
to the unfolding plot of the novel, is a miniature literary debate[28]
in ironic counterpoint to that between the canon and the curate. The
elements of parody in this "mock-*discorso*" between Sancho (the
absurd "ancient") and Don Quixote (the absurd "modern") are
important to observe. They set a tone that remains consistent in
Cervantes' many critical examinations of the Aristotelian literary
criteria and the problem of truth in literature in *Don Quixote* and
the *Persiles*. Moreover, they allow for some tentative conclusions
which, I think, the following chapters will bear out.

Cervantes is highly conscious of both the general and specific
aspects of the tradition of literary theorizing in the Renaissance and
generally sympathetic with its aims. It is undeniable that he voices

---

[27] *Del poema eroico*, pp. 136-137.

[28] It is no accident that Cervantes concludes the canon's discourse with the
phrase: "A este punto de su *coloquio* llegaban el canónigo y el cura . . ." and
entitles the chapter presenting Don Quixote and Sancho's discussion, which immediately follows: "Donde se trata del discreto *coloquio* que Sancho Panza tuvo
con su señor don Quijote." Cervantes uses the term *coloquio* to describe the conversation between Don Quixote, Sancho, and Sansón Carrasco in II, iii. The rich
allusiveness of the discussion to Aristotelian literary theory forms the basis for
Toffanin's interpretation of the *Quixote* (see *La fine dell' humanesimo*, Chap. XV).

through the canon some of his own opinions on art, that these opinions are expressed forcefully on several other occasions in his writings, and that the general plan of the *Persiles* was an act of conformity to the canon's Aristotelian principles. On the other hand he is suspicious about the burdens with which the critical movement saddled the creative artist and perhaps skeptical about its assumption that truth is within easy reach of reason's grasp. Consequently he does not hesitate to subject its major ideas to a careful examination and to assert openly his independence of many of them.

It is safe to assume that when Cervantes introduces the terminology and general principles of contemporary literary theory, he is aware of their meanings and implications. In this respect the passage discussed above is typical for many more, in which the artist wishes to debate with the neo-Aristotelians and to affirm his autonomy. The author will often bring up these notions and terms; generally they will reflect on the contexts in which they appear and the contexts will reflect on them. They will rarely be used as univocal standards of measurement, for they are as much a part of the fluid subject matter of Cervantes as they are comments upon that subject matter.

DON QUIXOTE'S DEFENSE OF THE ROMANCES

Following Don Quixote's release from the cage, the canon, moved to sympathy at the sight of the demented gentleman, offers a concise recapitulation of his arguments on the romances. He points to their offenses against verisimilitude and decorum ("dragons," "giants," "valiant women"), suggests their uncontrolled variety (a list of elements in which the word *tanto* appears more than fifteen times), and offers a dramatic, anecdotal explanation of his doctrine that the pleasure of reading books of entertainment is dependent upon the reader's acceptance of the literal truth of their subject matter. Admitting that his initial reaction to the fantastic elements of the romances is one of pleasure produced by their effect on his imagination, the faculty commonly associated with the *vulgo*, he adds that, as soon as he brings his intellect to bear on them, he discovers their falsity and hurls them into the fire in disgust.[29] He

---

[29] Riley (p. 183) finds in the canon's anecdote a possible echo of Alessandro Piccolomini's commentary on the *Poetics*. The distinction implicit in the statement

concludes by pointing out their pernicious effect on readers, proof of which is the condition of Don Quixote, and advising the *hidalgo* to seek pleasure, which the romances undeniably produce, in Holy Scripture (The Book of Judges) and historical accounts of great men, which offer both pleasure and edification.

Don Quixote now begins his lengthy rebuttal of the canon's arguments, proceeding along the lines laid down by traditional rhetoric. He briefly sums up what he considers to be the major arguments of the opponent, in this case the attack on the literal truth of the romances and their harmful effect on the readers, proceeds to a *refutatio* of these arguments, and concludes with a *confirmatio* of arguments in favor of the romances. In his refutation he accepts the canon's doctrine of verisimilitude and through ironic distortion illuminates the problematic foundations on which it rests; i.e., that in the last analysis belief depends on what the reader will accept as true. Refusing to state directly that the adventures of the knights-errant literally occurred, he shrewdly observes that their truth is universally *accepted*. It is "a thing so universally acknowledged and so accepted as truth, that anyone denying it, as

was very important for critics preoccupied with the problems of literal truth in literature and the dangers or pleasures of the fantastic. See for example Tasso's distinction between the normal fantasy (*fantasia sensitiva*), the kind employed by the sophist and responsible for such chimerical products as the flying horse of the romances (*imitazione fantastica*) and the intellectual fantasy (*fantasia intellettuale*), the kind employed by the poet, whose major concern is truth (*imitazione icastica*) (*Del poema eroico*, pp. 89-91). The general conservative tendency of the classicists was to admit the pleasures of the two spiritual faculties but to demand the reader's use of the intellect to censure any art which appealed only to the inferior faculties of the imagination and its allies, the senses, or in the case of allegory to see the deeper meaning beyond the literal level. In defending the veracity of the poets from the charges of that traditional detractor of poetry, Zoilo (who incidentally appears in Cervantes' *Viage del Parnaso* and his prologue to the *Novelas ejemplares*), Carvallo resurrects Lactantius' doctrine of *figura* and likens the poet to the Hebrew prophets, cloaking their revelations in the ambiguous figures of their prophecies. In doing so, he acknowledges the important distinction between the inferior and superior faculties of the soul: "Y si vemos pintado vn Angel a manera de vn mancebo y con alas, aunque la fantasia lo imagina assi, no por esso el entendimiento del prudente, concibe ser de aquella forma, como realmento no lo es, antes es incorporeo espiritu" (I, 101). Carvallo associates the temptations of the devil with a poetry that appeals solely to the lower faculties, comparing it curiously to the *cabeça de pulpo*, which tastes good but causes uncomfortable digestive aftereffects. On the other hand the defenders of the romances accepted the distinction but saw a positive value in an art which did appeal to the imagination alone.

you do, deserves the very punishment you say that you inflict on certain books when you have read them and they displease you."[30] Moreover, he adds that if one were to deny that Amadís existed, he would be forced to deny the historical reality of various other heroes, offering a curious list which begins with the Homeric figures, includes those of medieval chivalric romance, and ends with several of the historical-legendary figures of Spanish history.[31] The effect of this long listing is to suggest that truth is always a function of belief, that both historical and fictional reality depend on our willingness to accept their truth. Following closely on the canon's recommendation that Don Quixote read history and Holy Scripture, the passage has a retroactive implication that might have caused Cervantes trouble with the Inquisition if he had chosen to make the implication any more clear.

Like the argument between Don Quixote and Sancho, the exchange becomes much more meaningful if we observe its details against the background of the critical preoccupations of sixteenth-century literary theory. In presenting his list of heroes, Don Quixote is, in effect, laying bare the simple principle underlying the neo-Aristotelians' elaborate theories of verisimilitude. If the poet must strive to "deceive the reader with the semblance of truth" (*con la sembianza della verità ingannare il lettore*) as Tasso put it, or, in the canon's words, "wed the mendacious plots of fiction to the understanding of the readers," in the last analysis he is dependent on the reader. The problem immediately arises: what constitutes the reader and where does the outer edge of his capacity for belief (or his capacity to be deceived) lie? Much of Tasso's inexhaustible critical energy was spent on the problem of defining this hypothetical reader and drawing a line between what he can and cannot accept as plausible.[32] This line would lie somewhere between the points of

[30] ". . . una cosa tan recebida en el mundo, y tenida por tan verdadera, que el que la negase, como vuestra merced la niega, merecía la mesma pena que vuestra merced dice que da a los libros cuando los lee y le enfadan" (I, 495-496).

[31] To appreciate all the irony of the statement, we must recall the traditional use of the word *historia* to refer to the romances of chivalry in Spain, a practice which aroused the anger of serious historians in the sixteenth century.

[32] The weakness in Tasso's argument is apparent occasionally when, in order to allow the presence of certain marvelous elements in the epic poem, he resorts to the very argument which Don Quixote uses. For example, he claims that a poet

the giant Falafre and Suero de Quiñones, an historical personage, which mark the extremes of Don Quixote's list. In lumping all the heroes together, the defender of the romances is choosing to ignore all his opponents' efforts to trace the elusive line of verisimilitude, impudently suggesting the futility of such endeavors.[33]

Like Don Quixote's response to Sancho on the new methods of enchantment, his listing of legendary and historical heroes evokes a current topic of literary criticism, and does in fact rebut a serious theoretical objection with which he is confronted, in this case the canon's criticism of the falsity of the romances. However, as in the preceding "mock-*discorso*" there is more complexity to the refutation than is immediately apparent. Corresponding to the ridiculous misapplication of the argument of the "moderns" to modes of enchantment is Don Quixote's deliberate evocation of the basic weakness in contemporary theories of verisimilitude to suggest such patent absurdities as that his grandmother knew the dueña Quintañona and that he is himself the descendant of the historical-legendary hero Gutierre Quijada. Again the effect is of double-edged parody. The validity of the canon's critical objection, which

---

can employ angels, devils, fairies, and magicians who perform fantastic acts *because the masses believe that they exist,* adding that ancient poets realized that the deities that filled their works had no reality but wrote of them *because the masses accepted them* as literally true (*Dell'arte poetica*, pp. 7-8). Indeed Tasso's recommendation of subject matter from Sacred Scripture and history is based to a large degree on the fact that such matter is *accepted as true.*

[33] In the comic figure of the poet whom Berganza describes in the *Coloquio de los perros* Cervantes humorously shows what the canon's concern with defining the edge of belief can lead to. The young man has completed a history play concerning the Papacy. A ludicrous obsession with verisimilitude leads him to insist that the actors representing the twelve cardinals wear purple rather than scarlet robes. If the director does not have the robes, he will refuse to give him the play ("—Pues si me quita uno tan solo—respondió el poeta—, así le daré yo mi comedia como volar"). He reasons: ". . . cuando sucedió el caso que cuenta la historia de mi comedia era tiempo de *mutatio caparum,* en el cual los cardenales no se visten de rojo, sino de morado; y así, *en todas maneras conviene, para guardar la propiedad,* que estos mis cardenales salgan de morado; y éste es un punto que hace mucho al caso para la comedia. . . . *Yo no he podido errar en esto, porque he leído todo el ceremonial romano, por sólo acertar en estos vestidos*" (*Novelas ejemplares*, ed. Rodríguez Marín, [Madrid, 1917], II, 321-322). To appreciate the humor of this figure, we must recall the preoccupations of the theorists of the period with historical accuracy in the interests of verisimilitude and the humorless figure of Tasso, who spent years studying historical texts to assure his accuracy in details as trivial as the purple robes of Cervantes' poet.

has up to this moment been honored by a serious treatment, now suddenly dissolves before the calculated absurdity of Don Quixote's response. The absurdity of the response in turn destroys the validity of the serious literary consideration which lay behind the discussion as long as the serious level was maintained and suggests the absurdity of the entire mode of thinking on which it is based. In other words, a serious *discorso* turns suddenly into a "mock-*discorso*."

Cervantes concludes Don Quixote's refutation by returning to the dramatic methods which we have witnessed in the comic interlude of Sancho and Don Quixote's conversation about enchantment. The canon is puzzled by his adversary's lengthy argument and attempts to separate the true from the false in Don Quixote's list. His arguments are intricate and logical but conclude suddenly in an astonishing statement. He admits that he does not recall seeing in the national armory the huge peg (bigger than "the pole of a coach") of the wooden steed which bore the knight Pierres through the heavens, and in bewilderment attributes his oversight to shortsightedness. While providing a note of comedy of character, as the judicious canon suddenly appears in a new perspective as the befuddled pedant, the scene dramatically indicates that Don Quixote's rebuttal has been successful, that, just as Carvallo recommends in defining the aims of the *refutatio*, he has rendered his opponents' argument "doubtful," "uncertain," and "unprovable."[34]

Deprived of his original arguments, the bewildered canon is reduced to a conclusion similar to that of Don Quixote following the debate with Sancho: "Even if the peg is there, I still do not have to believe the stories of so many Amadises." Belief depends on the disposition of the individual; it is little more than an act of faith. Nevertheless, he is still unwilling to give in and restates categorically the standard argument of the classicists on the *vulgo* vs. the *culto* audience—that there is in fact an ideal reader with certain capacities for belief, and that what this reader accepts as real is in all probability real. He adds that it is incredible that Don Quixote, a man "endowed with such a good understanding," should believe in the fictions of the romances.

Don Quixote's response to this argument follows the pattern

[34] *Cisne de Apolo*, II, 109.

already set. He again accepts the canon's doctrine of verisimilitude and turns it back on him by absurdly misapplying it. His misapplication in this case is a favorable measurement of the romances by the doctrine. How can the romances be condemned as false, "presenting such an *appearance of truth*, for they tell us the father, mother, country, kindred, age, place, and the achievements, step by step, and day by day, performed by such and such a knight or knights"?[35] The force of the double-edged parody is fully appreciated only if we bear in mind the toils of the canon's kindred theorist, Tasso, to probe all the implications of that simple phrase "appearance of truth." Moreover, Don Quixote concludes the argument with a recommendation that the canon avoid the blasphemy of denying the reality of the knights-errant, assuring him: "I am advising you in these matters to act as a sensible man [*discreto*] should," impudently turning back on him his argument concerning the reader of "good understanding." Again the seriousness of the canon's criticisms disappears, and again the meaninglessness of the critical principles and system to which Don Quixote alludes is suggested.

At this point Don Quixote's *refutatio* is complete. He has concentrated his attack on the problem of verisimilitude, revealing the fundamental weakness in an aesthetic theory which makes pleasure contingent on the reader's accepting the subject matter of a work of art as literally true, and ridiculed the theory with a calculated mischievousness, distorting its serious principles through absurd misapplications of them.

The *confirmatio* of Don Quixote's rejoinder contains both literary and didactic arguments. The latter are brief and direct. Addressing himself to his adversary's claim that imaginative literature has a harmful effect on the citizens of a well-ordered republic, Don Quixote categorically affirms that such reading has had a beneficial effect on himself. In doing so, he recalls the spiritual values on which the system of chivalry is founded: "Since I became a knight-

---

[35] ". . . llevando *tanta apariencia de verdad*, pues nos cuentan el padre, la madre, la patria, los parientes, la edad, el lugar y las hazañas, punto por punto y día por día, que el tal caballero hizo, o caballeros hicieron?" (I, 499). The italics are mine.

errant, I have been valiant, courteous, liberal, well-bred, generous, polite, bold, gentle, patient, and an endurer of ordeals."[36]

The remainder of his argument is much more important for the light it sheds on Cervantes' literary theories, for it deals with the aesthetic flaws which his opponent has observed in the books of chivalry. It is based on two related principles which were traditionally invoked by the defenders of the romances to counter criticism by their rigidly classicist adversaries—success and pleasure. Don Quixote's oration on the pleasure which the reading of the romances invariably produces is prefaced by the assertion that the appeal of the genre is recognized universally: "They are read with universal delight and applause by great and small, poor and rich, learned and ignorant, plebeians and gentlefolk—in short, by all kinds of persons of every quality and condition."[37]

After recommending that the canon read the tales of chivalry to discover the pleasure which they offer, Don Quixote turns to the most important part of his argument. In his narration of the adventure of the Knight of the Lake, he attempts to bring the pleasures of romance literature to his present audience, which includes representatives of both the *cultos* (the canon and the curate) and the *vulgo* (Sancho and the barber). His introduction of the episode is significant in its emphasis on the sense of sight and on the value of an immediate, purely visual apprehension of the scene: "Could there be anything more delightful than to see displayed here and now before our eyes, as we might say, a great lake of pitch. . . ?"[38] Here Don Quixote is following standard precepts for

---

[36] ". . . después que soy caballero andante soy valiente, comedido, liberal, biencriado, generoso, cortés, atrevido, blando, paciente, sufridor de trabajos" (I, 501).

[37] ". . . son leídos y celebrados de los grandes y de los chicos, de los pobres y de los ricos, de los letrados e ignorantes, de los plebeyos y caballeros, finalmente, de todo género de personas de cualquier estado y condición que sean" (I, 499). The defense of the romances based on their success was common in the literary debate echoed in this dialogue. For example, in his praise of Ariosto (*Difesa del primo Infarinato*, 1590) Orlando Pescetti claims that the "universal consensus" is important in the evaluation of any poet and that the "universal consensus" has raised Ariosto to an exalted position (Weinberg, p. 1051). Similarly Lionardo Salviati (1585) defends Ariosto's work for the joy it offers all readers (Weinberg, p. 1009).

[38] "¿Hay mayor contento que ver, como si dijésemos, aquí ahora se muestra delante de nosotros un gran lago de pez. . . ?" (I, 499)

literary composition, expressed everywhere in sixteenth-century theorizing, from Castiglione's discussion of the ways in which the courtier should compose anecdotes[39] to the neo-Aristotelians' formulas for the epic poet. In Tasso's words the poet must strive for an *energia* of style, "which indeed with words places before [the reader's] eyes the thing, so that it seems to him that he is seeing it rather than hearing it."[40] However, Tasso's qualification (that the audience can feel it is witnessing the events only if it believes they are true) is implicitly and significantly absent in Don Quixote's account, which recalls the most fantastic themes of lake, cave, garden, and palace, all encompassed by the broader and omnipresent theme of medieval romance, the journey to the other world.[41]

The appeal to the pleasure of visual contemplation that begins the passage is a mere prelude to the stress on sensuous beauty in the description that follows. The pleasure of the audience in witnessing the scene is repeatedly recalled by the narrator: "Y ¿hay más que ver, después de haber visto esto, que ver salir por la puerta del castillo un buen número de doncellas. . . ? ¿Qué es ver, pues, cuando nos cuentan que, tras todo esto, le llevan a otra sala. . . ? ¿Qué el verle echar agua a manos, toda de ámbar. . . ? ¿Qué el hacerle sentar sobre una silla de marfil? ¿Qué verle servir todas las doncellas. . . ? ¿Qué el traerle tanta diferencia de manjares. . . ? ¿Cuál será oír la música. . . ?"[42] An interesting effect of this long

[39] *Il Cortegiano*, II, 43.

[40] ". . . la quale sì con parole pone inanzi a gli occhi la cosa che pare altrui non di udirla, ma di vederla" (*Dell'arte poetica*, p. 47). Renaissance poetics generally introduced the precept by recalling Aristotle's praise of the visual vividness in Homer's poetry and his recommendation that the poet put things before the reader's eyes (*Poetics*, xv, xvii). This emphasis on sight is a feature common to nearly all Cervantes' surrogates of the creating artist. More will be said of it in my examination of the most important development of the type of scene which Don Quixote's narration represents—Periandro's narration at the court of King Policarpo.

[41] See Howard R. Patch, *The Other World According to Descriptions in Medieval Literature* (Cambridge, Mass., 1950). Clemencín lists a wide assortment of vaguely similar episodes in romances and concludes unsympathetically that "de todos estos sucesos parece que hizo un potaje Don Quijote para forjar su aventura del *Lago ferviente*" (*Don Quijote de la Mancha* [Madrid, 1894], IV, 308).

[42] "After having seen this, could one have a finer sight than that of a number of maidens coming out of the door of the castle. . . ? Is it not something then to see that, when they tell us that after all this, they take him to another room. . . ? To see him sprinkle on his hands water all distilled of ambergris. . . ? To see him

series of queries emphasizing the sensuous experiences of the knight is the identification of the audience and the knight in the participation in the experience, as the audience's sensation of observing the scene from without merges into the knight's sensations within it. The effect, produced by the initial incantatory repetition of the verb *ver* and the succeeding ellipsis of the verb maintaining the point of view of the reader present, is made explicit at the end of the series, as the beautiful enchanted damsel tells her visitor things which "amaze the knight and astonish the readers." The narrator's consciousness of sensuous pleasure is apparent at nearly every moment of his account (e.g., the artfully arranged garden "whose verdure pleases the eyes" and in which "the sweet, untaught song of innumerable little bright-colored birds soothes the ear," "the sweet-smelling ointments," "fragrant and perfumed shirt," "sweet-smelling flowers," "deliciously cooked dishes," and the traditional gold and gems of the palace).

Like so many other elements of this discussion, the deliberate sensuous extravagance of Don Quixote's description is fully meaningful only if we recognize its allusiveness to the literary debate which lies in the background throughout his encounter with the canon. The notion that the romances appealed to the lower faculties, the imagination and the senses, and to the class which was most dominated by these faculties, the *vulgo*, had long been a weapon in the hands of the critics of the genre. As we have observed, it is implictly present in the canon's statement that the appeal of the romances to his imagination is undeniable and that only on subjecting them to examination by the higher faculties of the soul, i.e., the intellect, does he discover their worthlessness and cast them into the fire. The defenders of the romances refused to let this criticism go unanswered. In his *Della poesia romanzesca* (1596) Giuseppe Malatesta rejects outright the notion that true pleasure in reading is dependent on intellectual powers and upholds the senses as its ultimate source. His words could be taken as an abstract statement of the solution to the artistic problem and rebuttal of the canon's complaint which Don Quixote's recounted vision indirectly offers:

---

seated on an ivory chair? To see all the maidens serve him. . . ? And bring him such a variety of dishes? What must it be like to hear the music. . . ?"

This seems to me to be insolent curiosity, that I should feel in myself the effect of delectation and that somebody else should come along and try to confuse my own senses and tell me that this is not a true pleasure because it is not generated by the observance of the true poetic art, as if I were obliged to give more credence to the vanity of certain reasons of another than to the testimony of my very own senses. . . . Now if our sense is a good judge of pleasure and is able to recognize when a thing pleases it or annoys it, I do not wish that, since we must satisfy it, we should go about placing ourselves in servitude to certain vain reasons discovered by men who think that our senses can be moved more by arguments than by their own proper objects.[43]

Profusion in sensuous description is not the only characteristic of Don Quixote's narration which is significant in relation to the contemporary literary polemic over Tasso and Ariosto. Before directing his disparaging criticism at what he obviously considers to be the major flaw of the romances, their lack of verisimilitude, the canon had briefly touched on another aesthetic shortcoming of the genre, its lack of unity and reliance on untrammeled variety of episode, event, character, and detail as sources of *admiratio*.

It would certainly be false to suggest that the canon is insensitive to the aesthetic value of variety and the pleasures of the marvelous, which were normally associated with it. As we have observed, his envisioned romance is to utilize the "broad and spacious field through which the pen could run without any hindrance," to describe a great variety of characters and actions and, in so doing, to "hold in suspense" and "astonish" the reader. His attitude toward

[43] "Insolente curiosità mi par questa, che io senta in me stesso l'effetto della delettatione, & che altri voglia venire à sofisticarmi il proprio senso, & dirmi che questo non è vero diletto, perche non è generato con l'osseruatione della vera Arte Poetica, come s'io fossi tenuto di credere più alla vanità di certe ragioni altrui, che al testimonio del mio senso medesimo . . . Hora se il nostro senso è buon giudice del diletto, & sà conoscere quando vna cosa gli piace, ò gli annoia, io non voglio che douendo noi sodisfare ad esso ci andiamo à mettere in seruitù di certe vane ragioni ritrouate da huomini, che credono che i nostri sensi possano essere più mossi da gli argomenti, che da i proprij loro oggetti" (Weinberg, p. 1061 [Weinberg's translation]). Similarly, in defending Ariosto, Lionardo Salviati claims that the senses are more important than reason in the apprehension of a work of art (Weinberg, pp. 1005-1006).

the variety is marked by the same spirit of reconciliation that lies behind his allowance for the pleasure of the imaginary and insistence that it be achieved only within the confines of verisimilitude. The canon would doubtless agree with Tasso that, if variety is absent in a poem, the result will be the unbearable monotony which all theorists criticized in Trissino's historical epic, *L'Italia liberata*. At the same time, like Tasso, he would insist that variety must be carefully restrained; for, if exaggerated, it tends toward confusion ("Dico bene che la varietà è lodevole sino a quel termine che non passi in confusione").[44] In his comment on the lack of proportion in the romances, the absence of beginning, middle, and end in their plots, his introduction of the analogy of the deformed body, and his repetition of the word *tanto* to describe the monotony of their endlessly episodic construction, it is clear that the canon shares Tasso's theories on a controlled variety and like his Italian counterpart sees the variety in the romances as intolerable and in need of discipline if the ideal work, be it epic or romance, is to be created.

Like his rejection of the argument on the inferiority of the pleasures of the imagination and the senses, Don Quixote's answer to this criticism is contained in his account of the fantastic episode from romance. The allusion to the aesthetic problem of the senses through the deliberate concentration on sensuous detail is accompanied by the calculated evocation of the principle of variety by the exaggeration of detail.[45] Extravagant accumulation in asyndetic listings of objects of wonder suggests the multiplicity of phenomena in the subterranean world. In the lake there are "many serpents, snakes, and lizards, and many other sorts of savage and frightful creatures." There is a castle, whose "walls are of solid gold, turrets of diamonds, and gates of jacinth"; it is made "of diamonds, of carbuncles, of rubies, of pearls, of gold, and of emeralds." There are "small, innumerable, and bright-colored little birds." The reader's sensation of endless variety is heightened as single things are multiplied through various other stylistic devices, e.g., simple amplifications through

---

[44] *Dell'arte poetica*, p. 35.

[45] In addition to defending the value of the appeal to the senses of the romances, Malatesta asserts that the classical epic, exalted by the foes of Ariosto, is no longer viable because it lacks that quality which is indispensable for the pleasure of the audience, namely variety (Weinberg, p. 1063).

utilization of unnecessary synonym ("a strong castle or handsome palace," "sweet-smelling and perfumed," "embrace and contain"); simile ("a small stream, whose fresh waters glide like liquid crystal over delicate sand and little white stones, which resemble sifted gold and purest pearl"); and the use of adjectives with connotations of multiplicity and variety ("tanto concierto," "tanta diferencia de manjares," "infinitos pájaros," "intricados ramos," "jaspe variado," "mezclados entre ellos pedazos de cristal," "una variada labor"). The total effect of multiplicity is coupled with an effect of immediacy, heightened by the incantatory power of the asyndetic listings of objects (e.g., the list of gems) and the phonetic linkage of sentences or sentence units of parallel construction through anaphora (e.g., the five sentences beginning with "¿Qué," the series of sentence units "Aquí descubre un . . . acullá vee . . . acá vee . . . Acullá . . . ," and the repeated "ver").[46] The rapid rhythm of these listings, interrupted occasionally by swelling subordinate clauses describing one of the units, lends the account a tone of agitation and excitement that well suits the aims of the narrator, who would arouse *admiratio* in the reader as he beholds the infinite variety of the universe.

The number of unmistakable allusions in the dialogue to the topics of sixteenth-century literary debate concerning the value of the romances allows us to speculate at this point on the possible presence in Don Quixote's fantasy of one of the most venerated arguments in defense of poetry—the analogy between the poem and the cosmos. The analogy, which is at least as old as the ancient topics of praise of Homer and Virgil, appeared frequently in literary theories of the Renaissance,[47] and both opponents and defenders of the romances appealed to it in support of their arguments and principles.[48] The variety of the poem (the microcosm) mirrors the

---

[46] Clemencín's harsh criticism of the style of this passage is based on his failure to understand the author's intentions and to see that such effects as visual immediacy and verbal expansion and accumulation are functional. For example he criticizes Don Quixote's repetition of the verb *ver* three times in one sentence (IV, 305-306).

[47] See Durling, *The Figure of the Poet in Renaissance Epic*, pp. 123-128; Abrams, *The Mirror and the Lamp*, pp. 272-274.

[48] Defending the variety of the romances, Malatesta writes: ". . . par che il Romanzo imitando in questo i più marauigliosi effetti di colei che e Maestra di tutti gli artefici, della Natura dico, habbia procurato di far si che gli humani

plenitude of the universe, and the position of the poet in relation to his work is analogous to that of the divine creator—or his agent, nature—before his creation. Often theorists introduced this analogy, following closely the structural pattern of the ancient topics on Homer and Virgil: a rapid listing of the varied elements of the universe, coupled with a call to the reader to observe them, and a climactic statement that in the boundless variety of universe and poem there is a beauty that can be described paradoxically as a harmony of opposites (*dissimilium concordia*).[49] The linkage of the individual elements in the list by the repeated demonstrative adverbs "here" and "there," lends a pronounced conjurative power to the statements. Thus Don Quixote describes the wonders that his knight discovers in the "otherworld": "There the sky seems to him more transparent. . . . Here he discovers a small stream . . . there he sees an artfully constructed fountain . . . here he sees another. . . . There suddenly a strong castle appears to him. . . ." Near the end of this series he describes the "disordered order" of the fountain and proceeds to claim that "art, imitating nature, seems here to surpass her."[50]

If we are to allow that an echo of the celebration of variety in

---

ingegni, si ammirassero di vedere in un Poema quasi in un picciol mondo molte cose diuerse non conformi tra loro concorrere à produrre vn tutto cosi bene disposto, & ordinato" (Weinberg, p. 1062). See also Orazio Ariosto's comparison of the romance in its variety to the world (ibid., p. 1002). Tasso, on the other hand uses the argument to uphold unity of plot against the defenders of Ariosto, stressing the *unity-in-variety* dimension of the traditional analogy (*Dell'arte poetica*, pp. 35-36).

[49] For the remote origins and the persistence and universality of this notion of beauty in the western tradition, see Spitzer, *Classical and Christian Ideas of World Harmony*. It is important in Cervantes' concept of beauty, appearing not only in the passage under discussion, but also in his description of the music and dances of the pageant in Toledo which the wanderers of the *Persiles* witness: ". . . todas juntas componian vn honesto mouimiento, aunque de diferentes vayles formado . . . de todos estos sones redundaua vno solo, que alegraua con la concordancia, que es el fin de la musica" (II, 80).

[50] Compare for example the traditional topic in Tasso's famous formulation. As his all-embracing gaze follows the traditional descent from the heavenly bodies to the seas, fish, animals, brooks, fountains, lakes, fields, and forests, he falls into a similar pattern of evocation: ". . . e qui frutti e fiori, là ghiacci e nevi, qui abitazioni e culture, là solitudini e orrori; con tutto ciò uno è il mondo che tante e sì diverse cose nel suo grembo rinchiude, una la forma e l'essenza sua, uno il nodo dal quale sono le sue parti con discorde concordia insieme congiunte e collegate" (*Dell'arte poetica*, pp. 35-36).

art by use of the ontological analogy is audible here, it is significant that it is Don Quixote, the spokesman for the romances, to whom Cervantes gives the argument and not the canon, the classicist. The canon's praise of variety, which similarly includes an evocative listing, is based solely on the conventional argument that through variety the poet reveals his rhetorical virtuosity. There are no cosmic implications in his theory of an ordered variety; or, to put it another way, he cannot employ Tasso's most celebrated argument for unity in variety; for his opponent has appropriated that very argument to defend the romances.

If the "disordered order" which Don Quixote's knight beholds in the underworld paradise recalls the traditional cosmic analogy of the poet's creation, the emphasis on artifice in his fantastic description points to a corollary of the doctrine: the poet in respect to his created world is like the divine artificer before the macrocosm. Things are described not in their simple presence but rather in their reality as products of their creator's hand. A series of past participles attached to the objects almost invariably points toward the agent, the maker. The "apacible floresta" is *"compuesta"* of luxuriant trees. An "artificiosa fuente" is "de liso mármol *compuesta"*; another is "a lo brutesco *ordenada."* Its basin is studded with emeralds and seashells *"puestas* con orden *desordenada."* The fountain is described as a *"variada labor."* The miraculous palace is of such "admirable *compostura"* that, although it is *"formado"* of a variety of precious stones, "su *hechura"* is its most remarkable value.

Accompanying the celebration of artifice is the suggestion of the related notion of its superiority to nature. Above the garden paradise which the knight discovers at the bottom of the lake "the sky is more transparent" and "the sun shines with a newer brightness."[51] Don Quixote observes that the fountain "a lo brutesco," constructed of seashells and snail shells interspersed with shining crystal and emeralds, forms a "varied composition," in which art is seen to vanquish nature. In the literary context the fountain, in structure

---

[51] ". . . el cielo es más transparente"; "el sol luce con claridad más nueva." Clemencín criticizes Cervantes' use of *más* as a pleonasm, once again missing the importance of incantatory repetition and anaphora in the passage (IV, 306).

and value, must be interpreted as an analogue of the style which Don Quixote is praising in the romances.

In celebrating the artifice of the fountain, Don Quixote is indirectly proposing the liberation of art from the mimetic theories which dominated the mainstream of literary theorizing of the sixteenth century and which appear in various ways throughout the discourse of the canon and the curate (the stress on verisimilitude and imitation, the premise that pleasure in reading depends on belief, the observance of proportion in the external world, and the use of Cicero's famous mirror analogy in the critique of the contemporary theater). The hand of the artist, imitating that of God's creative agent, nature, can create a new reality superior to her products. To appreciate the significance of Don Quixote's fountain and his introduction of the ancient topic of art vs. nature, we must observe that the present historical moment was the eve of a full-scale revolution in literature against the empirically and historically oriented notion of verisimilitude which the sixteenth century had developed. It is important, too, to note that in contemporary reformulations of the art-nature duality, it was not uncommon for the traditional superiority of nature to yield to art.[52] Whatever a classicist such as Clemencín might think of the knight's diseased fantasies, it is nonetheless true that Don Quixote's grotesque fountain is very similar in detail to the fountains which were to capture the European fantasy for much of the seventeenth century.[53]

Indeed Don Quixote's proposed liberation of the fantasy marked the path which much of the art of the next decades would follow. As we shall observe below, other scenes in Cervantes' works in which he addresses himself to the problem of verisimilitude in its sixteenth-century formulation point in the same direction. However, it is important to observe that, if the literature which present-day historiography designates as baroque adopted the solution proposed by

[52] The nature-vs.-art controversy appears often in Cervantes' works. Below, in my examination of his use of the garden topic in the context of literary debate, I will discuss the matter in more detail.

[53] The grotto, the sea shells, and the spiraling forms of snail shells of Don Quixote's fountain are all features common to the baroque fountain as described by Jean Rousset (*La Littérature de l'âge baroque en France* [Paris, 1954], pp. 161-165).

Don Quixote and various other surrogates of the creating artist in Cervantes' works, Cervantes himself does not in his writing adopt that solution. In his interludes concerning literature he is constantly writing about the theoretical problem, and the flights of fantasy with which his characters taunt their classicist opponents are always subordinate to the problem. Cervantes' positive revolution against the strictures of classical literary theory was not toward an art based on the imaginary, i.e., Góngora, but toward an art based on historical, everyday reality, i.e., the modern novel.

In addition to the fantastic and sensuous subject matter, the amplification of detail, and the allusions to traditional doctrines on the analogies between poet and god, Don Quixote's rejoinder to the canon employs a specific narrative technique which is indirectly allusive to the Ariosto polemic. Like these other elements, it points toward the liberation of the artist from the aesthetic theories propounded by the canon. Although he attempts to evoke the visual presence of his subject matter and coax his audience into a state of accepting it as real, Don Quixote suddenly destroys the illusion of reality by interposing both himself and an alleged historical text containing his story between the audience and what he is witnessing: "Were I to set myself now to depict it [the attire of the damsels] as the histories describe it to us, I should never have done." Here we observe the familiar technique of the narrator of the romances, his freedom to intervene in his work, commenting on the events and characters, aiding the reader by prefaces and recapitulations, and instructing him to see the moral wisdom implicit in the events of the story. The narrative technique was one of the most controversial topics in critical discussions of the value of the romances. In general the classicists regarded this freedom unfavorably, preferring the more limited intervention of the ancient models for narrative methods, Virgil and Homer, and reaffirming Aristotle's recommendation that the poet speak as little as possible in his own voice in his narration.[54]

---

[54] Pigna defends the discursive techniques of Ariosto's freely intervening narrator, arguing that the genre had developed historically as an ensemble of fragmentary poems recited for an audience; the preface and recapitulation of the poet are necessary to unify all the fragments. Moreover, he offers a classical precedent for this type of narrative, the *Metamorphoses* of Ovid (*I romanzi*, pp. 44-48). Tasso

Don Quixote

Don Quixote's statement is more than a simple dismissal of the classicists' argument by deliberately adopting the romancers' methods of appearing in their works. In alluding to a preexisting historical text in a context in which an incredible event is being presented to a skeptical audience, Don Quixote is evoking the most famous poet of romance, Ariosto. As is well known, one of Ariosto's favorite tricks is to present an incredible event or description, and, as if anticipating objections in his audience on grounds of inverisimilitude, to disclaim personal control of the narrative and responsibility for its truth, mischievously asserting that the event is recorded in historical texts. As Robert M. Durling has recently pointed out, the real effect of this technique is to make the reader feel not that the poet is helplessly transcribing an old text but rather that he stands in absolute control of his creation, "that there is nothing in the poem but what he planned."[55] Don Quixote's disclaimer of authority is a slight modification on Ariosto's general procedure, as he apologetically states that he must condense the historical text in the interests of the reader.[56] Nevertheless, in casually overlooking the question of the credibility of the "historical" event, he increases the effrontery of his Ariostean claim, and reinforces the effect that he as author is in firm control.

In the context of the literary debate with the canon, Don Quixote's narrative method contains his final and most impudent thrust at his opponent's doctrine of verisimilitude. In basing his absurd account

---

examines these arguments sympathetically in the prologue of his early *Rinaldo* and decides to reject them in favor of the limited functions of the narrators of Virgil and Homer, claiming, like most of the critics of Ariosto, that the imitation is undermined by the presence of the poet before the reader (pp. 5-6). For Salviati and Sperone's criticism of the poet's entering his poem to comment on its action, see Weinberg, pp. 1023-1024.

[55] *The Figure of the Poet in Renaissance Epic*, p. 120. The century separating Cervantes from Ariosto witnessed the popularization of Aristotle's distinction between poetry and history, and this distinction adds a complicating dimension to Ariosto's gag in many of Cervantes' uses of it. Now history is in fact recognized as being stranger than fiction (an interpretation of *Poetics*, ix), and the playful narrator can offer wild fantasies as a "historian" rather than as a poet. More will be said of this below.

[56] Ariosto does in fact appear in his poem to express concern for the rhetorical principle of not fatiguing his audience, but these appearances are not used to poke fun at those who would question the credibility of his narration. (See Durling, p. 118).

on a "historical text," the knight is once again embracing and mis-applying the canon's theory on the necessary fidelity to truth in art. Once again the parody works against both an objection by the canon (here only implicit) to the fantastic account and the entire mode of thinking that lies behind the objection. Moreover, emerging from the humorous play that marks the scene is a serious artistic principle which is manifest in all of Cervantes' writings: the poet is a god standing above his creation and audience, and any attempts to restrict the freedom of his creative powers are unworthy of his serious consideration. The importance of this view of the poet in Cervantes' works and his debt to Ariosto will be explored further in an examination of his use of Cide Hamete Benengeli, the name-less narrator of the *Persiles*, and various specific episodes of literary significance in his works.[57]

CONCLUSION

At this point the literary debate has reached its end. In summary, the canon directs his attack on the romances of chivalry at all the flaws which Italian theorists had criticized in Ariosto's *Orlando Furioso* and the tradition of Spanish and French romance literature which lies behind that work. He concentrates on their aesthetic shortcomings, their lack of unity and verisimilitude, suggesting their failure to appeal to the higher faculties of the soul, those cultivated by the *culto* audience, and he notes briefly the dangerous influence which they can have on society. Recognizing the undeniable pleasure which their varied subject matter produces in the reader, he pro-poses the creation of a new type of romance (the epic in prose), which would eliminate the flaws of the original genre, conform to the Aristotelian aesthetic criteria (in their contemporary formula-tion, typified by the theories of Tasso on epic poetry), and at the

---

[57] See Durling's discussion of the narrative techniques of Ariosto in relation to the traditional analogy between the poet and the divine creator, pp. 123-132. Fol-lowing the completion of this work in its original form, I became acquainted with Maxime Chevalier's recently published book *L'Arioste en Espagne* (Bordeaux, 1966) and was pleased to see that, following a different approach from my own, he had reached certain conclusions concerning the impact of Ariosto on Cervantes which my study confirms. In the following pages I have not been able to indicate and discuss the specific areas of agreement between our works, but for those who know Chevalier's valuable book, they will be obvious.

same time preserve the appeal of variety and the marvelous so important in the success of the older romances. Don Quixote responds to the canon's theories by employing a method of parodistic argumentation to expose weaknesses underlying his opponent's aesthetic criteria. He then proceeds to invoke arguments which had been brought forward by Italian theorists in defense of Ariosto, affirming that the pleasure afforded by fantastic subject matter, sensuous detail, and variety of event and description in a literary context is indeed valuable. Moreover, in support of his argument for the pleasure of variety he recalls the traditional analogy between poem and cosmos to suggest that the romances reflect the disordered order of the universe.

In relation to Cervantes' creative production and his attitudes toward contemporary literary theorizing, the general implications of the dialogue are even more significant than its specific allusiveness to the controversy concerning the romances. Don Quixote's exposure of the weaknesses underlying the canon's conception of verisimilitude suggests Cervantes' suspicion of the fundamental direction of sixteenth-century critical thought, which would institutionalize an aesthetic doctrine based on an empirical-historical interpretation of Aristotle's concept of imitation. Like the Canon of Toledo the neo-Aristotelians are "short-sighted," preferring to confine the artist's vision to the surfaces, on which all lines and details appear in sharp relief, preventing him from turning toward the depths, in which outlines dissolve and reality becomes problematic. At the same time Don Quixote's celebration of the value of the creative powers of the artist or artificer and his ironic intervention as narrator between his story and audience suggest that for Cervantes the artist stands beyond all the norms and restrictions by which criticism would control his creative powers, as god above both his creation and his audience.

I BELIEVE that the length and detail of my analysis of the literary debate between Don Quixote and the canon is justified in view of the tendency in Cervantine scholarship to stress the normative side of Cervantes' aesthetic theories. This tendency overlooks the fact that the polarity marking his attitudes toward nearly every province of human experience is also present in his attitudes toward art.[58] His assertion that he is writing *Don Quixote* with the intention of ridiculing the romances of chivalry, his repeated remarks about the absurdities of that genre, his attacks on the Spanish national theater, his disparaging words on the capacities of the *vulgo*, to which both the romances and Lope's theater appealed, his repeated homage to Aristotelian-Horatian concepts of literary theory, his sympathetic treatment of the Canon of Toledo, and his submission to the theories of the canon in the general plan of the *Persiles* have all provided obstacles to a recognition of Cervantes' conscious and articulate suspicion of the mode of thinking and theoretical principles which underlie the Aristotelian critical movement and his sympathy for the artistic freedom which the romances represented.

Clemencín commented on Don Quixote's response to the canon: "The reader should be advised that the speaker is a madman, possessed of wide readings, erudition, and even a dash of ingeniousness, but bereft of any good sense."[59] If we recall how the studies of Toffanin and Castro showed that the achievement of Cervantes in discovering poetic value in the problematic realm of real human experience depended precisely on his conscious independence of those artistic restrictions which he so consistently honored and which the

[58] As Spitzer puts it aptly: "Man darf also nichts Extremes bei Cervantes zitieren, ohne die Gegengewichte und Gegenpolaritäten mitzuerwähnen, und nichts Rohes, ohne das 'Pedant-Feine' dazu, nichts Spitzes und Scharfes ohne das zugehörige Runde und Abrundende" ("Die Frage der Heuchelei des Cervantes," *Zeitschrift für Romanische Philologie*, LVI [1936], 144).

[59] Clemencín, IV, 262. The harshness of this judgment survives in contemporary Cervantine scholarship. In his humorless reading of the novel as a type of parable which reveals that "men, for a variety of selfish reasons, are all too prone to pervert truth and to jest with life," A. A. Parker presents Don Quixote as an arrogant megalomaniac, unworthy of representing the chivalric ideal, who appears "at his most foolish" in his answer to the compassionate Canon of Toledo (" 'Don Quixote' and the Relativity of Truth," *The Dublin Review*, No. 441 [Autumn, 1947], 28-37). Parker finds Sancho guilty of the same conceit in his lie about his flight on Clavileño. Below I will point out that Sancho's "journey to the other world" is analogous to his master's narration of the "Caballero del Lago" in its allusiveness to contemporary literary problems. As far as I know, B. W. Wardropper is the only critic who has suggested that the Canon of Toledo is an unreliable spokesman for Cervantes' literary theories. To be sure, he bases his interpretation on contradictions within the canon's arguments and not on Don Quixote's response. See "Cervantes' Theory of the Drama," *Modern Philology*, LII (1955), 217-221.

126

mad Don Quixote here attacks, we can now understand with no great difficulty why Cervantes entitled the chapter of Don Quixote's narration of the fantastic episode of romance to the canon "Of the learned (*discretas*) arguments between Don Quixote and the canon," why Cervantes refers to the account as "well-reasoned nonsense" (*concertados disparates*),[60] and why he adds that the subject matter and the "manner in which he had depicted the adventure of the Knight of the Lake" produced *admiratio* in the canon. Here Cervantes both affirms that Don Quixote is not speaking as a fool and adds a dramatic conclusion to the series of refutations that his hero has already forwarded to the canon's criticism. The canon acknowledged that *admiratio* is an effect which all good art must arouse in its audience but insisted that it can only be produced if the audience accepts the literal truth of the subject matter of the work of art. Since only the *vulgo* accepts the literal truth of the romances, a fact which is dramatically corroborated in Sancho's statement of belief in Don Quixote's promise to give him a *condado* at the close of his narration, the canon's response to the knight's fantastic adventure suggests either that he is not a *discreto* (obviously not the case) or that his basic principle that the pleasure of *admiratio* is contingent on the observation of the principle of verisimilitude in the work of art is unsound. We observe here another note of comedy of character at the expense of the neo-Aristotelian, who is suddenly revealed in a pose which contradicts his vigorously stated formulation of himself. As shall be pointed out in the following chapters, Cervantes often employs this type of comedy in his treatment of the embodiments of the Renaissance Aristotelian literary theories.

IN CONCLUDING my analysis, I would like to emphasize the fruitlessness of any attempt to arrest the fluid interplay of thought that marks

[60] Clemencín takes pains to explain that *concertados* means little more than the consistency of a sick mind in its absurdities (IV, 313). Recent scholarship has shown that Cervantes carefully designed the madness of his hero in accordance with contemporary psychophysical medical theories. It is the madness of melancholy, which on occasions can render its victims capable of perceiving and expressing truths of the highest order (see Harald Weinrich, *Das Ingenium Don Quijotes* [Münster, 1956], Chap. II, "Ingenium und Wahn").

the entire context of the *Quixote* for purposes of rendering it conveniently schematic. The multidimensionality of Cervantes' irony is never more evident than in Don Quixote's response to the canon, where a serious rejoinder to conventional attacks on the romance of chivalry is contained within what is obviously a parody of that very genre. As Cervantes writes in the *Viage del Parnaso* (p. 85), absurdities (*desatinos*) are pleasing in art only when they have a purpose. Don Quixote's vision does indeed have a purpose, but it is nonetheless an absurdity, a *disparate concertado*, and is presented as such. The standard of objectivity by which we measure the extravagance of the protagonist's envisioned romance is never absent. We are witnessing a reasoned discourse somewhere in Spain of the sixteenth century, where there are neither lakes of boiling pitch taunting us with the appeal of the unknown nor subterranean, bejeweled palaces in which enchanted fairies are awaiting the advent of their deliverer.

As if this were not enough, Don Quixote brings our point of reference into the heart of his narration, and the resultant travesty, the knight cleaning his teeth with toothpicks, makes us wonder whether the demented *hidalgo* is purposely playing with his awestruck audience or ironically indulging himself in the pleasure of contemplating what he knows very well to be a reality only in the world of the fantasy. Here we observe Don Quixote momentarily leaving the conventional polemic over the romances far behind and verging on that awareness of the paradoxical appeal of the fantastic precisely in its painful juxtaposition to the real which two centuries later the Romantic Movement was to discover and celebrate in Cervantes, his creator.[61] With the Romantics we may go on to interpret Don Quixote's vision as a response to the metaphysical tension between the real and the ideal, *Endlichkeit* and *Unendlichkeit*, which

[61] E.T.A. Hoffmann writes: "Sancho meinte, Gott solle den ehren, der den Schlaf erfunden, es müsse ein gescheuter Kerl gewesen sein; noch mehr mag aber wohl der geehrt werden, der den Traum erfand. Nicht den Traum, der aus unserem Innern nur dann aufsteigt, wenn wir unter des Schlafes weicher Decke liegen—nein!—den Traum, den wir durch das ganze Leben fort träumen, der oft die drückende Macht des Irdischen auf seine Schwingen nimmt, vor dem jeder bittre Schmerz, jede trostlose Klage getäuschter Hoffnung verstummt, da er selbst, Strahl des Himmels in unserer Brust entglommen, mit der unendlichen Sehnsucht die Erfüllung verheisst" (cited by Brüggemann, *Cervantes und die Figur des Don Quijote*, p. 226).

marked the birth of postclassical European civilization. With the benefit of 150 more years of human experience and the exploration of the irrational recesses of man's existence that these years have witnessed, we may see it as an exercise in wish-fulfillment, a flight from reality into the realm of the daydream,[62] or perhaps as a defense of the mythic mode of apprehending and dealing with the natural world as opposed to the scientific mode, here represented by the canon. Or we may prefer to understand the *hidalgo's* vision psychologically as in all probability Cervantes himself understood it— in terms of the contemporary theories of the humors.[63] As Cervantes clearly demonstrates, Don Quixote's illness is the madness of melancholy, and it is significant that, on concluding his fantastic account, he recommends that the canon read the romances because "they will banish any melancholy which he may feel and raise his spirits should they be depressed."[64]

Whichever interpretation we may prefer, we are nonetheless responding to the protean nature of Cervantes' parody, which, even as it would ridicule a literary genre, bears within itself a reasoned defense of that genre to its most eloquent critics and which, even as it would destroy the reality of the world of romance, nevertheless preserves and reshapes that world by paradoxically sharpening its fantastic contours against the cold background of reality. Here again we observe the dazzling multiplicity of perspectives contained in Cervantes' prose, or, put another way, the wonderful inconclusiveness of Cervantes' humor, its all-dissolving, yet all-inclusive character

[62] See Helene Deutsch's Freudian reading of *Don Quixote*, "Don Quijote und Donquijotismus," *Almanach der Psychoanalyse* (1935), 151-160.

[63] The clinical study of Don Quixote's madness with reference to sixteenth-century psychophysical medical theories is an area virtually untouched by Cervantine criticism up to this century. The initial essay of Rafael Salillas (*Un gran inspirador de Cervantes: el doctor Huarte de San Juan y su Examen de ingenios* [Madrid, 1905]), who first saw the relevance of Huarte de San Juan's *Examen de ingenios* to a full understanding of the madness of Don Quixote, has been followed up by the recent studies of Otis H. Green ("El 'ingenioso' Hidalgo," *Hispanic Review*, XXV [1957], pp. 175-193) and Weinrich (*Das Ingenium Don Quijotes*).

[64] Again the mad Don Quixote is the spokesman for a serious aesthetic doctrine. Cervantes echoes the words of his character: "Yo he dado en *Don Quixote* passatiempo/ al pecho melancolico y mohino," as he reviews his works in *Viage del Parnaso* (pp. 54-55). G. B. Guarini defends the utility of the pastoral tragicomedy against the rigid classicists, claiming that the new form is useful "per fine di purgar con diletto la mestizia degli ascoltatori" (see Leo, *Torquato Tasso*, p. 16).

which Friedrich Schlegel described as *Witz*, the fundamental principle of his envisioned *Universalpoesie*: "This artfully ordered confusion, this delightful symmetry of contradictions, this wonderful alternation of enthusiasm and irony, which is alive even in the smallest parts of the whole, seems to me to be indeed an indirect mythology."[65]

[65] Cited by Brüggemann, p. 52.

CHAPTER IV

The Narrator and His Audience
The Liberation of the Imagination

> You can baptize them and give them any names you like,
> fathering them on Prester John of the Indies or the Emperor
> of Trebizond; who, I have heard it rumored, were famous
> poets: and even if they were not, and some pedants and gradu-
> ates turned up to snap and growl at you behind your back in
> the name of truth, you need not bother about them a bit; for
> even if they convict you of a falsehood, they cannot cut off the
> hand you wrote with.
>
> A friend of Cervantes[1]

IN THE ANALYSIS of the literary discourse that concludes the first part of *Don Quixote*, we observed Cervantes' preoccupation with the problem that so insistently plagued Tasso. If the artistic quality of a work of art is contingent on its observation of the principle of verisimilitude, and if verisimilitude depends ultimately on the audiences' willingness to accept the literal truth of the subject matter, how is the poet to know how far he may strain their capacities for belief? For Don Quixote the matter presented no problem. He could mischievously put his finger on the difficulty raised by the canon's acceptance of the assumption underlying his theory of *admiratio* (i.e., that the pleasures of the marvelous presuppose audience belief), suggest its baffling consequences, and proceed to dismiss the whole problem as idle, postulating as valid an aesthetic pleasure which is in no way circumscribed by the notion of the possible.

Cervantes could not dismiss this perplexing problem of sixteenth-century literary theory as readily as his protagonist could. The ambivalence marking his attitudes toward nearly all areas of human experience, which criticism has come to regard as the basic principle of his *Weltanschauung* and artistry, is also in evidence in his relationship to contemporary literary theory. The artist is pulled

---

[1] ". . . los podéis bautizar y poner el nombre que quisiéredes, ahijándolos al Preste Juan de las Indias o al Emperador de Trapisonda, de quien yo sé que hay noticia que fueron famosos poetas; y cuando no lo hayan sido y hubiere algunos pedantes y bachilleres que por detrás os muerdan y murmuren desta verdad, no se os dé dos maravedís; porque ya que os averigüen la mentira, no os han de cortar la mano con que lo escribistes" (I, 22).

toward two opposing poles of critical thought, and the dialectic movement of the opposing tendencies overlays many of the scenes of the *Quixote* and the *Persiles* with a dimension of meaning that is not immediately apparent. At this point it is well to examine a series of related scenes from both works, which reenact dramatically the literary debate between the canon and Don Quixote and which illuminate the instability of the aesthetic foundations of the *Persiles*.

THE NARRATING AUTHOR VS. THE CRITICAL AUDIENCE

One of Cervantes' favorite structural devices is to bring storyteller and audience into his work. The most familiar case is the scene in the inn of Juan Palomeque el Zurdo, where people from various stations in society have assembled to listen to the history of the *Curioso impertinente* and the Captive's narration of his life story. In this situation the major elements are the lengthy stories themselves, which are told for the entertainment of the audience within and the reader. Nevertheless, it is important to point out that they are placed within the framework of literary debate by a foregoing discussion of the effects of the chivalric romances on various types of readers and by the curate's critical commentary on the *Curioso impertinente.*

As in the dialogue between the canon and Don Quixote, two basic critical tendencies are played off against one another and are held together as if by centripetal force in the all-embracing irony of Cervantes. The innkeeper and his family defend the romances in much the same manner as does Don Quixote in his response to the canon. Indeed Palomeque employs in his defense a description of the marvels of a knight's perilous journey to the otherworld, a description which prefigures Don Quixote's account of the Knight of the Lake.[2]

---

[2] This discussion, as well as the commentaries on the intercalated tales, looks backward to the scrutiny of Don Quixote's library, in which the issues are public morality and good taste in literature, and to Don Quixote's distinction between poetic and historical truth while discussing his penitence in the Sierra Morena (Chap. XXV), and forward to the debate between the canon and Don Quixote. In fact the curate's statement (". . . y si me fuera lícito agora, y el auditorio lo requiriera, yo dijera cosas acerca de lo que han de tener los libros de caballerías para ser buenos" [I, 325]) indicates that in constructing the scenes in Palomeque's inn, Cervantes was already considering the problems discussed more discursively

Don Quixote

The word dominating the observations of the innkeeper, his family, and Maritornes is *gusto*. The curate in turn argues that the romances should be banned because of their falsity and suggests that the innkeeper read *verdaderas historias*. At this point Cervantes introduces the type of parody which we observe in Don Quixote's treatment of the canon's theories of verisimilitude. The curate's example of a "true history," which he opposes to the absurdly fantastic tales of the innkeeper, is that of the historical figure Diego García de Paredes, who "with one finger stopped a mill-wheel turning at full speed."[3] Measuring the curate's general notion of plausibility against its specific aberrant application the parody suggests that in spite of his pedantic assertiveness, the *discreto*'s judgment is on no firmer grounds than that of the embodiment of the *vulgo*, Juan Palomeque el Zurdo. The thrust of the parody becomes much sharper as it embraces the two long stories which are now narrated. At the conclusion of the *Curioso impertinente* the curate criticizes the work as implausible for the breach of decorum observable in a husband as foolish as Anselmo. Following the curate's judgment Cervantes inserts the story of the Captive, not a work of literature but a real *historia verdadera*. In its implausibilities in both "plot" and "character" (i.e., we may assume that in the "typical daughter" the qualities of filial love and duty will be more effective than in Zoraida, who watches her father cast himself into the sea in rage and disillusionment before her unexplainable act) it does not fail to comment with retroactive irony on the curate's notion of verisimilitude, which, in accordance with the best theory of the day, would always limit artistic creation to the realm of the typical, always excluding the "improbable possibility" in favor of the "probable impossibility."[4]

---

and thoroughly in the debate. The position of the literary interludes in Part One of the novel reveals a gradual broadening in the scope of Cervantes' approach to literary problems and a sharpening of his critical focus as he addresses himself to the specific principles of the neo-Aristotelian theory.

[3] ". . . detenía con un dedo una rueda de molino en la mitad de su furia" (I, 323).

[4] The Captive introduces his narration with a clear statement of the distinction between the historical truth which is improbable (which, according to the Aristotelians, the poet must eschew) and the verisimilar: ". . . oirán un *discurso verdadero* a quien podría ser que no llegasen *los mentirosos que con curioso y pensado*

Cervantes & the Classical Aesthetic

The debate between the canon and Don Quixote marks a refinement in Cervantes' utilization of the audience-storyteller device and anticipates a series of scenes which culminate in Periandro's long narration in the second book of the *Persiles*. In these scenes the author presents dramatically the act of artistic creation in order to study the problems of authorial freedom and audience reaction and belief. Viewed within literary tradition they may be judged to be the logical development in the Renaissance climate of literary theorizing of the narrative situation observable in the romances of chivalry, in which the act of recitation is dramatized but the audience is, as it were, imagined. Here an important new dimension is added, for the audience is no longer simply present as imaginary listener, a captive who is bound to the narrator by a framework of shared values and beliefs and whose pleasure and belief in what the narrator recites are tacitly acknowledged by its silence. In Cervantes' scenes the "segnori e cavallieri inamorati, cortesi damiselle e grazïose" of Boiardo and Ariosto come to life as participants,[5] ceasing to be a generic totality and taking shape as individual perspectives representing different types of reactions, degrees of belief, and critical standards in relation to what is narrated. The resultant interplay between individual perspectives of members of the participating audience and the narrator is the subjection of the work of literature and the creative act to the refracting process which appears in Cervantes' examination of the problematic aspects of phenomenological (e.g., Mambrino's helmet) and moral (e.g., the galley slaves) realities.[6]

The series of scenes which I have chosen to designate as the "dramatic situation of narrating author vs. critical audience" can

---

artificio suelen componerse [i.e., fiction, which is circumscribed by the limits of the credible]" (I, 394). This is the distinction which in Cide Hamete Benengeli's hand becomes the basis for an elaborate hoax, as he presents himself as a historian and, as such, one who is obligated to present truth in spite of its occasional incredibility (see below).

[5] One can see also in the literary backgrounds of the structure of these scenes the frame device of Boccaccio's novellas and the scenes of sixteenth-century pastoral in which shepherds applaud each other's songs (see Riley, *Cervantes's Theory of the Novel*, pp. 33-34).

[6] See Castro, *El pensamiento de Cervantes*, p. 80: "Todo este mundo que nos rodea está, pues, en un tris, que se trate de un yelmo o de la noción de bien y mal."

be properly understood only if we examine them against the background of the critical movement of the sixteenth century. The structural debt to the *discorsi* is obvious. Many of the literary treatises employ the dialogue form, embodying different theoretical positions in the different speakers. Toward the end of the century it became increasingly fashionable to insert in the dialogue sample passages to represent specific ideas and styles or to be subjected to critical scrutiny from various points of view. Such was the structure of many of the dialogues involved in the literary polemic over Ariosto and Tasso,[7] the overtones of which are so clearly perceptible in the debate between the canon and Don Quixote. The scenes under discussion in *Don Quixote* and the *Persiles*, where recitation is followed by audience commentary, are clearly in this tradition.[8] The link between Cervantes' introduction of the audience as active par-

---

[7] See Weinberg, p. 1072.

[8] It is doubtful that there was one specific source for the recurrent scene of narrating author vs. critical audience in Cervantes' writings. The dramatic interplay of different perspectives on literature among the members of the audience, the humor that accompanies the interplay, and the background of Aristotelian principles all recall El Pinciano's dialogues. At the same time Cervantes had an important precedent for the introduction of a dramatic situation as a vehicle for refined literary theorizing within a work of fiction in Heliodorus' *Ethiopian History*. The long narration of Calasiris, which illuminates the shadowy origins of the wanderings of Theagenes and Chariklea, is punctuated occasionally by brief exchanges allusive to literary principles between the narrator and his audience, the youthful Gnemon. The aesthetic issue most often raised as the audience and the narrator both reflect critically on the style of the narration is that of unity (pp. 91, 92-93, 113, 175). In this respect the scene is most relevant to the Master Pedro episode, the mystifications of Cide Hamete Benengeli, and the most elaborate development of the scene in Cervantes' works, Periandro's narration. (The latter is clearly modeled on Calasiris' narration in its inclusion of both literary and nonliterary subject matter of the Greek romance and in its structural function in the work.) At the same time the irrepressible impulse to tell a story and the joy experienced by the artist in the creative act, observable in all Cervantes' surrogates of the artist, are important concerns of Calasiris' narration (pp. 86, 90, 121). Similarly the emphasis on visual immediacy, for which all narrators in Cervantes strive and which I would relate to the recurrent concern of Renaissance literary theory with *energia* of style, is shared by Heliodorus' artist and audience (p. 120). What is entirely absent in Heliodorus' examination of literary principles is, however, the dominant issue in Cervantes' use of the dramatic situation—the problematic aspects of the principle of verisimilitude. Here the influence of the Renaissance climate of literary criticism and the *discorsi* is most evident. (For the relation between the exchanges of Calasiris and Gnemon to Heliodorus' consciousness of structural problems in the composition of his prose narrative, see Victor Hefti, *Zur Erzählungstechnik in Heliodors Aethiopica* [Vienna, 1950], pp. 52-53.)

ticipants into his work and the *discorsi* goes beyond the level of simple structural and thematic similarity. Both the critical movement of the sixteenth century and Cervantes' sympathy for and independence of its aims must be seen as the results of the deep and complex changes in man's attitudes toward literature wrought by the historical-cultural movements and upheavals of the century. The renewed emphasis on the spiritual and ethical categories of man's existence which accompanied the Reformation and the Counter-reformation,[9] the orientation toward the problems of everyday living which characterized the humanist reform movement known for its inspirational leader as Erasmism,[10] and the proliferation of printed books and the attendant realization that literature could be a vital force in shaping people's attitudes are all interrelated factors contributing to the emergence of theoretical preoccupations with truth in literature, the relationship between literature and life, and the audience dimension as a factor conditioning artistic creation. The waning taste for the absurd adventures of the romances of chivalry, the discovery and exegesis of Aristotle's *Poetics* (interpreted to be sure in accordance with the spiritual needs of the age), and Cervantes' ambivalent relationship to both Amadís and Aristotle can be properly understood only if they are situated among these broader cultural phenomena.

In the debate between the canon and Don Quixote Cervantes presents for the first time in the novel the drama of artistic creation. As we have observed in our analysis of this scene, Don Quixote is a surrogate of the poet of epic and romance, addressing his audience and exhorting it to behold as present the realities of his narration. His tale is an indirect answer to the canon's criticism of the genre

[9] "Il primo impulso al concretarsi d'un problema critico nel cinquecento, venne da un problema morale, dopo del quale presero forma tutte le altre questioni più strettamente letterarie. Allora la poesia cercò di chiarire le sue origini, i suoi fini, i suoi rapporti con quella corruzione del mondo di cui la rivolta luterana aveva dato rapida e pungente consapevolezza. . . . È fenomeno rarissimo la rapidità con cui si concretò allora il problema critico: un decennio mutò l'aspetto della letteratura" (Toffanin, *La fine dell'umanesimo*, p. 8).

[10] Bataillon writes that the triumph of classicism in the second half of the sixteenth century owed much to the efforts of the Erasmists (". . . el terreno se lo habían ya abonado los humanistas discípulos de Erasmo, que buscaban a su vez una literatura verdadera, es decir, satisfactoria para la razón, y al mismo tiempo moral" [*Erasmo y España*, II, 393]).

Don Quixote

of the romance of chivalry and a celebration of an authorial freedom which the canon's Aristotelian mode of criticism would deny the narrator. Cervantes does not proceed, however, to examine the audience response to the narration, although representatives of the two fundamentally divergent perspectives of *vulgo* and neo-Aristotelian, which are significantly present in all his scenes constructed on the storyteller-audience relationship, are listening to the knight's tale.

THE CAVE OF MONTESINOS

It is in Part II of *Don Quixote* that Cervantes develops fully the possibilities of the narrator-audience situation. The most important scenes are Don Quixote's account of his vision in the Cave of Montesinos and Master Pedro's puppet show. The episode of the Cave of Montesinos contains some striking formal parallels to the debate between the canon and Don Quixote, which would suggest that there are deeper thematic links between the two scenes. The most obvious parallel is of course Don Quixote's evocation of the mythic theme so popular in romance literature, the knight's journey to the otherworld. There is the same descent into the depths of the earth, the same garden paradise, a similar "palace or castle," and an encounter with enchanted figures.[11] Again the knight describes the marvelous variety of the scene and its effect on him ("they held me in suspense and astonished me").

In addition to the similarity of the journeys to the otherworld, which in the former case Don Quixote narrates as an adventure

[11] María Rosa Lida ("Dos huellas del Esplandián en el *Quijote* y el *Persiles*," *Romance Philology*, IX [1955], 156-162) maintains plausibly that the direct literary source of Cervantes' scene is *Las sergas de Esplandián*, Chap. XCIX, where Montalvo, the author, visits an underworld palace guided by Urganda la Desconocida to behold the enchanted figures of his romance. The Arthurian reminiscences in the scene are observed by P. S. Barto, "The Subterranean Grail Paradise of Cervantes," *PMLA*, XXXVIII (1923), 401-411. J. G. Fucilla points out some echoes of Sannazaro's *Arcadia* in the episode in "The Cave of Montesinos," *Italica*, XXIX (1952), 170-173. A. Marasso observes the influence of the descent of Aeneas to the underworld in Cervantes' scene (*Cervantes: la invención del Quijote* [Buenos Aires, 1954], pp. 147-150). For the general similarity to the omnipresent mythic theme of the journey to the otherworld in romance literature, see Patch, *The Other World*, pp. 230ff. None of these critics observes anything more than a simple parody of the romance world in Cervantes' introduction of the scene. For some provocative comments on its implications concerning the craft of the novelist, see R. Hollander, "The Cave of Montesinos and the Key of Dreams," *Southern Review*, IV (1968), 756-767.

typical of the books of chivalry and in the present case recounts as a real experience (we infer from his condition when he is lifted from the cave that it is a dream vision), there is in both episodes a frame of literary debate surrounding the vision and reflecting critically upon it. Don Quixote is guided to the cave by the humanist cousin, a "famous scholar much given to the reading of books of chivalry." The literary ideals of this young man bear the stamp of the Renaissance critical movement. Like the canon he adheres to the Horatian principles of "edification" and "entertainment" and is preoccupied with the traditional Platonic concern about the relationship between literature and the well-being of the republic. If the canon represents the general aims and principles of the literary movement dominated by the figure of Torquato Tasso with his interest in the creation of the ideal epic and the perfect epic hero, the humanist represents another current of Renaissance literature, which produced encyclopedic compilations of curious facts modeled on Virgilius Polydorus' *De inventoribus*. This movement, which Bataillon associates with the Erasmian tradition of stressing the importance of truth in literature, was represented in Spain by such works as Pedro Mexía's *Silva de varia lección* and Antonio de Torquemada's *Jardín de flores curiosas*.[12] That the movements represented by the canon and the humanist were reconcilable is evident in Tasso's theories of fusing the marvelous and the verisimilar. The poet is to employ the curiosities of the natural world, which will elicit *admiratio* in the reader by virtue of their novelty and yet will not fail to maintain his belief, as their truth has the authority of scientific investigation behind it.[13] Nevertheless, Cervantes does not treat the humanist with the sympathy he shows for the canon. The uselessness of his literary endeavors is evident in the absurd facts which he claims to be seeking, i.e., "the first man to use ointments to cure himself of the French pox," and in his failure to match Sancho's

---

[12] See Bataillon, *Erasmo y España*, II, 241-244. De Lollis relates the popularity of such works to the decadent literary taste of the late sixteenth century which he terms "secentismo." The wonders of the world are presented to stupefy the reader (see *Cervantes reazionario* [Rome, 1924], pp. 178-180).

[13] Cervantes accepted this reconciliation in writing the *Persiles*, where he utilizes the oddities of Torquemada's collection, which he had allowed the niece to cast into the fire as absurd in the *Quixote* (I, vi).

natural wisdom in identifying the first acrobat in the world as Lucifer.

Cervantes' reasons for introducing the humanist at this juncture in the novel are more complex than the simple caricature would suggest. With his preoccupation with truth and authority the erudite young man is to represent the *culto* audience in Don Quixote's narration of the fabulous tale of the occurrences in the Cave of Montesinos. This is the same audience that is represented by the canon, and whereas the potential weakness in its aesthetic theories of the marvelous and verisimilitude is intimated through delicate parody in the literary debate of Part I, here the same weakness is exaggerated to the level of the grotesque.[14]

As in Don Quixote's description of the episode of the Knight of the Lake, the parody works on one level against the world of the romances. A standard of objectivity is brought into the narration, by which we cannot fail to measure the realities presented as distortions, e.g., the enchanted Dulcinea is in need of a loan of six *reals*. It is precisely the peculiar nature of the standard of objectivity, however, which gives a two-dimensional quality to the parody at hand. Don Quixote, Montesinos, and Durandarte intersperse in their description of the fantastic contours of the romance world a series of incongruous observations, which subject its phenomena to a process of analysis and explanation by contemporary standards of natural science. The first of these jarring shifts of perspective is in a curiously muddled syllogism in which Montesinos describes his discovery that Durandarte's heart was of great size: "I took out his heart with my own hands; and in truth it must have weighed two pounds,

[14] As a caricature, the humanist is closer to the absurd poet of the *Coloquio de los perros* than he is to the Canon of Toledo. Nevertheless, both figures represent an unhappy accommodation of the reality of the imagination to empirical reality, to which Cervantes knew the canon's attempt to define the reader's capacities for belief could lead. Without claiming that the humanist's interest in the *morbo gálico* contains a specific allusion to Fracastoro or Scaliger, I would like to recall a passage in the latter's influential poetics which demonstrates the degree to which the attitudes caricatured in Cervantes' figure were in fact brought to bear on literature during the Renaissance. Maintaining always that verse and not subject matter determine whether a piece of writing is poetry, Scaliger praises Fracastoro's work "De morbo gallico" as a divine poem. However, he finds a flaw: the poet claims that only human beings can contract syphilis, and Scaliger once saw a dog with the disease (*Poetices libri septem*, p. 315).

because, according to natural philosophers, a man with a larger heart is endowed with more courage than one with a small heart."[15] He adds that on leaving Roncesvalles with the heart of his beloved cousin, he sprinkled it with a bit of salt, "so that it should not smell bad, and arrive, if not fresh, at least dry" when delivered to Belerma, the lady of the fallen knight. Moreover, in describing the grief-stricken Belerma in her processions of lamentation, Montesinos is careful to point out that her haggard appearance is the effect of the haunting recollection of the loss of her lover and not of more natural causes: "And her sallowness and the rings round her eyes are not caused by the monthly disorders common to women."[16]

The complexity of the parody which these peculiar statements introduce goes beyond mere reduction of the fantastic to absurdity by its juxtaposition to the real. The real here is in effect the real of the natural scientist, and in its transparent misapplication to what is clearly fantasy it suffers a similar *reductio ad absurdum*. It is well to recall Don Quixote's feigned complicity with the Canon of Toledo concerning the "inverisimilitude" of the romances, a reductive technique which Cervantes may have learned from the narrative methods of Ariosto. As it were, the participating narrator (Don Quixote) brings the scientific-syllogistic perspective of a member

[15] ". . . le saqué el corazón con mis propias manos; y en verdad que debía de pesar dos libras, porque según los naturales, el que tiene mayor corazón es dotado de mayor valentía del que le tiene pequeño" (II, 705). To appreciate fully the irony we must remember that Cervantes is evoking a serious contemporary scientific doctrine on the physiology of the heart (see Clemencín, VI, 89) and employing the basic instrument of cognition of the natural scientists, the syllogism (see El Pinciano, *Philosophía antigua poética*, I, 74-75).

[16] "Y no toma ocasión su amarillez y sus ojeras de estar con el mal mensil, ordinario en las mujeres" (II, 707). Referring to these phenomena, Manuel Durán has observed in the episode an ambiguous "infiltración del prosaísmo en los sueños mismos del caballero" and skillfully analyzed its function in psychological terms. The knight is moving toward disillusionment; here "el subconsciente de Don Quijote continúa la labor despoetizadora de Sancho y la lleva mucho más lejos." (See *La ambigüedad en el Quijote* [Xalapa, 1960], pp. 210-228.) Madariaga's analysis is similar, although he interprets the *sanchificación* of Don Quixote as a conscious process. In the *realismo despiadado* the knight is treating the world of the romances with a cynical humor similar to that of Cervantes. (See *Guía del lector del "Quijote"* [Madrid, 1926], pp. 177-188.) I agree in large part that the psychological implications of the vision are important but wish to point out another dimension of the episode, in which the particular nature of the prosaic realities has an equally logical function.

of his audience into his imagined world and appears to submit to its demands. However, the inappropriateness of his scientific explanations indicates that his submission is a mere pose allowing him to underscore his belief that fantasy is indeed sadly no more than fantasy and at the same time to ridicule the humanist's perspective and the absurdity of his attempts to encroach upon the realm of literature of the imagination.

In a reversal which is typical of the fluidity that marks the contexts of Cervantine parody, the author utilizes the perspective of the *vulgo* to make his most direct thrust against the application to literature of the pedant's demand for empirical truth. Sancho is unwittingly drawn into Don Quixote's narration, when the latter reports that Montesinos is a bit concerned that "in the world up here" the history of his exploit holds that he employed a "dagger" and not a "thin stiletto sharper than an awl" in performing his feat of surgery on the corpse of Durandarte. The credulous squire interrupts his master's account: "That stiletto must have been made by Ramón de Hoces, the Sevillian." Although Don Quixote's answer, that "inquiry into this matter is of no importance, for it does not disturb or alter the truth and sequence of the history," is supported by the humanist, it is he who is interested in any factual or scientific material which Don Quixote can discover in his exploration of the cave and which he can add to his *Metamorfóseos* and his *Suplemento de Virgilio Polidoro*. At the conclusion of the account he announces enthusiastically his intention of adding to his encyclopedia the fact that playing cards were used in the time of Charlemagne, basing his conclusion on Durandarte's expression: "patience and shuffle the cards" (*paciencia y barajar*).[17] In their response to Don Quixote's narration both he and Sancho commit the blunder of the majority of literary theorists of the age, the confusion of artistic and empirical truth.[18]

[17] The humanist's penchant for allegory is but another aspect of the truth-oriented view of literature which he shares with most theorists of the age. Literature was seen as a source of facts (i.e., *docere*); even the most fantastic tales could yield "valuable information" when examined by an ingenious exegete. In his interpretation of Durandarte's phrase, Cervantes is parodying Renaissance methods of allegorical interpretation.

[18] Sancho Panza's belief that art mirrors external reality is most clearly presented in the episode in which he becomes a "participating narrator"—the tale of Torralba

Once the double-edged quality of its parody is recognized, the episode of the Cave of Montesinos points directly to the major problems of Renaissance literary theory—truth, verisimilitude, and the critical process which I refer to in Chapter I as the "legitimizing of the marvelous." It would be certainly false to equate Cervantes' caricature with the leading spokesman for this process, Tasso, who in his precepts for arousing *admiratio* consistently cautioned poets to avoid minutiae in details and extreme subtleties in scientific and philosophical matters.[19] Yet it is undeniable that Tasso's preoccupations with the dependence of *admiratio* on belief and with the poet's obligation to "increase as much as he can [the reader's] belief in the marvels of the work without diminishing his pleasure"[20] led to an unhappy accommodation of the imaginary realm of art to the scientific laws of empirical reality. Although Tasso's recommendations that the poet take advantage of the novelty of the unusual but verifiable detail would not countenance Montesinos' absurd insistence on describing the finer points of his surgical instrument and Sancho's attempts to specify to whom the dagger belonged, it is nonetheless well to remember that the Italian poet's insistent use of minutiae of a scientifically verifiable type in his *Liberata* provoked the criticism of Galileo that the work is like a room full of curiosities and antiques, dried chameleons and petrified crabs, and that the drought scene of Canto XIII is not poetry but a listing of all possible meteorological phenomena.[21] And if Tasso would never go to the extreme of render-

---

(I, 20). His absurd insistence that his account include the trials of each of Lope's goats as they cross the Guadiana causes his story to disintegrate and arouses the wrath of his "participating audience," Don Quixote.

[19] Tasso, *Del poema eroico*, pp. 109-110.

[20] ". . . accrescere quanto egli può fede alla meraviglia senza diminuire il diletto" (ibid., p. 111).

[21] *Scritti letterari* (Florence, 1943), pp. 96, 193. It is interesting that perhaps the greatest empirical mind of the age was one of the exceptional literary theorists who like Cervantes realized that truths of science and truths of literature rest upon entirely different grounds. Carlo Calcaterra writes that there was a "netta distinzione che il Galilei stesso e i galileiani facevano tra scienza e poesia, considerando quella come generata e avvivata dall'osservazione della natura e dall'esperimento, questa dal moto degli affetti, dall'entusiasmo, dall'immaginativa." He cites Galileo's words: "La natura non si diletta di poesia"; "Alla poesia sono in maniera necessarie le favole e finzioni, che senza quelle non può essere; le quali bugie son poi tanto aborrite dalla natura, che non meno impossibil cosa è il ritrovarne pur una, che il trovar tenebre nella luce" (*Il parnaso in rivolta* [Bologna, 1961], p. 207). Galileo's

ing Montesinos' preservation of Durandarte's heart against the decaying effect of time empirically sound by the addition of a little salt, he nevertheless was careful to justify the apparent suspension of activity at Jerusalem during the long journey of Carlo and Ubaldo to retrieve Rinaldo from the distant island of Armida by asserting that the armies of Goffredo spent the time constructing necessary siege engines.[22]

The acute concern for temporal consistency (which the humanist shares with Tasso and the Canon of Toledo) provides the basis for a small piece of comedy of character, which recalls Cervantes' methods of dealing with the neo-Aristotelian in the debate of Part One. The young scholar rejects the veracity of Don Quixote's narration, arguing that he did not spend enough time in the cave to see so many marvels, only to turn about and defend its credibility when Sancho asserts that his master must be lying: "Would Don Quixote lie? Why, even if he had wanted to, he had not time to compose and invent such a multitude of fictions."[23]

In his role as narrator of the adventure in the Cave of Montesinos, Don Quixote seems to acknowledge the critical principles of the *culto* audience, and bow to their authority, as he anticipates objections which this audience would raise to the subject matter narrated and answers these objections on its terms rather than his own, i.e., with statements that would seem to satisfy its rigid criteria of verisimilitude. The incongruity of these answers, however, in the present context serves to reduce to absurdity the critical principles seemingly acknowledged. The process of parody employed by the knight-narrator is continued at another level, one far closer to the actual reader, as the frame of literary debate which surrounds the

---

enthusiasm for Ariosto's powers of imagination and clarity of style and his evident lack of concern for the fashionable negative evaluation of the *Furioso* by contemporary standards of verisimilitude are logical in view of his sharp distinction between poetry and science. If Galileo saw a major adversary in those who would encumber science with constructs of the fantasy, Cervantes saw a major adversary in those who would inhibit the fantasy with notions derived from science. See Cassirer, *The Individual and the Cosmos in Renaissance Philosophy*, p. 156.

[22] See his letter, cited by Theophil Spoerri, *Renaissance und Barock bei Ariost und Tasso* (Bern, 1922), pp. 18-19.

[23] "Pues ¿había de mentir el señor don Quijote, que, aunque quisiera, no ha tenido lugar para componer e imaginar tanto millón de mentiras?" (II, 790).

episode of the Cave of Montesinos is closed by Cide Hamete Benengeli's retrospective comments that open the following chapter. It is now the Arab historian's turn to bring his audience into the work, and treat it just as Don Quixote has treated his participating audience.

Cide Hamete's statements have been foreshadowed in the title affixed to the chapter containing Don Quixote's fantastic account: "Of the wonderful things which the consummate Don Quixote said he saw in the deep Cave of Montesinos, the impossibility and magnitude of which cause this adventure to be deemed apocryphal."[24] The opening of the following chapter reasserts this judgment as the editor informs us that the Moorish chronicler has left a handwritten message in the margin of his manuscript. The first part of the message is a clear statement of the current Aristotelian doctrine of verisimilitude, his adherence to that doctrine, and his rejection of the incident of the Cave of Montesinos as apocryphal. Like his protagonist in his narration Cide Hamete seems to anticipate objections in his audience to the credibility of the exploit and to acknowledge and submit to the aesthetic assumptions underlying these objections. Yet as in the case of Don Quixote the submission is no more than apparent and almost simultaneously turns into parody of what seems to be affirmed. If the incongruity of the fashionable Aristotelian terminology (*contingibles y verisímiles*) in the mouth of the elusive Moor, who himself breaks all classical rules of decorum by swearing like a Christian,[25] is not enough to dissolve the value of his affirmation of Aristotelian doctrine, he proceeds to disavow directly what he has just upheld. He draws another favorite principle of the Aristotelian theorists, the corollary of verisimilitude—decorum of character—into the parodistic play to support his disavowal.

All the adventures till now have been feasible and probable, but this one of the cave I can find no way of accepting as true, for it exceeds all reasonable bounds. *But it is not possible for me*

---

[24] "De las admirables cosas que el estremado don Quijote contó que había visto en la profunda cueva de Montesinos, cuya imposibilidad y grandeza hace que se tenga esta aventura por apócrifa" (II, 702).

[25] See Carvallo, II, 122: ". . . gran indecoro seria si el Moro jurase por Christo, y el Christiano por el Alcoran."

*to suppose that Don Quixote, who was the most truthful gentle-
man and most noble knight of his age, could be lying.*[26]

The parody here is similar to that employed by Don Quixote with
the humanist, but at this level its object is not a character within the
work but rather the neo-Aristotelian mode of subjecting literature
to the laws of empirical reality and, what is most important here,
the reader who adopts this mode. The impudence of Cide Hamete's
play with the reader is heightened by his absurd reversal of re-
invoking the principle of verisimilitude to affirm what he had
previously denied by that very principle: "On the other hand, I reflect that he related and told *the adventure with all the circumstances detailed* and that he could not in so short a space have
fabricated such a vast complication of absurdities."[27] It is heightened
also by the concluding Ariostean-type assertion of helplessness and
disclaimer of authority for what he writes: "And if this adventure
seems apocryphal, it is not I that am to blame; and so, without
affirming its falsehood or its truth, I write it down. Decide for
yourself in your wisdom, reader; for I am not bound, nor is it in
my power, to do more."[28]

[26] ". . . todas las aventuras hasta aquí sucedidas han sido contingibles y
verisímiles; pero ésta desta cueva no le hallo entrada alguna para tenerla por
verdadera, por ir tan fuera de los términos razonables. *Pero pensar yo que don
Quijote mintiese, siendo el más verdadero hidalgo y el más noble caballero de sus
tiempos, no es posible*" (II, 713). The italics are mine.

[27] "Por otra parte, considero que él la contó y la dijo *con todas las circunstancias
dichas*, y que no pudo fabricar en tan breve espacio tan gran máquina de disparates"
(II, 713). The italics are mine.

[28] ". . . y si esta aventura parece apócrifa yo no tengo la culpa; y así, sin afirmarla
por falsa o verdadera, la escribo. Tú, letor, pues eres prudente, juzga lo que te
pareciere, que yo no debo ni puedo más" (II, 713). In view of the mystifying play
with Aristotelian criteria of the passage, it is not impossible that the concluding
statement contains a parodistic allusion to the widely repeated Aristotelian mandate
that the poet should speak as little as possible and leave matters of judgment up to
the reader's discretion. After repeating the principle and emphasizing the dangers
to plausibility of authorial interventions, Piccolomini adds, in words similar to
those of Cide Hamete: ". . . in tal guisa [the poet] vien' a mostrar superbia in
attribuire a se quello che ha da esser liberamente dei lettori e degli ascoltatori:
cioè il discorrere, il giudicare, il lodare, il biasimare o altra cosa fare che appartenga
a coloro che leggono; dovendo il poeta apparir come neutrale e lasciar libero il
giudizio agli altri sopra le cose che egli imitando narra." The passage is cited by
Riley (*Cervantes's Theory of the Novel*, p. 206), not in relation to Cide Hamete's

Cide Hamete's pose of helplessness and his conscious play with the reader leave us with the feeling that the Arab historian is in fact in absolute control of both his creation and his audience. At the same time his introduction of literary principles in a humorous context serves to emphasize Cervantes' independence of the neo-Aristotelian dogma and to suggest that, as far as Cervantes was concerned, the theorists' acute preoccupation with standards of credibility is irrelevant to the creation of fiction, which in the last analysis has no pretenses to being anything more than what it is, namely, fiction.

MASTER PEDRO'S PUPPET SHOW

After leaving the Cave of Montesinos and meeting the young soldier, one of the many youths in Cervantes' works who abandon the city and the court to seek adventure in distant lands, Don Quixote and Sancho arrive at an inn. Their arrival is followed shortly by that of an itinerant puppeteer, true to the Italian tradition of the *saltimbanco*, whose repertoire includes a clairvoyant monkey and a puppet show representing well-known episodes from the tradition of romance literature. An immediate link between his appearance and the adventure in the Cave of Montesinos is established as Don Quixote, complying with Sancho's suggestion, asks the monkey whether what he experienced in the cave was in fact true. The enigmatic answer of Master Pedro, "The monkey says that part of what your worship saw or experienced in the said cave is false and part verisimilar,"[29] does little to dispel the doubts that have been haunting the knight. It does, however, recall for us the fundamental theoretical problem which the narration of the underworld vision raised and the tone of parody pervading its treatment of this problem. The humor springing from Cide Hamete Benengeli's use of the

---

words in this episode, but rather as an example of current theories recommending authorial detachment, which may have influenced Cervantes' creation of the Moorish chronicler. I find unconvincing any arguments presenting the Moor as a device by which the author seriously seeks to stand apart from his text. On the contrary he is the means by which Cervantes continually asserts his personal powers over the reader and his independence of contemporary rules governing literary behavior.

[29] "El mono dice que parte de las cosas que vuesa merced vió, o pasó, en la dicha cueva son falsas, y parte verisímiles" (II, 727).

Aristotelian terminology is reinforced as a monkey, the traditional animal of parody par excellence,[30] flaunts the same principles.

After this introduction we are not surprised to discover a deeper thematic relationship between the ensuing scene and the episode in the cave. Again we observe the narrator-audience dramatic situation and the surrogate of the artist in the act of creation. Again Cervantes utilizes this situation to reflect on various literary problems, including those insistent preoccupations which we have been following, verisimilitude, audience belief, and authorial freedom.

The story which the puppets of Master Pedro perform is formally similar to the adventures of the Knight of the Lake and the Cave of Montesinos, presenting in another variation a traditional literary theme which had become omnipresent in medieval romance, the journey to the otherworld. Indeed Don Gaiferos himself offers the reader an imaginative link between his quest into Sansueña to rescue his wife from the forces of evil and the underworld journeys recounted by the protagonist: "He says that he is capable of rescuing his wife alone, even though she were imprisoned in the deepest bowels of the earth."[31]

Cervantes prefaces the performance with a line from the *Aeneid*, which identifies the expectant audience with the "Tyrians and Trojans" awaiting in silence the beginning of Aeneas' account of the fall of Troy. The evocation of Virgil is appropriate for the literary implications of the scene, for the youthful narrator begins his narration observing carefully the rules for epic composition which contemporary theorists had codified on the basis of Aristotelian-

---

[30] For Lope the monkey was "el animal que imita nuestro ingenio" (*Jerusalén conquistada*, III, 48; see ed. J. de Entrambasaguas [Madrid, 1951], I, 127). That the ape could be regarded despectively as a symbol of a servile, unimaginative type of imitation is evident in Lope's defense of the structure of his epic, in which he fails to follow the highly recommended *in-medias-res* formula for disposition. In claiming the superiority of invention to imitation, he recalls Poliziano's words: "Mihi verò longè honestior tauri facies, aut item leonis, quam simiae videtur" (p. 31). Similarly Carvallo (*Cisne de Apolo*, II, 182) differentiates the valuable imitation that an artist must practice from that of "la mona, que queriendo imitar y parecer al hombre, no le immita, ni parece en lo mejor que es el sentido, sino en la liuiandad de la risa y en las nalgas." For medieval associations of the monkey with the imitative faculty, see E. R. Curtius, *Europäische Literatur und Lateinisches Mittelalter* (Bern, 1948), pp. 524-525.

[31] ". . . dice que él solo es bastante para sacar a su esposa, si bien estuviese metida en el más hondo centro de la tierra" (II, 730).

Horatian dogma and the example of Virgil. He offers a concise proposition, a summary of his subject, and proceeds to an *in-medias-res* beginning. Moreover, in accordance with the rules, he demonstrates an acute concern for verisimilitude, offering an historical source of his poem ("the French chronicles") and adding, lest a theorist like the canon criticize his geography as including lands "that Ptolemy never knew nor Marco Polo visited," that the destination of his hero, the city of Sansueña, is in the present the city of Zaragoza.[32]

Following the pattern which we observe in nearly all Cervantes' scenes of this type, the youthful narrator exhorts the various spectators to behold as real the things and events described in the story of the rescue of Melisendra by her husband Don Gaiferos—the towers of Sansueña, Don Gaiferos at his chessboard, and the melancholy Melisendra gazing in despair toward France. His concern with the visual impact of his narration, which again recalls the precepts of the theorists and their praise of Virgil's *energia* in putting things before his readers' eyes, is evident in such phrases as "vean vuesas mercedes allí como está jugando," "adviertan con la vehemencia y ahinco que le riñe," "Miren vuestras mercedes," "ven como arroja," "Miren también un nuevo caso," "Vuelvan vuestras mercedes los ojos a aquella torre." Indeed the verbs "mirar" and "ver" are repeated no fewer than thirteen times and suggest that the young narrator like Don Quixote in his description of the episode of the Knight of the Lake is striving for the effect of conjuration.[33]

[32] This is exactly what the literarily self-conscious Cervantes of the *Persiles* does in justifying the one case in which real geography must be sacrificed for mythic geography. Although Thule was the ancient name for Iceland, by Cervantes' time geographers had adopted the modern name. Yet Thule, as the mythical end of the earth, is necessary in the allegorical movement of the work toward the center of the earth, Rome. Hence Cervantes is careful to justify its presence by having one of his characters state that the kingdom is known today by the name of Yslanda.

[33] As will be made clear in the following chapters, nearly all of Cervantes' figures of the poet have affinities with the magician. Here it is important to observe the religious connotations of the word *retablo*; Master Pedro's stage, illuminated by candles, is an altar, on which the spectator witnesses *misterios* of figures which are described at one point as *reliquias* and whose demolition occurs in "less than two Credos." Moreover, in advertising the "seventy thousand" marvels which can be witnessed on his magical stage, the puppeteer cites the words of the Gospel: "Operibus credite, et non verbis." In his provocative analysis of this scene George Haley has suggested that there are magical implications in the narrator's wand

Don Quixote

Following his exemplary beginning, the narrator begins to slip away from the strict formal controls which he has initially observed and finds himself admonished by his critical audience. Twice he is interrupted by Don Quixote, who curiously enough in this scene finds himself cast in the role of representing the school of criticism which he has ridiculed in those scenes in which his role was that of narrator. His first interruption criticizes the narrator's failure to observe the principle of unity, the *línea recta*, and cautions him to avoid the confusion that digressions generally produce. The validity of his assertion is acknowledged by Master Pedro, who is as it were both participant and arbiter in this brief scene of literary discussion. The latter offers the next criticism, censuring the narrator's recourse to a learned (*culteranista*) allusion (the youth apostrophizes the fleeing Gaiferos and Melisendra, wishing them the long life of Nestor) and recommending simplicity in style.

At this point Don Quixote raises his second objection, condemning the narrator's failure to meet the demands of verisimilitude. In his description of the havoc that fills the city of Sansueña as the Moors discover the presence of Don Gaiferos, the boy states that the sound of tolling bells echoes from the towers of the mosques throughout the city. Don Quixote will not allow this:

> "No, no!" interrupted Don Quixote. "In this matter of the bells Master Pedro is not proceeding properly, because they do not use bells among the Moors, but kettle-drums and a kind of trumpet like our clarion; and this about ringing the bells in Sansueña is most certainly complete nonsense."[34]

Master Pedro now turns about to reject Don Quixote's criticism, and he does so on no uncertain terms: "Don't worry about childish trifles, Don Quixote, or expect perfection, for you never find it,"[35] adding

---

("The Narrator in Don Quijote: Maese Pedro's Puppet Show," *Modern Language Notes*, LXXX [1965], 145-165). I interpret the *retablo* of Master Pedro as the hallowed region of the imagination, with which man can commune only through the ministrations of the poet.

[34] "—¡Eso no!—dijo a esta sazón don Quijote—. En esto de las campanas anda muy impropio maese Pedro, porque entre moros no se usan campanas, sino atabales, y un género de dulzainas que parecen nuestras chirimías; y esto de sonar campanas en Sansueña sin duda es un gran disparate" (II, 733).

[35] "No mire vuesa merced en niñerías, señor don Quijote, ni quiera llevar las cosas tan por el cabo, que no se le halle" (II, 733).

that the success of the implausible works of the Spanish theater, "which are greeted not only with applause but with admiration," is sufficient proof of the irrelevance and pedantry of the strict application of the notion of verisimilitude.

Although it is tempting to dismiss Master Pedro's statements and Don Quixote's acquiescence as a simple slap at the theater of Lope, their significance in Cervantes' consistently critical examination of the fashionable notion of verisimilitude should not be overlooked. Master Pedro's rejoinder to Don Quixote recalls in fact the latter's rejection of the canon's theories. In the same way, the puppeteer's introduction emphasizing pleasure as the aim of his art ("And in order *to give you pleasure* and *to give everybody in the inn pleasure free of charge*, I wish to set up my puppet show")[36] recalls the defenses of the romances by Juan Palomeque el Zurdo and his family and Don Quixote in the first part of the novel.

Cervantes' conclusion of the scene is both a masterpiece of comedy of situation and character and a fitting conclusion to the interplay of literary discussion that punctuates the performance of Master Pedro's puppets. The borderline between the realm of the imagination and that of real life could not be more clearly drawn for the group of spectators. The characters in the performance are lifeless figures of papier-mâché separated from the surrounding world by the enclosure of the *retablo*. Despite the narrator's concern for geographical verisimilitude, his setting, Sansueña, suggests that all that the poet wants his audience to see is a reality only in the distant reaches of the imagination.[37] Indeed, as if this were not enough, the author brings the standards of objective reality into this dream world by presenting the romance figures in a series of comic poses, e.g., the hapless Melisendra dangling by her skirts as she descends from the tower, Gaiferos hurling the chessboard in rage, and Melisendra wiping her mouth, which has been defiled by her Moorish captor's kiss. These incongruities, which recall the reductive technique of Don Quixote in his description of the Knight of the Lake cleaning his teeth with a toothpick, are of course con-

---

[36] ". . . y por *darle gusto*, quiero armar mi retablo y *dar placer a cuantos están en la venta*, sin paga alguna" (II, 726). The italics are mine.

[37] See Harry Levin, "The Example of Cervantes," *Contexts of Criticism* (New York, 1963), pp. 79-96.

sistent with the overall pattern of the work of rendering the chivalric world ridiculous. However, in the literary drama contained within the present scene, they have the additional function of serving as *Verfremdungseffekte*, by which the author willfully heightens his audience's consciousness that what it is witnessing is art and not life and obliquely suggests that the pleasures of the imagination are all the more enjoyable precisely if we are aware of their unreality.

Don Quixote seems to be the member of the audience most conscious of the fictitious quality of the narration and least likely to fall to the seductive appeal of the imagination. And yet, almost immediately following his criticism of the lack of verisimilitude in the envisioned scene, he forgets that the characters are of papier-mâché and that the stage is a stage and attempts to enter the world of fantasy to aid the Christians in their flight. The scene of violence and carnage at the expense of the defenseless papier-mâché figures of Master Pedro is of course a dramatic representation of Don Quixote's madness,[38] but it is also a significant conclusion to the literary discussion that accompanies the representation. Here retroactive irony is at work at the expense of the theoretical point of view maintained by Don Quixote throughout the scene. We recall the *admiratio* that the canon could not help feeling as he heard Don Quixote's narration of the adventure of the Knight of the Lake, which flouted all his aesthetic principles, and the *admiratio* which is produced, as Master Pedro points out, by the "absurdities" of the Spanish stage. Don Quixote's attack is once again dramatic proof of the appeal of the fantasy, which is independent of the laws governing empirical reality, even as it is a vindication of the poet's freedom from observing such laws.

[38] Ortega's analysis of the scene is a classic in the history of Cervantine criticism. He reveals how the process by which Don Quixote is swept across the border separating the realm of myth from that of everyday reality in this scene contains the clearest representation in the work of the madness of the hero, which in turn represents the psychological condition of normal man as he copes with everyday experience ("lo que en él es anormal, ha sido y seguirá siendo normal en la humanidad" [*Meditaciones del Quijote* (Madrid: Revista de Occidente, 1958), p. 114]). In the unprecedented presentation of the interaction between both realms in a work of fiction, Cervantes added a "third dimension" to literature and created a new genre, the modern novel: "El arte se enriquece con un término más; . . . Ahora tenemos que acomodar en la capacidad poética la realidad actual" (pp. 108-109).

Cervantes & the Classical Aesthetic

CLAVILEÑO AND THE BRAYING ASS

The parallelism in the adventures of the Cave of Montesinos and Clavileño has often been pointed out. Both the underworld experience of Don Quixote and the flight of Sancho are variants of the traditional journey to the otherworld of romance literature.[39] In each case the world of fantasy is measured beside the world of everyday reality and suffers a humorous reduction. Moreover, in both episodes a character recounts a fantastic experience to a skeptical audience and must defend his credibility against its vigorous objections. In the Clavileño episode the roles of the knight and the squire are reversed: the "quixotized" Sancho becomes the participating narrator and defends artistic fantasies, while Don Quixote appears as the principal spokesman for empirical orientation in contemporary literary theory.

Like many of his literary forbears on the aerial journey Sancho Panza discovers the insignificant size of the world when it is viewed from the heavenly perspective. He tells his audience that, on looking downward, he found the earth to be as small as a mustard seed and its inhabitants as small as hazelnuts. The duchess is apparently not interested in the moral implications of the comparisons, for she immediately objects that Sancho Panza must be lying, employing impeccable syllogistic reasoning to support her argument: A hazelnut is larger than a mustard seed. If Sancho saw a man as large as a hazelnut on the earth, he could not possibly have seen the earth, for it would have been entirely covered.

Sancho is undaunted by the duchess' argument and proceeds to describe his encounter with the seven little goats. At this point Don Quixote raises his objection. He doubts that his squire could have dismounted from Clavileño and amused himself with the goats, for they reside beyond the region of fire (i.e., the constellation of the Pleiades is beyond the fiery area separating the air from the circle of the moon and the outer circles). Consequently, before reaching them, one would naturally have to suffer burns. The knight's syllogistic reasoning leads to the abrupt conclusion that "as we are not burnt, either Sancho is lying or Sancho is dreaming

[39] For the aerial journey, see Patch, *The Other World*, pp. 22-26.

152

("... y pues no nos asuramos, o Sancho miente, o Sancho sueña" [II, 836]).

Don Quixote's reasoning recalls a passage in the work of a writer who in all probability was Cervantes' model in the creation of the humanist, the critical audience in the episode of the Cave of Montesinos—Antonio de Torquemada. In his extensive discussion of the location of the earthly paradise, Antonio, the chief authority in Torquemada's dialogue takes up the matter of the altitude of the mountain on which Eden was created, a matter complicated by Strabo's belief that the summit touched the circle of the moon and by the authority of the Old Testament, which states that the great flood covered all mountains of the earth. Antonio attacks Strabo's opinion, recalling arguments by Thomas Aquinas and Duns Scotus to the effect that, if the mountain reached the circle of the moon, it would have to pass through the region of fire and would be consumed. He supplements these arguments by pointing out that the water of the four streams which, according to Genesis, descend from Eden could not pass through the contrary element fire, and that, if the mountain were so high, it would be visible from all points of the earth.[40]

The absurdity of the application of this type of reasoning to dispute Sancho's claim to have frolicked with his heavenly flock is the same absurdity that surrounds its implicit application as Don Quixote defends the plausibility of the delivery of Durandarte's gift to Belerma, i.e., the heart was kept fresh by a sprinkle of salt. The process of parody is not so complex as that observable in the Montesinos episode, for the narrator Sancho does not formulate and parody the audience's objections as does the ingenious Don Quixote. He simply refuses to be daunted by these objections and answers them in the Ariostean way, heightening the extravagance of the fantasies which he claims to be true. Nevertheless, the object of parody—the objections of the literary critic oriented toward empirical reality to the creative artist's freedom—is in both cases the same. Once again, Cervantes' literary interlude ends with the critic in a state of confusion. Don Quixote, the member of the audience most certain that Sancho was either lying or dreaming, approaches

[40] *Jardín de flores curiosas*, pp. 101-102.

153

his squire and whispers: "Sancho, if you want me to believe what you saw in the sky, I wish you to accept my account of what I saw in the Cave of Montesinos. I say no more."[41]

An echo of Cervantes' debate with the neo-Aristotelians is audible in the episode of the Braying Ass, which immediately follows Don Quixote's destruction of Master Pedro's puppets. In the brief scene the author does not employ a participating narrator to defend poetic freedom. He merely allows the reader to contemplate the quibblings of a critical audience as it comments on "poetic text." Don Quixote and Sancho encounter an army of villagers, whose standard depicts an ass braying in a triumphant posture. The inscription beneath the emblem reads: "No rebuznaron en balde/ el uno y el otro alcalde" (II, 740).[42] The knight has apparently not forgotten the recent offense to his academic scruples in Master Pedro's breach of temporal verisimilitude, for he immediately transposes the new adventure into the sphere of literary abstractions. He recalls the account of the magistrates' fruitless search for the missing ass (II, xxv) and criticizes its inaccuracy: a magistrate (*regidor*) is not a mayor (*alcalde*); therefore the narrator made a serious error. Sancho Panza offers an explanation which overcomes the difficulty: "It is perfectly possible that the magistrates who brayed then have come in course of time to be mayors of their village, and so they can be called by either title."[43] In the objection and the explanation, both "sixteenth-century theorists" miss the fundamental point—poetic effect (*en balde-alcalde*) can scarcely be achieved if the poet is the "slave of the facts."[44]

[41] "Sancho, pues vos queréis que se os crea lo que habéis visto en el cielo, yo quiero que vos me creáis a mí lo que vi en la cueva de Montesinos. Y no os digo más" (II, 837).

[42] "They did not bray in vain/ our mayors twain."

[43] ". . . bien puede ser que los regidores que entonces rebuznaron viniesen con el tiempo a ser alcaldes de su pueblo, y así, se pueden llamar con entrambos títulos" (II, 740).

[44] It is worth recalling Tasso's words "io ho peggiorati i versi onde ho tolta la parola *mori*; ma così bisognava, perchè gli arabi non son mori nè tartari" (see above, Chap. II, n. 64); for they reveal that the neo-Aristotelians could allow the type of objection to poetic license raised here by Don Quixote to destroy a poetic context. Moreover, they demonstrate the theorists' concern for historical accuracy, which is implicit in Sancho's justification of the poet's alteration.

Don Quixote

CIDE HAMETE BENENGELI

In view of the emergence of narrative literature at the focal point of critical attention in this century, it is not surprising that much recent Cervantine scholarship has devoted its energies to Cervantes' use of the fictitious-authorship device in the *Quixote*. Without troubling itself with discrediting Pierre-Daniel Huet's seventeenth-century interpretation of the presence of the Moor Cide Hamete Benengeli as indicating Cervantes' belief that the genre of prose romance originated in Arabic literature,[45] this scholarship has indeed revealed that the device is far more complicated than is immediately apparent and has a function within the novel directly related to its major themes.[46]

On its simplest level of significance the presence of the Arab chronicler is a resumption of one of the conventions of chivalric romance, the repeated assertion by the narrator that the subject matter of his work is historical and is recorded as such. On some rare occasions the appearance of Cide Hamete Benengeli has no function other than to evoke the romance convention in the narration of Don Quixote's adventures and could indeed be replaced by the more general *la historia* without altering the significance of

---

[45] *Traité de l'origine des romans*, p. 206.

[46] For literary, etymological, and historical sources for "Cide Hamete Benengeli," see Geoffrey Stagg, "El Sabio Cide Hamete Venengeli," *Bulletin of Hispanic Studies*, XXXIII (1956), 218-225. The closest literary precedent is the "original" historian of Pérez de Hita's *Guerras civiles de Granada*, Aben Hamin. The word "Cide" suggests that Cervantes may have had in mind the holy men of Algiers of the epoch of his captivity, the marabouts, who like Cide Hamete Benengeli were wise magicians. R. S. Willis suggests a possible parodistic relationship between the Moorish narrator, the repeated phrase *dice la historia*, and the fragmentary character of many of Cervantes' chapters and the structure of Arabic historiographical works, the fragments of which are often introduced by the expression *qala*, corresponding to the phrase "says the historian" (*The Phantom Chapters of the Quixote* [New York, 1953], pp. 100-103). For studies that concentrate on the function of the narrator within the novel, see, in addition to those of Riley, Gerhardt, Trueblood, Wardropper, and Castro (cited below), Käte Hamburger's "Don Quijote und die Struktur des Epischen Humors," *Festgabe für Eduard Berend* (Weimar, 1959), pp. 191-209; Wayne Booth's "The Self-Conscious Narrator in Comic Fiction before *Tristram Shandy*," *PMLA*, LXVII (1952), 163-185; Norman Friedman's "Point of View in Fiction," *PMLA*, LXX (1955), 1160-1184; Ruth Snodgrass El Saffar's "The Function of the Fictional Narrator in *Don Quijote*," *Modern Language Notes*, LXXXIII (1968), 164-177; Louis Rubin's *The Teller in the Tale* (Seattle, 1967), Chap. I.

the context in which it appears (see for example pp. I, 135, 273; II, 929, 988).[47]

Just as Don Quixote is a parody of the chivalric hero, be it Amadís or Orlando, Cide Hamete is similarly a parody of the chronicler of old, be it Turpin, Maestro Elisabat, or simply the *historia*, and their descendants in the false chronicles of the sixteenth century.[48] Whether or not the decision to employ such a device came to Cervantes as an afterthought, his delayed introduction of the Moorish historian into the novel has the curious effect of making us feel that he is a part of the imaginary world of the protagonist, who, as if by a sheer act of will creates his chronicler.[49] On his first sally the knight addresses a historian of the future ("sage enchanter, whoever you may be"— "sabio encantador, quienquiera que seas") and offers him the sentence by which he can begin his history. Seven chapters later such a magician-historian does in fact appear, and from that moment on he begins to play an increasingly important role in the novel.

In many of the scenes containing overt parody of the conventions of the romance world, as has been demonstrated above, the protean nature of Cervantine parody allows for the coexistence of various levels of significance, if indeed at times there seems to be a tension arising from the simultaneous presence of these levels. In the case of Cide Hamete the same is true. While being a caricature of a literary device, he occasionally speaks neither as parody nor in parody but as a serious spokesman for the opinions of the author. Whether Cervantes was consciously obeying the current literary theory, derived from Aristotle's *Poetics*, that the narrator should always maintain a stance of detachment by expressing personal opinions through one of his characters is difficult to determine. Nevertheless, it is clear that Cide Hamete Benengeli is speaking for Cervantes in his exclamation of sympathy for Don Quixote as the proud knight discovers

[47] Admittedly this is an oversimplification. The characterization of Cide Hamete in other commentaries, and the fact that he is indeed a Moor, a member of a race "known for its love of lying" (*siendo muy propio de los de aquella nación ser mentirosos*), bring by implication the complex effects of parody which we shall examine below even to these insignificant intrusions.

[48] See D. José Godoy Alcántara, *Historia crítica de los falsos cronicones* (Madrid, 1868), pp. 9-10; Bruce W. Wardropper, "*Don Quixote*: Story or History?" *Modern Philology*, LXIII (1965), 1-11.

[49] See Riley, *Cervantes's Theory of the Novel*, p. 209.

holes in his stockings and despairingly contemplates the dishonor that the sight of mended stockings would bring upon a knight-errant. The narrator's interjected statement expands into a satirical comment on the manners of the time and on the illusory quality of worldly honor, recalling Lazarillo's words of indignation and sympathy at the sight of his master's preference of starvation to dishonor:

> How miserable is the man of birth who is always regaling his honor while he dines poorly behind closed doors. . . . How miserable is he, I repeat, whose honor is terrified at the thought that someone may discover from a mile off the patch on his shoe, the sweat marks on his hat, the threadbareness of his coat, and the hunger in his stomach![50]

Similarly it is evident that Cervantes is speaking when Cide Hamete judges the Duke and Duchess to be madder than Don Quixote in their elaborately contrived staging of the resurrection of Altisidora, another of the many jokes which they enjoy at the expense of their guest (II, 1041), when he offers the well-known justification of his inclusion in Part One of the *Curioso impertinente* and the *Capitán cautivo* in terms of the pleasure of variety in fiction (II, 849), and when he expresses the hope that Avellaneda and others may let the bones of Don Quixote rest in peace at the conclusion of the novel (II, 1067-1068).

For our purposes it is neither the Moorish narrator's nonfunctional poses, in which he merely echoes a traditional literary device, nor his serious, discursive role, in which he is a vehicle for the author's judgments, that is of primary interest. It is rather a second dimension of his parodistic function in the novel, a function which he shares harmoniously with his translator and the editor of the translation (that is, the *yo*, whom we may, if we wish, call Cervantes, who refers first to various *autores* and the annals of the Mancha in which the events of Don Quixote's first sally are recorded, then to the *autor* who broke off his narration of the battle between Don Quixote and the Biscayan, and finally to his discovery of the Arabic manu-

---

[50] "¡Miserable del bien nacido que va dando pistos a su honra, comiendo mal y a puerta cerrada . . . ¡Miserable de aquel, digo, que tiene la honra espantadiza, y piensa que desde una legua se le descubre el remiendo del zapato, el trasudor del sombrero, la hilaza del herreruelo y la hambre de su estómago!" (II, 853).

script and a translator in Toledo). Here we observe three points of vision, from which reflections are made on both the deeds of Don Quixote and Sancho as historical events and on the documentary enclosure of these deeds in the narrated history.[51] What unites all three perspectives is their intense awareness of the critical notions which the preceding hundred years of theoretical writings have produced. True to the tradition of the chroniclers of the romances, they maintain their right to interject gratuitous comments on the events they record, but unlike their moralizing ancestors they allow a new literary preoccupation to color many of their observations.

An examination of the most significant passages reveals a pattern closely related to what we have observed in Cervantes' use of the dramatic situation structured on the audience-narrator relationship. For the effect of the words of the commentator in these passages is to bring the reader into the work and assert the same power over him that the participating narrator exercises over his listeners in the scenes discussed above. Cide Hamete Benengeli, the translator, and the editor mockingly assume the point of view of a certain type of reader, thereby bringing that point of view into the work, as an imaginary but nonetheless functional participant, and by absurdly applying the principles which they seem to be assuming and acknowledging in accord with the reader, render them meaningless. The technique is basically the same as that which Don Quixote employs in ridiculing the humanist in his narration of the events in the cave of Montesinos.

Cervantes frequently utilizes the possibilities of the fictional-narrator device to reduce to absurdity the restrictions which contemporary literary theories would impose on the artist. One of the clearest examples is Cide Hamete's retrospective commentary on the Montesinos episode, which, as has been pointed out, evokes Aristotelian notions and terminology both to defend and to reject the authenticity of Don Quixote's account and concludes by turning

---

[51] Castro has recently observed ("Cide Hamete Benengeli: el cómo y el por qué," *Mundo Nuevo* [February, 1967], pp. 5-9) how a result of the accretion and preservation of participating, multiple authors is the treatment of the work itself and its process of becoming as an *experienced* reality, just as all things and people within it are presented as realities experienced within the lives of a human being. Thus the creation of the novel itself becomes "novelized."

to another Aristotelian notion to justify his leaving the matter un-
resolved. We might add that the circularity of this pattern of
thought as well as the refusal to stay the circular motion by arriving
at a decision is perfectly consistent with Cide Hamete's preoccupation with the endless cyclical flux which marks the world of tem-
porality: "Everything in this life goes in cycles, or rather round-
about . . . time revolves in this continuous wheel."[52]

In a similar passage, which introduces the encounter with the
enchanted Dulcinea in Toboso, Cide Hamete mentions specifically
the objections of the imagined audience and playfully attempts to
evade its criticisms by stressing his role as *historian*. He thus invokes
the popular Aristotelian distinction between poetry and history and
suggests that, although history is often not verisimilar, the historian
must always remain true to his duty of recording things as they are.

> Finally he wrote the mad deeds down, although with fear and
> misgivings, just as our knight performed them, without adding
> or subtracting one atom of truth from the history, or taking
> into account any accusations of lying that might be laid against
> him.[53]

Here we observe an ingenious modification on the simple Ariostean
disclaimer of responsibility; the narrator no longer simply falls
back in assumed helplessness on the authority of the "historical
text," but rather on that of "truth," which the theoretical writing
of the century has consistently admitted to be stranger than fiction,
and on the duty (or freedom) of the historian to record it faithfully. The incongruity of this justification in what is obviously a

[52] ". . . ella [esta vida] anda todo en redondo, digo, a la redonda . . . y así
torna a andarse el tiempo con esta rueda continua" (II, 922). Mia I. Gerhardt (*Don
Quijote: la vie et les livres* [Amsterdam, 1955]) offers an excellent analysis of the
various narrative poses of Cide Hamete Benengeli, but fails to explore the parodistic
allusiveness of his comments to Aristotelian theory, assuming that the author generally shares the criticism of his text which the Moor voices. Thus she interprets
his comments in this scene as illustrative of Cervantes' concern for verisimilitude;
he wants to inform his reader that Don Quixote did in fact either lie or dream
(p. 12).

[53] "Finalmente, aunque con este miedo y recelo, las [las locuras de Don Quijote]
escribió de la misma manera que él las hizo, sin añadir ni quitar a la historia un
átomo de la verdad, sin dársele nada de objeciones que podían ponerle de
mentiroso" (II, 601).

fictional context once again renders absurd the particular theories invoked and underscores the complete control of the narrator—in this case, the ironical Moor—over both his creation and his reader. The point is driven home as the chronicler, faithful to "historical precision," proceeds to write that "Don Quixote retired into the thicket, or oak wood, or forest, beside great El Toboso."[54]

Cide Hamete's assumed role of "historian" and the equivocation implicit in the term (i.e., in the sixteenth century "historians" were both historians according to Aristotle's distinction between poetry and history and historians of *libros de caballerías*, which continued to be entitled as they had been through the Middle Ages, *historias*) are utilized often by Cervantes for a humorous play between the editor, the translator, and the Moorish historian. In the same scene the editor criticizes Cide Hamete's failure to specify whether the three peasant lasses were mounted on three young asses or fillies ("for the author does not tell us which, although it is more credible that they were she-asses, as these are the ordinary mounts of village women") only to retract his criticism ("as nothing much hangs on it, there is no reason to stop and clear up the point").[55] The humor of Cervantes' intrusion is multiform, beginning as a feigned attack on the chronicler for failing to do his duty as historian, but almost immediately turning full circle around to mock those whose excessively pedantic interpretation of verisimilitude would in effect confuse the poet's function with that of the historian. This humorous play is repeated in two later passages in the novel, in which the editor again criticizes the chronicler for failing to mention an "important" fact. In one case it is whether Don Quixote spent the night "among some thick oak or cork trees" ("for on this point Cide Hamete does not observe his usual meticulousness"). In the other, it is whether Don Quixote was leaning against a "beech tree or a cork tree" ("for Cide Hamete Benengeli does not specify what tree it was").[56]

[54] ". . . don Quijote se emboscó en la floresta, encinar o selva junto al gran Toboso" (II, 601).

[55] ". . . que el autor no lo declara, aunque más se puede creer que eran borricas, por ser ordinaria caballería de las aldeanas"; "como no va mucho en esto, no hay para qué detenerse en averiguarlo" (II, 604).

[56] ". . . que en esto no guarda la puntualidad Cide Hamete que en otras cosas suele" (II, 972); ". . . que Cide Hamete Benengeli no distingue el árbol que era" (II, 1032).

On another occasion it is the translator's turn to indulge in this type of literary play. The fifth chapter of the Second Part describes a conversation in which Sancho Panza attempts to convince his wife Teresa of the wisdom of his decision to sally forth with Don Quixote once again. His arguments include rhetorical flourishes and an ingenious piece of casuistry, utilizing remarks he once heard at a sermon and turning unexpectedly into an assertion of one of Cervantes' favorite ethical doctrines—nobility is to be measured by deeds and not ancestry. All this baffles the simple Teresa, who begs her husband, "Don't break my head with your haranguing and fine words."[57] The chapter is introduced by a parenthetical remark, in which the translator expresses the opinion that the chapter is apocryphal "because in it Sancho's style is much superior to what one would expect of his limited understanding, and his remarks are so subtle that he [the translator] believes it is impossible that Sancho could understand them."[58] The text of the chapter is interrupted twice by similar parenthetical observations, both invoking the well-known Aristotelian-Horatian doctrine of decorum to judge the chapter to be apocryphal. In all three intrusions, the translator emphasizes that he is not responsible for the passage and is including it out of a sense of duty as translator. In the acknowledgment of the "impossibility" of the scene and the mischievous reliance on "history," in this case Benengeli's text, Cervantes is again employing Ariosto's favorite trick for asserting his absolute control over his work. What is different in the Spaniard's use of the transparent hoax is that the audience's objection, imaginary, or at the most, implicit in Ariosto's work, appears now in careful formulation, i.e., the doctrine of decorum. It is no overstatement to say that the subtle difference observable explains much in terms of the developments in critical thinking that occurred between 1516 and 1616.

Perhaps the most outright mockery of the restraint which classical theories of decorum would impose upon an artist is made by the editor in commenting on certain chapters that Cide Hamete wrote but failed to include in his history. It is rumored that the Moorish

---

[57] ". . . no me quebréis más la cabeza con vuestras arengas y retóricas" (II, 576).
[58] ". . . porque en él habla Sancho Panza con otro estilo del que se podía prometer de su corto ingenio, y dice cosas tan sutiles, que no tiene por posible que él las supiese" (II, 570).

chronicler composed several chapters on the deep friendship between Rocinante and Sancho's ass but refrained from inserting them "in order to preserve the propriety and decorum proper to so heroic a story" ("por guardar la decencia y decoro que a tan heroica historia se debe" [II, 619]). Again we observe the humorous attribution of contemporary critical concerns and terminology to the evasive Moor. At this point, however, the editor decides to complicate the matter, first stating that at times Cide Hamete forgot this restraint and then inserting a detailed description of the two animals resting placidly in a meadow, which the careless Moor did in fact include. As if the shift were not enough, the editor proceeds to recount to us some details which Cide Hamete did indeed edit out of this particular description, being careful to absolve himself of responsibility for their accuracy by leaning on the authority of those who spread rumors about the missing chapters. The mystifying phrase introducing the digression on animals: "I say that they say that the author left in writing that . . ." ("Digo que dicen que dejó el autor escrito que . . ."), followed by the hyperbolic comparison of the friendship of the ass and Rocinante to that of Nisus and Euryalus and the detailed description of all that men have learned from animals might be described as Ariosto's trick exploited for the ultimate in absurdity and, needless to say, the apex of the spiraling parody calculated to dismiss the serious literary principle of decorum.[59]

At the same time the introduction of the Aristotelian definitions in the humorous interplay between the editor, the translator, and the chronicler can be utilized by Cervantes to reflect on the thematic problems in the surrounding context. In these cases the parodistic treatment of theoretical terminology and questions of authorial freedom and belief becomes a point of departure for thematic concerns of a nonaesthetic nature. Such is the translator's intrusion in the episode of the Caballero del Verde Gabán, in this case not to complain humorously about the chronicler's omission

[59] Decorum in respect to the traditional separation of the styles, the principle which Cervantes here introduces, should be distinguished from decorum in respect to typical behavior and consistency in the portrayal of characters, the theoretical issue in the translator's criticism of Sancho's conversation with Teresa.

of "important historical" details but rather to edit out a passage of description which he regards as unessential in the history of Don Quixote.[60] What initially seems to be no more than a continuation of the humorous badinage based on equivocations in aesthetic terminology and restrictions which literary theory would impose on a narrator becomes a significant thread in the delicate web of irony in which Cervantes envelops Don Diego de Miranda and the way of life he represents. The translator refuses to transcribe as "unsuitable to the principal purpose of this history" Cide Hamete's detailed description of the house of Don Diego. Compounding the irony only suggested by this omission is the passage immediately following, i.e., a passage that he does *not* delete. It is undoubtedly the most detailed description of Don Quixote in the work, a calculated inclusion of all possible minutiae (II, 662-663). Here it is not simply another conscious and impudent reversal on the part of the narrator to assert his freedom from the very restrictions which he seems to be acknowledging. Following immediately on the statement that the details of Don Diego's house are unimportant, the detailed passage has the effect of telling us *what indeed is important*. It is the narrator's most direct hint that the subtle irony we observe in Don Quixote's humorously magnanimous suggestion that Don Diego withdraw from the field of adventure to tend his "quiet decoy partridge" and "bold ferret" is shared by the author. Moreover, it sets a tone for the scenes that follow in Don Diego's house,

[60] Alan S. Trueblood observes the importance of what Cervantes purposely omits in this scene in relation to the ironic treatment of Don Diego de Miranda and goes on to explain the opposition between Cide Hamete and the author-editor as often representing the Aristotelian opposition between historical truth and poetic truth ("Sobre la selección artística en el *Quijote*: '. . . lo que ha dejado de escribir,'" *Nueva Revista de Filología Hispánica* X [1956], 44-50). The conclusion is correct but should be qualified by the observation that the two narrators are constantly in motion in representing poetry and history. Although Cide Hamete is the "historian" and in this passage must indeed be reprimanded by Cervantes the poet, the cases discussed above show that Cervantes was just as willing to allow the Moor in his "historical" text to be truer to poetic truth than the editor, who would occasionally burden his text with the irrelevant details of the historian. Such shifting of roles among the narrative voices is analogous to Don Quixote's shifting from the role of the creating artist in his confrontations with the canon and the humanist to the role of the pedant in the Master Pedro and Clavileño episodes. Again we observe the fluidity that is everywhere apparent in Cervantes' poetic context and the difficulty of the task of the critic, who must render that fluidity meaningful in some static scheme.

as it were, establishing a frame of reference within the literary context, by which we cannot avoid interpreting as ironic the author's famous comparison of the house in its marvelous silence to a *monasterio de cartujos*.[61]

In conclusion, the most important function of the fictitious-authorship device in the *Quixote* resides in the series of commentaries which the editor, the translator, and the "author" make concerning the creation of the novel. The uniformity which marks the tone of these three voices allows us to refer to all of them by the name of the protean figure who dominates this commentary, Cide Hamete Benengeli. The Moorish historian-author repeatedly scrutinizes his creation according to the most fashionable literary theories

[61] Bataillon is right in seeing a parallel between the canon and Diego de Miranda, who in his opinion are the only two important figures in the world of the *Quixote* whose role is simply the expression of ideas (*Erasmo y España*, II, 417). We can assume that the literary theories of the canon are shared by his counterpart, who prefers the *honesto entretenimiento* of historical and religious literature and refuses to allow a romance of chivalry to cross the threshold of his house. Similarly we may infer safely that the canon would approve of the moderation, order, and charity that mark the life of Don Diego. While Bataillon is correct in observing Cervantes' evident sympathy for the ideals embodied in these two figures, he takes the dangerous step of extracting ideas from Cervantes' poetic context and fails to observe the delicate irony pervading the contexts in which they appear. The parallels in Cervantes' use of these figures in fact go beyond those observed by Bataillon. Just as Don Quixote's account of the Knight of the Lake is juxtaposed to the canon's statement of literary ideals, so the adventure of the lions is significantly inserted following Don Diego's description of his life of peace and piety. Admittedly each of these rebuttals is made by a madman and each is to some extent a burlesque of the ideals by which the madman is acting. Nevertheless, as we have shown, Cervantes puts discreet arguments in the mouth of Don Quixote in the former case, and in the latter states as directly as he can his preference for the demented knight to the Caballero del Verde Gabán. Again double-edged parody must be recognized.

It is safer to see Don Quixote's confrontations with the canon and Diego de Miranda as the confrontations of two radically different modes of thinking that pull Cervantes in opposite directions and find resolution only in his irony, which allowed them to coexist as opposites. On the one hand the normative, or classical, encompassing the great rationalist movements of the Renaissance—in natural philosophy, experimental science, in literary thought, the Aristotelian tradition, in ethical thought, Christian humanism—on the other hand, the vitalistic or mythic, exalting the freedom of the individual's creative imagination to deny the relevance of the laws of nature, to disregard the normative modes of reason, and to transmute the external world according to its own internal laws. One of the clearest indications of the tension between the appeals of these modes of thinking in Cervantes is the consistently ambivalent play of his various narrators with what represents the flowering of the Renaissance rationalist tradition in literary matters, the Aristotelian standards of criticism.

of the day, but his introduction of literary principles is always accompanied by mystifications, sophistry, evasions, and equivocations of one sort or another. In the resultant play we witness a consistent parodistic dismissal of the value of the theories invoked, specifically those concerning verisimilitude, decorum, poetic truth, and historical truth.

In large part the position of Cide Hamete concerning literary theory is one of negation. He is articulately aware of an adversary, the Horatian-Aristotelian dogma of the Renaissance, and he continually subjects it to a ridicule, which in its mildness comes from a position of unshaken superiority. To define Cide Hamete Benengeli as a representative of a literary principle is more difficult. However, in one of his commentaries a hint of a positive doctrine can be discerned. Following what is clearly Cervantes' own justification for the inclusion in Part One of the *Curioso impertinente* and the *Capitán cautivo* in terms of the principle of variety, Cide Hamete Benengeli begins his familiar play with Aristotelian literary criteria. He seemingly submits to the classicists' rigid standards of disposition ("In this, the second part, he decided not to insert any tales, either detached or connected, but to include some episodes, something like them, which arise out of the actual happenings themselves, and even these sparingly"). But he then dissolves the serious value of his submission by asking for praise "not for what he writes but for what he has refrained from writing." The pose of submission is immediately followed by the statement: "*He confines and encloses himself within the narrow limits of the narrative, though he has the skill, the capacity, and the intelligence to make the whole universe his subject. . . .*"[62] In the Moor's ironic renunciation before his critics, we hear both a plea for the liberation of the creative artist and an affirmation of the godlike freedom which enabled his creator, Cervantes, to defy the "narrow limits" set by the Aristotelians. In defying those limits, Cervantes broadened the boundaries of

---

[62] ". . . en esta segunda parte no quiso ingerir novelas sueltas ni pegadizas, sino algunos episodios que lo pareciesen, nacidos de los mesmos sucesos que la verdad ofrece, y aun éstos limitadamente"; ". . . no por lo que escribe, sino por lo que ha dejado de escribir"; ". . . y pues *se contiene y cierra en los estrechos límites de la narración, teniendo habilidad, suficiencia y entendimiento para tratar del universo todo . . .*" (II, 849). The italics are mine.

literature to encompass the entire universe—from the airy regions of Clavileño's flight to the fields which witness the frustrations of the amorous Rocinante, from the realm of eternal values which remain untarnished by Don Quixote's inadequacies in imposing them on reality, to the "countless beatings" (*infinitos palos*) which the implacable historian to the dismay of his protagonist will not exclude in the interests of poetic truth. ("'And tell me what is said of me,' said Sancho, 'for they say I'm one of the principal presonages in it'.")[63]

---

[63] "Y de mí—dijo Sancho—; que también dicen que soy yo uno de los principales presonajes della" (II, 561).

PART THREE:
CERVANTES AND THE CLASSICAL AESTHETIC
Persiles y Sigismunda

CHAPTER V

The Critical Examination of
Literary Theory in the *Persiles*

LITERARY THEORY AS A THEME OF THE *PERSILES*

IT IS CLEAR that the Canon of Toledo's plan for the ideal book of chivalry was Cervantes' general formula for the *Persiles*, and it is tempting to believe that the hundred pages which the canon claims to have written and abandoned are Cervantes' first sketch of his final work. Just how far the composition of the *Persiles* can be related to the suggestive literary dialogue is conjectural. Nevertheless, Cervantes' desire to follow the classical rules—unity, verisimilitude, decorum, the legitimized marvelous, rhetorical display, moral edification, and instructive erudition—is everywhere evident in the *Persiles*, both in subject matter and structure and in the various comments of the self-conscious narrator concerning criteria governing his creative and selective processes.

In view of the author's submission to classical theory, the last thing which we would expect to find in the *Persiles* is a continuation of his critical engagement with the neo-Aristotelians. And yet it is there throughout the work, usually as an undertone sustained in a dialogue within the narrative voices, but on two occasions as an undisguised literary debate. It is the dialogue which we have heard before, between the canon and Don Quixote and between their subsequent incarnations in the dramatic situation of narrating artist vs. critical audience. What is more astonishing, however, is that, although the canon would seem to have had his way at last in Cervantes' creation of his prose epic, the literary debates which it contains, like those of the *Quixote*, generally move toward the assertion of an *anticlassical* position on literary theory.

To be sure, the anticlassical spokesmen of Cervantes' final work must face opposition that is far more stubborn than that which Don Quixote, Master Pedro, and Cide Hamete Benengeli overcome in the *Quixote*. In the debates of the *Persiles*, victories are often ambiguous and shift freely from side to side, particularly when they appear in the narrator's commentary. Their ambiguity suggests that

Cervantes himself was caught up between two conflicting views of art and that the untroubled disengagement from classical theory which we observe in the *Quixote* was, in the composition of the *Persiles*, a slow and painful process.

The introduction of problematic aspects of contemporary literary theory and the assertion of an anticlassical point of view on literature bring a double ambivalence to the total context of the *Persiles*. On the one hand the prose epic presents, alongside of the traditional heroic deeds and conflicts, the personal drama of Cervantes as a creative artist in the production of the work. Indeed, if there is any actor or any action of the *Persiles* which is treated "novelistically," it is the personality of its creator and his trials in creating the work.[1] On the other hand, by introducing the anticlassical voice and allowing its triumph, Cervantes appears to be undermining the aesthetic foundations of his work even as he is building upon them.

THE INTERLUDE OF THE COUNTERFEIT CAPTIVES

The episode of the counterfeit captives (*Persiles*, III, x) reveals Cervantes' mastery of the art of the *entremés*. The brief dramatic scene, consisting almost entirely of dialogue, moves rapidly toward a crisis, the moment of potential disaster and highest comic intensity, and concludes with the happy resolution of the crisis. Two former captives in Algiers have become entertainers, wandering through the villages of Spain, reciting the history of their sufferings, and illustrating it with various pictures on a portable canvas. Periandro, Auristela, and their fellow pilgrims arrive in a village and discover that the captives are performing their show. In the audience are the two magistrates of the town, who comment on the performance of the captives. One of the magistrates, who has been a prisoner in Algiers, begins to suspect the veracity of the performers' *historia* and decides to put them to a test, demanding detailed information about Algiers. He quickly catches the youths in the lie, and deter-

---

[1] I do not wish to exaggerate here the similarity of the *Persiles* and the *Quixote*. In spite of the inclusion in the *Persiles* of the drama of its creation and Cervantes' literary debate with the neo-Aristotelians, the differences between the two works are far more important than their similarities. However, I do not agree with M. Singleton that there is in the *Persiles* "casi nada de lo que preocupaba al Cervantes maduro" ("El misterio del 'Persiles,'" p. 240).

mines to punish them severely. They confess that they are in reality students and have abandoned the university of Salamanca to see the world and to follow the paths of glory, serving Spain in the wars in Italy and Flanders.

The dialogue that follows recalls Cervantes' *entremeses* and many humorous scenes of the *Quixote* in exploiting for comic effects equivocation in the understanding of words (e.g., *iniuria—luxuria*), the outspoken aberration of a person who holds himself to be normal, and good comedy of situation (e.g., the confusion of asses and magistrates). As is usually the case in Cervantes' *entremeses*, comic effect serves a serious intention.[2] In the midst of the raillery marking the dialogue, the author allows the students to express one of his most cherished ideals: "There are no better soldiers than those who are transplanted from the seats of learning to the fields of war"[3] and to raise the related problems of justice, mercy, and revenge, each a recurrent concern in Cervantes' writings. The Cervantine principle of justice tempered by mercy does indeed prevail.[4] The magistrates not only pardon the students but vie with one another for the honor of having them as dinner guests. The scene ends humorously as the magistrate who has been in Algiers promises to inform his guests about the details of the city of their "captivity," so that in the future their act will be more convincing and profitable.

Comedy of situation and character, and the beloved themes of *las armas y las letras* and justice, all familiar elements in the writings of Cervantes, give this little scene a particular liveliness and color. Yet there is still another dimension of the episode, which,

---

[2] See L. Pfandl ("Die Zwischenspiele des Cervantes," *Neue Jahrbücher für Wissenschaft und Jugendbildung*, III [1927], 301-323), who judges Cervantes' *entremeses* to represent the high point of the genre.

[3] ". . . no ay mejores soldados que los que se trasplantan de la tierra de los estudios en los campos de la guerra" (II, 107).

[4] The student's admonition: "Los juezes discretos castigan, pero no toman vengança de los delitos; los prudentes y los piadosos mezclan la equiedad con la justicia, y, entre el rigor y la clemencia, dan luz de su buen entendimiento" is the same solution to these problems which Cervantes presents in the equally comic situations of Sancho's tribunal and the *entremés*, *La elección de los alcaldes de Daganzo*. It recalls Don Quixote's advice to his squire: "Cuando pudiere y debiere tener lugar la equidad, no cargues todo el rigor de la ley al delincuente; que no es mejor la fama del juez riguroso que la del compasivo" (II, 841).

171

although partially hidden from the modern reader, is perhaps the author's most important reason for including it in the *Persiles*. In the exchange between the students and the magistrate Cervantes is presenting dramatically the contemporary theories on the creation of the verisimilar plot (the *fingida historia*) and some of the major problems raised by those theories.

In its literary dimension the *entremés* of the counterfeit captives is a recreation of the *retablo* of Master Pedro. In both episodes an itinerant showman whose art and livelihood depend on fraud depicts a traditional type of scene calculated to arouse the empathy of the audience: a demonic otherworld where the forces of evil hold the heroes in bondage. Each scene is to end with the deliverance of the captives from their persecutors, but in each case the intervention of a member of the audience cuts the rescue short. In both scenes Cervantes employs the confrontation of the narrating artist and the critical audience to examine the essential critical problem of verisimilitude and audience belief. As it turns out, Master Pedro discovers that his success in capturing the belief of his audience leads to his ruin. The counterfeit captives, on the other hand, discover that their failure to do the same almost lands them in the galleys. In each case, however, the demands of verisimilitude are stated—whether in the pedantic formulation of Don Quixote or in the singularly nonliterary objection of the magistrate to the lies of the narrator—and *rejected* by the artists.

The allusiveness of the *entremés* to contemporary literary ideas can be observed in many details. In accordance with the current theory of narrative poetry that the poet must "place things before his reader's eyes," the student narrator exhorts his audience to see the events described as present (the repeated *aquí veys* . . .). Moreover, he follows the recommended pattern of disposition, beginning *in medias res* at a low moment in the fortunes of the protagonists, and proceeds to follow the standard precepts for inspiring belief in his story, founding it on a historical situation and inserting various details which are geographically and historically accurate.[5]

[5] Following the exposure of their fraud, the students speak of the "historical research" lying behind their narration, offering a concise statement of the way in which contemporary criticism recommended the poet's use of history as a guarantee

The Turkish galleys that preyed upon Christian coastal cities and ships, the enslaved captives who are depicted rowing in these ships, the dungeon of Tetuan, Algiers as the center of piracy and slavery were all historical realities for the Spaniard of the time. Even the barbarous Dragut, whom the student describes whipping him and his comrades with the severed arm of a Christian, was a known historical personage, and the type of cruelty attributed to him was regarded as plausible. Similar acts of barbarity committed by the Turks are recorded in nonfictional works of the epoch.[6] Similarly the student is following contemporary theory perfectly as he injects a few Turkish words into his account and imitates the diabolic language of the raving Dragut: "... a mi me suena agora el *rospeni*, el *manahora* y el *denimaniyoc* ..." (II, 102).[7]

In its first interruption of the narrator, the critical audience (i.e., the magistrate) offers a favorable judgment of his artistry, acknowledging that his process of "deceiving with the semblance of truth" has been effective: "It seems to me that he is telling the truth, and that his general statements indicate that he is not a counterfeit captive."[8] However, by coincidence the magistrate has witnessed the historical events of the narration ("the feigned history") at first hand and decides to test the narrator "on particulars." The young man defends himself very well in responding to the mayor's probing questions but yields in exasperation when the latter wants to know how many fountains and gates there are in Algiers, confessing shortly thereafter that his history is in fact a lie.

The magistrate's presence at the recitation of the history as well as the stern rebuke (the threat of one hundred lashes and the galleys) which the students suffer at his hands recalls dramatically

---

of plausibility: "... nos informamos de algunas cosas de las de Argel, que nos parecio ser vastantes y necessarias *para acreditar nuestro embeleco*" (II, 105). El Pinciano writes that "mentir con arte es muy dificultoso" (*Philosophía antigua poética*, II, 60) and recommends that poets use historical subject matter, "algunas verdades como rafas" in order to "tener firme la tapiería de sus ficciones" (II, 98).

[6] See Schevill's notes, *Persiles*, II, 308-310.

[7] In praise of Homer, "non sol facitor de' versi, ma di parole," Tasso writes: "Né trasporta solamente i nomi vicini da' vicini, ma i lontani da' lontani, purché adolisca l'auditore e, rempiendolo di stupore, l'incanti con la meraviglia" (*Del poema eroico*, pp. 245-246).

[8] "... parece que va diziendo verdad, y que en lo general no es cautiuo falso" (II, 103).

a conclusion which Tasso reached in his exploration of the difficulties which the composition of a verisimilar plot creates. To inspire belief, the poet must attempt "to persuade that the things treated by him are worthy of belief and authority, and he attempts to gain this opinion and this belief in the minds [of the audience] through the authority of history and through the fame of illustrious names."[9] Tasso qualifies this recommendation of the historical subject by counseling the poet to limit his choice to medieval history. As very little precise information is known about this period, the poet can use his inventive powers for episodic amplification without fear of making a factual error. The theorist goes on to warn of the potential dangers in the choice of subject matter from contemporary history. Such an undertaking as a poem on Charles V would be foolishly audacious and place deadening limitations on the poet's inventive powers. The audience knows too much about the subject and is certain to discover some historical inaccuracies in its literary adaptation. "Men cannot bear being deceived about those things which they know through their own experience or which they have been informed about by the report of their parents or grandparents."[10] Insofar as they utilize historical occurrence and *nomi illustri*, the students observe Tasso's recommendations and are initially successful. However, they neglect his important qualification and by an unfortunate coincidence find themselves to be in a situation dreaded by poets of the neo-Aristotelian school, in the presence of an audience which knows more about their subject than they themselves and will not tolerate being deceived by the poet: "I was a slave in Algiers five years, and I know that you have not said a single thing to show that you were ever there."[11]

[9] ". . . di persuadere che le cose da lui trattate siano degne di fede e d'autorità, e si sforza di guadagnarsi ne gli animi questa opinione e questa credenza con l'autorità dell'istoria e con la fama de' nomi illustri" (*Del poema eroico*, p. 85).

[10] "Non possono soffrire gli uomini d'esser ingannati in quelle cose ch'o per se medesmi sanno, o per certa relazione de' padri e de gli avi ne sono informati" (*Dell'arte poetica*, p. 10). Repeating Tasso's arguments, Cascales recommends historical events which occurred between three hundred and five hundred years in the past, ". . . pues no podrá haver quien con vista de ojos se lo contradiga" (*Tablas poéticas*, p. 134).

[11] "Yo he estado en Argel cinco años esclauo, y se que no me days señas del en ninguna cosa de quantas aueys dicho" (II, 105).

If the magistrate's presence and reaction to the *cose finte* of a work based on a subject from recent history seem to justify the precepts on the selection of subject matter which Tasso offers the epic poet, his insistence on examining the details of the Algiers of the students' narration to discover that it was in fact a feigned city recalls a specific topic of sixteenth-century critical discussions concerning the general problems of verisimilitude and artistic freedom. It was thought that Virgil had modeled his description of Carthage on the Spanish port of Cartagena. The resulting problem caused quite a bit of concern among the theorists and pedants, who felt that such freedom came close to altering known history, a sin which would endanger the credibility of the entire work of a poet, and they at times took pains to justify the alterations of the prince of poets. For example, Tasso exonerated Virgil by drawing a painfully subtle distinction between categories of geography and topography and asserting that Virgil's description of Carthage must be considered in the latter category. If it were geographically important, it would indeed be an error, if only a minor one. But Virgil's intention was merely to create a beautiful port, and, in imitating Cartagena, he achieved his purpose. In case this justification might be considered inadequate, Tasso adds another. If minor aspects of Virgil's description do not correspond to Carthage as we know it, it is nevertheless quite plausible that these aspects in Carthage could have changed since the time of the events described, for, as natural history shows, minor topographical changes are very frequent. Such were the tortuous processes of thought that literary theory of the sixteenth century was forced to undertake in its failure to transcend the traditional suspicion of poetry as falsehood and its consequent empirical-historical interpretation of the Aristotelian notion of verisimilitude.[12] The magistrate's concern for

[12] *Del poema eroico*, pp. 170-171. El Pinciano too must deal with the problem, asserting that it is not impossible that there was in the epoch of the Dido episode a port in Africa similar to Cartagena. He goes on to justify Virgil's error in assuming that there were stags in Africa by claiming that "pudo ser en algún nauío lleuado algunos [cieruos] y auer produzido y criado al tiempo que fué Eneas en aquellas riberas. Y como quiera que sea, queda el precepto de verisimilitud inuiolable" (*Philosophía antigua poética*, II, 77-80). This was the age in which the pedantic Scaliger saw in a geographical error in a poem of Silius a justification for Plato's exile of the poets from the republic (*Poetices libri septem*, p. 289).

fountains and gates is a humorous distortion of a major current of Renaissance critical thought.

The student's rejoinder to the attack of the magistrate is simple, but it recalls words which we have heard before. Yielding finally before his tormentor's question concerning the number of fountains in Algiers, he states simply: "The question is idiotic!" Later he refers to the value of such information as "a childish trifle (*niñería*) not worth three farthings." The youth's retort recalls the words of Master Pedro in response to Don Quixote's concern about the bells of Zaragoza: "Don't worry about childish trifles (*niñerías*)." In a more general way it recalls Don Quixote's ironic play with the canon's notion of verisimilitude, his mockery of the humanist in his concern with literature as a source of facts of "scientific" authority, Cide Hamete's calculated reduction to absurdity of the fashionable notions of the neo-Aristotelian critical movement, and the editor–Cide Hamete interplay ridiculing those who would apply the historian's criteria of truth to the poet's subject. Again we observe the narrator's assertion of the idleness of the restrictions with which the critic would burden him.

Within the scheme of literary problems that overlie the scene, the magistrate's exoneration of the students in the *entremés* is Cervantes' assertion of his independence of the basic tendency of a critical movement that would institutionalize artistic creativity. A final touch of Cervantine humor is observable at the close of the scene, when the magistrate, whose objections to the narrator's story bear the weight of the entire critical movement of the sixteenth century, admits that he cannot read. Like the literary episodes of the *Quixote*, the *entremés* concludes with the neo-Aristotelian in a somewhat ridiculous posture.

The influence of Ariosto on Cervantes is never more apparent than in the various scenes in which his narrators assert their mastery over their subject matter and their listeners. We have observed how the audience, which was so fully at Ariosto's disposal, comes to life in Cervantes' works and assails the narrator with criticisms, subjecting his tale to examination and judgment by the critical standards which evolved in the theoretical writings of the century separating the two writers. However, there is one scene in the *Furioso* which anticipates both the major literary problem of the following years and Cervantes' manner of dealing with it. In tone and detail it is very similar to the episode of the counterfeit captives.

In Canto XLII of *Orlando Furioso* Ariosto, in the manner of Cide Hamete, brings the critical perspective of his audience into his work and allows it to cast doubts on the veracity of an event which he has just related—the battle on the island of Lipadusa. He admits: "Here Federigo Fulgoso is somewhat in doubt whether or not my story is true."[13] Like the magistrate in the *Persiles*, Federigo Fulgoso has actually visited the place where the literary event is set. He has sailed along the Barbary Coast and gone ashore on the island of Lipadusa, the terrain of which he remembers to be so mountainous and unpropitious to chivalric battle that he "does not hold it to be verisimilar that in that mountainous rock six knights, the flower of the world, could do mounted battle."[14] Ariosto seems to acknowledge the validity of the standards of judgment on which the objection is based, for he proceeds to honor it with an explanation. The terrain of Lipadusa is indeed unsatisfactory for horsemanship, but it is only so because an earthquake subsequent to the great battle piled rocks on what had been an ideal field for jousting. The explanation is of course "scientifically possible," but so unlikely that Ariosto's joke is perfectly clear. Like Don Quixote in his explanation of the scientific plausibility of the delivery of Durandarte's heart to Belerma, Ariosto feigns submission to the demands of his skeptical audience in order to ridicule its notion of verisimilitude in literature. Ariosto's response to Federigo Fulgoso is admittedly more articulate than the student's retort to the magistrate, "the question is idiotic," but both amount to the same categorical dismissal of the restrictions on artistic creation of the type formulated by the neo-Aristotelian critical movement, which the two artists, Ariosto and Cervantes, frame chronologically.

The episode of the counterfeit captives is introduced by an important commentary of the discursive narrator of the *Persiles*. It

[13] "Qui de la istoria mia, che non sia vera,/ Federigo Fulgoso è in dubbio alquanto" (*Orlando Furioso*, ed. S. Debenedetti and C. Segre [Bologna, 1960], pp. 1428-1429).

[14] "né verisimil tien, che ne l'alpestre/ scoglio sei cavallieri, il fior del mondo,/ Potesson far quella battaglia equestre."

177

is a brief digression on literary problems and has the dual function of stating the basic aesthetic criteria on which the *Persiles* is founded and of establishing a frame of reference for the interpretation of the ensuing scene. In its latter function it is similar to Cide Hamete Benengeli's commentaries framing the episode of the Cave of Montesinos. To my mind it is one of the most puzzling paragraphs in all Cervantes' writings; hence I record it in its entirety, putting the key words and phrases in italics.

> Long pilgrimages involve various events, and, as variety is composed of different things, it is necessary that their occurrences be different. This is demonstrated well in *this history*, the threads of whose various incidents are broken off and leave us in doubt as to where we should knot them together; because all that happens is not good to be narrated, and may be passed over without being noticed and without worsening *the history*. There are some actions which, because of their greatness, should be passed over in silence, and there are others which, because of their humbleness, should not be told, *although it is one of the merits of history [historical writing] that whatever has been written in it has the relish or seasoning of the truth that goes along with it; which fabulous history [la fábula] does not have*. In it it is necessary to flavor the occurrences with such *preciseness* and correct taste and with such *verisimilitude* that, in spite of its lie, which would clash with the understanding, it produces a true *harmony*.
>
> Profiting then by this truth, I shall say that the beautiful band of pilgrims, pursuing their journey, arrived at a place, *neither very large, nor very small, the name of which I do not remember*.[15]

[15] "Las peregrinaciones largas, siempre traen consigo diuersos acontecimientos; y como la diuersidad se compone de cosas diferentes, es forçoso que los casos lo sean. Bien nos lo muestra *esta historia*, cuyos acontecimientos nos cortan su hilo, poniendonos en duda dónde serà bien anudarle; porque no todas las cosas que suceden son buenas para contadas, y podrian passar sin serlo y sin quedar menoscabada la *historia*: acciones ay que, por grandes, deuen de callarse, y otras que, por baxas, no deuen dezirse, *puesto que es excelencia de la historia que, qualquiera cosa que en ella se escriua, puede passar al sabor de la verdad que trae consigo; lo que no tiene la fabula, a quien conuiene guissar sus acciones con tanta puntuali-*

The first sentences present no great problem. Cervantes alludes to the principle of variety, pointing out the advantages which the journey as a structural basis offers the poet, who would present to his reader *diversos acontecimientos*. The sentence recalls Tasso's praise of Homer's use of the journey for variety: "Therefore because of the diversity of countries described in three journeys and the multitude and novelty of things seen, the variety is necessarily very great."[16] Cervantes offers *esta historia*, i.e., the *Persiles*, as an example of the principle. It is important to observe here that the term *historia* in its first appearance means "story" and has no connotations of historiography. Cervantes proceeds to refer to his control of the complicated dispositional techniques of "raveling" and "unraveling" (*anudar* and *soltar*), which all theorists of the age recommended for the effect of suspense and for which Heliodorus' prose epic was universally recognized as an unsurpassable model.

Although the ideational content of the first sentences is clear, they contain an intentional mystification, which weakens the foundations on which we stand as we judge what follows. In its phrasing and repetition of sounds, the second half of the first sentence appears to introduce the final members of a syllogism (the pairings *cosas-casos* and *diversos-diversidad* are deceptive enough to make us hear the terms of a syllogism) and forces us to consider the first part of the sentence as the major premise. Like Montesinos' syllogism on the size of Durandarte's heart, it is willfully muddled. There is no conceptual link between the major premise and what follows; the terms of the minor premise are identical (i.e., it is a tautology); and the conclusion restates the minor premise in ambiguous wording. The baffling conclusion, which is "illustrated" immediately by the example of the *Persiles* ("bien nos lo muestra esta historia") sets the tone for a more skillful type of sophistry, which begins with the second and third appearance of the term

---

dad y gusto, y con tanta *verissimilitud*, que, ha despecho y pesar de la mentira, que haze dissonancia en el entendimiento, forme vna verdadera *armonia*.

"Aprouechandome, pues, desta verdad, digo que el hermoso esquadron de los peregrinos, prosiguiendo su viage, llegò a vn lugar, *no muy pequeño ni muy grande, de cuyo nombre no me acuerdo*" (II, 100).

[16] "Laonde per la diversità de' paesi descritti in tre peregrinazioni, e per la moltitudine e novità delle cose vedute, grandissima conviene che sia la varietà" (*Del poema eroico*, p. 147). See Riley, p. 124.

179

historia and the introduction of the term *fábula* into the commentary. It is based on the equivocations inherent in aesthetic terminology in the age, specifically on the double meanings of the two widely used terms *fábula* and *historia*.

Sixteenth-century Aristotelian criticism employed freely the term *fábula* to refer to two very different phenomena in literature. On the one hand it was used, as by the Canon of Toledo, as a despective term to refer to literature which abdicated any pretense to verisimilitude. Such literature was justifiable aesthetically only if it was written with ulterior moral purposes, e.g., *fábulas apólogas*, namely the Aesopian Fables. It was adjudged totally reprehensible if its aim was simply the pleasure of the imagination or senses, e.g., the *fábulas milesias* and the romances of chivalry. In the first book of the *Persiles* Cervantes exploits this meaning of the term. Mauricio suspects that the metamorphosis of Rutilio's wolf into a witch was an illusion, and Arnaldo adds: "The same must be true of what the fables [*las fábulas*] tell of the transformation of King Arthur of England into a crow, a thing so much believed by that wise nation that no one will kill a crow throughout the island."[17] On the other hand *fábula* was employed in the Aristotelian literary system as the "soul" of the poem, the plot. Here far from being a pejorative term it was a critical rubric of the highest importance, one discussed by all theorists, whose admitted intention was the determination of how the artist was to construct his *fábula* properly.[18]

[17] ". . . y lo mismo deue de ser lo que las fabulas cuentan de la conuersion en cueruo del rey Artus, de Inglaterra, tan creyda de aquella discreta nacion, que se abstienen de matar cueruos en toda la isla" (I, 118).

[18] ". . . la ánima de la poesía es la fábula, lo qual Aristóteles dize . . ." (El Pinciano, *Philosophía antigua poética*, I, 204). ". . . digo que la fábula es imitación de la obra. Imitación ha de ser, porque las ficiones que no tienen imitación y verisimilitud, no son fábulas sino disparates, como algunas de las que antiguamente llamaron Milesias, agora libros de cauallerías" (II, 8). How curious that a few pages further on in his tract El Pinciano can observe: "Ay tres maneras de fábulas, vnas que todas son fición pura, de manera que fundamento y fábrica todo es imaginación, tales son las Milesias y libros de cauallerías" (II, 12) (the other two are the moral fable [e.g., Esopo] and the fable founded on truth and verisimilitude, the latter consisting of main plot and episode [see II, 14])! In Tasso we observe the same flexibility in the usage of the term: after the poet has chosen an adequate subject (i.e., of grandeur and verisimilitude), he gives it the form of an epic plot. Thus it becomes the *favola*, which is the "forma e anima del poema; e tale è da Aristotle giudicata." Tasso proceeds to give precepts to "formare la testura della

The term *historia* was employed with a similar flexibility in the sixteenth century. On the one hand it continued to be used, as in the previous century, to designate a work of narrative fiction (i.e., a "story"), in prose or verse, whether the patently false accounts of the knights-errant or the verisimilar narrations in accordance with the rules (i.e., Amyot's *historia disfrazada* and Don Quixote's *historia fingida* [II, 1000]).[19] On the other hand the term was employed to refer to a work of historiography, the type of work which Diego Gracián de Alderete opposed to the false histories of the romances. Aristotle's influential distinction between poetry and history did much to dissociate this use of the term from its firmly established literary usage, and the Renaissance neo-Aristotelian critics were much more careful to avoid a confusion in their use of the term *historia* than in their use of the term *fábula*, consistently avoiding its literary usage.[20]

Cervantes can use the term *historia* seriously to refer to a work

favola" (*Dell'arte poetico*, p. 14). Nevertheless, he can refer to *le favole* of Apuleius, in which "il poeta vuol solo piacere a gli orecchi e fa quasi professione di falsità e di bugia" (*Del poema erocio*, pp. 83-84), and the "bellissima favola e la dottissima allegoria del ramo d'oro" (p. 94). Carvallo is more consistent in using the term, failing to employ it in describing the verisimilar plot. He distinguishes two types of fiction—"verisimiles y fabulosas." The latter "se bueluen a diuidir . . . en fabulas visibles, y corporeas, como son las de Hisopo" and "fabulas intelectuales," by which Carvallo means simple allegory, i.e., figures of abstract ideas (I, 80-83).

[19] See Wardropper, "*Don Quixote*: Story or History?" 1-11. It should be pointed out that the usage of *historia* to designate books of chivalry was more deeply entrenched in Spain than in France and Italy; for the term "romance," which in France and Italy had always provided an alternative designation and which was to gain full acceptance following the humanist historians and Aristotelians' opposition to the free use of the term *historia* in the sixteenth century, had come to refer specifically to the ballad in the fifteenth century and was hence excluded as a possibility to replace *historia*. At the same time *novela* was an Italianism, a pejorative term, associated with the short story in the ribald tradition of Boccaccio and offered no alternative. It was not until the seventeenth century, in moralizing attacks on literature, that "novela" came to acquire the broader meaning of "prose narrative." Thus *historia* as meaning a "long fictional work," generally in prose, but possibly in verse, survived in Spain throughout the sixteenth century (see Werner Krauss, "Novela-Novella-Roman," in *Gesammelte Aufsätze*, pp. 50-67).

[20] However, Carvallo's tract indicates that the traditional literary usage of the term *historia* did indeed survive in the context of literary theorizing. Although he appropriates various notions and terms from the neo-Aristotelians, this theorist cannot be considered an Aristotelian in his fundamental didactic and allegorizing approach to literature. Unlike Tasso and El Pinciano, he uses *historia* in the traditional, non-Aristotelian way, claiming that in *historias* ". . . se vsa contar algunas fictiones en estylo historico." He refers to Ariosto's *Orlando Furioso* and the *Aeneid* as *historias* (*Cisne de Apolo*, II, 40-41).

of fiction, entitling his last work *Historia septentrional* and having Don Quixote voice the formula for the verisimilar plot: "Feigned histories are only good and pleasing insofar as they adhere to truth or the appearance of truth."[21] At the same time he can exploit the other range of meaning of the term (i.e., its allusiveness to Aristotle's distinction between poetry and history) for humorous equivocation at the expense of the reader and the Aristotelian literary critics. As has been pointed out above, Cide Hamete Benengeli's favorite hoax is based on this allusiveness.[22]

To return to the introduction to the episode of the counterfeit captives, it is clear that the narrator employs *fábula*, in the Aristotelian sense, as meaning the "soul of the work," the verisimilar plot. Cervantes presents here in a discursive way what the following *entremés* presents dramatically—the formula for the creation of the verisimilar plot, or, in other words, the formula for the *Persiles* itself. His definition of *fábula* is perfectly in accord with that of the theorists: "In it [*la fábula*] it is necessary to flavor the occurrences with such preciseness and correct taste and with such verisimilitude that, in spite of its lie, which would clash with the understanding, it produces a true harmony." In every detail this definition echoes the principles of the Canon of Toledo: the poet must lie with such skill that the lie appears to be truth to his reasoning audience. For the rational powers of the soul will regard an implausibility as a failure in proportion and will be unable to experience pleasure in contemplating it ("The mendacious plots of fiction [*las fábulas mentirosas*] should be wedded to the understanding of the readers . . .").

We can infer that the episode which immediately follows is intended as an illustration of this definition. Both the transitional phrase introducing the recital of the student rogues ("Profiting then by this truth, I shall say that . . ."), the literary implications of the dramatic scene, and the mayor's desire to give the student some lessons in the composition of his *fingida historia* make the connection between preface and episode perfectly clear. It is probable that Cervantes conceived the *entremés*, just as he had con-

[21] ". . . las historias fingidas tanto tienen de buenas y de deleitables cuanto se llegan a la verdad o la semejanza della" (II, 1000).
[22] See also *Don Quijote*, I, xxv; II, iii.

ceived the entire *Persiles,* as a vindication of the Aristotelian aesthetic principles. In its general plan it does indeed support these
principles—the students fail in their attempt to construct a plausible
fábula simply because they cannot "flavor its occurrences with such
preciseness," and they are pardoned with the simple admonition to
continue their efforts, paying more attention to verisimilitude.
Nevertheless, as we have discovered, Cervantes cannot grant the
Aristotelians the final word, and in the student's retort to the
pedantic mayor, he allows his desire for artistic liberation to assert
itself. This aspect of the *entremés* is also reflected in the discursive
introduction, for the movement toward the unequivocal definition
of the verisimilar plot generates a countermovement toward humorous deflation of the entire context. In effect Cervantes turns on
himself just as Don Quixote turns on the Canon of Toledo and the
various surrogates of the creating artist in the *Quixote* turn on
their critical antagonists.

The effectiveness of the countermovement, which originates in
the muddled syllogism of the first sentence, hinges on the potential
equivocation in the term *historia.* In his first two references to the
term the narrator means the *historia fingida,* or in other words, the
verisimilar *fábula,* which is exemplified by the *Persiles* and which
he will define more precisely in the sentences which follow. Indeed
his comments on his selective processes ("There are some actions
which, because of their greatness, should be passed over in silence,
and there are others which, because of their humbleness, should
not be told") recall the standard precepts of the Aristotelians for
the construction of the ideal plot. The poet should avoid writing
about events and people of such fame that his audience will already
know them in detail. Describing them, he will find his powers of
arousing *admiratio* and his license to invent or modify details severely limited.[23] At the same time in accordance with the lofty aims of
epic poetry he must avoid *acciones baxas.*[24]

[23] ". . . l'azioni di Carlo sono state così grandi e così laudevoli, anzi così meravigliose c'hanno più tosto tolta che data a' poeti l'occasione d'accrescerle" (*Del
poema eroico,* p. 99). The precept may also allude to Tasso's admonition that the
poet avoid sacred history as his subject; for he dare not use his inventive powers
with such sacrosanct matter (*Dell'arte poetica,* p. 9).

[24] ". . . lasci da parte le necessarie, come il mangiare e l'apparecchiar le vivande
. . . Sdegni ancora il nostro poeta tutte le cose basse . . ." (Tasso, *Del poema eroico,*
p. 112). The passage here recalls Don Quixote's appeal for "poetic truth" in the

At this point the narrator inserts a short clause which violently obstructs the straightforward development of the passage: "although it is one of the merits of history that whatever is written in it has the relish or seasoning of the truth that goes along with it."[25] Here we experience a jarring change in perspective. *Historia* is no longer employed in its traditional literary sense as the equivalent of *fábula*, but is suddenly viewed as the polar opposite of *fábula*. For Cervantes suddenly uses the term in its Aristotelian sense as meaning historiography as opposed to poetry.[26] Furthermore, as the narrator jumps from one potential meaning to the other with no mediating explanation, the *Persiles* itself suddenly appears as *real history* as opposed to *historia fingida* or *fábula*, which the narrator proceeds to define. It remains perfectly clear to the reader, however, that the *Persiles* is not the history which Aristotle distinguishes from poetry, and that, in presenting it as such, the generally sober narrator of the *Persiles* has introduced Cide Hamete's favorite hoax into his narration. Offering, as he does, the *Persiles* in its metamorphosis from *historia*-fiction into *historia*-historiography, as a foil for his definition of *fábula*, the narrator's commentary concludes with a curious piece of nonsense: an artistically constructed *fábula* (the *Persiles* as *historia fingida* or verisimilar fiction) is momentarily considered to be *historia*-historiography and presented as the antithesis of an artistically constructed *fábula*.

---

famous literary colloquy of II, iii. He wishes that his historian had left out certain *cosas bajas*—the *infinitos palos*. ". . . las acciones que ni mudan ni alteran la verdad de la *historia* no hay para qué escribirlas, si han de redundar en menosprecio del señor de la *historia*. A fee que no fué tan piadoso Eneas como Virgilio le pinta. . ." (II, 560). Sansón Carrasco promptly informs him that his historian is a historian according to Aristotle's definition and not according to the commonly accepted equation of *poeta* and *historiador* which Don Quixote was echoing.

[25] If this clause were omitted, the ambiguity of the passage would be insignificant. The minor mystifications—the muddled syllogism and the forgetfulness of the narrator as to the name of the village—would be insufficient to counteract the serious statement of aesthetic doctrine.

[26] Cervantes' figure of speech, which he develops in his definition of *fábula* that immediately follows (i.e., the poet must *guissar sus acciones* with verisimilitude), recalls El Pinciano's discussion of Aristotle's distinction between history and poetry: ". . . el poeta escriue lo que inuenta y el historiador se lo halla guisado" (*Philosophía antigua poética*, II, 11). The poet must *guissar*, but his product, the *fábula*, must be verisimilar.

What makes this passage ultimately ambiguous is its failure at this point to break down in a humorous play as do all similar passages in the *Quixote*. The irony of Cide Hamete Benengeli's favorite equivocation is not exploited further by the narrator. Instead it is stifled as he expresses his definition of Aristotelian *fábula* in all seriousness.[27] The passage produces not the effect of clearly developed parody but rather of ambiguity or confusion in terminology. It would appear that the movement of the passage reflects an inner dialogue within the narrator, which parallels that enacted in the dramatic episode which it introduces as well as that lying behind all Cervantes' scenes in which the creating artist confronts a critical audience. However, in the case of the narrator of the *Persiles*, who is always conscious of the generic principles on which the epic in prose is based, the voice of classicism has the final say. Seen another way, the movement of the passage represents a silencing of the voice of Cide Hamete Benengeli, which the narrator cannot fully control, by the Canon of Toledo.[28]

At the close of the dramatic episode of the counterfeit captives Cervantes deliberately establishes the link, suggested by the narrator's prefatory commentary, between his epic in prose and the ideal *fábula* which the students attempt to create. The magistrate asks the pilgrims: "Do you bring with you a picture to show us, do you bring another history to relate and make us believe it true, al-

[27] It could be argued that the play with the term *historia*, which precedes the definition of the term *fábula*, does in fact dissolve the foundation of the reader's base of observation to such an extent that he cannot accept the definition as unequivocal. In other words, although Cervantes does not explicitly exploit the potential equivocation in the term *fábula* as he does in the term *historia*, the shock effect of the double meaning of *historia* predisposes the reader to suspect the "other" connotations of *fábula*, i.e., as meaning "absurdly inverisimilar fiction." Tieck's words on the elusiveness of Cervantes' parody are very applicable to this puzzling passage: ". . . man fast nirgend mit Sicherheit angeben kann, ob man deutlich sieht, oder nur geblendet ist" (cited by Brüggemann, *Cervantes und die Figur des Don Quijote*, p. 53).

[28] The silencing of Cide Hamete Benengeli (i.e., the refusal to develop the parody) is not entirely successful; for, immediately following the statement that the poet must *guissar sus acciones con tanta puntualidad* and verisimilitude, the narrator turns about to flout his own principle in introducing the episode which would illustrate it. In words familiar to everybody he writes: ". . . el hermoso esquadron de los peregrinos, prosiguiendo su viage, llegò a un lugar, *no muy pequeño ni muy grande, de cuyo nombre no me acuerdo*."

though falsehood herself may have composed it?"[29] Even if we have forgotten that Periandro has commissioned an artist in Lisbon to create such a picture to record the memorable exploits of the pilgrims in the northern part of the world, we cannot fail to overlook the obvious parallel Cervantes is drawing. Actually the parallels between the students' narration and the *Persiles* go beyond those which Cervantes points out. For the ambivalence in the resolution of the aesthetic problem posed here underlies the whole work. The student's answer, "the question is idiotic," springs from the depths of Cervantes' artistic consciousness and may be more articulate than the author would have liked to admit.[30]

[29] ". . . traeys algun lienço que enseñarnos, traeys otra historia que hazernos creer por verdadera, aunque la aya compuesto la misma mentira?" (II, 109).

[30] The ambiguity of Cervantes' literary intentions in this miniature analogue of the *Persiles* is heightened by the fact that, although they seem to be following the classicists' formulas for plausibility, the students cannot resist sounding a note of literary parody, which is always at one level the willful destruction of any illusion of reality in a literary context. The student's unexpected comment: "Este baxel que aqui veys reduzido a pequeño, porque lo pide assi la pintura, es vna galeota de ventidos bancos" (II, 102), has the effect of bringing the perspective of objectivity into his narration, suddenly confronting the audience with the contrast between the fictional quality of his work and actuality. The type of humor produced by the shift in perspective is employed by all Cervantes' surrogate poets; it is observable, for example, in Don Quixote's unexpected introduction of toothpicks into the world of his fantasy and in Master Pedro's concern to describe Melisendra dangling by her skirts. It is more striking in the present case in that the students are very preoccupied with verisimilitude and the other classical rules. This consistent use of the *Verfremdungseffekt* suggests that Cervantes is not simply employing his participating narrators negatively, as spokesmen for critical answers to the theories formulated by the neo-Aristotelians, but indeed is endowing them for brief moments with his own awareness of the paradoxical joy in the contemplation of the tension between the realms of actuality and the fantastic, with his own "romantic irony."

CHAPTER VI

Periandro's Narration

THE HERO AS POET

THE LONG NARRATION of Periandro to his fellow wanderers and his hosts, assembled in the palace of King Policarpo (*Persiles*, II, x-xx), is Cervantes' most significant use of the dramatic situation of the narrating author vs. the critical audience to examine the literary problems which preoccupied him throughout his career as a creative artist. It is important to recognize at the outset the function of the account in relation to various aesthetic demands of the genre to which the *Persiles* belongs: its structural necessity in the *in-medias-res* scheme of disposition,[1] its exaltation of the protagonist in accordance with the Renaissance conception of the ideal hero, its introduction of marvelous episodes for the arousal of *admiratio*, and its wealth of literary reminiscences from the tradition of heroic literature.

The extremely literary quality of Periandro's narration serves as a convenient point of departure for a consideration of the account in its peculiar, nongeneric dimension, for the series of conscious evocations of themes from the tradition of epic and romance literature has a broader function than simply adding marvelous subject matter to the *Persiles* and associating the epic in prose and its hero with illustrious literary models. Unlike his literary forbears—Odysseus, Aeneas, and Calasiris—Periandro is not only an epic hero but also an epic poet as he relates the story of his wanderings and sufferings. Similarly his audience is not the anonymous group at the courts of Alcinous and Dido, which we can assume listens to the recitation of the hero in sympathy and wonderment. Periandro faces an audience which includes both those who are willing to listen passively and enjoy his account and those who are preoccupied by literary concerns and do not hesitate to reflect critically on the

---

[1] It is the method by which the poet reveals what lies behind the *in-medias-res* beginning. In Chapter II I pointed out how El Pinciano frequently praises the disposition of the *Odyssey*, the *Aeneid*, and the *Aethiopica*, underscoring the structural importance of the narrations of Odysseus, Aeneas, and Calasiris. El Pinciano refers to Calasiris' account as a delayed prologue. In its structural necessity in the *Persiles* Periandro's narration is analogous to those of these ancient figures.

literary qualities of his narration.[2] Once again we observe the dramatic situation which we have followed through the *Quixote*, as the narration of the creating artist is punctuated by the interruptions of his critical audience.

Periandro's use of the terminology of formal rhetoric reveals immediately his consciousness of the literary quality of his narration: "Since you desire, sirs, that I relate to you my history, I wish that its preamble and beginning be this: that you contemplate my sister and me. . . ."[3] Moreover, these opening words recall specifically two methods employed by Cervantes' other surrogate poets. There is the same use of incantatory anaphora and rhythm which marks Don Quixote's conjurative description of the underworld in his rejoinder to the canon (the eight words beginning with *qu* or *c* and the pairing of the synonymous *esdrújulos*—*preámbulo* and *principio*).[4] Periandro will occasionally return to these incantatory linguistic patterns in the course of his narration. Moreover, Periandro asks the ladies and gentlemen of his audience to see as real the subjects which he describes (*que nos contempleys*). Throughout his account the hero will repeat the exhortation: "Veys me aqui, señores que me estays escuchando hecho pescador" (I, 251). "Contemplad, señores, a mis marineros" (I, 265); "Volued, señores,

[2] It should be pointed out that throughout Book I various characters are called on to narrate their *historias*, and Cervantes is concerned to describe the reaction of their audience to their tales and style of presentation (see I, 84, 88, 91, 108). Moreover, both the storytellers and their audience usually reveal a rhetorical consciousness and occasionally allude to the fundamental aesthetic criteria which come under examination in Periandro's narration. Thus the audience reminds Antonio of the dangers in narrating too much (I, 45). Rutilio recognizes both the problem of verisimilitude (I, 54) and that of unity (I, 57, 62). Although there is no critical examination of literary theory in these scenes and the classical principles are implicitly accepted by audience and narrator, we observe in them the germs for the development that occurs in Periandro's narration in Book II and in the episode of the counterfeit captives of Book III.

[3] "El principio y preambulo de mi historia, ya que quereys, señores, que os la cuente, quiero que sea este: que nos contempleys a mi hermana y a mi, . . ." (I, 225) It is well to observe that throughout Periandro's narration there are none of the equivocations in the use of the term *historia* which Cide Hamete finds so convenient in the *Quixote* and which the narrator of the *Persiles* employs in introducing the episode of the counterfeit captives. There are no implications of Aristotle's distinction in the background; the term means simply "story."

[4] Although *principio* is not, strictly speaking, an *esdrújulo*, it can be metrically equivalent to *preámbulo*.

los ojos, y hazed cuenta que veys salir del coraçon de vna peña" (I, 276). In these cases we observe the narrator following the recommendations of contemporary literary theorists that the poet infuse into his narration that *energia* which provokes the audience to see as present whatever he describes.

As Periandro proceeds with his narration, other details appear which are important in strengthening the identification of the hero with the poet. Describing the eagerness of the most appreciative member of Periandro's audience to hear the tale, Cervantes associates his hero with Hercules, a symbol of eloquence well-known in the age ("... the beautiful Sinforosa, hanging upon his words, as if in the chains which came from the mouth of Hercules").[5] The hero describes his sensations as he prepared to persuade the fishermen to abandon their plows for the lance and to follow him to a life of adventure in an oration rich in many of the rhetorical flourishes that the handbooks of classical oratory recommend: "A certain spirit entered my breast, which, without changing my being, yet made me feel as if I were more than a man." The allusion is to the traditional divine fury which takes possession of the poet, at once compelling him to speak with the words of the gods.[6]

Moreover, Periandro embellishes his narration with many of the rhetorical devices which contemporary literary theorists recommended in their discussions of *elocutio* and on two occasions draws praise from members of his audience for the elegance (*donaire*)

---

[5] "... la bella Sinforosa, estando pendiente de sus palabras como con las cadenas que salian de la boca de Hercules ..." (I, 244). For the meaning of the myth in contemporary interpretations (e.g., Cartari, Alciati), see Schevill's note to this passage (I, 345). It is not surprising that we discover the myth in the episode of Master Pedro's *retablo*, where Cervantes again presents a figure of the poet: "... pendientes estaban todos los que el retablo miraban, de la boca del declarador de sus maravillas" (II, 729).

[6] "... vn cierto espiritu se entrò entonces en mi pecho, que, sin mudarme el ser, me parecio que le tenia mas que de hombre" (I, 248-249). "... en bano procura ser Poeta, el que no saliere de si, esto es el ordinario juyzio, y no se leuantare a otro mas alto juyzio, y no se trasportare en otro mas delicado seso del que antes tenia, sacandole este furor como de si, y transformandole en otro mas noble sutil, y delicado pensamiento, eleuandose y embelesandose en el, de tal suerte, que pueda dezir, que esta fuera de si, y no sabe de si ..." (Carvallo, *Cisne de Apolo*, II, 192-193). The theme of the divine fury, originally formulated in Plato's *Ion* and *Phaedrus*, was one of the popular topics of sixteenth-century critical discussion (see Leo, *Torquato Tasso*, pp. 88-90).

of his style (I, 238, 244). For example, he employs the traditional Homeric simile as Tasso had recommended, as a method of including unusual information in his poem and producing the effect of *admiratio*. As the rowers await the signal for the beginning of the boat race, Periandro states that they are "spirited and impatient at the delay, just as is the generous hound of Ireland when his master refuses to release him from the cord to run down the prey which he has just spied."[7] At the same time he cannot suppress an impulse to parody, which he shares with all other of Cervantes' surrogate poets, and occasionally undercuts his own rhetoric. For example, he mixes the terms of an epic simile in a striking antithesis that draws attention to the artificiality of the figure, i.e., to the inadequacy or limitations of the analogy on which it is based: "The thieves, who like hungry wolves, attacked the flock of innocent sheep, and carried off, if not in their mouths, yet in their arms, my sister Auristela."[8]

There is another important aspect of Periandro's narrative style, which associates him not with the poet in general, but with a specific poet—Ariosto. In Periandro's opening statement we hear the familiar words "I want it to be" ("quiero que sea"), which suggest that we are confronted with the voice of a narrator who in

[7] ". . . impacientes por la tardança, y fogosos, bien ansi como lo suele estar el generoso can de Irlanda, quando su dueño no le quiere soltar de la traylla a hazer la presa que a la vista se le muestra" (I, 234).

It is not my purpose to catalogue the various rhetorical figures employed by Periandro in his analogic process of poetic creation. A few examples will suffice to indicate his rhetorical consciousness: prosopopoeia: ". . . parecio que la tierra se quiso auentajar al mar, y el mar a la tierra en ofrecer la vna sus carnes y la otra sus pescados" (I, 230); a synecdoche which turns into an extravagant metaphor: "Despojad essos arboles [masts of a ship] de tan mal fruto [the cadavers of the treacherous crewmen whom Sulpicia has slain]" (I, 269); antithesis and hyperbole: "La fiesta de mis pescadores, tan regozijada como pobre, excedio a las de los triunfos romanos" (I, 244). One of Periandro's favorite devices is a type of word-play (zeugma), based on the insertion of a word into a context which employs simultaneously its figurative and literal expressive value, provoking an unexpected shift from one level of meaning to another: ". . . hizo muestra de aquel tesoro a los ojos de mis pescadores, cuyo resplandor, quiça, y aun sin quiça, cego en algunos la intencion que de ser liberales tenian" (I, 269); ". . . como mi ventura andaua siempre en los ayres, vno de tierra soplò, y hizo apartar el nauio" (I, 248).

[8] ". . . los ladrones, los quales como hambrientos lobos, arremetieron al rebaño de las simples ouejas, y se lleuaron, si no en la boca, en los braços, a mi hermana Auristela" (I, 245).

the tradition of Ariosto is careful to establish his presence in his work and to reveal his firm control of both his creation, the *historia*, and his reader. The intrusive voice of the narrator reflecting both on the events of his narration and on his manner of composition continues to sound in Periandro's account with the result that the subject of the narration includes not only the events and deeds of the protagonist but also the process of epic composition. His commentaries on the events of the *historia* range from the brief Homeric generality on the ways of the world: "But the way in which things turn out is different from what one would imagine" and "as the fortunes of mortals for the most part hang suspended on delicate threads which are easily snapped and destroyed by inconstancy"[9] to an explanation of the specific moral to be drawn from one of the events described (I, 244), to a long, moralizing reflection on his present state of happiness, which serves as a preface to one of the episodes of his narration (I, 295). In the last example we observe the type of authorial intrusion which Ariosto employed in the introduction of many of his individual cantos.[10]

In those commentaries of Periandro suggesting his rhetorical self-consciousness, the voice of Ariosto is more clearly discernible, as for example, in the "quiero que sea" of the opening passage, in which he deliberately reveals his control of his narration.[11] His words announcing the abrupt fragmentations of his episodes recall Ariosto's technique ("I request of you, gentlemen, that we leave the matter at this point, for tonight I shall conclude it"),[12] particularly when he makes such pronouncements in the humorous pose of helplessness before the demands of his "independent" subject matter:

[9] "Pero son diferentes los fines y acontecimientos de las cosas de aquello que se imagina" (I, 235); "como las venturas humanas esten por la mayor parte pendientes de hilos delgados, y los de la mudança facilmente se quiebran y desbaratan" (I, 244).

[10] Pigna refers to the preface with a moral as a characteristic of the genre of romance, likening its effect to that of the chorus in a Greek tragedy (*I romanzi*, p. 46).

[11] See, for example ". . . e *vo' narrarne* inanti/ Che di Rinaldo e di Gradasso io canti" (*Orlando Furioso*, XXXII; cited by Durling, p. 115). To be recalled are Don Quixote's rhetorical concerns in his narration of the adventure of the Knight of the Lake and Cide Hamete's constant discussion of the composition of his work.

[12] ". . . os ruego, señores, dexemos estos en este punto, que esta noche le dare fin" (I, 237).

191

"I take my leave of you for the present, as the second exploit forces me to rest in order then to take it up."[13]

If Periandro's own words describing his processes of composition associate him with the poet Ariosto, the narrator of the *Persiles* reinforces the association. In describing the narrative methods of his hero, he employs the terms which Ariosto himself had constantly used to describe his complicated manner of composition and which sixteenth-century theorists, deriving the same metaphor from Aristotle's *Poetics*, consistently employed in dealing with the topic of the disposition of the plot: the narrative thread, the knot of complication, and the skillfully interwoven fabric of the successful work of art: "Periandro repeated some of the words which he had pronounced earlier so that he could catch up the thread of his history in an orderly way" and "he again picked up the thread of his adventures."[14] Moreover, at one point in his narration, one of the critical members of his audience reacts to the skillful *anudar y soltar* (the "tying" and "unraveling" of the knots of the narrative) with the pleasures of suspense and surprise, which theorists associated with the technique when perfected, and praises Periandro for his skill in "linking up the chain" of his "splendid history."[15]

[13] ". . . yo me despido agora, porque la segunda hazaña me fuerça a descansar para entrar en ella" (I, 263).
[14] ". . . voluio Periandro a repetir algunas palabras antes dichas para que viniesse con concierto a anudar el hilo de su historia" (I, 243); "Los [sus sucessos] voluio anudar" (I, 244). "Di molte fila esser bisogno parme/ A condur la gran tela ch' io lavoro" (XIII, cited by Durling, p. 118). It should be pointed out that, while the theorists used the same terminology, they never suggested that the poet make the act of composition one of his themes. In doing so, Cervantes is far closer to Ariosto, than to either the theorists, who wrote so much in elaborating on the implications of the *tela*, or his acknowledged model, which was held to be a model for techniques of *atar* and *soltar*—Heliodorus' *Ethiopian History*.
[15] Rutilio's exclamation: "¡Valame Dios . . . y por que rodeos y con que eslabones se viene a engarçar la peregrina historia tuya, o Periandro!" (I, 284), is one of the clearest examples of the way in which literary theory becomes dramatized in Periandro's narration. The analogy of the chain was second only to that of the fabric in theoretical discussions of plot (according to Giraldi Cintio in the perfect plot the poet "si ha preso a dire con continuo filo e continua catena . . ." [*De' romanzi*, p. 30]; similarly Pigna writes [*I romanzi*, p. 42] that episodes must be *concatenati* with the *favola* or main plot). Rutilio's admiration is occasioned by Periandro's mastery of the highly recommended *in-medias-res* technique of disposition and recalls one of the theorists' specific arguments for its use, that based on the pleasures of witnessing the *difficulté vaincue* (see Pigna's statement of this argument above, Chap. I).

Like his allusions to his manner of composing his tale, Periandro's unceasing interest in the audience's reaction to his narration reveals the rhetorical awareness of the poet. His most frequent concern is with the credibility of his subject matter, but such concern, like that of Ariosto, is no more than a rhetorical pose, which he assumes in order to mock criticism which would point to its incredibility. When the *muchos y extraños sucessos* of his wanderings seem to reach beyond the outer limits of the possible, he acknowledges their incredibility and asks the audience to believe as an act of courtesy: "A strange thing, and one which demands that your courtesy help to give it accreditation!" and "For what I am now to narrate, no intelligence could grasp it, indeed there is no courtesy which could accept it as truth."[16]

Periandro's concern for the way in which his audience responds to his tale provides a key to an understanding of the most important dimension of his narration—its use of literature. On the one hand, his introduction of many episodes of an unmistakable literary derivation is but one more factor reinforcing the identification of the hero with the poet in the scenes under examination. As is well known, Renaissance rhetorical and literary theory accorded to the imitation of the classics an important role in the education of the artist and in his actual creations. Thus Periandro is following contemporary precepts as he describes in brilliant detail the figure of the warrior maiden Sulpicia, whom the Renaissance audience could not fail to associate with such classical figures as Hippolyte, Penthesilea, and Camilla and their modern descendants, Ariosto's Bradamante and Tasso's Clorinda.[17] Similarly Periandro appears

[16] "¡Caso estraño, y que ha menester que la cortesia ayude a darle credito!" (I, 251); ". . . a lo que resta por dezir, falta entendimiento que lo perciba, y aun cortesias que lo crean" (I, 276).

[17] For the literary tradition of the warrior maiden, see Gilbert Highet, *The Classical Tradition* (Oxford, 1949), p. 155. Like other literary topics of Periandro's narration the warrior maiden had become a common subject of critical discussion in the age and had been drawn into the sphere of Aristotelian-Horatian theories and terminology. The problem which the topic raised was the plausibility or decorum of such a figure. Generally the figure was determined to be unsuitable according to modern standards of decorum (see Minturno, *L'arte poetica*, pp. 49-50; El Pinciano, *Philosophía antigua poética*, II, 76; the Canon of Toledo seems to share this view, mentioning as one of the "disparatados casos" of the romances "tantas mujeres valientes" [I, 494]). As I shall point out in the examination of

to have literary models in mind in his description of Sulpicia's nocturnal slaughter of her servants, who lie in drunken slumber, a description which in its gruesome wine-blood antithesis would recall the similar scenes of carnage which Nisus and Euryalus and their modern descendants, Medoro and Cloridano, wreaked in the slumbering ranks of their enemies.[18]

On the other hand, such literary reminiscences have a function beyond that of adding splendor to the poet's narration and marvelous notes to the total context of the *Persiles*. Periandro as epic poet is reciting to an audience of highly critical sensibilities. In addition to the ladies, who listen with pleasure and unquestioning faith in the truth of what the narrator recounts, there are the implacable neo-Aristotelians, led by the Renaissance scientist and magician, Mauricio, who do not hesitate to measure Periandro's poetic creation by their critical standards. Cervantes carefully selects the episodes of literary reminiscence as occasions for critical responses by this audience. In the course of the ensuing exchange between members of the audience and between audience and narrator, Cervantes introduces the two basic critical notions of the Canon of Toledo and his fellow neo-Aristotelians—unity and verisimilitude—and subjects them to critical scrutiny.

Throughout Periandro's narration abstract aesthetic problems are the basis for a dramatic conflict which is resolved in comedy. As the lively humor of the various exchanges between participants is dependent on the topical nature of the neo-Aristotelian criteria in the sixteenth and seventeenth centuries, the modern reader can ap-

---

Periandro's treatment of the garden and the flying horse, Cervantes is using the account of his protagonist to assert his independence of the Aristotelian movement. In doing so, he purposely evokes "topics of the marvelous" which the movement had rejected on the grounds of inverisimilitude.

[18] Carvallo writes that "el que entiende el arte mucho se ayuda y fauorece de la immitacion," adding that "nada bueno se puede en estos tiempos dezir, sin tener a quienes immitar en ello" (*Cisne de Apolo*, II, 172-173) and recommending the imitation of the famous poets. Cervantes followed the contemporary practice with no reservations (see *Don Quijote*, I, 237; *Adjunta al Parnaso*, p. 133; Riley, *Cervantes's Theory of the Novel*, pp. 61-67). On the importance of the principle of the imitation of models (to be distinguished always from the Aristotelian concept of imitation [mimesis]) in the Renaissance, see Hermann Gmelin, "Das Prinzip der Imitatio in den romanischen Literaturen der Renaissance," *Romanische Forschungen*, XLVI (1932), 83-360.

preciate it only if he bears in mind those two fundamental aesthetic dilemmas which beset the critical movement—the reconciliation of the demands of verisimilitude and the marvelous and those of unity and variety—as well as the tireless labors of such figures as Torquato Tasso to resolve them.[19] The most important episodes in the unfolding literary drama are Periandro's descriptions of the fishermen's wedding, in which the fundamental problem is unity; the marvelous horse, in which the focus shifts to verisimilitude; and the garden paradise, where both problems are examined. In the pages that follow I propose to analyze the details of these episodes, including the horse and the garden, which I designate as "topics of the marvelous," in a separate chapter.

The implications of Periandro's narration are more far-reaching than the limitations of its focus—the specific critical notions of unity and verisimilitude—would indicate. In reality this most literary interlude of the *Persiles* amounts to a trial of literature, in which the stakes are much higher than those in Pero Pérez and Master Nicolás' inquisitorial examination of Don Quixote's library. At stake here is the freedom of the creative imagination and the value of its ageless creations. It is not without purpose that Cervantes crowds Periandro's account with literary reminiscences, for his surrogate poet would summon to the defense of artistic freedom the cumulative weight of the entire tradition of imaginative literature. In a sense Periandro's narration is the rebuilding of Don Quixote's library.

THE FISHERMEN'S WEDDING: THE PROBLEM OF UNITY

Periandro begins his narration with the longest of the various episodes of which it is composed. In relation to his principal subject, his wanderings and sufferings with his beloved Auristela, the episode accounts for the initial separation of the lovers. However, a large part of his account is devoted to two incidents in which his

---

[19] "Diversissime sono, ilustrissimo Signore, queste due nature, il meraviglioso e 'l verisimile, e in guisa diverse che sono quasi contrarie fra loro; nondimeno l'una e l'altra nel poema è necessaria, ma fa mestieri che arte di eccellente poeta sia quella ch'insieme l'accoppi" (Tasso, *Del poema eroico*, p. 96). "È certo assai agevol cosa e di niuna industria il far che 'n molte e separate azioni nasca gran varietà di accidenti; ma che la istessa varietà in una sola azione si trovi, *hoc opus, hic labor est*" (p. 140).

participation is little more than that of a passive witness—the wedding of the fishermen and the boat race which follows. As we examine the literary overtones of these scenes (*Persiles*, II, x-xii), it is well to bear in mind the distinction between the concept of inner unity and that of external unity. The former, since the Romantic Movement's discovery and celebration of the thematic unity of the *Quixote*,[20] has marked the modern critical approach to Cervantes' works. The latter (i.e., the logically constructed plot containing nothing irrelevant to its development and conclusion) dominated critical thinking of the Renaissance and lay at the heart of the aesthetic controversy in which Cervantes and many of his contemporaries were involved.

To be sure, the pastoral interlude of the wedding is significant within the thematic context of both the *Persiles* and all of Cervantes' writings. In it the author examines the nature of love, dramatically stating a conclusion of his neo-Platonic doctrines: beauty of the soul and virtue is ultimately more important than beauty of the body. By arrangement of their elders two young couples are to be wed. Conveniently enough one member of each sex is extremely beautiful and one is ugly. Beauty is paired with beauty, Carino with Seluiana, and ugliness with ugliness, Salercio with Leoncia. On the eve of the wedding Periandro and Auristela wander into the community. Interpreting their arrival as a miracle, Carino seizes the opportunity to inform the hero that he is in love not with the beautiful Seluiana, whom he is to marry, but rather with the ugly Leoncia: "In the eyes of my soul, Leoncia, for the virtues which I discover in her soul, is the most beautiful woman in the world."[21] It is rare for Cervantes to explore this theoretical consequence of the neo-Platonic theories of love and present a tension between corporeal and spiritual beauty, but he does return to it at a most important juncture in the work. At the conclusion of the heroes' wanderings and at the moment when their sufferings

---

[20] See, for example, Solger: "Nirgends sind die Episoden schöner, als in Cervantes' *Don Quijote*, wo die eingeschalteten Novellen dem Gedichte wesentlich sind und immer allegorische Beziehung auf den Hauptgedanken des Ganzen haben" (cited by Brüggemann, *Cervantes und die Figur des Don Quijote*, p. 75).

[21] ". . . a los ojos de mi alma, por las virtues que en la de Leoncia descubro, ella es la mas hermosa muger del mundo" (I, 230).

are to be rewarded with Christian marriage, Periandro's love must endure the sight of a physically repulsive Auristela, whose physiognomy has been transformed by the sorcery of Hipolyta's Jewish magician. Periandro survives the trial, for like the fisherman Carino he looks upon his beloved with the eyes of the soul and sees only her spiritual goodness. His love is superior to that of his rival, the Duke of Nemours, who, driven to despair by the corporeal decay of Auristela, abandons his suit and returns to France.[22]

There is another problem that the wedding raises which is a recurrent thematic concern in Cervantes' writing: the conflict between parental authority and the inclinations of children in the arrangement of marriages. Here as in the episodes of Ysabel Castrucho and Feliciana de la Voz later in the romance, the problem is resolved in favor of the freedom of children to make their own decisions: "I cannot think it reasonable for a man to consent that a burden, which must endure for life, should be fixed upon his shoulders not by his own but by the wishes of others."[23] In its treatment of this theme as well as in many structural details, the scene of the fishermen's wedding is strikingly similar to the episode of the "Bodas de Camacho" in *Don Quixote*. In both, the author describes the pageantry of a wedding in rural circumstances, and links the episode into the main narrative thread by having the hero intervene in the festivities to settle a conflict between parental authority and the wishes of the parties involved and to free the latter to alter the marriage. Moreover, the pageantry of the wedding culminates in the one case in a dance of competing allegorical

---

[22] A similar situation occurs in *La española inglesa*, as Ricaredo is exposed to the sight of his beloved Isabela completely transfigured by the poisons of the Queen's servant. Like Periandro his love survives the test; for he is in love with her soul. It is characteristic of Cervantes, however, that he refuses to dwell on this possibility of his theory of ideal love. In both cases the spiritual love of his heroes is rewarded by the complete restoration of the beauty of their beloved. On the neo-Platonic theory of love in Cervantes' works, see Otis H. Green, *Spain and the Western Tradition* (Madison, 1963), I, 185-206.

[23] ". . . no puedo yo pensar en que razon se consiente que, la carga que ha de durar toda la vida, se la eche el hombre sobre sus ombros, no por el suyo, sino por el gusto ageno" (I, 231). Cervantes' awareness that the problem is much more complex than this solution suggests is evident in his varying treatment of the subject. See, for example, the episode of Leandra and Vicente de la Rosa in *Don Quixote* (I, li). For a study of Cervantes' attitude toward marriage, see M. Bataillon, "Cervantès et le 'mariage chrétien,' " *Bulletin Hispanique,* XLIX (1947), 129-144.

figures, in the other in a race of boats conceived as an allegorical contest. In both episodes the allegorical participants are the various topics of the love debates in the tradition of the sentimental and pastoral romances, e.g., *Amor, Interés, Buena Fortuna, Diligencia.*

The thematic relevance of the fishermen's wedding and the boat race in the context of the *Persiles* and the other writings of Cervantes is not our concern at this moment. It is rather the relation of the scene to the literary problems which lie behind Periandro's entire narration. It is significant that the audience that has assembled to listen to the hero's tale is interested neither in the philosophical issues raised by the episode nor in the problems of traditional love debates which the allegorical designations of the competing ships recall. The preoccupations of this audience are almost exclusively literary, and the literary standards of judgment of its most outspoken members are those dictated by the neo-Aristotelian critical canons. Reflecting on Periandro's description of the fishermen's wedding and the boat race, the audience's major concern is their problematic relevance as an episode in a properly constructed *historia.*

In the commentary that interrupts Periandro's account, Cervantes examines critically a major theoretical problem of contemporary literary theorists, namely, the implications of the Aristotelian criteria of unity in epic composition. At the center of the controversy was the *episode* and the poet's liberty in employing it. In general, the critical movement reaffirmed Aristotle's judgment that unlike tragedy the epic is to a large degree dependent on the episode for its success. For example, Tasso restated Aristotle's discussion of the startling simplicity of the basic plot of the *Odyssey* and its dependence on episodic additions and praised Virgil's reliance on episodes to give the story of Aeneas' journey the breadth and variety required in epic poetry.[24] Moreover, theorists maintained that the use of the episode, like the use of the unchronological disposition, is one of the major factors differentiating the poet from the historian. The widely acknowledged failure of Lucan's *Pharsalia* as poetry was in part due to his failure to employ the episode as a means of embellishing

[24] *Del poema eroico*, pp. 146-148.

the historical facts and his resultant confusion of the poet's aim with that of the historian.[25]

The use of the episode raised structural problems analogous to the thematic problems which I have referred to as the "legitimation of the marvelous." The interrelationship of the two areas of problem is evident if we recall that the marvelous was in large part dependent on variety and the invented matter which the poet must add to the historical foundation of his plot. The episode was the structural unit enabling the incorporation of varied and generally feigned matter.[26] In both cases poetic license was the crucial issue, and theorists delineated structural boundaries for the legitimate episode which the poet must not overstep, just as they did for marvelous subject matter. They generally set these limits by recalling Aristotle's analogy of the plot of a tragedy to a body, which the contemplator can embrace in one view; his statements on the laws of probability and necessity, which must link events of the plot; and his somewhat contradictory demands for single action and varied episodes in an epic plot. The plot must have magnitude, but its totality must be perspicuous. In other words it must be of a length which can easily be embraced by the memory, and in it all must follow as if by necessity. The neo-Aristotelian critics were unanimous in limiting the use of episodes in accordance with this theory of plot,[27] and in insisting that the poet avoid the overly lengthy

[25] See Minturno, *L'arte poetica*, p. 25; Tasso, *Del poema eroico*, pp. 113-114; El Pinciano, *Philosophía antigua poética*, III, 170-171.

[26] See Minturno, *L'arte poetica*, p. 24; Tasso, *Del poema eroico*, pp. 145-148; El Pinciano, *Philosophía antigua poética*, III, 170-171. Carvallo defined the episode as the part of the plot in which "es licito fingir" (*Cisne de Apolo*, II, 42).

[27] Thus Tasso recommends the use of episodes as a means of giving a poem the proper length but, recalling Aristotle's passage, adds: "Grande dunque sarà convenevolmente quella poesia in cui la memoria non si perda né si smarisca, ma, tutta unitamente comprendendola, possa considerare come l'una cosa con l'altra sia congiunta e dall'altra dependente. Ma viziosi senza dubbio sono quei poemi che sono simili a i corpi che non possono esser rimirati in un'occhiata." He proceeds to define episodes as "azioni fuor della cosa di cui si tratta, le quali si pigliano d'altra parte e sono estrinsiche," but adds that the episodes must be related to the main plot in narrating events which either hinder or aid the hero in his movement toward his goal (*Del poema eroico*, pp. 125, 145-148). We observe the importance of *degree* in Minturno's definition of the episode as a digression independent of the main plot but "non sì fuori, che sia strana da lei [la favola]" (*L'arte poetica*, p. 18).

episode and that he be careful to employ a "legitimate bond" (*legittima legatura*) to integrate his episode into the main plot, to which it must then remain subordinate. If it becomes independent of the main action, the unity of the entire poem is destroyed, for the work becomes a series of separate actions, i.e., "episodic."[28]

Periandro's departure from the main thread of his *historia* to describe the fishermen's wedding and the boat race is Cervantes' conscious introduction of episode into his narration as an aesthetic problem. The event itself is rich in literary associations with the tradition of epic poetry, recalling at once perhaps the most venerable conventional episode, that of athletic competition and martial games. Indeed in his discussion of the important function of the episode, Tasso recommends that the poet "in games should be ornate and effective, and he should place things before the eyes [of the reader], and he should not describe everything which is done, but rather the most celebrated and illustrious deeds, as well as those which are simulacra of war or its exercise, as did Virgil and Homer, the one at the burial of Patroclus, the other at the grave of Anchises."[29] Whether or not Cervantes had this particular passage in mind in composing this scene of the *Persiles* is hypothetical. Nevertheless, Periandro does just as Tasso recommends, exhorting his audience to see as real the events described and modeling the boat race very closely on that of the festivities at the grave of Anchises (*Aeneid*, V).[30]

That Cervantes' introduction of an episode typical of the epic tradition and widely discussed in critical circles is an occasion for

[28] Pigna writes of episodes: "Due parti massimamente hauer doueranno: & che del tenore della propria materia: & che del tutto con essa concatenati siano. Il poema ogni volta che di questo auertimento sia priuo, Episodico chiamerassi: cio è disordinato & disconforme" (*I romanzi*, p. 42).

[29] ". . . ne' giuochi sia ornato, efficace, e ponga le cose inanzi gli occhi, e non descriva tutti quelli che si fanno, ma i più celebri e illustri, e quelli che sono quasi simulacri della guerra o sua essercitazione, come fecero Virgilio e Omero, l'uno nell'essequie di Patroclo, l'altro nella sepoltura d'Anchise" (*Del poema eroico*, p. 110).

[30] The description of the boat race is one of several passages of the *Persiles* in which Cervantes' borrowings from Virgil are observable not only in general outline but also in specific detail. For a comparison of the texts of the *Persiles* and Velasco's translation of the *Aeneid*, which Cervantes undoubtedly used, see Schevill, "Studies in Cervantes," *Publications of Yale University*, XIII (1908), 530-534.

the raising of a critical problem is evident in the author's description of the reactions of the various listeners at the end of the account of the boat race. Although Mauricio and Ladislao judge Periandro's narration to have been "somewhat long and very little to the purpose, for in a narration of his own misfortunes, he had no reason to relate the pleasures of others," the audience is generally pleased with the story: "Nevertheless, they liked it and remained eager to listen to his history to its end."[31] Here we observe the two opposing tendencies of critical thought (the rules vs. pleasure) which we observed in the confrontation between Don Quixote and the Canon of Toledo and which will continue to dominate much of the critical reflection on Periandro's narration. From the point of view of the neo-Aristotelian, Mauricio, the hero's digression is not properly integrated into his main action. In the *Aeneid*, the boat race is part of the scene of festivities at the tomb of Anchises, which reaches its climax in the apparition of the old man's ghost before Aeneas to exhort his son to continue on his destined course to Italy and to announce the descent to the underworld. In Periandro's narration the protagonist is merely a witness to a boat race between participants who have no role in his wanderings. The narrator makes no attempt to establish those links (*legittime legature*) to the main plot which the Aristotelians deemed so necessary for the justification of the ornamental episode. Both Mauricio's reproof of the irrelevance of the episode (*larga y no muy a proposito*) and its answer praising the episode for the pleasure which it produces recall that fundamental dialogue of sixteenth-century literary theorizing which echoes through Cervantes' writing, the dialogue between the classicists and the defenders of the romances.[32]

[31] ". . . algo larga, y traida no muy a proposito, pues, para contar sus desgracias propias, no auia para que contar los plazeres agenos"; "Con todo esso, les dio gusto, y quedaron con el esperando oir el fin de su historia" (I, 238).

[32] *L'arte poetica* of Minturno, whose most extensive criticism of the romances concerned their structural disorder rather than their inverisimilitude, is most relevant to this scene. His principal interlocutor condemns the romances in their use of "molti Episodii, molto dalla principal facenda, e dalla materia lontani, e per niuna conueneuole ragione quiui introdutti." Vespasiano, representing the *vulgo*, answers: "Ma con tutto ciô piû uolentieri si canta, ò si legge qual si uoglia canto de gliamori, e de'fatti di Rinaldo ò d'Orlando, che qualunque . . . de'migliori Sonetti del Petrarca" (pp. 25-26). Although Minturno rejects this opinion unequivocally, the argument associating the pleasure with structural looseness was

The critical dialogue becomes complicated by new dimensions and takes a more dramatic form in the succeeding interruption, in which abstract ideas appear in the form of their representatives and engage in humorous conflict. As it employs literary topics as elements of humor in a dramatic exchange between members of an audience and a narrator, the scene recalls the episode of the counterfeit captives as well as the series of scenes in the *Quixote* which I have analyzed. Periandro promises his audience many more episodes: "There is no point at which the changes of my fortune cease, nor are there boundaries which enclose them" (". . . que las vueltas de mi fortuna no tienen vn punto donde paren ni terminos que las encierren" [I, 252]). As if in confirmation of Tasso's belief that "variety is praiseworthy up to that point beyond which it turns into confusion" ("la varieta è lodevole sino a quel termine che non passi in confusione"),[33] Arnaldo interrupts to voice his displeasure: "No more . . . no more, Periandro, my friend; for, although you do not tire of telling your misfortunes, it is wearisome for us to listen to them, as there are so many."[34]

The similarity between the dramatic exchange and a passage in Tasso's *Del poema eroico*, which forms a prelude to an examination and rejection of the structural looseness and uncontrolled variety of the romances, demonstrates clearly the way in which the literary dialogues of the sixteenth century nourished the creative art of Cervantes.

> I add that indeterminateness arises from multiplicity, and this progress could go on infinitely, unless some limit is preestablished for it or circumscribed about it by art. Wherefore Aristotle says in the *Problems* that we are wont to hear much more willingly those histories which set forth only one thing rather than those others in which more are recounted, because we are more attentive to and can understand better those things which are more known. But the single thing is more known because

---

presented by others as a valid defense of the new genre. See Pigna, *I romanzi*, p. 44.

[33] *Dell'arte poetica*, p. 35.

[34] "No mas . . . no mas, Periandro amigo; que, puesto que tu no te canses de contar tus desgracias, a nosotros nos fatiga el oyrlas, por ser tantas" (I, 252).

it is well defined; on the other hand, things which are many partake of infinity. The poet who treats a single plot, when it is finished, has reached his end; he who weaves more of them will be able to weave four or six or ten, nor is he obligated more to this number than to any other number. Accordingly he will be unable to determine with certainty the point at which it is fitting to halt.[35]

Periandro responds to the attack of the neo-Aristotelian prince with a mysterious statement, which is significant both in its allusiveness to two arguments which had been advanced by various theorists to defend Ariosto and the romances from an unfavorable judgment according to the classical standard of unity and in the peculiar style which it employs: "I, my lord Arnaldo, am like a place, one in which all things fit and nothing is out of place; and in me all things which are misfortunes take place, although, because I have found my sister Auristela, I would gladly say that such misfortunes are fortunes."[36] On the one hand the statement alludes to the thesis forwarded by Giraldi Cintio and others that in the ideal romance there are indeed many actions, but that there is a unity that is based on the presence of one outstanding hero, who towers above the others.[37]

[35] "Aggiungo che dalla moltitudine nasce *l'indeterminazione,* e questo progresso potrebbe *andare in infinito,* senza che le sia dall'arte *prefisso o circonscritto termine alcuno.* Laonde dice Aristotele ne' *Problemi* che *noi più volentieri sogliamo udire quelle istorie ch'espongono una cosa solamente,* dell'altre dalle quali più ne sono raccontate, perché siamo più attenti alle cose e possiam meglio intendere le più note. Ma l'uno è più noto perch'è definito; all'incontro le cose che son molte participano dell'infinito. Il poeta ch'una favola tratta, finita quella, è giunto al suo fine; chi più ne tesse, o quattro o sei o dieci ne potrà tessere, né più a questo numero che a quello è obligato. *Non potrà aver dunque determinata certezza qual sia quel segno ove convenga fermarsi*" (pp. 127-128); the italics are mine.

[36] "Yo, señor Arnaldo, soy hecho como esto que se llama lugar, que es donde todas las cosas caben y no ay ninguna fuera del lugar, y en mi le tienen todas las que son desgraciadas, aunque, por auer hallado a mi hermana Auristela, las juzgo por dichosas" (I, 252).

[37] The romance is a modern genre and hence not subject to all the rules formulated by the ancients. Giraldi asserts that Aristotelian rules are not applicable to all heroic poetry but only to that presenting a single action (see *De' romanzi,* pp. 26-29). Pigna similarly finds in the central hero a unifying principle in romance literature (*I romanzi,* p. 25). It is important to bear in mind the extremely topical character of the Aristotelian critical apparatus and of its generalizations. The appearance of similar statements in the writings of various theorists makes the question

On the other hand Periandro is speaking as one of Cervantes' various surrogates of the creating artist, and, as has been pointed out above, his narrative techniques allow little doubt that Cervantes fashioned him in the mold of Ariosto, the most influential poet of romance. In the chapter under discussion, which begins with the narrator's statement of the universal moral principle to be derived from the episode of the boat race and concludes as the narrator rapidly sums up the recounted actions and breaks off his narration, Periandro is following particularly closely the practice of Ariosto. It is interesting that his Ariostean summary and allusion to the many episodes that still await the audience provoke the interruption of Arnaldo and the ensuing critical examination of unity. For in Renaissance critical writing this narrative technique was a subject of discussion which was closely related to the problem of unity and variety. Thus Pigna points to the important role that the narrator's interventions to recapitulate and offer moral reflections play in the introduction of cantos in the romances. He attributes the development of the technique to the romances' wealth of subject matter and their original composition for a listening audience.[38] In terms of the critical problem raised by the scene, Periandro represents a narrative principle exemplified by Ariosto—

---

of sources as difficult and as idle as the question, for example, of where a present-day writer acquires his knowledge of Freudian commonplaces. The similarity in detail between Tasso's statement and the scene under discussion is revealing in terms of the way in which Cervantes employed critical ideas in a humorous, literary context. However, it would be dangerous to assume that Cervantes was working with Tasso's text. Pigna's defense of the variety of the romances contains a similar passage, which, while it does not offer close correspondences in detail, nevertheless, in its broad outline presents a more complete discursive formulation of the critical exchange in Cervantes' scene. For it provides the subject matter not only for the humorous exchange between Periandro and Arnaldo, dramatizing the danger of the openness of the uncircumscribed plot, which in its episodes could expand infinitely, but also for Periandro's critical response to this danger. Discussing the necessity of one action of one man in the perfectly constructed epic, Pigna observes that ". . . piu attioni di termine mancherebbono: & ne verrebbe il processo in infinito: & piu fini farebonno"—all of which destroys unity, which is "la perfettione d'ogni materia." He proceeds to admit that romance presents many actions but claims that its multiplicity is unified in a single hero who towers above the other characters, and "cosi il gire in infinito si toglie" (pp. 25-26).

[38] Ovid is the classical prototype of the romance narrator, and Pigna praises his technique in unifying so much diverse matter (see *I romanzi*, pp. 47-48). The strict classicists condemned the technique of free authorial interventions, recalling Aristotle's praise of Homer for not speaking in his own voice.

it lies in the power and the freedom of the narrator's voice itself to impose order on a subject which in its variety of actions would inevitably resist the order which the Aristotelian criteria of unity would demand. Undoubtedly Periandro's assertion that he is the center at which all the actions of his narration meet contains an allusion to the theory that unity in the poem of many actions is in the hero. It is allusive also to a theory far more important in Cervantes' artistic undertaking, the absolute freedom and power of the artist, who, in a symbolical gesture that would answer the Aristotelian precept that the poet not speak in his own voice, places himself at the very center of his creation.

As a final commentary on Periandro's rejoinder to Arnaldo it is necessary to observe the peculiar formulation of his argument and the abrupt shift from the literary to another level of meaning, a shift highlighted by the verbal magic of the zeugma, as the evasive narrator conjures up two distinct meanings from the single word *lugar.* Here we observe Periandro following the same pattern of distortion, misapplication, and evasion which Don Quixote and Cide Hamete Benengeli practice in dealing with the serious principles of the literary theorists. He is ironically dismissing any restrictions which his audience would impose on his creative freedom. His authorial impudence and heedlessness of Arnaldo's objection is underscored as he concludes the discussion with the words: "If possible, I will bring my story to an end tonight, although it is yet hardly begun."[39]

In spite of the leap away from the level of literary theory that concludes Periandro's humorously formulated, theoretical defense of the variety of his interminable narration, the dramatic exchange

---

[39] "Esta noche, señora, dare fin, si fuere possible, al cuento, que aun hasta agora se está en sus principios" (I, 252-253). Responding on another occasion to one of the numerous requests of the audience that he abbreviate his narration, Periandro replies: "Si hare . . . si es possible que grandes cosas en breues terminos puedan encerrarse" (I, 285). The exchange recalls Cide Hamete Benengeli's ironic submission to the Aristotelians on the question of the episode: ". . . y pues se contiene y cierra en los estrechos límites de la narración, teniendo habilidad, suficiencia y entendimiento para tratar del universo todo . . ." (II, 849). It should be recalled that the Moor presents the same opposing aesthetic principles—pleasure vs. the rules—which we observe in this scene before he reaches his conclusion. He complains that writing of "un solo sujeto" is boring and laments that he cannot include "otras digresiones y episodios más graves y más entretenidos."

immediately returns to the literary problem under examination. Representing dramatically the unlearned audience, Transila admits that she understands nothing of Periandro's refined arguments: "Speaking for myself, Periandro, I do not understand this explanation . . .", but proceeds to offer him a familiar defense. She requests that he continue his story, acknowledging that he has been successful in presenting his subject as real before her eyes and in arousing suspense in his audience:

> I understand only that it will be a great evil indeed if you do not satisfy our desire to know the events of your history, which seem to me to be so grand that many tongues will tell of them and many envious pens will write of them. The sight of you as a captain of brigands has me in suspense; I judged that your brave fishermen merited such a name. And I shall be waiting, still in suspense, to discover what was your first deed and your first adventure.[40]

Once again we hear the argument based on pleasure and success, by which Don Quixote rebuts the Canon of Toledo's attack on the romances and which the members of Juan Palomeque el Zurdo's family affirm when the curate criticizes their reading habits.[41]

The final critical commentary on Periandro's inclusion of the episode of the fishermen's wedding and the boat race appears at the conclusion of the episode in which the hero encounters the dishonored King Leopoldio of Danea and dissuades him from avenging himself on his unfaithful wife. Puzzled by the problematic relevance of the episode, Mauricio cannot help recalling the

[40] ". . . sólo entiendo que [el mal] le será muy grande si no cumplis el desseo que todos tenemos de saber los sucessos de vuestra historia, que me va pareciendo ser tales, que han de dar ocasion a muchas lenguas que los cuenten y muchas injuriosas plumas que la escriuan. Suspensa me tiene el veros capitan de salteadores; juzgué merecer este nombre vuestros pescadores valientes, y estare esperando, tambien suspensa, qual fue la primera hazaña que hizistes, y la auentura primera con que encontrastes" (I, 252).

[41] Transila's reaction emphasizing the pleasure of suspense as she anticipates the outcome of Periandro's adventures recalls Pigna's defense of the multiple actions and fragmentations in their development in the romances. When such techniques are used, "l'animo resta sospeso & ne nasce perciò vn desiderio che fa diletto: essendo che vn certo ardore è causato, che è di douer la fine della cosa sentire." The epic poet cannot arouse this pleasure so easily, for he is limited to a single action of a single man (see *I romanzi*, p. 45).

opening scenes of the narration. The brief dramatic exchange between him and his daughter restates the critical problem, and once
again the anti-Aristotelians have the final word:

> The agreeable way in which Periandro told the story of his
> strange adventures gave pleasure to every one of his hearers,
> except Mauricio, who, whispering in the ear of Transila, his
> daughter, said: "It seems to me, Transila, that Periandro might
> relate the events of his life in fewer words and in a more suc-
> cinct discourse. *I do not see why he need detail, so very mi-
> nutely, all about the fishermen and their festivals, nor yet their
> marriages, for though episodes may be admitted to ornament
> a tale, they should not be as long as the original story itself.*
> But the fact, I suspect, is, that Periandro likes to display his
> inventive powers [*la grandeza de su ingenio*] and show what
> fine language he can use." "It may be so," said Transila, "but
> all I know is, *whether he is expansive or succinct in what he
> relates, all is good and gives one pleasure to hear it.*"[42]

Here we observe, in its clearest formulation in the entire scene, the
fundamental opposition between the aesthetic principles of the
classical school and the aesthetic of pure pleasure which marks all
the confrontations of narrating author and critical audience in the
works of Cervantes. The surreptitious gesture of the pedantic
Mauricio as he expresses the serious critical doctrine recalls those of
two other befuddled spokesmen for the neo-Aristotelian canons,
who find themselves forced to make ambivalent judgments of narrations which abuse their standards of verisimilitude: Don Quixote
following Sancho's account of his celestial goat-herding and Master

---

[42] "A todos dio general gusto de oir el modo con que Periandro contaua su
estraña peregrinacion, si no fue a Mauricio, que, llegandose al oido de Transila, su
hija, le dixo:

—Pareceme, Transila, que con menos palabras y mas sucintos discursos pudiera
Periandro contar los de su vida; porque *no auia para que detenerse en dezirnos
tan por estenso las fiestas de las varcas, ni aun los casamientos de los pescadores,
porque los episodios que para ornato de las historias se ponen, no han de ser tan
grandes como la misma historia*; pero yo, sin duda, creo que Periandro nos quiere
mostrar la grandeza de su ingenio y la elegancia de sus palabras.

—Assi deue de ser—respondio Transila—; pero lo que yo se dezir es que, *ora se
dilate o se sucinte en lo que dize, todo es bueno y todo da gusto*" (I, 264). The
italics are mine.

207

Pedro's monkey, following Don Quixote's account of the adventures in the Cave of Montesinos.

To understand Cervantes' independent position in relation to the neo-Aristotelian movement as well as to appreciate fully the tone of playfulness that accompanies his introduction of the critical dogmas, we must observe how the steadily increasing anger of the implacable Mauricio lends this extended situation of narrator vs. audience a humor which escapes the modern reader. The dependence of this humor on the extremely topical character of even the finer points of the critical writings of the sixteenth and seventeenth centuries is most evident in the following interjection of the exasperated neo-Aristotelian. Periandro reaches the conclusion of another episode typical of the tradition of epic poetry, his encounter with the warrior maiden Sulpicia, which seems to have very little bearing on his principal subject. In an obvious evocation of Virgil's Palinurus and another "great moment" of imaginative literature, he proceeds to describe himself abandoning his post at the helm to do some stargazing. The scientific Mauricio is incapable of viewing the stars in the perspective of poetry and voices his displeasure:

> "I would lay any wager . . . that Periandro is going to give us a description of the whole celestial sphere, as if an explanation of the movements of the heavens had anything to do with what he is telling us. For my part I wish he would bring his story to an end, for the desire that I have to get away from this place is such that I really cannot trouble myself with knowing which are fixed, and which, wandering stars, and *all the more because I myself know more about their movements than he can possibly tell me.*"[43]

There is comedy of situation here as the professional astrologer is detained from his long-awaited embarkation by Periandro's description of the heavens. Yet the comedy of situation is merely

---

[43] "Apostarè . . . que se pone agora Periandro a descriuirnos toda la celeste esfera, como si importasse mucho a lo que va contando el declararnos los mouimientos del cielo. Yo, por mi, desseando estoy que acabe, porque el desseo que tengo de salir de esta tierra no da lugar a que me entretenga ni ocupe en saber quales son fixas o quales erraticas estrellas; *quanto mas, que yo se de sus mouimientos mas de lo que el me puede dezir*" (I, 271-272). The italics are mine.

the first step in a movement toward an intellectual humor based on literary principles. Mauricio's impatience is the result of the narrator's failure to observe the critical canon which he, Mauricio, represents. Although it is not treated with much sympathy in the context of the entire narration, it is, nevertheless, based on a well-reasoned theoretical point of view. However, in Mauricio's final statement, he himself shatters his image as a respectable representative of an intelligent point of view and appears suddenly as a ridiculous figure. This abrupt shift is based on the evocation of a specific doctrine of the critical movement.

It was a commonplace of Renaissance criticism that the poet, like the ideal orator, should know something about every science. The notion was coupled with the ready admission that the poet could not equal the knowledge of the specialists in any one field and should not try to do so. As Giraldi Cintio writes, the poet must consult the experts of the various fields of knowledge, for example "the astrologers of the heavens" for "it would be too great a burden for him, if he had to learn all that before he could devote himself to writing."[44] Mauricio is of course the Renaissance scientist and master of astrology. The subtle humor of his protesting that his knowledge of the stars is superior to that of Periandro originates in the incongruity of this utterance of a Mauricio, the specialist resentful of the presumption of the novice, from the mouth of a Mauricio, who, as we know, is not only an expert astrologer but also an expert literary theorist who should be well aware of the poet's necessary reliance on the superior knowledge of the specialists and consequently of the folly of his own objection.

Here we observe Cervantes employing one of the classic patterns of comedy of character at the expense of the neo-Aristotelian, who is compelled by circumstances unwittingly to act in contradiction to his formulation of himself. The humor in Mauricio's comment is essentially the same as that which springs from the sober canon's admission in bewilderment that he did not notice the huge peg of

---

[44] ". . . cogli astrologhi del cielo . . . troppo gran peso gli si darebbe, s'egli tutto ciò avesse ad apparare prima che a scrivere si desse" (*De' romanzi*, p. 219). In another context the narrator of the *Persiles* alludes to the popular doctrine: ". . . que, en el arte de la marineria, mas sabe el mas simple marinero, que el mayor letrado del mundo" (I, 302).

Pierres' flying horse in the national armory, from Don Quixote's sudden transformation from a pedantic Aristotelian into a most credulous spectator in the scene of Master Pedro's *retablo*, and from the *primo humanista*'s use of deductive reasoning both to defend and to deny the authenticity of Don Quixote's vision in the Cave of Montesinos.

In conclusion, Periandro's description of the fishermen's wedding and the boat race appears in the same context of literary debate which we have observed in Don Quixote's conversation with the Canon of Toledo and in the numerous scenes in which the process of artistic creation is presented dramatically in the *Quixote*. Once again the same fundamental aesthetic principles are presented in dramatic conflict, as the narrator, exemplifying an aesthetic based on pleasure and artistic freedom, must counter the restrictions which an audience representing the neo-Aristotelian canons of the sixteenth-century critical movement would impose upon his creative freedom. Unlike most of the encounters between audience and artist in Cervantes' works, here the critical issue raised by the audience is unity and not verisimilitude. Nevertheless, the conflict and its resolution follow the familiar pattern.

The neo-Aristotelian criteria are reduced to the role of components of a context of humor, a humor which arises from the incongruity of their juxtaposition to other elements in the context. The humor is generally benign, as for example in Mauricio's surreptitious gesture accompanying the statement of an Aristotelian principle, in the association of the principle of unity with Arnaldo's physical discomfort and Mauricio's impatience to resume his journey, or in the latter's exasperation at the pretentiousness of Periandro's amateurish astrology. Nevertheless, at times a serious intention gives the humor a particularly pointed quality, as for example in Periandro's evocation of a valid literary principle to defend his narrative technique and in his deliberate play with his audience, both of which recall Cide Hamete's methods of dealing with the neo-Aristotelians and his readers.

Viewed within the total context of the *Persiles*, the humor acquires a broader and a more aggressive dimension, for what is raw material for comedy, dissolving in the comic exchange between the various participants in the scene, are those very criteria on which the *Persiles* is founded. In this context it is an equivocal humor, recalling the ambiguity of the introductory passage to the episode of the counterfeit captives. In Periandro we observe once again the emergence of the narrative voice of Cide Hamete Benengeli, which triumphantly declares its independence of any critical restrictions and affirms its absolute control over its creation. The irrepressible narrative voice of Periandro continues to defy that of him who originally conceived the *Persiles* (i.e., his own creator), as the focus of the literary controversy broadens to include the principle of verisimilitude. The occasion is Periandro's account of his visit to the island paradise.

CHAPTER VII

Topics of the Marvelous

THE GARDEN PARADISE

ONE OF THE BEST indications of the breadth of Cervantes' literary awareness is to be found in his various treatments of what may be the oldest theme of world literature, the description of the paradisiacal regions of the otherworld. It is undoubtedly one of his favorite topics, appearing at nearly every stage of his literary development, assuming various forms, and evoking a wide variety of the elements of a deep and persistent literary tradition. In its different forms, from the classical landscape that provides a stage for the shepherds' homage to the dead Meliso in the *Galatea* to the fantastic paradise of Periandro's dream, it affords a convenient means by which we can gauge the changing preoccupations of Cervantes. Indeed a theme of such pronounced topical character is only of interest in the way in which an author selects and fashions it as a vehicle of his own vision of reality. Our principal concern is of course Cervantes' use of the garden paradise in the *Persiles*. Nevertheless, since one of the commonplaces of Cervantine criticism is the *difference* between the *Persiles* and the *Quixote* and the *similarity* of the *Persiles* to the *Galatea*, it is useful to take advantage of the presence of this topic in each of the works to test the validity of this belief. Moreover, the significance of Periandro's vision of paradise can only come into sharper focus when viewed against the background of the other works.

The Garden Paradise as an Expression of World Order:
The Galatea

In his early work *La Galatea* Cervantes was cultivating a genre which, following the publication of Sannazaro's *Arcadia* (1502), had become increasingly popular among the refined social and literary circles during the sixteenth century.[1] In attempting to discover the spiritual forces which animated the Renaissance bucolic,

---

[1] A general study of the development of this genre in Italy, Spain, and France can be found in Mia Gerhardt's *La Pastorale* (Assen, 1950).

critics and historians have pointed to a variety of factors. E. W. Tayler observes that civilized man's constant yearning for the simple and natural, which he embodies in pastoral fiction, is a psychologically plausible reaction to the refinement and complexity which he finds in his society.[2] Others have offered a more historical explanation of the literary phenomenon, relating the Renaissance cult of nature to specific aspects of the humanist movement. The Florentine neo-Platonists celebrated God's creative agent, nature, and its highest creation, man the microcosm, as reflections of divine beauty. They maintained that through contemplation of nature and human perfection, man could ascend to a mystical communion with the creator.[3] The absorbing preoccupation of the humanists was not, however, metaphysics but ethics, and in this area of thought too they turned to the natural order, envisaging the possibility of man's moral perfectibility through his discovery of and adherence to the laws of nature.[4] Moreover, the importance of the cultivation of the study of classical antiquity and the prestige which the first poet of the idealizing bucolic, Virgil, enjoyed as prince of poets, have been recognized as contributing factors in the self-conscious attempts of the writers of the period to resurrect the spirit of his eclogues.[5] It is perhaps best to view the creation and the popularity of the sixteenth-century pastoral romance as a coalescence of these various factors without attempting the impossible task of seeking a single cause.

[2] "Buccolic fiction requires before all else a poet and audience sufficiently civilized to appreciate primitive simplicity, to recognize that the gain of Art means the loss of Nature. . . . After all, nostalgia for natural simplicity is a sentiment denied those who have experienced only natural simplicity" (*Nature and Art in Renaissance Literature* [New York, 1964], p. 5).

[3] For the importance of neo-Platonic ideas on nature, "este concepto de la naturaleza, como fuerza codivina, mística e ineludible," in the age and in the works of Cervantes, see Castro, *El pensamiento de Cervantes*, Chap. IV. For neo-Platonic theories of love in the creation of the *Galatea* and a bibliography on Cervantes' sources, see Otis H. Green, *Spain and the Western Tradition*, I, 185-191.

[4] For the ethical implications of nature in Renaissance thought, see Castro, op.cit.; José Antonio Maravall, *El humanismo de las armas en Don Quijote* (Madrid, 1948), p. 217.

[5] Menéndez y Pelayo interprets the origins of the pastoral romance exclusively in terms of literary influences: ". . . se derivó . . . de la intención artística y deliberada de reproducir un cierto tipo de belleza antigua vista y admirada en los poetas griegos y latinos. Ninguna razón histórica justificaba la aparición del género bucólico: era un puro *dilettantismo* estético" (*Orígenes de la novela*, II, 185).

213

The pastoral romance envisions man in a state of perfection, living in harmony with a universal order that is everywhere visible in an ordered and beautiful nature. It is a vision of happiness in simplicity, "des Vollglückes in der Beschränkung," to borrow Jean Paul's definition of the idyl. In tending flocks, singing, dancing, and competing in rustic games, the blessed of the bucolic paradise find all the joy that is missing in the real world, which is represented by the highly refined society of the courtier. Only does an occasional shadow fall on their world of light, the brief tragedy of an unrequited love.[6]

It is not surprising to discover in Cervantes' *Galatea*, which must be situated in the Sannazaro-Virgilian tradition,[7] the artist's most extensive description of a pastoral paradise and a paradise which is constructed almost exclusively according to classical and not oriental or Celtic models.[8] In the final book of the work nearly all the characters gather to make a pilgrimage to the tomb of the beloved shepherd Meliso in the Valley of the Cypresses. They journey along the Tagus, reach the cemetery, perform various rites of homage, deliver eulogies, and listen to the song of the nymph Caliope, who rises miraculously in the flames issuing from the tomb of the fallen shepherd.

The general outlines of the episode were probably inspired by the rites, processions, lamentations, and games at the tombs of Androgeo and Massilia in *Prose* V, X, and XI of Sannazaro's *Arcadia*, which themselves are reminiscent of Aeneas' return to

[6] "Erstlich kann die Leidenschaft, in so fern sie heisse Wetterwolken hinter sich hat, sich nicht mit ihren Donnern in diese stillen Himmel mischen; nur einige laue Regenwölkchen sind ihr vergönnt, vor und hinter welchen man schon den breiten hellen Sonnenschein auf den Hügeln und Auen sieht" (*Vorschule der Aesthetik, Sämtliche Werke* [Weimar, 1935], XI, 241-243). How different are the violent *chiaroscuros* of the heavens above the rugged landscapes of the *Persiles*.

[7] In emphasizing the unity of Cervantes' work, Avalle-Arce devotes most of his study of the *Galatea* to nongeneric elements, which prefigure the novelistic vision of reality that informs the *Quixote* (see *La novela pastoril española* [Madrid, 1959], pp. 197-231). While traces of a spirit opposing the idealizing tendency of the pastoral romance are undoubtedly present in the work, they are few. The *Galatea* remains a conventional work, and to my mind the scene of the funeral of Meliso is a high point in the development of the genre to which it belongs.

[8] Here and below in my study I refer to the categories which Howard R. Patch employs in his study of the paradise theme in various literary traditions (*The Other World*).

Sicily to perform rites of homage at the grave of Anchises (*Aeneid*, V).[9] What concerns us here, however, is not the episode in its entirety but rather Cervantes' description of the pastoral cemetery, in which he does not follow Sannazaro. The outstanding characteristics of the Valley of the Cypresses are the symmetrical arrangement of real objects of nature and the implied presence of the ordering hand of its creator. The garden is located within four gentle hills which rise evenly to form a rectangular enclosure ("On one part of the bank of the famous Tagus, there rise in four different and opposite quarters four green and peaceful hills, walls and defenders as it were of a fair valley which they contain in their midst")[10] and is approached by four avenues extending from the edges of the hills. A second natural wall, in the form of a row of evenly spaced cypresses, all of equal height ("set in such order and harmony that even the very branches of each seem to grow uniformly, and none dares in the slightest to exceed or go beyond another"),[11] stands along the four converging avenues and surrounds a central green. The spaces between the cypresses are planted with rose bushes and jasmines, whose branches and petals intermingle. Evenly spaced, gentle brooks flow down from the hills and converge in the open circular area. The center of the garden is marked by a marble fountain which surpasses in artistry the famous fountains of Tivoli and Trinacria. Between the wall of cypresses and the outer wall formed by the hills are the marble and jasper sepulchers of the shepherds whose remains are worthy of such a cemetery.

The geometrical symmetry and order that is everywhere evident in this scene is reflected stylistically in the measured, evenly flowing prose of Cervantes. At no point do we hear the agitated movement of language based on uncontrolled accumulations of nouns

---

[9] See Michele Scherillo's introduction to his edition of the *Arcadia* (Turin, 1888), pp. cclv-cclx; also Francisco López Estrada's *Estudio crítico de la Galatea* (La Laguna de Tenerife, 1948), pp. 95-99.

[10] "Levántanse en una parte de la ribera del famoso Tajo, en cuatro diferentes y contrapuestas partes, cuatro verdes y apacibles collados, como por muros y defensores de un hermoso valle que en medio contienen" (*La Galatea*, II, 171-172).

[11] ". . . puestos por tal orden y concierto, que hasta las mesmas ramas de los unos y de los otros parece que igualmente van creciendo, y que ninguna se atreve a pasar ni salir un punto más de la otra" (II, 172).

and adjectives in long asyndetic listings which characterizes his subsequent descriptions of the garden paradise. Here Cervantes achieves an even cadence by moderation in descriptive language and the repeated balancing of two units, employing frequently the ornamental epithet to preserve parallelism:

Cierran y *ocupan* el espacio que entre *ciprés* y *ciprés* se hace, mil *olorosos rosales* y *suaves jazmines*, tan *juntos* y *entretejidos*, como suelen estar en los vallados de las guardadas viñas las *espinosas zarzas* y *puntosas cambroneras*. De trecho en trecho destas apacibles entradas, se ven correr por entre la *verde* y *menuda* yerba *claros* y *frescos* arroyos de *limpias* y *sabrosas* aguas (II, 172).[12]

The balancing in pairs can be observed in nearly every sentence of the passage ("altos e infinitos cipreses," "blanco y precioso mármol," "orden y concierto," "largas y apacibles calles," "verdes y apacibles collados," "muros y defensores," "el remate y fin").[13]

It is important to observe the moderation in the descriptive style of this passage. Just as there is no uncontrolled enumeration of object, there is similarly little emphasis on concrete details which would individualize objects. Brooks, cypresses, hills, and rose bushes are present no more than in their generic reality, as their modifying adjectives are usually attributive rather than descriptive. It is similarity rather than difference, unity rather than variety, harmony rather than discord that inform the author's vision of the natural world in his pastoral romance. Moreover, although natural objects appear in an impossibly perfect geometrical pattern, they nonethe-

---

[12] "The space there between *cypress* and *cypress* is *closed* and *occupied* by a thousand *fragrant rose-bushes* and *pleasing jessamine*, so *close* and *interwoven* as *thorny brambles* and *prickly briars* are wont to be in the hedges of guarded vineyards. From point to point of these peaceful openings are seen running through the *short green* grass *clear cool* streamlets of *pure sweet* waters." The italics are mine.

[13] In its even cadence and slow movement the passage is a good example of the prose rhythm which Hatzfeld, in observing "ganz bestimmte breit-ruhige Dämpfungsmomente des Gesamtstiles" in the *Quixote*, has designated as "Schäferstil" and attributed to the strong influence of the conventional, classical literary modes in Cervantes' artistic education (see *"Don Quijote" als Wortkunstwerk* [Leipzig, 1927], pp. 222-223).

216

less do not cease to be real. The transmutation of the natural world into some higher reality by metaphor, an important characteristic of Cervantes' subsequent paradise descriptions, is significantly absent in the *Galatea*.

The literary tradition behind Cervantes' garden paradise is that which lies behind the entire genre of the pastoral romance, that of classical antiquity. Its prototype is the garden of King Alcinous in the *Odyssey* and its imitations in the Greek romances, all of which present a gentle, bountiful nature of remarkable symmetry and order and reflect man's desire for harmony and peace.[14] Indeed, as the procession moves along the Tagus toward its destination, Elicio compares the Valley of the Cypresses to the garden of Alcinous and describes three features of it which recall the garden paradise of the Homeric tradition—a pleasant zephyr blows constantly in the valley, extremes of cold and heat are unknown in its climate of perpetual spring, and the trees produce fruit in abundance.[15]

In describing the paradise of the *Galatea,* Cervantes introduces a problem which is perhaps as old as civilization itself—the relationship between art and nature. Elicio's allusion to the garden of Alcinous is preceded by the words: "And the skill of its inhabitants has wrought so much that nature, incorporated with art, is become an artist and art's peer, and from both together has been formed a

[14] ". . . der späte Grieche sucht in der Natur wohl, statt der Verwirrung der Menschenwelt, eine ewig in gleichem Masse bewegte Harmonie, statt des hastigen Getümmels der Stadt die beschauliche Andacht auf stiller Flur. . . . Das Ideal dieser Art der Naturempfindung ist die Natur als Garten" (Erwin Rohde, *Der Griechische Roman und seine Vorläufer*, pp. 544-545). For similarity in spirit of the Virgilian bucolic and the Renaissance pastoral romance, see Hellmuth Petriconi, "Die Verlorenen Paradiese," *Romanistisches Jahrbuch*, X (1959), p. 179.

[15] The academic problem of a specific source for Cervantes' garden paradise need not concern us, and is indeed probably impossible to solve. Probably the "purest" examples of the enclosed garden topic which he could conceivably have known are in Homer's *Odyssey*, Longus' *Daphnis and Chloe*, and Achilles Tatius' *Clitophon and Leucippe*. Like the Valley of the Cypresses, each of these rectangular gardens presents real objects of nature with no fantastic transmutation, and in each the movement of the description proceeds from the outer edge toward the central object (by the time of the Greek romance these two procedures had been standardized in the rhetorical codes of the sophists, where the garden appeared as one of the standard pieces of the writer and orator [see Otmar Schissel, "Der byzantinische Garten: seine Darstellung im gleichzeitigen Romane," *Sitzungsberichte der Akademie der Wissenschaften in Wien*, CCXXI (1942), 1-9, 19]).

third nature to which I cannot give a name."[16] As the traditional art-nature duality appears in nearly every paradise description in Cervantes' writings, and as its variations are meaningful in relation to the author's changing preoccupations in shaping the literary topic, it is necessary to summarize briefly its major implications in the thought and writings of the time.

According to the most recent study of the subject the terms "art" and "nature" are "as ubiquitous and pivotal in Renaissance thought as the pairing of 'heredity' and 'environment' in a modern textbook of social psychology."[17] The terms had a wide variety of meanings and areas of application, and it is not surprising to find them used inconsistently by a single writer, in one context as complementary and in another as opposed terms. Cervantes' writings could be used to demonstrate nearly every facet of this multidimensional controversy. Perhaps its most important frame of reference was philosophical and ethical:[18] nature could be viewed either as a source of natural wisdom and presented as superior to society in its artifice and hypocrisy, or as a state of barbarity which civilization, exemplified by the city, must overcome.[19] In Cervantes' works we can observe frequent examples of this aspect of the controversy, both pro-nature: Don Quixote's speech on the happy state

[16] "Y la industria de sus moradores ha hecho tanto, que la naturaleza, encorporada con el arte, es hecha artífice y connatural del arte, y de entrambas a dos se ha hecho una tercia naturaleza, a la cual no sabré dar nombre" (II, 170).

[17] Tayler, *Nature and Art in Renaissance Literature*, p. 2. See also Elias L. Rivers' illuminating observations on the subject in his study of Garcilaso's Third Eclogue ("The Pastoral Paradox of Natural Art," *Modern Language Notes*, LXXVII [1962], 130-144).

[18] If the categories which I establish in what follows (the ethical-philosophical, the aesthetic, and the educational) represent an oversimplification, I think that they are useful in an attempt to deal meaningfully with an area of thought and terminology which presents so many superficial contradictions. Admittedly it is never possible to isolate entirely the ethical from the aesthetic moment of the concept of nature; nevertheless, it seems fair to say that in almost all cases one usually dominates a given context. Thus the aesthetic moment in the celebration of nature, which was rooted in Renaissance neo-Platonism, is most important in the funeral scene of the *Galatea*. On the other hand, the ethical moment, which derived from the humanists' preoccupation with man's moral nature and their belief that he can achieve an inner perfection in solitude and through contact with nature, is the dominating force in Don Quixote's speech to the goatherds.

[19] The philosophical context of the popular Renaissance controversy is probably the original context in which the problem was formulated (see Arthur O. Lovejoy and George Boas, *Primitivism and Related Ideas in Antiquity* [Baltimore, 1935]).

of man in the Golden Age, his recurrent denunciations of the artificiality of the life at the court, Sancho's natural wisdom in the Barataria episode, his respect for the proverb as a source of wisdom, and the *beatus-ille* motif of Soldino in the third book of the *Persiles*; and contra-nature: the overall movement of the *Persiles* from the rugged island of the barbarians toward the city of Rome, the center of civilization.[20]

At the same time art and nature were popular terms in the numerous theoretical writings concerning the education of the humanist and poet. Here art and nature were generally held to be complementary, in accordance with Horace's influential recommendations for the formation of the poet.[21] Cervantes was also aware of this aspect of the duality. Don Quixote tells Diego de Miranda that the poet is born but perfects himself in his vocation by diligent study and that "this is so because art is not better than nature, but perfects her; so nature combined with art and art with nature, will produce a most perfect poet."[22]

And finally there was an essentially aesthetic context in the art-nature controversy, in which the traditional view of art as the *simia naturae* (i.e., the likening of the creative act of the artist to that of God's creative agent, nature [*natura naturans*]) was invoked, and evaluations of the creations of the respective creative forces, art and nature, were made. The conventional solution was the assertion of the superiority of nature's creative power and its created objects to those of art, which in the last analysis merely imitates both the creative act of nature and nature's objects in its own act of creation. In the words of Erasmus, "Much better in every respect are

[20] The flexibility with which Cervantes employs the ancient topic in an artistic context is most apparent in *La Gitanilla*, where the Gypsy world of nature is presented both as a positive counterweight to the corrupt city and court and as a demonic counterweight to the regenerate order exemplified by the city to which the hero returns.

[21] "Natura fieret laudabile carmen an arte,/ Quaesitum est; ego nec studium sine divite vena/ Nec rude quid possit video ingenium: alterius sic/ Altera poscit opem res et conjurat amice" (*Epistola ad Pisones*, ll. 408-411).

[22] ". . . la razón es porque el arte no se aventaja a la naturaleza, sino perficiónala; así que mezcladas la naturaleza y el arte, y el arte con la naturaleza, sacarán un perfetísimo poeta" (II, 650). In praising a Master Orense, unknown to Cervantine scholarship, Mercury states: "Su natural ingenio, con la ciencia/ y ciencias aprendidas, le leuanta/ al grado que le nombra la excelencia" (*Viage del Parnaso*, p. 63).

the works of Nature than the adulteries of Art."[23] In spite of the superiority generally conceded to nature, there was a tendency in Renaissance writings to see the two creative forces as complementary at this level too. For example, Fray Luis de Granada generally maintains that nature, God's creative agent, is vastly superior to art.[24] However, he believes that man's imitation of the divine process in creating artifacts is one of the major proofs of man's dignity and his likeness to God, and he acknowledges that both nature and art have important functions in the universe: "And just as God created this world full of natural works, so art has nearly made another new world of artificial things."[25] On the other hand the balance could occasionally lean toward art, and in the late sixteenth and seventeenth centuries the appearance of the terms in an opposition which was resolved in favor of art became very frequent. Probably the best known statement of the superiority of art to nature is Sir Philip Sidney's "Her [Nature's] world is brasen, the Poets only deliuer a golden."[26] In Spain Baltasar Gracián wrote: "Art is the complement of nature and another, a second entity, which beautifies it in the utmost degree and even strives to surpass it in its creations . . . without the aid of artifice, nature would remain unrefined and rude."[27]

At this point it is well to return to the subject at hand, which is the consideration of Cervantes' use of the garden paradise topic. The implications of the art-nature controversy in the aesthetic sphere are those which are most relevant to it. Cervantes seems to as-

[23] Cited by Tayler, pp. 32-33. Cervantes can at times approximate this point of view (see *Viage del Parnaso*, p. 94) just as he can assume the other possible positions in the controversy (see below).

[24] ". . . vemos la conformidad del arte con la naturaleza que Dios crió, aunque primero fué la naturaleza que el arte" (*Del símbolo de la fe*, ed. B.A.E., VI, 252). Granada offers the wonders of the human body (*el mundo menor*) in proof of the inimitable powers of nature. The painter requires days to reproduce the images which the eye can compose in an instant (p. 257).

[25] "Y así como Dios crió este mundo lleno de obras naturales, así el arte ha hecho cuasi otro nuevo mundo de cosas artificiales" (ibid., p. 264).

[26] *An Apologie for Poetrie, Elizabethan Critical Essays*, ed. G. G. Smith (Oxford, 1904), I, 156.

[27] "Es el arte complemento de la naturaleza y un otro segundo ser que por estremo la hermosea y aun pretende excederla en sus obras . . . sin este socorro del artificio, quedara [la naturaleza] inculta y grosera" (*El Criticón*, ed. Romera-Navarro [Philadelphia, 1938], I, 243).

sociate the theoretical problem with the *locus amoenus*, for it appears as consistently in his descriptions as do the various objects traditionally associated with the paradise topic, i.e., trees, flowers, fountains, et cetera. Moreover, its variety of formulations and resolutions spans all the possibilities which we observe in the writings of his contemporaries. In the *Galatea* Elicio's words: ". . . la naturaleza, encorporada con el arte, es hecha artífice y connatural del arte, y de entrambas a dos se ha hecho una tercia naturaleza" (II, 170) present the conventional conception of the two forces as complementary in their workings. However, it is well to note that nature is subtly given the dominant role by Cervantes. Nature is in fact conceived as a divine artificer which enables art to surpass itself in its creations.

Cervantes' solution of the art-nature controversy in favor of nature is logical in the *Galatea*, for the romance was conceived as an expression of a vision of a world order created by God through His creative agent, nature. At one point man, the supreme creation, is described as the product of the so-called *mayordomo de Dios*: "But that which made them wonder most and raise their thoughts, was to see the frame of man so well-ordered, so perfect, and so beautiful, that they came to call him a world in little; and so it is true that in all the works made by God's steward, nature, nothing is of such excellence."[28] At the same time both man and nature (*natura naturata*), the creations of nature (*natura naturans*), bear within themselves the divine spirit. As the shepherds approach the Valley of the Cypresses, Elicio asserts that "God, for the same reason that they say He dwells in Heaven, makes here His sojourn for the most part."[29] His description of the scene reaches its climax as he praises the beauty of the shepherdesses who are born in the region and turns to Galatea as the outstanding example. In the narrator's recapitulation of Elicio's speech the identification of the beauty of

[28] "Pero lo que más los admiró y levantó la consideración, fue ver la compostura del hombre, tan ordenada, tan perfecta y tan hermosa, que le vinieron a llamar mundo abreviado, y así es verdad, que en todas las obras hechas por el mayordomo de Dios, naturaleza, ninguna es de tanto primor" (II, 61).

[29] ". . . Dios, por la mesma razón que dicen que mora en los cielos, en esta parte haga lo más de su habitación" (II, 170).

221

woman and that of nature is more explicit: "He had praised the banks of the Tagus and the beauty of Galatea."

Cervantes' most concentrated expression of the harmony between the creator, nature, and man is the garden paradise, where nature, the hand of God, has guided the hand of art, where a nature of order and symmetry receives the fallen Meliso and allows heaven to raise "in its starry abode the blessed soul of the body that lies there,"[30] and where the song of the birds accompanies the lamentation of the human beings in an indescribable dirge.

The Garden Paradise and Literary Parody: Viage del Parnaso

Brief mention must be made of the garden paradise which Cervantes presents in his literary satire in the form of a mock-epic, the *Viage del Parnaso*. As the paradise appears here as a purely literary phenomenon, it provides a convenient transition from the philosophical context of the *Galatea* to the contexts of complicated literary problems surrounding the gardens of the *Quixote* and the *Persiles*.

In his mock-epic Cervantes describes the haunt of Apollo and the Muses high on Mount Parnassus, which is to be the setting of the defeat of the vulgar poetasters by the true disciples of Apollo. The description of the *locus amoenus* is brief and, in keeping with the tone of the work, hyperbolic. We observe once again a comparison of the garden to that of Alcinous and the Hesperides. Although there is a minimum of descriptive detail, several of the traditional elements are noted hastily: eternal spring, fruit, ivy, and several of the trees of classical literature—namely, the myrtle, the oak, and the laurel. The parodistic tone that sounds throughout the work can be perceived also here: "Along with being a garden, it was an orchard, a grove, a wood, a meadow, a delightful vale, for it bears all these titles at once."[31]

What is most interesting in the description is Cervantes' introduction of the art-nature controversy twice within fifteen lines of poetry. Both art and nature are conceived as positive creative agents,

---

[30] ". . . en su estrellado asiento la bendita alma del cuerpo que allí yace" (II, 173).

[31] "Iunto con ser jardin, era vna huerta,/ vn soto, vn bosque, vn prado, vn valle ameno,/ que en todos estos titulos concierta" (p. 52).

as it were, engaged in competition to embellish the beautiful garden. After introducing the garden by observing that both nature and art are displaying their best talents in its creation, Cervantes proceeds to the description in three tercets and then returns to the theme:

> Naturaleza y arte alli parece
> andar en competencia, y está en duda
> qual vence de las dos, qual mas merece.[32]

The double appearance of the topic in what is a schematically drawn garden paradise according to the classical models suggests that for Cervantes the art-nature controversy was one of the traditional formulas of paradise description. We have observed its appearance in the paradise of the *Galatea* and its thematic coherence in the work. Here it is simply one more ornament of a garden, which itself has no function more serious than that of being one of various traditional topics of idealizing literature which Cervantes travesties.

The Garden Paradise, Psychology, and Literary Problems: Don Quixote

In *Don Quixote* Cervantes employs the garden paradise topic in the parallel episodes of the Knight of the Lake's journey to the lower regions and the protagonist's descent into the Cave of Montesinos. As I have pointed out above, both episodes have a function within a surrounding context of literary debate, the former touching on a variety of problems concerning the aesthetic merits of the romances, the latter dealing with the specific problem of verisimilitude and audience credibility. In what follows I hope to show by examination of the style and sources of the paradise descriptions how Cervantes created the gardens of his masterpiece as humorous rebuttals to the judgments of the romances advanced by the Aristotelian critical movement and the principles on which these judgments were founded. Here the paradise is no longer an expression of the neo-Platonic theories of universal harmony and man's inherent perfection which animate the *Galatea*. It is rather a symbol

[32] "There it seems that nature and art are competing, and it is uncertain which of the two is the victor, which is the more worthy" (p. 51).

of the traditional aspect of imaginative literature which was causing most concern in contemporary critical writings, the marvelous.

In the garden episodes of the *Quixote* the moderation in descriptive matter characteristic of the pastoral romance has yielded to a multiplicity of detail presented in long sentences which swell with accumulations and listings.[33] The geometrical lines of the Valley of the Cypresses are nowhere visible in the disordered mass of phenomena which the amazed Knight of the Lake discovers confronting him on all sides ("Aquí descubre . . . acullá vee . . . acá vee . . ."). Real objects of nature are present, but their reality immediately dissolves in a fantastic transmutation through simile. The water of the brook becomes liquid crystal, and the sand and pebbles of its bed become sifted gold and pearls. The clarity of the sun ("el sol luce con claridad más nueva") and the transparentness of the heaven of the *locus amoenus* are unknown in the world above. Indeed the dominant feature of the garden is its artificial and unnatural quality, a quality distinguishing it sharply from the harmonious synthesis of art and nature represented by the garden of the *Galatea.* Once again Cervantes introduces the art-nature controversy into his description of the garden paradise, but now the balance has tipped in favor of art. In the creation of the marvelous fountain of marble, jasper, and emeralds, "el arte, imitando a la naturaleza, parece que allí la vence" (I, 500). In the underworld paradise we observe an emphasis not only on artifice but also on its dazzling effects on the senses of the observer (the detailed account of sensuous experiences "que suspenden al caballero y admiran a los leyentes").

The chaotic variety of the subterranean world of pleasure is reflected stylistically in the rhythmical movement which marks the prose of the passage. The effect of repose in the description of the Valley of the Cypresses, arising from the succession of evenly flowing sentences based on the balancing of paired elements, is here totally absent. Instead we hear an agitated rhythm produced, on the one hand, by overloaded sentences, as the author compresses an

---

[33] Here I take my specific examples from the Knight of the Lake episode, but the *conclusions* concerning style and sources are applicable to the Montesinos episode as well.

abundance of detail into the knight's utterances, on the other hand, by sentences which swell with parallel syntactical units and accumulations of adjectives, nouns, and verbs in long listings. The former have a retarding effect on the movement of the passage, as overly crowded individual units seem to break the syntactic bonds holding them in the sentences and establish themselves as independent units (". . . acá vee otra a lo brutesco ordenada, adonde las menudas conchas de las almejas con las torcidas casas blancas y amarillas del caracol, puestas con orden desordenada, mezclados entre ellas pedazos de cristal luciente y de contrahechas esmeraldas, hacen una variada labor . . ." [I, 500]). The latter have an opposite effect of energy and rapid movement, particularly when the parallelism of the accumulated elements is reinforced by anaphora ("sin entrar . . . sin ponerse . . . sin despojarse . . ." or "de diamantes, de carbuncos, de rubíes, de perlas, de oro, y de esmeraldas"). In many cases these two rhythmical tendencies of the prose of the passage alternate within single sentences, and the resultant overall effect is what could be described as an agitated rhythm. In conclusion it is perhaps useful to point out a minor detail which well illustrates the disappearance of both the moderation in detail and the rhythmic evenness of the *Galatea* in the description of the underworld paradise. Both works present a common motif of the paradise tradition, the singing of the birds: the *Galatea*: "Juntábase a esto la dulce armonía de los pintados y muchos pajarillos que por los aires cruzaban" (II, 176); *Don Quixote*: ". . . y entretiene los oídos el dulce y no aprendido canto de los pequeños, infinitos y pintados pajarillos que por los intricados ramos van cruzando" (I, 500).[34]

The striking differences between the garden paradise of Don Quixote's vision and that of the *Galatea* indicate that, in creating the former, Cervantes had turned to a nonclassical tradition for his model. In his study,[35] Howard R. Patch has illuminated the depth and richness of the literary tradition which lay behind the gardens of the medieval romance. The ornate and fantastic motifs of the

[34] "To this was joined the sweet harmony of little bright-colored birds, that were flitting through the air"; ". . . and the sweet and untaught song of the tiny, innumerable, and bright-colored little birds which flit about the interlacing branches delights his ears."

[35] *The Other World according to Descriptions in Medieval Literature.*

otherworld visions of the ancient orient, which were preserved and given renewed life in the Celtic and old Germanic traditions and flowered in the medieval visions of the Christian Earthly Paradise and the Garden of Love of courtly love; the motifs of darkness, mystery, and magic, which seem to be the product of the northern European fantasy; and indeed many of the themes and motifs of the literature of classical antiquity had all become possessions of a common literary tradition from which the writer of romance could nourish his creations.

Cervantes' parodistic scenes, like the scenes of the romances which he no doubt had in mind as he created them, reveal a rich combination of elements from this eclectic tradition. For example, the perilous descent through darkness to an underworld realm of delightful gardens guarded by frightening creatures is as old as the Gilgamesh epic. The variant pattern of the descent through a water barrier, actually the case in the episode of the Knight of the Lake, appeared frequently in Celtic mythology.[36] The double fountain of the type which Cervantes' knight discovers was common in the Islamic, classical, and Celtic traditions of paradise description.[37] Other important elements of Don Quixote's vision—the use of highly ornamental metaphor to describe nature, the extreme ornateness of the palace, the emphasis on the sensuous beauty of the region and the sensuous pleasure which the knight experiences, and the attentions of his hostesses—are traceable ultimately to the oriental tradition of the garden paradise.[38]

Our present concern is not what was the specific source of the episode of the Knight of the Lake, but rather what the general source, the garden of romance, reveals about Cervantes' selective processes and how it functions in the context of the *Quixote*. It might be argued that Don Quixote's vision of a subterranean paradise, in which nature is replaced by a higher reality, is a landscape of the mind, in this case a sick mind yearning for an escape from a

[36] See Patch, pp. 11, 43.

[37] See Patch, pp. 36, 15, 17.

[38] See Patch, p. 15. The motif of maidens who, like those who meet the Knight of the Lake, receive, undress, bathe, and feed their guests and ensure their general physical well-being, is a peculiarity of Celtic and Islamic mythology and appeared frequently in medieval romances (p. 32).

world which it has come to find intolerable. While it is undeniable that Don Quixote is indulging himself in the pleasures of a wish-fulfillment daydream, the psychological verisimilitude of the vision should not obscure its thematic necessity in relation to the problems formulated in the context which immediately frames it—the literary debate between Don Quixote and the canon.

In Chapter III, I pointed out certain features of the garden of romance which were well suited to Don Quixote's intentions of undermining the canon's neo-Aristotelian criticisms of various moral and aesthetic flaws in the books of chivalry. In the attributes which had crystalized around it in its literary tradition—teeming variety of detail, subordination of the natural to the artificial and ornate, exaggeration of a sensuous apprehension and enjoyment of reality, and the unrestrained use of the fantastic—it represents in concentrated form those qualities which the "ancients" censured and the "moderns" celebrated in the works of Ariosto and other romancers.

There is still another important aspect of Cervantes' creation of a romance paradise within the literary debate between the canon and Don Quixote. In the writings of contemporary theorists the topic of the garden paradise was, like the pagan deities and monsters, Virgil's nymph-ship transformation, and the hippogryph, one of various elements from the tradition of imaginative literature which had acquired through repeated examination a particular allusiveness to the literary controversy concerning belief, verisimilitude, and the marvelous. Thus Julius Caesar Scaliger, to whom one can always look for the extreme form of pedantry that the accommodation of the empirical-instructive mode of thought to literary theory in the Renaissance could easily produce, censured the poets of the ideal landscape for placing together trees that could not possibly grow together in a real forest.[39] The example which caused most concern among the theorists in all these matters was Ariosto, and it is not surprising that the fantastic garden of Alcina should come under fire in their writings. The conservative literary theorist Tommaso Campanella, for example, was always suspicious of the lie as morally reprehensible and found invented subject matter in

---

[39] See Curtius, *Europäische Literatur und Lateinisches Mittelalter*, p. 201.

literature difficult to tolerate in any context.[40] However, he allows the poet to present *cose finte*, if verisimilitude is maintained, and he is even willing to permit some implausibilities if they are accompanied by a moral lesson and if the element of the marvelous does not overshadow that lesson. Campanella cites, as examples of a poet's failure both to observe verisimilitude and to subordinate the marvelous to the exemplary, Ariosto's land of Alcina and hippogryph as well as the paradise of Tasso's Armida.[41] In fact the lack of verisimilitude in the episode of Armida's garden remained a cause of some discomfort for Tasso. In response to Silvio Antoniano's suggestions concerning revisions of the *Liberata*, he promises to cut out of his text various marvelous elements which his censor "either condemns as an inquisitor, or does not approve as a poet" ("o condanna come inquisitore, o non approva come poeta"), among them a metamorphosis of knights into fish, a "miracle of the tomb, which is in truth too strange," and a vision of Rinaldo. At the same time he asserts that he will maintain some of the censured marvels, e.g., the garden of Armida and the enchanted forest, but his weak justification of their inclusion, which amounts to a concession to the very forces which Cervantes continually mocks, suggests his insecurity with what he feels to be a flaw in his work: "As for the enchantments of Armida's garden and the forest, the truth is . . . I would not know how to cut them out without causing obvious damage to the whole."[42]

The pedantry of a Scaliger or the inhibitions of a Tasso are representative of an entire movement in literary theorizing, and it was this movement which Don Quixote and Cervantes were addressing in their description of the underworld paradise. The garden, a topic of that controversial area of aesthetic theorizing,[43] the

[40] See Weinberg, p. 1066.

[41] Tommaso Campanella, *Poetica*, pp. 120, 158-159.

[42] "Ben è vero che gl'incanti del giardino d'Armida e quei de la selva . . . io non saprei come troncare senza niuno o e senza manifesto mancamento del tutto" (Tasso, *Le lettere*, I, 144).

[43] An interesting appearance of the garden in the critical writing of the time is to be found in Ugo's long and detailed poem describing the earthly paradise in El Pinciano's *Philosophía antigua poética* (I, 253-261). Here the impossibly beautiful garden of innumerable trees, flowers, springs, and precious stones is presented in an entirely different critical focus. It is given as an example of the possibility of a

marvelous, becomes a vehicle for Cervantes' humorous assertion of his independence of the Aristotelian dogma. In the *Persiles*, the epic in prose modeled according to neo-Aristotelian doctrines, he reasserts this independence, and in doing so he once again has recourse to the garden paradise as a topic of the marvelous.

The Garden Paradise and the Liberated Imagination: *Persiles y Sigismunda*

If the episode of the counterfeit captives recalls Master Pedro's puppet show in the way in which it poses and resolves certain literary problems, Periandro's account of his visit to the mysterious island recalls Don Quixote's narration of the adventure of the Cave of Montesinos. In both episodes Cervantes utilizes the narrator-audience situation to study the problems of belief and authorial freedom. In both the two fundamental types of audience as defined by conventional theorists are present to reflect on the narration— the unquestioning, enthusiastic audience, identified generally with the *vulgo* and women, and the highly critical audience, identified with the educated humanist (the *culto*) and the neo-Aristotelian literary school. In both episodes Cervantes employs the archetypal theme of imaginative literature, the journey to the otherworld, and utilizes the traditional dream vision as a way of rendering plausible an episode dominated by the fantastical.[44]

In describing his vision, Periandro employs the narrative technique which we observe in Don Quixote, Master Pedro, Cide

---

description—i.e., a painting in poetry—and as an example of how imitation is to be distinguished from true reproduction. The fantastic garden is contrasted with a hypothetical verse description of the real gardens of Aranjuez and the Escorial, which would be merely history in verse and not poetry. It is interesting that El Pinciano fails to discuss the garden in terms of its problematic verisimilitude, although the skepticism of Scaliger, Campanella, Tasso, and Periandro's learned audience is implicit in the words of disbelief of the character El Pinciano, here speaking in his occasional role as philistine in the discourse: "¿Por qué llamáys poesía perfecta a esta descripción priuada de toda imitación?" (p. 263).

[44] The ambiguity of Don Quixote's motivation and his apparent failure to realize that his experience was a dream is of psychological interest but does not affect the literary dimension of the scene. In the *Persiles*, the literary is the dominating dimension, and Periandro's refusal to reveal that his experience was a dream vision until he has captured the belief of his audience must be interpreted as an analogic representation of the way in which the artist manipulates his illusions and controls his audience.

Hamete Benengeli, and the counterfeit captives' confrontations of their respective audiences. In all cases the narrator presents his subject matter as truth, exhorting his listeners to "see" it. At the same time he unexpectedly inserts details which remind the audience of the fictional quality of the narration. In Periandro's description of the disappearance of "seven or eight" of his men, we hear the familiar intentional imprecision of Cide Hamete Benengeli. In his assertion that the river is of diamonds "as is normally said" (*como suele dezirse*), we witness the *Verfremdungseffekt* of the type which the counterfeit captives employ when reminding their audience that the ships of their narration are small because of the size of their canvas. Such comments reveal a ludic spirit in the narrator, who, by playfully deflating his poetic context, underscores the dependence of both that context and its audience on his wishes.

Of all the adventures contained in Periandro's narration, his journey to the otherworld is the richest in literary reminiscences. In its imaginative synthesis of various motifs of epic and romance traditions, it is one of the outstanding examples of the eclectic and self-consciously literary character of the *Persiles*. For example, the account begins with the familiar garden paradise, which in Renaissance epic had become a necessity whether as functional thematic element or merely as ornament (*ecphrasis*). The description of the figure Sensuality, a beautiful woman with a wand mounted on a cart drawn by apes, is evocative of a variety of motifs of the tradition of island sorceresses, from Circe down to her most famous Renaissance descendants, Alcina and Armida. The retinue of girls, whose strange song enchants the listener and seems to turn him into stone and who seize and bear into the mountain several of Periandro's men, as well as the sorceress' chariot in the form of a wrecked ship, represents an imaginative evocation of the Sirens.

Cervantes links these literary motifs to the major thematic thread of the work by employing them in an allegorical representation of the ordeals and triumph of his protagonists. Auristela appears as the goddess Chastity and banishes the procession of sorceress, her apes, and her attendants. The maidens, Continence and Modesty, then assure Periandro that they will protect his beloved through all the trials that await her on the journey to Rome.

The literary details and sources of Periandro's vision of the other-world are meaningful in relation to the literary debate which is carried on throughout his narration. Once again Cervantes turns to the fantastic gardens of romance literature, which the neo-Aristotelian theorists were censuring as examples of inverisimilitude (see above). The setting of the paradise is a mysterious island ("an island unknown to any of us") in remote waters at the northern extremity of the world. The sorceress' palace is a hollow crag, which miraculously opens while strange music sounds and the beautiful women come forth. All these elements were products of the Celtic imagination which frequently appeared in the medieval romance. Generally the *imram*, the island, and the *sid*, the hollow hill, were not conjoined, for each one, containing marvelous gardens, palaces, and maidens, was conceived as a complete otherworld, at which the hero must arrive after perilous approach.[45]

Cervantes' free combination of literary motifs as well as certain structural aspects of the vision suggest that his immediate inspiration came not from traditional literature but rather from the contemporary spectacular form of drama—the court masque. This genre was nourished by a wide variety of fantastic themes from the literature of antiquity and medieval romance and obviously was in no way restricted by the principles of neo-Aristotelian aesthetic theorizing. The thematic structure of the vision (the momentary triumph of forces of evil followed by their flight before the forces of goodness and the restoration of order); the importance of scenic effects over dialogue; the processional form of the pageant (the ape-drawn chariot bearing the sorceress, succeeded by the group of maidens and their leaders, Chastity, Continence, and Modesty); the music which accompanies their movements; and the courtly setting for the narration and the involvement of the audience in the unfolding drama, all are general conventions of the masque. Moreover, there are striking similarities in detail between the vision and the contemporary spectacles, indicating beyond a doubt that Cervantes modeled his scene on them.

Jean Rousset has studied the spectacular drama (*le ballet de cour*) as one of the dominant artistic forms of expression of the

[45] See Patch, pp. 27-59.

period of the Baroque, and recognizes the strong inspiration which this form found in the scenes of Armida's island paradise and the enchanted forest in Tasso's *Gerusalemme liberata*. He relates such features as the sorceress, the changing scenery, and the transformations of men into beasts to the preoccupations of the age with mutability, motion, and the deceptive quality of earthly experience. Rousset's examples offer obvious correspondences to Periandro's vision. The garden, the temptress, the mountain which opens up (i.e., the Celtic *sid*) as music plays and from which a procession emerges, and the chariot drawn by beasts are recurrent details of this genre, which by 1600 had become popular all over Europe.[46] In relation to the literary problems which inform Periandro's entire narration, Cervantes' introduction of the court masque into the *Persiles* represents his deliberate selection of a genre in which the untrammeled cultivation of the fantastic was the norm in order to examine critically the Aristotelian criterion of verisimilitude.[47]

The garden which we observe on the *imram* of this masque is with minor variations the same as that of Don Quixote's underworld paradise. The same natural objects are there—the brook, the pleasant fields, and the grove of trees. Both descriptions emphasize the sensuous beauty of the *locus amoenus* and its effect on the observer ("que nos suspendieron las almas y alegraron los sentidos" [I, 274-275]), and both abound in the traditional, oriental paradise motifs of precious stones and metals. The differences between the gardens are minor, but they are meaningful in relation to our study; for they suggest that the focus in which the garden paradise of the *Persiles* was created was exclusively literary. The disorder

---

[46] For example, Rousset describes a masque at Naples, which has all these features in addition to the ape-drawn chariot of Cervantes' figure of Sensuality: "On vit la montagne . . . s'ouvrir et produire un théâtre . . . Alquise, fille d'Urgande, sur un chariot conduit par deux singes . . . elle commande à la montagne de s'ouvrir, on en voit sortir des oiseaux de toutes espèces, douze tambours et fifres, huit pages et quatre chevaliers" (*L'Age baroque*, p. 16).

[47] Viewed in terms of the overall thematic structure of the *Persiles* the masque is an emblematic presentation of the basic cycle of bondage and restoration on which the work is based. As such it can be viewed as an example of the way in which the author assimilates matter from a wide variety of conventional literary forms to his underlying theme of *los trabajos*. The Italian novella, the romance of chivalry, the classical epic, the biblical legends, and traditional comedy and farce are other genres which he exploits in the same way.

of Don Quixote's description, which we observe in the multiplicity of things named and described and in the agitated rhythm of his statements, is significant as it both mirrors his mental disorder and contains an oblique literary defense of the variety of the romances. In Periandro's account all disorder vanishes, and the agitated rhythm of the prose is replaced by a rapid movement, which is free from the constant interruptions which disturbed the flow of the former passage. Variety is indeed an important attraction of this garden, but its variety is presented in a series of carefully constructed sentences dominated by syntactic parallelism and listings. These qualities suggest composition by literary formula, an effect which is not offset by the abundance of details in the listings. For example, the traditional element of the paradise, perennial temperate weather, is described: "There all was spring, all was summer, all was estival mildness, and all was pleasant fall, all delightful beyond belief."[48]

The highly schematic character of this paradise description is nowhere more evident than in the orderly enumeration of the phenomena which appeal to the senses of the visitor.

> What we observed gratified all our five senses: our eyes, with its grace and beauty; our ears, with the soft murmuring of the fountains and rivulets and with the song, formed of untaught voices, of the innumerable little birds, which, hopping from tree to tree and from bough to bough, seemed as if they were detained as captives in that area, captives who did not manage to recover their liberty and did not wish to; our sense of smell, with the fragrance which the herbs, the flowers, and the fruits exhaled; our taste, with the proof which we made of their sweetness; our touch, with the feeling which they afforded our hands, which made us believe we held in them the pearls of the South, the diamonds of the Indies, and the gold of Tebir.[49]

[48] ". . . todo alli era primauera, todo verano, todo estio sin pesadumbre, y todo otoño agradable, con estremo increyble" (I, 275).

[49] "Satisfazia a todos nuestros cinco sentidos lo que mirauamos: a los ojos, con la belleza y la hermosura; a los oydos, con el ruydo manso de las fuentes y arroyos, y con el son de los infinitos paxarillos, que, con no aprendidas vozes formado, los quales, saltando de arbol en arbol y de rama en rama, parecia que en aquel distrito tenian cautiua su libertad, y que no querian ni acertauan a cobrarla; al olfato, con el olor que de si despedian las yeruas, las flores y los frutos; al gusto, con la prueua

Cervantes & the Classical Aesthetic

The single sentence swells with accumulations of elements at all
levels, opening up into five parallel syntactic units each of which
opens up in a continuing syntactic expansion and an amplification
of detail. Yet the multiplicity remains bound to the single sentence,
for the parallelism in listing keeps all in firm control. The overall
effect is one of plenitude but a plenitude that is controlled and
suggestive of a schematic, indeed almost formulaic, planning of the
passage on the part of the author.

There is another significant development in Cervantes' re-creation
of Don Quixote's garden paradise in the *Persiles*. The last sentence
of the passage cited above recalls the metaphorical transmutation
of nature which we observe in the preceding work. The fruit which
delights Periandro and his companions turns into pearls, diamonds,
and gold. Periandro's description actually goes beyond that of Don
Quixote in this respect; for in the latter's metamorphosis of the
natural world the use of the simile allows the natural object to be
preserved. In the *Persiles* the natural world actually disappears and
is replaced by the fantastic. Don Quixote's knight discovers a "small
stream, whose fresh waters glide like liquid crystal over delicate
sand and little white stones, which resemble sifted gold and purest
pearl."[50] Periandro relates: "We treaded on the delightful shore, the
the sands of which (without any exaggeration) were all of grains
of gold and minute pearls."[51] On disembarking, his party enters the
pleasant fields of the island, "meadows whose grass was green not
because it was grass, but rather because it was emeralds."[52] Like the
knight the visitors discover a brook, in which flows not water
"but rather streams of liquid diamonds, which appeared, as they
meandered through the meadows, like crystal serpents."[53] Here the

---

que hizimos de la suauidad dellos; al tacto, con tenerlos en las manos, con que nos
parecia tener en ellas las perlas del Sur, los diamantes de las Indias y el oro del
Tibar" (I, 275).

[50] ". . . arroyuelo, cuyas frescas aguas, que líquidos cristales parecen, corren sobre
menudas arenas y blancas pedrezuelas, que oro cernido y puras perlas semejan"
(I, 500).

[51] ". . . pisamos la amenissima ribera, cuya arena, vaya fuera todo encarecimiento,
la formauan granos de oro y de menudas perlas" (I, 274).

[52] ". . . prados cuyas yeruas no eran verdes por ser yeruas, sino por ser esmeraldas"
(I, 274).

[53] ". . . sino corrientes de liquidos diamantes formados, que, cruzando por todo
el prado, sierpes de cristal parecian" (I, 274).

234

conscious withdrawal from reality in the narrator's imagined world proceeds one step further as a stream of flowing diamonds is imaginatively transmuted further into crystal serpents.[54] It is interesting that in the passage in *Don Quixote* Cervantes chooses objects of artifice, the fountain and the palace, to indulge his fantasy in the use of the traditional ornamental motifs of jewels and precious metals. In the *Persiles*, where the fantastic quality of the vision is heightened, there is no need for architecture, as nature itself becomes the object of marvelous artifice. In this respect the garden looks forward to the final false paradise of the *Persiles*, the storeroom of the courtesan Hipolyta in Rome, a completely artificial paradise in which the song of caged birds is the only vestige of the sorceress' garden.

The popular controversy over art and nature, which Cervantes, like other authors of the epoch, seems to have associated with the literary topic of the garden paradise, is introduced by Periandro in an interesting variation on the way in which it appears in the gardens of the *Galatea*, the *Quixote*, and the *Viage del Parnaso*. On entering the pleasant grove, the company discovers trees of various types, laden with all the fruits which are known to man and beautiful objects which could not have been placed there by the hand of nature. Periandro and his men gaze in astonishment at the beauty of the fruits, unable to distinguish them from the beautiful objects of artifice which they resemble: "From some hung clusters of rubies which looked like cherries, or cherries which looked like droplets of rubies."[55] The pairing of nature and an art that is perfect by the traditional standard that "art is only perfect when it looks like nature"[56] is more subtly introduced in the following lines. The

---

[54] The double metamorphical transmutation is a perfect example of the style which baroque poetics (e.g., E. Tesauro, M. Pellegrini, B. Gracián) would soon canonize under the heading of *conceptismo* and associate with the central creative faculty, the *ingenio*. Hugo Friedrich summarizes Tesauro's theories on the workings of *ingenio*: ". . . blitzartiges Erfassen von Analogien zwischen Entferntestem, verblüffendes Zusammenziehen von Nichtzusammengehörigem, ruhelose Beweglichkeit, Nicht-Endenwollen im Spiel des Kombinierens . . . die Aufgabe des sprachlichen Erzeugens von sonst nicht Existierendem" (*Epochen der Italienischen Lyrik* [Frankfurt, 1964], pp. 630-631).

[55] ". . . de algunos pendian ramos de rubies que parecian guindas, o guindas que parecian granos de rubies" (I, 275).

[56] See Tayler, p. 34. The *locus classicus* is Longinus, *On the Sublime*, xxii.

fusion is visible in the individual fruits themselves, which seem to be the products of a harmonious interworking of the hands of the two great creative powers.

> From others hung apples that had one cheek of rose and the other of the finest topaz; on another branch there appeared pears, whose fragrance was of ambergris and whose color was of those which form in the sky when the sun is setting.[57]

The striking similarity between the art-nature topic in its present, ambiguous formulation and the way in which it appears in other works of literature of the Renaissance invites immediate comparison, which leads us to the uniqueness of Cervantes' preoccupations in the shaping of his garden. Perhaps the most similar formulation of the traditional quality is in Spenser's description of the Bower of Bliss, where the knight Guyon must experience the temptations of the flesh and survive the debilitating effect of sensual indulgence. The Bower is the realm of an enchantress and takes the form of the garden of pleasure. Here nature and art appear, as in Periandro's dream, in a harmonious collaboration, and in their creations the artificial and the natural are indistinguishably intermingled.[58] In the Bower there is a grapevine on which hang grapes which look like rubies and emeralds. Intermingled with the real there are grapes of burnished gold, "So made by art to beautify the rest," and from the fruits of this marvelous vine the temptress Excess extracts her sweet potion to offer her victims. In Tasso's garden of Armida there is a formulation of the nature-art duality which is again formally similar to that of the *Persiles*, as a harmonious interworking of art and nature produces creations in which the artificial and the natural cannot be distinguished from one another.[59] In both

[57] ". . . de otros pendian camuesas, cuyas mexillas la vna era de rosa, la otra de finissimo topazio; en aquel se mostrauan las peras, cuyo olor era de ambar, y cuyo color de los que forma en el cielo quando el sol se traspone" (I, 275).

[58] "The art, which all that wrought, appeared in no place" (II, xii, 58) and "One would have thought, (so cunningly the rude/ And scorned partes were mingled with the fine,)/ That Nature had for wantonesse ensude/ Art, and that Art at Nature did repine;/ So striving each th'other to undermine,/ Each did the others worke more beautify" (II, xii, 59); see Edmund Spenser, *The Poetical Works*, ed. F. J. Child (Boston, 1855), II, 147-148.

[59] After listing the beautiful objects of Armida's garden, Tasso writes: "e quel che 'l bello e 'l caro accresce a l'opre,/ l'arte, che tutto fa, nulla si scopre./ Stimi

poems this interworking represents a corruption of the two creative forces, serving as it does the demonic forces which would ensnare the Christian hero.

A. Bartlett Giamatti has recently pointed out that the ancient topic of the garden paradise functions in the poems of Tasso and Spenser as a thematically and structurally integrated element. It both forms the background for the presentation of essential moral conflict and its resolution and represents one of the forces involved in the conflict. The sensuously delightful aspects of the garden and the ornamental motifs of jewelry and precious metals are symbolic of the attractions of fleshly and material pleasures. Similarly the harmonious interworkings of nature and an art which is manipulated by the temptress and the difficulty of the visitor in distinguishing the real from the artificial are meaningful in relation to the power of illusion in life and the problems of the Christian in coping with the illusory nature of earthly experience.[60]

Up to a certain point it is valid to interpret Periandro's dream in terms of the moral issues that dominate the scenes in the works of Spenser and Tasso. The details of the garden, the way in which the art-nature controversy is used, the fact that the island is the haunt of a sorceress who captures men and is served by animals, as well as the visual, allegorical representation of the resolution of the moral conflict which is part of the central thematic substance of the *Persiles*, do in fact support such an interpretation. However, it is important to recognize that the moral implications of the vision are secondary to literary concerns. Cervantes makes no direct connection between the delights of the garden and the theme of worldly temptation. There indeed seems to be no attempt to relate the garden paradise to the sorceress and the allegorical pageant which crown the vision. The critical audience's interruptions, which separate the appearance of the figures of Sensuality and Chastity from the description of the garden, serve both to thrust the entire narration into the perspective of literary problem and to isolate the two

---

(sì misto il culto è co 'l negletto)/ sol naturali e gli ornamenti e i siti./ Di natura arte par, che per diletto/ l'imitatrice sua scherzando imiti" (XVI, 9-10); see B. Maier, ed. (Milan, 1963), p. 526.

[60] See *The Earthly Paradise and the Renaissance Epic* (Princeton, 1966), pp. 201, 271-272.

scenes from each other. And with the absence of any internal links between them, we actually read them as separate episodes. Moreover, the problem of art and nature and the difficulty of distinguishing rubies from grapes or cherries in the context of the *Persiles* have none of the obvious moral overtones which they are given in the English and Italian works.

All the difficulties involved in finding coherence in the episode in relation to such common themes in the literature of the Counterreformation period as the illusory quality of earthly experience and the corruption of nature, temptation, and sinfulness can be overcome only if we realize that these metaphysical and ethical issues were simply not Cervantes' central concern in the creation of the scene.[61] As in all other episodes of Periandro's narration the author's principal interest is in problems of an exclusively aesthetic or literary nature. His purpose is the depiction of a fantastic paradise as a topic of the marvelous, to be reflected upon by a critical audience. The force of literary association compelled him to make the rich combination of elements which form the texture of the episode: the *imram* garden paradise, the hollow hill, the reminiscences of Circe and the Sirens, the apes, the strange music, the disappearance of the men in the sorceress' dwelling, and the art-nature controversy, which in its various possibilities for formulation had come to be as persistent a topic of late Renaissance paradise descriptions as the archetypal pleasant grove and brook.[62]

[61] As I shall point out in another study, on other occasions Cervantes does in fact employ the garden paradise in a context informed by the principal ethical and metaphysical issues of the *Persiles*. The two most important are Feliciana de la Voz's description of the heavenly paradise, which represents the goal of all the wanderers of the *Persiles*, and the false paradise of the courtesan Hipolyta, from which the hero must escape.

[62] In view of the extreme literary eclecticism which we discover in the description of the garden of Periandro's dream, it is important to distinguish Cervantes' use of the traditional theme from its purely ornamental use in various works of his contemporaries. In late antiquity the description of the garden became one of the favorite rhetorical exercises of both Greek and Latin writers and continued to be an occasion for the display of poetic virtuosity throughout the Middle Ages (see Rohde, *Der Griechische Roman und seine Vorläufer*, p. 545 and Curtius, *Europäische Literatur und Lateinisches Mittelalter*, p. 200). In the age of Cervantes, which in its literary production has been likened to late antiquity by literary historians (see Friedrich, *Epochen der Italienischen Lyrik*, pp. 616-618 and Curtius, pp. 292-293), it is not strange to discover the garden paradise description once again fre-

That Cervantes conceived and created this paradise in a context of literary problems is evident in the humorous scene of audience commentary which follows Periandro's unexpected conclusion of his account. The enthusiasm with which he evokes the poetry of Garcilaso as he addresses the goddess Chastity shatters his dream and causes his vision to vanish ("rompi el sueño, y la vision hermosa desaparecio"). The scene recalls the inn of Palomeque, where the enthusiastic statements of the innkeeper's family about the romances of chivalry are followed by the sobering notes of the curate's neo-Aristotelian criticism of the genre. The first to comment are the ladies, whose empathy has been aroused by Periandro's narration and who have never doubted its veracity, despite the fantastic events and the narrator's occasional parodistic comments.[63] In disappointment and disbelief at his abrupt destruction of the illusion of reality of his account, Costanza comments: "Then, my lord Periandro, were you only sleeping?" She adds that she had been about

---

quently used as pure *ecphrasis*. It could be argued that the dominant tendencies of this manneristic literature—high literary self-consciousness, emphasis on the rhetorical and formal ("Überfunktion des Stiles" [Friedrich, p. 546]), and literary eclecticism—are all present in Periandro's description. Moreover, in its highly ornate and metaphorical character and in its careful elaboration of the effects of the landscape on each of the five senses of the viewer, it is not altogether unlike that greatest rhetorical display in garden descriptions of the age, Marino's garden of Venus (*Adone*, Canto VI), with its five separate gardens for the individual senses and its combinations of real and artificial fruits in the trees. What is important to note in Cervantes' context, however, is its conscious use of the ornamental and the freely imaginative to raise an abstract problem of literary theory. What at first glance appears to be pure *ecphrasis* becomes an integrated, meaningful element in the author's examination of the aesthetic problems of verisimilitude and unity. It is not present simply as a vehicle for the arousal of *admiratio* (*meraviglia*) through a dazzling display of poetic talent and imaginative flights from the real world as is that of Marino. (For examples of garden *ecphrasis* from Spanish literature of the Baroque, see Lope's *Jerusalén conquistada*, Book V, and Góngora's *Soledad primera* II, 572-629.) The resolution of the aesthetic problems raised in the literary discussion of Periandro's account may indeed suggest the validity of the aesthetic principle underlying the creations of Lope and Marino. Nevertheless, Cervantes is writing about the problem.

[63] The willful introduction of notes of literary parody (once again it serves as a *Verfremdungseffekt*), the trickery of refusing to tell his audience that the experience was a dream until after having captured its belief, and the final defense of the joy that the dream provides, as well as the absence of psychological (Don Quixote), financial (the counterfeit captives), and racial (i.e., all Moors are liars) motives in Periandro's presentation of the lie as truth, suggest that Periandro is the purest representative of the spirit of romantic irony among Cervantes' many narrators and perhaps, as he acts in this scene, the one closest to Cervantes.

to ask Auristela where she had been during the time preceding her appearance with the figures of Continence and Modesty on the island. The humor arising from her reaction recalls that in Sancho Panza's interruption of Don Quixote's account of the adventure of the Cave of Montesinos to volunteer information on the knife which Montesinos used to extract the heart of Durandarte. In both cases the narrator presents an obviously fantastic episode, and the listener finds himself drawn into the world of fantasy. The humor surrounding Constanza's commentary is compounded by Auristela's assertion that Periandro's narration had almost convinced her of the truth of the episode, an astounding admission in view of the fact that she was said to participate in the island encounter in the company of Continence and Modesty.[64]

At this point Mauricio, the representative of the learned audience, speaks out, offering a scientific explanation for the belief of the ladies. He maintains that the powers of the imagination are so great that through them such illusions as Periandro's vision imprint themselves in the memory and remain in it, "as if they were truths, although they are lies" ("siendo mentiras como si fueran verdades"). His words recall the Canon of Toledo's allusion to the distinction between the intellectual faculty (that which demands and appreciates verisimilitude) and the inferior imaginative faculty and to the power of the lies of the romances to appeal to the latter. Following the comment of the disapproving Mauricio, Arnaldo, the other spokesman for the learned audience, asks Periandro to refrain from including any more dreams in his narration. Periandro's response is significant; it affirms the aesthetic theories of both sides of the literary debate between the canon and Don Quixote: " 'The pleasure that my dream gave me,' replied Periandro, 'made me unaware of

[64] It is possible that this humorous scene of *trompe-l'oeil* was inspired by a scene in Cervantes' literary model for Periandro's narration, Calasiris' relation of the fortunes of Theagenes and Chariklea to Gnemon. On describing Chariklea's appearance before the temple of Diana to meet Theagenes, the excited Gnemon interrupts: "¡Veislos allí . . . !" The bewildered Calasiris asks: "¿Adónde están?", to which Gnemon replies: "Parecióme padre, que los vía . . . aunque están ausentes; tan claramente y tan al propio me los ha representado vuestro cuento" (Heliodorus, *Historia etiópica*, p. 120).

the fruitless nature of digressions in any narrative, which should be concise and not amplified'."[65]

The ambivalence of his statement, in its acknowledgment of both the appeal of the dream, with which the romances had been associated since Petrarch's disparaging remark "sogno d'infermi e fola di romanzi," and the inappropriateness of the dream in literature in accordance with the Horatian-Aristotelian critical canon, is the ambivalence underlying all of Cervantes' examinations of literature and literary theory.[66]

If at the conclusion of this scene the voice of the canon seems to have the final word in Periandro's apparent submission to the learned members of his critical audience, the continuation of his narration at the beginning of the following chapter witnesses the resurgence of the voice of Don Quixote. Periandro immediately engages in the type of authorial play which we observe in Cide Hamete Benengeli's use and abuse of Aristotelian terminology. Having just sworn to abide by the Aristotelian principles in his narration, he resumes his *historia* by alluding to the dream episode, which has been judged to be irrelevant. He asserts that on the following day he asked his companions whether they had seen their kidnapped wives in the company of Auristela on the mysterious island. Whether this statement in itself contains an ironic thrust at the critics of his narration is not clear. Nevertheless, it serves to

---

[65] "—El gusto de lo que soñe—respondio Periandro—me hizo no aduertir de quan poco fruto son las digressiones en qualquiera narracion, quando ha de ser sucinta, y no dilatada" (I, 279).

[66] Again I wish to emphasize that the debate which I have analyzed in Chapter III echoes and reechoes throughout Cervantes' writing. Perhaps the critical exchange most similar in detail to the one under examination is in Alférez Campuzano's criticism and justification of his redaction of what may have been a dream, the conversation of the dogs Cipión and Berganza: "Pero puesto caso que me haya engañado, y que mi verdad sea sueño, y el porfiarla disparate, ¿no se holgará vuesa merced, señor Peralta, de ver escritas en un coloquio las cosas que estos perros, o sean quien fueren, hablaron?" (*El casamiento engañoso y coloquio de Cipión y Berganza* in *Novelas ejemplares*, II, 205). Behind Campuzano's problem, which reappears at the end of the narration ("Aunque este coloquio sea fingido y nunca haya pasado . . ." and "no volvamos más a esa disputa" [pp. 339-340]), lies a common judgment in the writings of the Aristotelians: in their inverisimilitude the Aesopian fables belong to a very low class of literature and are justifiable only because they can be read allegorically.

recall the entire episode as a background for his following remark, which, to be sure, renders it retroactively ironic: "For two months we continued cruising about these seas, and nothing worthy of any consideration happened to us, although we purged them of more than sixty pirate ships."[67]

In a ten-word account of the destruction of sixty ships, deliberately subordinated within the concessive clause, Periandro offers his learned audience both the "single subject," which according to the rigorous Aristotelians must never be eclipsed by episode and digression, and, juxtaposed to the fantastic dream vision, the "historical-verisimilar" truth, which must never be undermined by the poet's insertion of an implausible occurrence. It is the truth which Periandro's critics would demand in his narration and which he himself has just acknowledged to be his only valid subject. However, the nature of the comment makes it perfectly obvious that Periandro is telling his opponents that, in effect, their restrictions compel the poet to be a bore. Following closely on his pretended submission to the rule, Periandro's ironic dismissal of its validity recalls the many humorous reversals of Cide Hamete Benengeli in his calculated misapplications of the neo-Aristotelian principles. In content and tone the interchange is particularly similar to his statements introducing Chapter XLIV of the second part of the *Quixote*: his claim that "to write about a single subject is an unendurable ordeal" as he justifies his inclusion of the intercalated novellas, his reluctant submission to the Aristotelian restrictions on the question of unity which follows, and his immediate turnabout to request praise for what he has failed to write.[68]

[67] "Dos meses anduuimos por el mar sin que nos sucediesse cosa de consideracion alguna, puesto que le escombramos de mas de sesenta nauios de cossarios" (I, 280).

[68] The general parodistic treatment of the Aristotelian critics and their standard notions throughout Periandro's narration, as well as the narrator's elusiveness in toying with the members of his audience, suggests an interpretation for the ambiguous sentence by which he introduces the description of the procession on the island: "*Volued*, señores, *los ojos*, y hazed cuenta que *veys* salir del coraçon de vna peña, como nosotros lo *vimos*, sin que la *vista* nos pudiesse engañar, digo que *vimos* salir de la abertura de la peña, primero vn suauissimo *son*" (I, 276; italics added). The incantatory repetition of the verb *ver* and the exhortation of the audience to see represent an evocation of the critical demand that the narrator present his matter with stylistic *energia* (see above). However, the intention seems to be parodistic. Both the extravagance of the repetitions and the ridiculous climax (*un son*) of a

Conclusion

Close analysis of function, content, style, and sources indicates that Cervantes' repeated recourse to the literary theme of the garden paradise must be judged in terms of changing preoccupations and artistic intentions. In his pastoral romance, the *Galatea*, the garden is subordinated entirely to the philosophical concerns which inspired the work. Like the pastoral genre in general the *Galatea* was animated by Renaissance neo-Platonism, with its conception of a universal order visible in the natural world and in man, the microcosm. Cervantes found in the garden of Greek literature, in its carefully controlled nature and geometrical symmetries, an ideal expressive medium for a vision of harmony and order. The garden cemetery, the Valley of the Cypresses, from which the souls of the fallen shepherds ascend to their celestial dwelling, is Cervantes' fullest poetic realization of the neo-Platonist vision of world order.

In *Don Quixote* the garden appears in an entirely different context, as the philosophical concerns which find expression in the *Galatea* are replaced by an interest in the psychological condition of the protagonist and in problems of literary theory. The focus in which the fantastic subterranean world of Don Quixote's envisioned romance comes into clear view is that of the controversy in contemporary critical circles over the problematic aesthetic value of the romances of chivalry, and such specific theoretical concerns as pleasure in art, the function of the lower and higher faculties in the apprehension of the work of art, verisimilitude, the fantastic, variety, and unity. In the scheme of literary debate that frames Don

---

sentence which is unnaturally extended for the sake of heightened visual anticipation serve to distort this overworked idea of contemporary theorists. It is possible that, in constructing this sentence, Cervantes had in mind the labors of such theorists as Giraldi Cintio and Tasso. The former devotes two pages to describing what the romance brings to the eyes of the reader, employing the verb *vedere* no fewer than ten times and concluding: "Queste finalmente sono quelle [cose, i.e., rhetorical ornaments] che ci apportano le cose vive vive, spirando negli occhi" (*De' romanzi*, pp. 212-213). The latter's particular sentence "necessaria è in lui [lo stile] l'energia la quale sì con parole pone inanzi a gli occhi la cosa che pare altrui non di udirla, ma di vederla" (*Dell'arte poetica*, p. 47) may well have inspired Periandro's persiflage. It is worth recalling that the garden paradise was offered by Pigna as an episode in which *energia* was particularly necessary (*I romanzi*, pp. 101-102).

243

Quixote's account the garden is to represent the romances and form part of a critical response to the canon's classicist criticism of the modern genre. Cervantes turns to the fantastic gardens of medieval romance for his model, presenting a highly metaphorical description swelling with accumulations of sensuous detail. By implication his description rejects the canon's principles of verisimilitude, unity, and the primacy of the intellectual apprehension of art. On the positive side, it celebrates an art of the free fantasy, which recognizes no limits in its transformations of reality and which would justify itself solely in terms of its pleasurable appeal to the reader's senses and imagination.

In the *Viage del Parnaso* Cervantes returns briefly to the garden theme, and again the surrounding context is dominated by literary concerns. As in *Don Quixote* the problematic character of the topic in relation to the Aristotelian criterion of verisimilitude lies behind his creation of the garden of the Muses on Mount Parnassus. However, here Cervantes' solution to the aesthetic problem is simpler than that which we observe in Don Quixote's response to the canon, in which double-edged parody works against both the nontruths of the world of the romances and the most refined arguments of their critics. The *Viage del Parnaso* is a mock-epic, and like all mock-epics it is restricted to a limited range of parody. The garden paradise is one of many standard topics of traditional idealizing literature which in their patent unreality become the vehicles for the unequivocal humor of unsophisticated travesty.

In the *Persiles* the garden reappears in a literary context, and once again it is its problematic value in terms of Aristotelian criteria—here unity as well as verisimilitude—which lies behind its inclusion. Here we observe a return from the realm of the burlesque to the complex interplay of critical thought that deepens the fantastic vision of Don Quixote. It is fundamentally the same garden paradise, in which variety and sensuous beauty are the principal attributes and the realities of nature submit to the transmutations which the fantasy demands. Moreover, it is presented by a narrator to an audience which includes several persons obsessed by the same critical principles by which the canon condemns the romances—unity and verisimilitude. In their inclusion of the garden vision, the narrators, Periandro and Don Quixote, are deliberately flouting these principles. Like Don Quixote, Periandro employs the garden as a literary topic of the marvelous to assert the artist's independence of the restrictions on creative freedom which the Aristotelian movement had formulated and to suggest the validity of an art founded solely on pleasure. Moreover, both surrogate poets suggest the inadequacies of the criterion of verisimilitude as it had been interpreted by the neo-Aristotelians and imply that audience belief cannot be viewed in terms of empirical belief. For they are careful to allow the fictional quality of their narrations to appear clearly, yet impudently ask their audiences to believe what they narrate.[69]

It should be observed that in all of Cervantes' evocations of the literary tradition of the garden paradise, the topic is integrated into the deeper thematic texture of the work. The garden paradise had always been a favorite topic of the literary tradition of *ecphrasis*, and its purely ornamental use was frequent in the works of Cervantes' contemporaries. To be sure, Cervantes found in his garden descriptions an opportunity for the arousal of *admiratio* and a display of artistic talent, just as did such poets as Spenser and Tasso. Nevertheless, just as the ornamental value of the topic is subordinated to ethical and philosophical problems in the *Faerie Queene* and the *Gerusalemme liberata*, so in the *Galatea*, the *Quixote*, and the *Persiles*, the fundamental philosophical or literary concerns of the works dictate the inclusion of the garden and the particular form that it takes.

THE MARVELOUS HORSE

In Periandro's description of the breaking of King Cratilo's horse (*Persiles*, II, xviii-xx), the central literary focus shifts away from the problem of unity to that of verisimilitude.[70] Again Cervantes chooses

[69] Ortega's unhistorical evaluation of the *Persiles*: "El *Persiles* . . . nos garantiza que Cervantes quiso la inverosimilitud como tal inverosimilitud" (*Meditaciones del Quijote*, p. 88) is curiously valid in a way in which he did not realize. It is applicable not to the work as a whole, in which Cervantes carefully observes the rules for verisimilitude (i.e., the "legitimate marvelous") developed by sixteenth-century theorists, but rather to the extended narration of Periandro, where Cervantes allows his protagonist to voice a plea for the freedom of the creative imagination.

[70] Again formal and thematic parallelism should be observed between the complex of scenes based on the dramatic situation of the narrating author vs. critical

a theme of pronounced literary overtones to confront the critical problem. The marvelous horse as a topic of imaginative literature is probably as ancient and ubiquitous as the theme of the other-world paradise. Perhaps its earliest appearance is in the *Patashantra* of India, in the form of the miraculous wooden horses which bear their riders to realms known only to the imagination. By the late Middle Ages such horses and aerial journeys had entered the mainstream of European literature, perhaps through the pseudo-Callisthenes' popular account of the life of Alexander the Great, which describes the ascent of the hero in a basket carried aloft by flying creatures, perhaps through the translation of the vast collection of oriental tales, the *Thousand and One Nights*. In any event, such creatures were not uncommon in romances of chivalry, and Clavileño is one of their most famous descendants.[71] The imagination of classical antiquity too produced a tradition of marvelous horses, the most famous being the winged Pegasus, who bore Bellerophon on his unsuccessful flight toward the realm of the gods, and Alexander's Bucephalus.

The important role of the horse in the system of chivalry is well documented in the medieval romances, which abound in episodes involving extraordinary horses and feats of horsemanship. For example, a popular incident is that which Laura Hibbard has called the "Vain Pursuit," in which a knight under pursuit by his enemies spurs his horse to leap from a high rock into the sea below.[72] The development of the marvelous attributes of the horse and the increasing exaggeration of feats of horsemanship in the verse ro-

---

audience in the *Persiles* and the *Quixote*. Just as the episode of the counterfeit captives and Periandro's dream vision of paradise are to some extent reworkings of the episode of Master Pedro's *retablo* and the underworld journeys of the Knight of the Lake and Don Quixote, the episode of Periandro's leap is a reenactment of Sancho's flight on Clavileño.

[71] See J. Gillet, "Clavileño: su fuente directa y sus orígenes primitivos," *Anales Cervantinos*, VI (1957), 251-255. For a more widely ranging discussion of the literary tradition of marvelous horses, see Pio Rajna, *Le fonti dell'Orlando Furioso* (Florence, 1900), pp. 115-116.

[72] The incident discussed by Hibbard is found in *Boeve de Haumtone* (see "Jaques de Vitry and Boeve de Haumtone," *Modern Language Notes*, XXXIV [1919], 408-411). On the reappearance of the incident in romance literature, see Christian Boje, "Über den altfranzösischen Roman von Beuve de Haumtone," *Zeitschrift für Romanische Philologie*, Beiheft XIX (1909), 96-100.

mances of the Italian poets have been traced by Rajna. The Baiardo of Pulci could think, and, although possessed of no supernatural physical endowments, he was able to make an occasional leap across the Straits of Gibraltar.

All these marvelous horses were alive in the literary tradition in which artists of the Renaissance nourished their creations, and the uniqueness of Periandro's horse, Clavileño, and even Rocinante can be fully understood only when one considers their remote and illustrious ancestry. However, there was one horse which above others dominated the fantasy and thought of the Renaissance artists and theorists. The famous hippogryph of Ariosto was indeed modeled on Pegasus, but as Rajna observes, through imaginative association, he bore with him on his flights the tradition of marvelous horses in all its multiformity.

Curiously it was in part due to the extraordinary popularity of Ariosto's work all over Europe that the theme of the marvelous horse acquired a new dimension. The period of enthusiasm for the *Furioso* coincided with the emergence of the neo-Aristotelian movement, and the theorists who professed faith in the new critical tenets did not hesitate to test their strength against the universally read work. In the ensuing controversy perhaps the example most frequently cited of Ariosto's abuse of the artistic imperative of credibility was the hippogryph, which in defiance of all natural law bears Ruggiero to the distant land of Alcina and Astolfo to the circle of the moon.

In his discussion of the range of possibilities for poetic creation allowed by the Aristotelian limitation of verisimilitude, Tasso offers a list of legitimate subjects, i.e., subjects which either occurred or conceivably could have occurred, including the Trojan War, the wrath of Achilles, and the piety of Aeneas, and a list of subjects which the poet must avoid: "But Centaurs, Harpies, and Cyclopes are not a proper or principal subject of poetry, *nor are the flying horses and the other monsters which fill the plots of romances.*"[73] Even the defenders of the romances tacitly acknowledged that the

[73] "Ma i Centauri, l'Arpie e i Ciclopi non sono adeguato o principal subietto de la poesia, né *i cavalli volanti e gli altri mostri de' quali son piene le favole di romanzi*" (*Del poema eroico*, p. 88; see also the list on p. 93; the italics are mine).

hippogryph presented difficulties in their recourse to allegorical interpretations to justify its inclusion in the work. Pigna, for example, could differentiate the romance genre from epic and tragedy in that it is not dependent on the truth of historical occurrence for its subject matter and indeed can invent it as does comedy. Nevertheless, claiming Aristotle as his guide, he insists that plausibility be maintained by the poet. Consequently, when he must defend Ariosto's implausible hippogryph, he maintains that the winged horse is parallel to the classical Pegasus and the gryphon and is hence an emblem of glory and that one of the beauties of romance as a genre is its presentation of wisdom by mysterious means.[74]

The result of the emergence of the critical spirit and the exposure of traditional literature to its scrutiny was in the case of marvelous horses and horsemanship the same as that which we observed in the case of the island paradise. Both became associated with a particular aesthetic problem from which they would never again regain their independence. In other words, both would appear henceforth not only as topics of a literary tradition, but in addition as topics of a critical tradition, bearing within themselves the sign of their own problematic character within the framework of the dominant critical mode of thought.[75] Thus when Lope de Vega wishes to defend the verisimilitude of his *Peregrino en su patria*, he writes: "Our Pilgrim should appear fabulous to nobody, for in this painting there

---

[74] See *I romanzi*, pp. 21-22, 90.

[75] It is natural that the intense consciousness of the problematic nature of such venerable literary topics rendered them favorite topics for parody directed against fantastic literature. We have observed Cervantes' parodistic treatment of the garden paradise in his mock-heroic *Viage del Parnaso*. In a similar vein he introduces the winged horse Pegasus into his narration, associating him with other illustrious horses of literature and with the aesthetic principle of *admiratio* ("cosas nueuas oyras de gusto ricas" [p. 109]), proceeding to describe his absurdly fantastic qualities (he eats only amber and musk served on cotton), and amid the hyperboles injecting the reductive notes of travesty (the envy of Rocinante and the poets who gather his excrement for inspiration). Rocinante and Pegasus represent well the two basic reductive tendencies which, as Harry Levin has observed, mark the extreme points between which Cervantes' parody ranges—"mock-epic, which magnifies vulgarity, applying the grand manner to commonplace matters; and travesty, which minimizes greatness, reclothing noble figures in base attire" ("The Example of Cervantes," in *Contexts of Criticism*, p. 86). This type of parody of the topic of the marvelous is significantly absent in the episodes of Periandro's leap and the island paradise.

is no horse with wings."[76] It is not surprising that half a century later, when the major tendencies of the sixteenth-century critical movement had been directly challenged under the aegis of a new, reinterpreted Aristotle, and poets had cast off the bonds with which the great critical demands of unity and verisimilitude had shackled their creative powers, Emanuele Tesauro should recommend the creation of fabulous animals in poetry, and that one of his contemporaries should celebrate the freedom of the fantasy with the phrase "Far better are hippogryphs than sheep" ("meglio ippogrifi che pecore").[77]

In Periandro's feat of horsemanship Cervantes is once again using literature to confront literary criticism. As in the case of the island paradise, the episode is purposely schematic and eclectic. In the description of the setting and the event, abundance of detail is sacrificed in favor of brief outline, yet all the outlines are evocative of elements of the literary and critical traditions which are being examined.[78] The general similarity of the scene to Alexander's

---

[76] ". . . a ninguno parezca nuestro Peregrino fabuloso, pues en esta pintura no hay caballo con alas" (p. 299). The statement accompanies Lope's allusion to Tasso's theories of verisimilitude.

[77] See Friedrich, *Epochen der Italienischen Lyrik*, pp. 633-634. El Pinciano criticizes poets who would sacrifice verisimilitude for the sake of the marvelous, referring to "hombres deste siglo" who are "tan mentirosos; los quales por poner admiración dirán que vieron bolar vn buey" (*Philosophía antigua poética*, II, 103). Above we have observed how Campanella censures both Alcina's garden and the hippogryph as violations of verisimilitude. The continuing association of the flying horse with an art that would defy the demands of plausibility is observable in Hobbes' prefatory remarks to Davenant's epic *Gondibert* (1651): "There are some that are not pleased with fiction, unless it be bold, not onely to exceed the *work*, but also the *possibility* of nature. They would have impenetrable Armors, Inchanted Castles, invulnerable bodies, Iron Men, flying Horses . . . [But] as truth is the bound of Historicall, so the Resemblance of truth is the utmost limit of Poeticall Liberty. . . . Beyond the actual works of nature a Poet may now go; but beyond the conceived possibility of nature, never" (cited by Abrams, *The Mirror and the Lamp*, p. 267).

[78] As in the case of the island paradise, it is important to distinguish Cervantes' introduction of the horse episode from the pure *ecphrasis* which we observe in the works of such writers as Lope and Marino. Again we are dealing with a traditional ornamental motif, and the temptation to see its introduction as an occasion for a display of artistic virtuosity or the simple arousal of *admiratio* is undeniable. De Lollis censures the episode as an example of decadent mannerism. (Cervantes "nel *Persile* ha pei 'disparates' una carità che malvolentieri si lascia controllare dalla saggia estetica del canonico" [*Cervantes reazionario*, p. 185]). It is revealing to compare Cervantes' sketch, which seems purposely simple, to the horses of Marino (conveniently assembled by Calcaterra [*Il parnaso in rivolta*, pp. 24-26]) or to the

breaking of Bucephalus has been pointed out (with some sarcasm) by De Lollis. Like Philip of Macedon, King Cratilo of Bituania has a beautiful horse of fiery disposition, which defies all those who attempt to tame him. Periandro determines to break the horse, leaps onto the saddled animal, and, clutching him tightly, rushes toward a high rock overlooking the ocean. Undaunted, the hero spurs his mount onward, and in a mighty leap rider and horse plummet downward. Periandro survives the fall, although he is thrown from his mount and rolls across the frozen surface of the sea. To prove that the horse is broken, he attempts to force him to leap once again, and the cringing beast refuses.

The literary associations of the episode reach beyond Plutarch's account of Alexander and Bucephalus. The dimension of spectacle, the assembled masses who view the scene, the sudden noise announcing the appearance of the horse, Periandro's leap onto his mount, and the theme of horse-breaking, all recall the final scene of Cervantes' acknowledged model, the *Aethiopica*. Aroused by the cries of the throng assembled for the sacrifices in Meroe, Theagenes leaps onto an unsaddled horse and, clinging to its mane, he pursues a bull, which he breaks much to the satisfaction of the aged King

---

horses of Lope's *Jerusalén conquistada* (see for example the marvelous Cisne [Book IV] and the horses of Agusto and Tisandro [Book X]) or to the well-known horse of Rosaura (*La vida es sueño*), which Calderón associates with the ubiquitous topic of the marvelous, the hippogryph; for all are occasions for dazzling metaphorical transmutations and displays of poetic talent. (To be sure, in the case of Calderón there is a complex allegory conjoined with the *ecphrasis*.)

It could be argued that the apparent resolution of the critical problem which Periandro's account represents points toward the aesthetic of the free imagination which lay behind such creations as Marino's horses and gardens. However, it is important to realize that Cervantes is not interested simply in indulging his fantasy or displaying his poetic talents in his use of familiar topics of the marvelous. He is principally interested in an abstract problem, the tension between two divergent tendencies in critical thinking. All that we have observed indicates that the advocacy of creative freedom voiced so consistently by his various narrators was negatively oriented, i.e., it was directed against the restrictions on creative freedom demanded by the prevailing Aristotelian critical movement. The positive or creative dimension of his response to this critical tension in fact did not lead him to the cultivation of the fantasy, i.e., to Lope or Marino. Rather, it led him to that which both the Aristotelian critical movement and the literary movement associated with the marvelous excluded from the realms of serious literature, the everyday world of human experience, and the ambiguous role of the fantasy within it, i.e., the novelistic.

Hydaspes.[79] The rocky crag above the sea, the spurring of the horse onward, and the leap into the sea seem to be modeled on the "Vain Pursuit" theme of romance literature.[80] Perhaps the most significant of the evocative details which form the texture of the episode is Periandro's simple statement "I made him fly through the air" (le hize bolar por el ayre"), which could not fail to suggest both those absurd *cavalli volanti* criticized by Lope and Tasso and the aesthetic problem associated with them. Mauricio's reaction to Periandro's account of the incident reinforces the suggestion, as he critically reflects on the episode and judges it to be implausible.

The form of Mauricio's unspoken commentary recalls Cervantes' favorite technique of dealing with the critical movement in *Don Quixote*.

The terrible leap of the horse, which resulted in no injury, was a hard thing for Mauricio to bear. He wished that there had been at least three or four broken legs, so that Periandro would not leave the belief in so outrageous a leap so entirely up to the courtesy of the listeners.[81]

Initial humor springs from the abrupt shift of the focus in which we witness the scene. The adventure narrated by the hero does indeed have literary overtones (e.g., Bucephalus, the "perilous leap," the hippogryph), but we view it as part of his biography, a heroic deed which he performed at some point in his wanderings. Mauricio's comment, however, abruptly transposes the adventure into an entirely different sphere, that of literary abstractions. He intro-

---

[79] See *Historia etiópica*, pp. 408-409.

[80] Cervantes describes the leap very briefly, but once again the few outlines are suggestive. Hibbard sees the essential elements as the rock, the leap, and the sea, the only elements which appear in Periandro's account. It is interesting to compare Cervantes' lines with the account of Jaques de Vitry, which may be the first written appearance of the incident: ". . . llegué a la punta de vna peña que sobre la mar pendia, y, apretandole de nueuo las piernas . . . le hize bolar por el ayre y dar con entrambos en la profundidad del mar" (I, 311); and ". . . ab una parte cacumen prerupte rupis habebat, ex alia parte mare profundissimum subjacebat." Like Periandro the knight spurs his horse on and leaps "in abissum maris" (Hibbard, p. 409).

[81] "Duro se le hizo a Mauricio el terrible salto del cauallo tan sin lission: que quisiera el, por lo menos, que se huuiera quebrado tres o quatro piernas, porque no dexara Periandro tan a la cortesia de los que le escuchauan la creencia de tan dessaforado salto" (I, 312).

duces the problem of audience belief and compels us to examine the verisimilitude of the adventure.

The humor that we experience in the unexpected shift of perspective is immediately compounded by Mauricio's peculiar manner of evoking the principle of verisimilitude: i.e., if Periandro and his horse had broken three or four legs, the account would have been plausible. Cervantes proceeds to give these elements of humor a parodistic direction in the delicate touches indicating that Mauricio is annoyed by the tale and serious in his objection: because the leap produced no injuries, it is "unbearable" and "outrageous"; he wishes that there had been "at least three or four broken legs." A more inappropriate subordination of human experience to abstract realities than that of the pedantic Mauricio would be difficult to imagine. It is probable that the force of Cervantes' parodistic intention dictated his departure from the usual dialogue pattern in the various scenes of audience commentary since in the dramatic movement of dialogue it is more difficult for an author to control the perspective of his reader and make his point forcefully. In any event what we observe in Mauricio's unspoken commentary (the desire for three or four broken legs) amounts to a willfully absurd misapplication by the author of the principle which sixteenth-century criticism had taken such pains to formulate, that of the legitimate marvelous. It is the type of misapplication which in the *Quixote* we observe in the absurd sprinkling of salt by which Don Quixote answers the pedants' objections to the implausibility of Montesinos' delivery of Durandarte's heart to Belerma.

Following the parodistic treatment of Mauricio's notion of verisimilitude, Cervantes addresses himself directly to the theoretical problems of belief and authorial freedom. Observing that Mauricio is not content to allow audience belief to be a question of courtesy, he adds:

> But so great was the credit which Periandro had with them all, that they did not yield to their doubt of his credibility, for, just as it is a punishment of the liar that, when he tells the truth, he is not believed, so it is the glory of the well-accredited truth-teller that, when he tells a lie, he is believed. And as the

private thoughts of Mauricio did not interfere with his discourse, Periandro continued, saying . . .[82]

For De Lollis, who failed to situate the episode of the fantastic leap in the perspective of literary controversy, these words could be meaningful only in reference to the oppression of free thought and the sacrifice of morality to expediency which he associated with the Counterreformation.[83] Viewed in terms of the literary problems which underlie the scene, the words become more coherent than De Lollis imagined. As Don Quixote had intimated in his humorous thrusts at the canon's doctrine of verisimilitude, the conditions for audience belief are far more complicated than the empirically minded theorists of the neo-Aristotelian movement preferred to believe. In the last analysis belief depends simply on the audience's willingness to accept as true what the narrator offers. Moreover, there is a suggestion here that belief is a matter of courtesy, which recalls both Don Quixote's whispered words to Sancho at the close of the Clavileño episode that he is willing to believe the narration of the adventures in the sky if his squire is willing to believe his account of the descent to the Cave of Montesinos, and the discourtesy of the magistrate, who repeatedly interrupts the counterfeit captives in their account of their captivity. In acknowledging that the audience can *decide to believe*, Cervantes suggests that the

[82] ". . . pero el credito que todos tenian de Periandro, les hizo no passar adelante con la duda del no creerle: que, assi como es pena del mentiroso que, quando diga verdad, no se le crea, assi es gloria del bien acreditado el ser creydo quando diga mentira. Y como no pudieron estoruar los pensamientos de Mauricio la plática de Periandro, prosiguio la suya diziendo . . ." (I, 312).

[83] "Sempre—in via generale—una morale relativa, da contro-riforma, quella che ammette 'vanto' (*gloria* dice testualmente Cervantes) là dov'è menzogna (*mentira*). Si direbbe che quelle povere coscienze, poichè non eran più padrone di sè, rinunciavano ad ogni punto fisso di orientazione" (*Cervantes reazionario*, p. 185). De Lollis proceeds to offer a psychological explanation, imagining Cervantes taking comfort in the words that a good man can lie. Here the critic approaches without quite reaching the theory of Cervantes' "heroic hypocrisy," which Ortega had advanced ten years before (see *Meditaciones del Quijote*, p. 86) and which Castro was to elaborate more thoroughly in the following year (1925; see *El pensamiento de Cervantes*, pp. 261-292). Castro's theory stirred up a controversy in Cervantine scholarship of the succeeding years. For bibliography on the subject as well as a systematic critique of the theory, see Spitzer, "Die Frage der Heuchelei des Cervantes." A sober reevaluation of the theory can be found in M. Bataillon, *Erasmo y España*, II, 407ff., which gives a more comprehensive view of the Counterreformation.

fundamental misfocus in the neo-Aristotelians' approach to the problem of belief lies in their concentration on the objects of imitation rather than on the reader's apprehension of those objects. At the same time the courtesy of the reader, or his "willing suspension of disbelief" must be captured by the narrator, and once again we discover the association of deception (*mentir*) with the function of the poet which we observe in nearly all theoretical writings on literature of the age. It is he who glories in passing off his lies as truth, or in the words of Cervantes ". . . es gloria del bien acreditado el ser creydo quando diga mentira."[84] Where Cervantes differs from the neo-Aristotelians is not in his advocacy of the precept "deceive with the semblance of truth," which they unanimously recommended, but rather in his refusal to accept the limited capacities for belief[85] which the Aristotelians presupposed in the ideal reader and their resultant restrictions on the poet's freedom. Here Cervantes comes as close as he ever does to making the aesthetic discovery that managed to continue eluding literary theorists for the next two hundred years—that aesthetic belief is of an order entirely different from that of empirical belief.

THE ADVENTURE of Periandro's leap is the final episode in the extended narrator-audience situation that occupies a central place in the second book of the *Persiles*. Viewed in terms of the structural and aesthetic principles on which the romance is based, the protagonist's long recitation enables the author by subsequent exposi-

---

[84] That the glory of the poet depends on his ability to deceive with lies recalls the recommendations of Minturno: "Trouasi un modo d'approuare, nel quale il parer dell'humano intelletto s'inganna." The poet must strive to give his fictions "la somiglianza del vero, e la uertû del mentitore parer le [the events linked in his fictional context] fà simili à quelle, che necessariamente accadono. Ingannasi adunque il nostro intelletto, ou'egli delle cose, che auuengano, questa differenza non conosca. Ma Laude grande è del Poeta, che alle cose finte acquista mirabil fede" (*L'arte poetica*, pp. 41-42). The idea continued to be echoed by theorists throughout the next century. Bouhours writes: ". . . il est permis, il est même glorieux à un Poete de mentir d'une manière si ingenieuse" (cited by Abrams, *The Mirror and the Lamp*, p. 269).

[85] It goes without saying that Cervantes' fascination with the problematic aspects of man's capacity for belief, here viewed exclusively in terms of a literary problem, is fundamental to the entire conception of *Don Quixote* and that irony celebrated by the Romantics in his work, which would recognize the attraction and value of the incredible in human experience precisely because of its incredibility.

tion to provide the reader with necessary information concerning the events leading up to the opening scene of the work. It represents what El Pinciano describes as a delayed prologue, on which the *in-medias-res* structure is dependent, and corresponds to the recitations of Odysseus, Aeneas, and Calasiris in the ancient epics. Moreover, Cervantes employs it to add the necessary elements of the marvelous to his prose epic through the hero's account of heroic and strange incidents resonant with overtones from the literary tradition of epic poetry and romance.

In the context of the literary controversy, which lies behind Periandro's narration, we have observed how the focus shifts gradually to encompass the two basic aesthetic problems which dominated much of the neo-Aristotelian critical thinking, from the initial critical confrontation of the demand of unity in the scene of the fishermen's wedding, to the examination of both unity and verisimilitude in the dream of the island paradise, and thence to the account of the fantastic leap, in which the aesthetic focus becomes exclusively the problem of belief and verisimilitude. In all cases the narrator offends against the accepted critical canons and is admonished by the critical members of his audience. If Periandro seems at times to acknowledge the validity of the arguments of his adversaries and to submit to them, his submission is in each case illusory. Almost immediately he reasserts his narrative freedom, as it were, impudently flouting the principles which he seems willing to accept. Periandro rarely responds to his critics with theoretical justifications, but we can infer, from his occasional observations and his conscious failure to accept the critics' terms, that in opposition to the classical principles of unity and verisimilitude he represents the aesthetic which Don Quixote sets forth in his debate with the Canon of Toledo, an aesthetic based entirely on pleasure and the freedom of the artist from the restrictions that the classical rules would place on his creative powers in his task of providing pleasure.

It is characteristic of the *Persiles* that the tension between critical audience and creating narrator is never adequately resolved. Even as the narrator (i.e., in the broader context of the work, not the character Periandro) enters the episode of Periandro's leap to poke fun mildly at the indignant Mauricio, he resumes the narration of the romance shortly thereafter by suggesting that perhaps the judgment of Mauricio was correct. Formally we observe the frame of a dialogue between two conflicting voices of the narrator enclosing and echoing the dialogue between Periandro and his critics:

> I do not know whether I am certain, so that I would dare to affirm it positively, that Mauricio and some of the other listeners were pleased that Periandro put an end to his account, because most of the time accounts which are long, although they may be of great importance, are wont to be tiresome.[86]

The significant aspect of this passage, however, is its purposeful ambiguity. The opening part of the sentence with its double reservation establishes distance between the author and all that follows, and the final part, which contains an affirmation of an opinion which may or may not be that of Cervantes, is literally a mass of qualifications (las mas veces," "aunque sean," "suelen ser"). The qualifications and ambiguity do not, however, turn into the transparently parodistic equivocation of Cide Hamete Benengeli at the expense of Aristotelian principles. We are left with the impression of a Cervantes who was quite literally caught in the opposition between two divergent aesthetic tendencies. As in that ambiguous *fábula-historia* passage which introduces the adventure of the counterfeit captives, we perceive in the narrator's words a note of stifled parody, as the voice of the canon once again succeeds in silencing the irrepressible Cide Hamete Benengeli.

[86] "No se si tenga por cierto, de manera que osse afirmar, que Mauricio y algunos de los mas oyentes se holgaron de que Periandro pusiesse fin en su plática, porque las mas vezes, las que son largas, aunque sean de importancia, suelen ser desabridas" (I, 317).

CHAPTER VIII

The Narrator of the *Persiles*

Unlike the skillfully conceived triptych of historian (Cide Hamete Benengeli)-translator-editor, who are coherent in all their elusiveness, the narrator whose words we occasionally hear in the *Persiles* seems to speak with two conflicting voices, which never reach an adequate resolution. In the analysis of the discursive comment which introduces the episode of the counterfeit captives we discovered the simultaneous presence of a voice which we could liken to that of Cide Hamete Benengeli as it attempts to introduce the humorous play on the concept *historia,* typical of many comments in the *Quixote,* and a sober voice reminiscent of that of the Canon of Toledo, which abruptly cuts short the development of the humorous equivocation to offer in all seriousness the Aristotelian definition of the verisimilar plot—i.e., the plot of the *Persiles* itself. Similarly the two voices are audible in the commentary interspersed amid Periandro's narration, in which we discover support for both the freely inventive narrator and his pedantic critics.

It is illuminating to trace the vicissitudes of the authorial voice through the *Persiles,* for a pattern quickly emerges which parallels that which we have observed in the dramatic examinations of literary theory in the scenes analyzed above. Corresponding to the opposing tendencies that mark the critical exchanges between the participating authors and their critical audiences is an ambivalence at two levels in Cervantes' use of the narrator of the *Persiles.* One lies in Cervantes' conflicting notions concerning the general role of the narrator and the extent to which he is allowed to intervene in his narration. Here the opposition is between the neo-Aristotelian conception of the narrator's limited function and the conception of the narrator, exemplified by the romances of chivalry, as a vehicle for widely ranging, discursive commentary. At the same time there is an ambivalence *within* the voice of the narrator. In his various commentaries which are informed by literary concerns we observe once again the recurrent literary debate which we have traced through the *Quixote* and the *Persiles,* from its most discursive

257

formulation in the argument between Don Quixote and the Canon of Toledo to its most dramatic presentation in Periandro's narration.

The Restrained Narrator and Classical Literary Theory

Throughout the first book of the *Persiles* the narrator seldom appears in his narration. As has been pointed out above, the work was originally conceived as a continuation of the genre of classical epic poetry and modeled on the celebrated "prose epic" of Heliodorus. This artistic plan undoubtedly dictated Cervantes' apparent intention of avoiding authorial digressions and dispensing with the discursive fictitious narrator of the romance tradition, which he had so successfully revolutionized in the chronicler of the *Quixote*. The singer of classical epic is traditionally anonymous, and his appearances in his text are limited to such formalities as proposition, invocation, and apostrophe or to an occasional brief comment on the events of the narration.[1] As Robert M. Durling has recently pointed out, Tasso, whose precepts and example seem to have influenced Cervantes' plan of the *Persiles*, was led by his theories and his desire to re-create the classical epic to the resurrection of the anonymous narrator of Homer and Virgil.[2]

In addition to the example of the ancients, Aristotle's words on the role of the narrator had to be reckoned with by all artists of the Renaissance. One of the widely divulged parts of the *Poetics*, the impact of which can be assessed properly only if we situate it beside the theorists' outspoken veneration for the classical epic, was Aristotle's statement of praise for Homer: "Homer, admirable in all respects, has the special merit of being the only poet who rightly appreciates the part he should take himself. The poet should speak as little as possible in his own person, for it is not this that makes him an imitator."[3] Thus El Pinciano can repeat the injunction: the

---

[1] For the limited range of these comments, see Richard Heinze, *Virgils Epische Technik* (Leipzig, 1908), pp. 368-373.

[2] *The Figure of the Poet in Renaissance Epic*, p. 185.

[3] *Poetics*, xxiv, p. 93. In rejecting the narrative technique of the verse romances, Tasso writes: ". . . né il principe dei poeti Virgilio, né Omero, né gli altri antichi gli [the discursive prologues which often introduce the cantos of the romances]

epic poet "deve hablar lo menos que el pueda," and should employ characters to express his judgments and ideas.

The theorists offered various elaborations on the Aristotelian principle. For example, El Pinciano claims that by speaking through characters, the poet can state his moral principles more honestly and freely, provide more variety, infuse more pathos into the narration, and follow the *in-medias-res* structural demands more easily.[4] Similarly Tasso asserts that the poet displays his inventive powers in interspersing in various parts and voices in the poem the direct commentary which the discursive narrator of romance inserts at the beginning of his cantos. At the same time Piccolomini condemns the arrogance of the poet who forces his own judgments on the reader.[5] However, the theorists' primary concern in invoking and interpreting Aristotle's words was their curious preoccupation with credibility in the fictional work. By intruding to make a judgment, the author betrays himself as an interested party and arouses suspicions in the reader about his veracity. Thus Castelvetro praises Homer's detachment as an example of the narrative technique of the *narratore indifferente* as opposed to the *narratore passionato*, who in expressing judgments and beliefs "diminishes the listeners' faith that he is telling only the truth."[6] Whatever reasons they chose to present, the classicists were in agreement in favoring the narrative technique of the prince of poets, Virgil, over that of his most formidable modern rival, Ariosto, and consequently the limitations on authorial intervention in accord with the practices of the former over the freedom which the discursive narrator of the latter assumed throughout his work.[7]

---

abbiano usati, ed Aristotele chiaramente dica ne la sua *Poetica* . . ." and proceeds to cite the passage from Aristotle (prologue to the *Rinaldo*, p. 5).

[4] *Philosophía antigua poética*, III, 208-209.

[5] See Riley, *Cervantes's Theory of the Novel*, p. 206.

[6] ". . . diminuisce la credenza degli ascoltatori che egli dica puramente la verità" (*Poetica d'Aristotele*, p. 55). Although the bases of this plea for authorial detachment should be distinguished from modern theories condemning the intrusions of a narrator in favor of "objectivity" and the preservation of the illusion of actuality in the novel, both notions are founded on the failure to deal adequately with the distinctions between fictional reality and actuality (see Durling's discussion of the matter, pp. 252-253).

[7] As far as I know, theorists did not invoke Heliodorus as an example of the authorial detachment recommended by Aristotle. Nevertheless, his narrative tech-

Cervantes & the Classical Aesthetic

In the first book of the *Persiles* Cervantes seems to be observing the injunction of Aristotle and his modern commentators. For in approximately half of the book the narrator disappears completely behind various of his characters, who relate the stories of their wanderings: Antonio and his wife Ricla, Rutilio, Manuel de Sosa, Mauricio, Transila, and the captain of the ship serving King Policarpo. The characters have the privilege of making comments on the action and voicing general principles about the ways of the world.[8] A typical example is Periandro's sententious generalization as he requests that Arnaldo put him ashore among the barbarians: "For in cases of danger or difficulty, the advice and the undertaking should be settled together at once."[9] Similarly Auristela voices one of Cervantes' favorite themes: "As the light shines

---

nique would offer Cervantes a good example of the observation of the classicists' rule, for his narrator seldom makes his presence felt by voicing an opinion of his own (see Victor Hefti, *Zur Erzählungstechnik in Heliodors Aethiopica*, p. 82).

[8] For the importance which the neo-Aristotelians attached to such *sententiae* in poetry, see Cascales, *Tablas poéticas*, pp. 68-72. He asserts that epic poetry should use them much more sparingly than tragedy and that the epic poet should express many of them through his characters.

In addition to direct discourse, Cervantes occasionally uses *erlebte Rede* to introduce such sententious commentary into his work. For example, the narrator inserts a generalization on jealousy into his description of Auristela's frightened thoughts about Periandro's encountering his rival Arnaldo. Whether the author was conscious of this effect or not, we interpret the generalization as emerging from the consciousness of Auristela rather than from the narrator. The evocative element, which E. Lorck sees as necessary to establish the context for *erlebte Rede*, provoking the reader to expect the character's discourse (see *Die "Erlebte Rede": Eine Sprachliche Untersuchung* [Heidelberg, 1921], pp. 11-15), is here provided in the words "turbóse Auristela." The description of the series of thoughts which follows leads to a rhetorical question and then the general statement, at which point we find ourselves still witnessing the consciousness of Auristela: "No quisiera ver juntos a los dos amantes . . . y mas que ¿quien le quitaria a Periandro no estar zeloso, viendo a los ojos tan poderoso contrario? Que no ay discrecion que valga ni amorosa fee que assegure al enamorado pecho, quando, por su desuentura, entran en el zelosas sospechas" (I, 52). A similar attribution of a general statement of the narrator to one of his characters by *erlebte Rede* appears later, as the notion "es mejor casarse que abrassarse" is inserted amid a description of the ponderings of the troubled king Policarpo (I, 286). Other examples of this narrative technique of authorial withdrawal in the *Persiles* can be found in II, 83 and 94. For examples from the *Quixote* and the *Novelas Ejemplares* of Cervantes' use of this device, see Friedrich Todemann, "Die erlebte Rede im Spanischen," *Romanische Forschungen*, XLIV (1930), 132-138.

[9] ". . . en los casos arduos y dificultosos, en vn mismo punto han de andar el consejo y la obra" (I, 14).

brightest in darkness so is hope most firm in time of trouble."[10] In the part related by the narrator Cervantes rarely allows him to assert his presence by such generalizations and judgments, particularly in the opening chapters of the work.

In the few early appearances of the narrator, one finds him clothed in the garb of the classic poet. To be sure, Cervantes dispenses with the classical proposition and invocation in his modern epic, apparently following El Pinciano's recommendations concerning the quantitative parts of the prose epic and the example of Heliodorus. Nevertheless, his narrator's second appearance is in the statement of a topic similar to these and equally resonant of the tradition of classical poetry—the expression of diffidence: "But how can tongue express or pen describe what were the feelings of Periandro, when he saw that the now free, but lately condemned victim, was his own Auristela?"[11] Moreover, in one of his two longest appearances in the first book, the poet again appears in his classical robes. The apostrophe of jealousy and Auristela, in spite of its rhetoric, is reminiscent of the Virgilian apostrophe in its introduction of the poet's emotions occasioned by the situation of his characters in the work:

O Mighty power of jealousy! O infirmity, that art so planted in the heart, that thou canst only be uprooted thence with life itself! Ah! beauteous Auristela, stay and reflect ere you allow yourself to become a prey to this cruel suffering! But who can restrain thought within bounds, which is so light and subtle, that bodyless it passes through stone walls, enters human bosoms, and penetrates the deepest recesses of the soul?[12]

[10] ". . . assi como la luz resplandece mas en las tinieblas, assi la esperança ha de estar mas firme en los trabajos" (I, 67).

[11] "¡Que lengua podra dezir, a que pluma escriuir, lo que sintio Periandro quando conocio ser Auristela la condenada y la libre!" (I, 24).

[12] "¡O poderosa fuerça de los zelos! ¡O enfermedad, que te pegas al alma de tal manera, que sólo te despegas con la vida! ¡O hermosissima Auristela! ¡Detente, no te precipites a dar lugar en tu imaginacion a esta rabiosa dolencia! Pero ¿quien podra tener a raya los pensamientos, que suelen ser tan ligeros y sutiles, que, como no tienen cuerpo, passan las murallas, traspassan los pechos, y veen lo mas escondido de las almas?" (I, 148). The scene of Auristela's jealousy introduces the series of episodes at the court of Policarpo, which fills the greater part of Book II. As the wanderers' visit to this utopia is occasionally allusive to the Dido episode of the *Aeneid* (see Schevill,

Midway through the first book of the *Persiles* Cervantes' narrator begins to come forth from the shadows to comment more frequently on the course of the events of his tale. His observations can preserve a classical ring, as in his words following the arrival of his despairing wanderers at the island of snow, words which recall the pathos of Virgil's narrator: "Miserable and fearful indeed are the perils of the ocean, since they who had experienced them could rejoice to change them for the worst the land could offer."[13] Occasionally, however, he proceeds to speak in the sententious tone more typical of the narrator of medieval romance than of the classical singer. Thus after observing Auristela and Periandro's sympathetic reaction to Manuel de Sosa's song of woe, the narrator comments: "Those who love quickly recognize the passion in another, and seek fellowship with them who know how to pity and sympathize with their own weaknesses."[14]

In addition to pathos and sententiousness, concerns of a more literary type, e.g., the necessity of marvelous and instructive subject matter in the lofty genre, can provoke the narrator's intrusion, as in his general comment on wines: "The cups flowed with exquisite wines, which so improve when they travel by sea from one extremity of the world to another, that they are unequaled by the finest nectar."[15] It is important to observe, however, that such general statements are inserted sparingly throughout the rest of the first book. Moreover, Cervantes' narrator avoids voicing such moral judgments on his characters' actions as those which had become

---

"Studies in Cervantes," *Publications of Yale University*, XIII [1908], 475-548), it is probable that Cervantes was conscious of the nature of the Virgilian apostrophe. Heinze has shown how Virgil went beyond Homer's limitations on subjective intrusions by his narrator, particularly in the Dido episode, where he departs from the ideal of objectivity which he generally maintains throughout the rest of the work (see p. 369). Both the topic of diffidence and the apostrophe are among the various literary devices of classical and romance literature which in *Don Quixote* Cervantes parodies in the commentaries of his Moorish narrator (see, for example, II, 657).

[13] "Miserables son y temerosas las fortunas del mar, pues los que las padecen se huelgan de trocarlas con las mayores que en la tierra se les ofrezcan" (I, 127).

[14] ". . . que los enamorados facilmente reconcilian los animos, y trauan amistad con los que conocen que padecen su misma enfermedad" (I, 66).

[15] ". . . se llenaron las taças de generosos vinos: que quando se trasiegan por la mar de vn cabo a otro, se mejoran de manera que no ay nectar que se les yguale" (I, 101).

typical of the narrator's style in the medieval romances and which sixteenth-century Aristotelians found particularly damaging to an author's credibility in a work of literature.

The Disintegration of the Classical Narrator and the Emergence of the Discursive Narrator

The final paragraph of the first book of the *Persiles* signals a change in Cervantes' use of the narrator. The narrator suddenly appears as an editor, transcribing the text of an original author, and immediately allows himself the privilege of making editorial comments on its composition. The words introducing the fictitious author recall the interplay of authorial voices in the *Quixote*:

> And at this part of their *history* the author of the first volume leaves them and passes to the second, wherein things will be related which *although they do not surpass truth, yet go beyond what one could conceive, since they could scarcely enter into the most lively and expansive imagination.*[16]

Unexpectedly the singer of classical epic is replaced by the fictitious author and editor of an original text, a narrative situation associated with the genre which the *Persiles* was to unseat, the romance of chivalry. Moreover, for the first time criteria governing the composition of the work are presented directly as one of its subjects. The metamorphosis proceeds one step further, for the new authorial voice immediately introduces the favorite hoax of Cide Hamete Benengeli and his editor. Alluding to the familiar distinction between the historian and the poet, truth and verisimilitude, and taking advantage of the equivocation contained in the range of meanings in the term *historia* in contemporary usage, the editor asserts that as historian the author of the *Persiles* is free and obligated to recount the truth, which is of course much stranger than fiction. As in Cide Hamete Benengeli's similar claims, the extravagance of the pretense to be writing history is perfectly obvious, and we realize that we are facing a narrator who is turning aesthetic

---

[16] ". . . en el qual punto dexa el autor el primer libro desta granda *historia*, y passa al segundo, donde se contaràn cosas que, *aunque no passan de la verdad, sobrepujan a la imaginacion, pues a penas pueden caber en la mas sutil y dilatada sus acontecimientos*" (I, 153). The italics are mine.

theory into an elaborate joke on his reader. The sober voice of the classical narrator, which Cervantes maintains throughout his first book, has yielded to that of Ariosto's trickster. His words form a prelude to the following book and Periandro's narration, much of which is dominated by a humorous, dramatic exploitation of potential tensions in contemporary literary problems.[17]

The first paragraph of Book II develops the device of the fictitious author further along familiar lines. The editor is not merely transcribing the author's text. He is translating it, and like Don Quixote's translator exercises the right to delete irrelevant matter: "But in this translation, and it is a translation, I omit as something impertinent, something aired and bespoken everywhere, the author's definition, and I proceed with the facts."[18] Here he shows himself to be much more conscious of the demands of historical writing than the "original historian." Moreover, as in the case of Cide Hamete Benengeli, Cervantes gives his fictitious author a real personality and exploits it for humorous purposes. What the editor must delete in the interests of the truth of the history is a long digression of chapter length on jealousy, which unfortunately the original author included because "he knew more about being a lover than an historian."[19] Following the narration of Book I, in

---

[17] I do not wish to deal with the problem of dating the *Persiles* here; however, the changing role of the narrator suggests both that a period of some time may have intervened between the composition of the first book and the remaining three books and that the final three books bear some resemblance to the *Quixote*. The resemblance would seem to be sufficient to call into question Singleton's arguments for an early dating of the entire *Persiles*, which depend to a great extent on his conclusion that none of the preoccupations of the "mature Cervantes" are visible in the *Persiles*. Could it not be that, when Cervantes has the Canon of Toledo say he has written more than one hundred pages of the perfect book of chivalry, Cervantes is thinking of the first fragment of the *Persiles*, which he wrote after 1596, the date of El Pinciano's tract, and was not to complete until the years following the publication of *Don Quixote I*?

[18] ". . . pero en esta traducion, que lo es, se quita por prolixa, y por cosa en muchas partes referida y ventilada, y se viene a la verdad del caso" (I, 155). Compare the words of the editor of the *Quixote* (discussed above): ". . . pero al traductor desta historia le pareció pasar estas y otras semejantes menudencias [included by the original historian, i.e., Cide Hamete Benengeli] en silencio, porque no venían bien con el propósito principal de la historia; la cual más tiene su fuerza en la verdad que en las frías digresiones" (II, 662).

[19] ". . . sabía mas de enamorado que de historiador" (I, 155). The type of digression to which the editor is alluding was common in the romance of chivalry (see for example, *Amadís de Gaula*, ed. B.A.E., XL, 323).

which a sober tone is uniformly maintained, the sudden transformation of the anonymous epic narrator into the incongruous figure of the fool in love and the introduction of a humorous interplay between fictitious author and translator are astonishing.

The following chapter of the *Persiles* continues the interplay, beginning with a similar humorous thrust by the translator at the fictitious author, and once again the literary problem of artistic selectivity and authorial presence are elements of a context of humor.

> It seems that the capsizing of the ship capsized or, to put it better, confounded the judgment of the author of this history, because he offered four or five beginnings to this second chapter, almost as if he were not certain as to the end toward which he would proceed. Finally he resolved the difficulty by stating that fortune and misfortune generally come together and that perhaps there is no means of separating the one from the other. Grief and happiness are so closely coupled that equally foolish are the sad man who despairs of remedy for his sorrows and the happy man who is confident amid his fortune. All of this can be easily understood if one considers this strange event.[20]

The initial humor, springing from the ingeniously incongruous vision of the author standing both within his work as a character subject to the vicissitudes of its plot, and without as creator, befuddled in his creative endeavor by the frightening events of his own creation, takes a mildly aggressive turn at the expense of the heavily sententious style of the freely intervening narrator of the romance of chivalry.[21]

To interpret the unexpected appearance of the romance narrative situation and its humorous exploitation at this juncture of the work

---

[20] "Parece que el bolcar de la naue bolco o, por mejor dezir, turbò el juyzio del autor de esta historia, porque a este segundo capitulo le dio quatro o cinco principios, casi como dudando que fin en el tomaria. En fin, se resoluio diziendo que las dichas y las desdichas suelen andar tan juntas, que tal vez no ay medio que las diuida; andan el pesar y el plazer tan apareados, que es simple el triste que se desespera y el alegre que se confia, como lo da facilmente a entender este estraño sucesso" (I, 159).

[21] A similar sententious intrusion on adverse and prosperous fortune can be observed in *Amadís de Gaula*, p. 110.

as a parody of a favorite literary device of an outmoded genre is to ignore the context surrounding it, for the *Persiles*, unlike *Don Quixote*, was conceived as anything but a parodistic attack on the romance of chivalry. To understand the emergence of the fictitious author, we must recall rather the anticlassicist tendency of Cervantes and the double-edged irony surrounding the figure of Cide Hamete Benengeli, which enabled him not only to represent parodistically the digressively sententious narrator of medieval romance, but also to ridicule the most eloquent critics of that genre and to defy any attempts to limit his creative freedom.

To be sure, we might say that in both of the exchanges under examination an Aristotelian voice in the editor is mocking and silencing that of his opponent. Nevertheless, the humor of the voice is very un-Aristotelian,[22] and the mere appearance of this real personality, the *loco enamorado*, who can be disturbed by the misfortunes of his characters, and whom we see in the elusive act of artistic composition, literally standing as god over *quatro o cinco principios* of his creation and puzzling over how he will proceed to manipulate the destinies of his characters or draw the appropriate moral lesson from the example, can only be seen as an incongruous element in the overall texture of the *Persiles*. Its significance resides precisely in its incongruity, for it is the first clear indication of Cervantes' deep uneasiness with the aesthetic conception of his work. In spite of being cut short, an irrepressible voice in Cervantes has uttered a plea for artistic freedom. The plea will be resumed, and asserted with more forcefulness, shortly thereafter in Periandro's narration as the protagonist and his Aristotelian opponents will reincarnate the figures of the original author and the critical editor-translator and continue their dialogue.

An indication of the instability surrounding Cervantes' literary intentions in the *Persiles* is his abandonment of the fictitious author as a functional device almost immediately following its introduction. It would appear that the artist suddenly recalls an intention which he has momentarily forgotten, that of producing the masterpiece that is to rival Heliodorus' *Aethiopica*. He fails to expand the voice of the *loco enamorado* into the fully developed personality of

---

[22] To be recalled is Tasso's theory that humor is inappropriate in epic literature.

a Cide Hamete Benengeli and avoids exploiting the interplay allowed by the double vantage point to make comments on the composition of his text and to introduce literary problems. Occasional allusions to an original text recall the narrative situation, but in these cases the fictitious author is not characterized and at times is replaced by the term *historia*. Such allusions are nonfunctional and can be viewed as simple vestigial mannerisms of the narrative situation of the romance of chivalry (see I, 190, 212, 323).

However, following the brief interlude with the fictitious author, an important change occurs in Cervantes' use of the narrator, suggesting that he has cast off some of the restraint which his classical theories imposed on him and to which he successfully submitted throughout Book I. Although the fictitious author who must bear the abuse of a critical editor disappears, the narrator establishes himself now at the center of his narration, and his widely ranging discursive comments become as central to his work as do the heroes and events which he describes.

The new freedom of the narrator is immediately apparent in the first chapter of Book II, in which in addition to a long epic apostrophe (see below) and two allusions to the original author, we discover the narrator intervening no fewer than four times with those general statements which by and large he expresses through the voices of his characters in the preceding book. There is a sententious comment on the power of death: "The figure of death, whatever the garment in which it appears, is frightful, and, when it seizes a person in full possession of his powers and health, unawares, it is formidable."[23] In addition there is an observation on the emotions of the shipwrecked traveler, allowing Cervantes the use of literary paradox in referring to the victims' pleasure in the embraces of a broken plank.[24] Another inserted remark emphasizes

---

[23] ". . . la figura de la muerte, en qualquier trage que venga, es espantosa, y la que coge a vn desapercebido en todas sus fuerças y salud, es formidable" (I, 156-157).

[24] This type of authorial intrusion, which simply embellishes the text with a display of poetic wit, adding the marvelous of lofty language, recommended by all theorists, is infrequent in the *Persiles*. Another example appears near the end of Book II, as Cervantes describes the attributes of sailors in a perfect balance of antithetical elements: ". . . mejor les (marineros) huele la pez, la brea y la resina

the verisimilitude of the failure of the ship to sink as it drifts help-lessly. The remaining comment by the narrator in this brief chapter is the first of a series of digressions on problems of love and court-ship which fill Book II of the *Persiles*. Although he has deleted a long commentary on jealousy by the fictitious author, the narrator allows himself the privilege of remarking that the power of jealousy is such that even the fear of imminent death cannot remove it from the mind of him whom it possesses.

As we have observed before, Book II of the *Persiles* is modeled on the Dido episode of the *Aeneid* and consists (apart from the long narration of Periandro) of a complex web of love intrigue in which nearly all the characters of the courtly society of King Policarpo's palace are enmeshed. In this situation it is only natural that the narrator's comments should return over and over again to such themes as the proper conduct of a gentleman and a lady in courtship (I, 197), the danger of self-deception in love (I, 209), the power of love to turn a king from the responsibilities of his office (I, 212, and 291), the power of jealousy (I, 181-182), the evils of revenge (I, 173), and the qualities of a good counselor (I, 177).

In many cases such statements concerning ethical problems are accompanied by judgments of the conduct of the characters, as the author makes no effort to observe the theorists' mandate that moral judgment should be the privilege of the reader. Thus a gen-eral remark on the folly of the old man who pursues a young woman contains an adverse judgment of King Policarpo's lust for Auristela (I, 205). Similarly the aged king becomes an example of the harmful effects which hypocrisy produces in him who practices it (I, 211). A judgment of the malicious poet Clodio be-comes the occasion for a digression on the literary-ethical problem of the satirical poet, the *maldiziente agudo* (I, 185-186).[25] A brief

---

de sus nauios, que a la demas gente las rosas, las flores, y los amarantos de los jardines" (I, 293). The most important case of such ornamental commentary is the second epic apostrophe (see below).

[25] The presence of Clodio in the *Persiles* is one more indication of the im-portance of the literary *discorsi* in the work. He dramatically represents both the conventional view of satire as a low form of literature and the consequences of the irresponsible practice of satire which various contemporary theorists men-tioned—the exile of the poet (". . . a Ouidio con ser tan excelente Poeta lo dester-raron de Roma . . . y Iuuenal celebre Poeta Español estuuo desterrado en Egypto,

observation on chivalric virtues accompanies the praise of Renato's courtesy ("who, as he was a knight, and courtesy is ever to be found in those who profess knighthood . . .").[26] On the other hand the narrator can make his presence felt simply in a judgment of his characters ("This conversation passed between our two pretended lovers, but in fact impudent knaves").[27] In length the authorial intrusions in the second book of the *Persiles* range from the brief parenthetical remark to the extended digression, in which the heavily sententious tone of the sermon can be perceived as the author may appear as *yo* and like the medieval romancer address his readers as *vosotros* (see I, 178, 181-182, 206).

In the final two books of the *Persiles* the narrator continues to occupy the central position that he appropriates for himself at the beginning of Book II. The range of his discursive commentary extends from a variety of brief *sententiae* (see, for example, "kinship warms the blood which will freeze in the greatest friendship" and "it rarely happens that good intentions are carried into effect without any hindrances"), to occasional remarks of a satirical nature ("if all contentions ended in this way [the narrator refers to the simple betrothal of young peasants by a vow and a clasp of hands], the solicitous quills of notaries would dry up and lose their plum-

---

por ciertas poesias que hizo perjudiciales. . . . Y es lastima embilezcan aora la malicia de algunos Poetas vna arte de tanto prouecho para las Republicas" [Carvallo, *Cisne de Apolo*, II, 224]). Clodio has been exiled from England because he has forgotten the moral mission of poetry and allowed maliciousness to enter his verses. Mauricio approves of his punishment: ". . . dignamente, los satiricos, los maldizientes, los mal intencionados, son desterrados y echados de sus casas sin honra y con vituperio" (I, 97). Cervantes is consistent in voicing his distaste for satire, condemning it in *Don Quixote* (II, 651), and boasting in *Viage del Parnaso*: "Nunca voló la pluma humilde mia/ por la region satirica, baxeza/ que a infames premios y desgracias guia" (p. 55); in both cases he mentions the fate of the exiled Ovid. Compare: *Don Quixote*: "Si el poeta fuere casto en sus costumbres, lo será también en sus versos [this is Strabo's maxim, which was omnipresent in Renaissance criticism]; la pluma es lengua del alma: cuales fueren los conceptos que en ella se engendraren, tales serán sus escritos" (II, 651); *Persiles*: "Es tan ligera la lengua como el pensamiento, y si son malas las preñezes de los pensamientos, las empeoran los partos de la lengua" (I, 98).

[26] ". . . el qual, como era cauallero, a quien es anexa siempre la cortesia. . ." (I, 303).

[27] "Estas razones passaron entre los dos fingidos amantes y atreuidos y necios de veras" (I, 201). See also I, 219 and 222.

age"),[28] to the extended digressions which open many of the chapters. (See for example the introductory comment of the first chapter of Book III on mutability[29] or that of the eighth chapter on the river Tagus.) What distinguishes these authorial intrusions from those of the preceding book is a shift in focus from aspects of amatory and courtly conduct to considerations of a purely literary nature. Some of Cervantes' most significant statements about literature in general and the specific genre which the *Persiles* represents appear in Book III. As most of them are meaningful in relation to the ambivalence which marks the literary poses of the discursive narrator, I have chosen to discuss them in the second part of this chapter.

LITERARY AMBIVALENCE IN THE DISCURSIVE NARRATOR

The Conservative Voice: the Assertion and Defense of the Generic Principles

Whether speaking in the subdued tones of the classical narrator in Book I or with the unrestrained garrulity of the medieval romancer in the rest of the work, Cervantes' narrator always reveals an acute preoccupation with the literary principles by which the *Persiles* was conceived. In view of Cervantes' general intentions in the work and the limited range of commentary which he initially allows his narrator, it is not surprising that throughout Book I,

---

[28] ". . . que el parentesco calienta la sangre que suele elarse en la mayor amistad" (I, 144). ". . . nunca los buenos desseos llegan a fin dichoso sin estoruos que los impidan" (II, 41). ". . . que si con esta verdad se acabaran todos los pleytos, secas y peladas estuuieran las solicitas plumas de los escriuanos" (II, 83).

[29] It is instructive to compare this statement with that of Cide Hamete Benengeli, opening Chapter LIII of the second part of *Don Quixote* (II, 922-923). Both narrators exploit venerable commonplaces of the Christian tradition of *vanitas* and mutability. In the *Persiles* the words are reminiscent of Saint Augustine, in the *Quixote*, of Ecclesiastes. In both, the philosophical value of the statement is subordinated to the example in the literary context, in the one case to the utterly incongruous example of Sancho's government, which vanishes in smoke and shadows, in the other case to the example of Arnaldo's decision to abandon his courtship of Auristela. Whereas the effect of the former context is one of humor, as the traditional words of wisdom are uttered by a *filósofo mahomético* and are referred to the humorous demise of governor Sancho, the effect of the latter is one of heavy sententiousness, as the appropriateness of Arnaldo's change of mind as an example of the venerable utterance is questionable but not doubtful enough to be humorous.

the latter's few comments concerning literary matters should be both brief in length and conservative in tone. They draw attention to the principles governing the author's selective processes and consistently underscore the *appropriateness* or *legitimacy* of elements which he includes in his narration.

In a brief intrusion following the scene of recognition in which Transila takes off her veil, revealing herself to her father Mauricio, the narrator both underscores the effect of *maravilla* of anagnorisis, which was recommended by all theorists of the time, and defines the conditions for the arousal of the effect in the reader: "It surely can be believed that such a *novel* and *unexpected* case stirred up *wonder* in the spectators."[30] On another occasion the narrator comes forward as "I," invoking the "legitimate marvelous" to justify his inclusion of a seemingly irrelevant description. Following their arrival in Golandia, the weary travelers enjoy a feast featuring the meat of marvelous birds, "which are raised in those parts in a strange way, so strange and wonderful in fact that I am obliged to give an account of it here." The narrator proceeds to offer a detailed account of the way in which the natives of Ybernia and Irlanda implant stakes at the edge of the ocean, which in the process of decay engender the delicious bird called Barnaclas.[31] A tone of self-

[30] "Sin duda se puede creer que este caso de tanta *nouedad* y tan *no esperado* puso en *admiracion* a los circunstantes" (I, 82). The italics are mine. For the marvelous as an effect of anagnorisis in contemporary literary theory, see above, Chapter I. Tasso uses the narrator's intervention similarly to point out and underscore the effect of *meraviglia* produced by peripeteia and recognition (see Durling, pp. 189-192).

[31] ". . . que se crian en aquellas partes, de tan estraña manera, que, por ser rara y peregrina, me obliga a que aqui la cuente" (I, 84). In inserting the digression on the marvelous bird, Cervantes is following Tasso's suggestion that the poet find subject matter that is both verisimilar and marvelous in the accounts of the strange lands in the northern part of the world (". . . di Gotia e di Norveggia e di Suevia e d'Islanda . . . si dee prender la materia di sì fatti poemi [*Del poema eroico*, p. 109]). Antonio de Torquemada, whose *Jardín de flores curiosas* supplied Cervantes with much of the marvelous subject matter for the *Persiles*, describes the northern countries as full of "cosas maravillosas en aves y animales y en las hierbas y plantas, y tan diferentes de las comunes y ordinarias, que no dexan de poner admiración," offering as an example the genesis of such a bird as the narrator of the *Persiles* describes (see pp. 279, 321). The appearance of the narrator is particularly significant in this case, as it not only reveals Cervantes' acute literary self-consciousness, but also prefigures the narrator's series of humorous poses of being dominated by "real" events of his fictional world. The latter, of course,

Cervantes & the Classical Aesthetic

justification is more audible when the narrator appears to call our attention to the *legitimacy* of a wondrous event in his narration, as in the brief, parenthetical remark which he appends to the description of the wanderer's recourse to the methods of the American Indian in kindling a fire: "they also kindled a fire by rubbing two dry sticks together, *a trick which is well known and widely practiced.*"[32] In addition to justifying the marvelous in subject matter and plot, the narrator is concerned to point out the relevance of a traditional vehicle of the marvelous in language, appending to his epic apostrophe of jealousy the explanation: "This has been said because [in Auristela] . . . long-suffering yielded place to suspicions."[33]

Although the classical restraint on the range of his commentary disappears at the end of Book I, the narrator continues to insert brief remarks of the type which we observe in the early chapters, and occasionally they are informed by the same conservative literary theories. In Book II such comments are infrequent, for in literary matters the new narrative voice reflects a new orientation and speaks usually in parody. Nevertheless, the apologetic voice can reassert itself. For example, the narrator underscores the legitimacy of a marvelous occurrence by appending to his description of the capsized ship the phrase "This is one of the dangers . . . which can befall a ship."[34] He explains his abbreviation of a description with the precept: "Simple details neither demand nor suffer long narrations,"[35] and alludes to the commonplace in Renaissance poetics that the knowledge of the specialist in matters concerning his field of

---

marks his narrative technique following the completion of his metamorphosis from the impersonal "classical" narrator into the playful, self-deprecating narrator which Ariosto had created.

[32] ". . . hizieron assimismo fuego, ludiendo dos secos palos el vno con el otro, *artificio tan sabido como vsado*" (I, 68). The italics are mine. Again Tasso's theories on the legitimate marvelous should be recalled: ". . . di paesi di nuovo ritrovati nel vastissimo Oceano oltre le Colonne d'Ercole si dee prender la materia de sì fatti poemi" (*Del poema eroico*, p. 109). The historians of the Indies were a source of much of Cervantes' marvelous subject matter. Garcilaso de la Vega el Inca writes how the Indians kindle their fires "con dos palillos rollizos delgados . . . barrenando uno con otro" (see the introduction of Schevill and Bonilla to their edition of the *Persiles*, p. xxix).

[33] "Esto se ha dicho, porque . . . rindio el sufrimiento a las sospechas" (I, 148).

[34] ". . . es vno de los peligros . . . que le puede suceder a vn vaxel" (I, 157-158).

[35] ". . . pues las menudencias no piden ni sufren relaciones largas" (I, 301).

272

study is superior to that of the most encyclopedic poet (I, 302).

The most interesting of the intrusions of the conservative literary voice in Book II is in one of the few instances in which Cervantes employs the interplay of fictitious author and critical translator. Here the issue is the marvelous in language, or, more specifically, the artificiality of a venerable convention of the genre—the epic apostrophe. Above we observed how Cervantes' narrator of Book I employs an apostrophe of the classical type and how, even as he does so, he betrays his literary self-consciousness by appending an explanation for his introduction of the literary convention. Following the introduction of the humorous interplay between translator and fictitious author in Book II Cervantes inserts his second epic apostrophe, but now he makes no attempt to observe the restraint characteristic of Homer and Virgil in the use of the device.[36]

Unlike the preceding intervention describing Auristela's jealousy, which is to play an important role in the scenes of intrigue at the court of Policarpo, the apostrophe is no longer functional in the movement of the narrative. It merely highlights an unexpected change of fortune in the wanderings of the heroes. Moreover, it is twice as long as that of Book I, as the narrator proceeds to address Auristela, Transila, and Ricla in succession, and is the occasion for a display of rhetorical flourishes and wit in an accumulation of antitheses founded on the double opposition between expected happiness and its frustration by unforeseen disaster, and between the unexpected suffering on earth and the reward of eternal salvation:

Farewell, O chaste thoughts of Auristela! Farewell, O well-founded intentions! Cease, ordeals so honored and holy! No other mausoleums, no other pyramids, no other spires can you expect, except those offered by these badly bitumened planks. And you, O Transila, bright example of maiden purity, can celebrate your marriage, if not in the arms of your betrothed Ladislao, in those of your discreet and ancient father, and with the hope that he will have brought you to a better bridal bed!

[36] In ancient literature the ornamental use of the apostrophe did not gain ascendance over its functional use until Ovid and later poets (see Johann Endt, "Der Gebrauch der Apostrophe bei den lateinischen Epikern," *Wiener Studien*, XXVII [1905], pp. 106-129).

And you, O Ricla, whose desires have brought you to your rest, clasp in your arms your children Antonio and Constanza, and bring them into the presence of Him who has taken away your life to make it better in heaven![37]

Following the apostrophe the translator reflects on the author's reasons for employing it, affirming the logic of its inclusion: "... y la certeza de la muerte de los que en ella [la naue] yuan, puso las razones referidas en la pluma del autor desta grande y lastimosa historia." It might be argued that, in attributing the insertion of the apostrophe to a fictitious author, Cervantes' translator's comment bears the formal stamp of the familiar disclaimer of responsibility and feigned reliance on an original text which Ariosto and the various narrators of the *Quixote* (see above) employ in justifying the insertion of absurd events in their narrations. Similarly it might be argued that just as Ariosto takes advantage of his "removal" from a preexistent text to allow himself the pleasure of the fantastic, Cervantes utilizes the same method to allow himself the pleasure of some rhetorical flourishes in a well-worn literary device. Yet there is an important difference in intention and effect between the Ariostean withdrawal and that implied by the statement of the translator of the *Persiles*. In attacking the credibility of their insertions and denying responsibility for them, Ariosto and his successors are playing a joke on the reader, mocking the latter's demands for plausibility in the fictional context and in fact underscoring the dependence of the inserted matter on the author's hand. In effect they are using the insertions of elements of questionable appropriateness in the work for humorous purposes.

In the *Persiles*, however, Cervantes has no intention of making a joke out of his inclusion of something which did, however, disturb his aesthetic sensibilities. His translator's observation does not ridi-

---

[37] "¡A Dios, castos pensamientos de Auristela; a Dios, bien fundados dissinios; sossegaos, pasos, tan honrados como santos; no espereis otros mauseolos ni otras pyramides ni agujas que las que os ofrecen essas mal breadas tablas! Y vos, ¡o Transila!, exemplo claro de honestidad, en los braços de vuestro discreto y anciano padre podeis celebrar las bodas, si no con vuestro esposo Ladislao, a lo menos con la esperança, que ya os aura conduzido a mejor talamo. Y tu, ¡o Ricla!, cuyos desseos te lleuauan a tu descanso, recoge en tus braços a Antonio y a Constança, tus hijos, y ponlos en la presencia del que agora te ha quitado la vida para mejorartela en el cielo" (I, 158).

cule the inappropriateness of the rhetoric of the fictitious author or the *historia,* nor does it offer an intentionally absurd justification for its inclusion. It rather invokes a valid literary argument to justify the original author's recourse to the apostrophe. As is well known, Homer chooses crucial moments in the developing action of his narrative to address his words to his characters and underscore the significance of the moment. On two occasions it is the *certeza de la muerte,* to borrow Cervantes' translator's words, which inspires his doing so.[38] As the justification is serious and as the apostrophe itself falls far short of the limit at which parodistic distortion begins,[39] the translator's remark represents a *serious* disclaimer of responsibility. Far from being a playful pose, it successfully establishes distance between the author and his work. Such removal undoubtedly allowed Cervantes to be more comfortable with a device which in the *Quixote* he could enjoy and keep at safe distance through parody.[40] It is no surprise that a fully articulated parodistic voice in the narrator of the *Persiles* emerges immediately following this apostrophe (see below, the following section of this chapter).

In Book III literature becomes one of the central themes of the work, and the conservative authorial voice reasserts itself with more

[38] See Endt, pp. 106-107. See Homer's apostrophes of Menelaos, *Iliad,* IV and VII.

[39] It is important to distinguish this use of the apostrophe from that of Cide Hamete Benengeli, where overt parody of the literary device allows Cervantes the joy of exploiting its grandiloquence even as he ridicules it. A comparison of this authorial intrusion with that of the Moor at the conclusion of the adventure of the lions ("¡Oh fuerte y sobre todo encarecimiento animoso don Quijote de la Mancha . . . etc." [II, 656-657]) reveals the difference immediately. The narrator uses the occasion not for a display of rhetorical ingenuity but rather for an endless accumulation of accolades, celebrating the knight's victory with "hipérboles sobre todos los hipérboles." Moreover, the editor's comments following the outburst, far from seeking to justify its inclusion, suggest its irrelevance. This type of parody of narrative techniques in Cide Hamete's interventions includes also the medieval romancer's habit of inserting long, sententious digressions in his narrative as well as apostrophes of people outside the romance, presumably in his audience, and exhortations that they observe the moral significance of the events of the romance (see Weinrich's observations in *Das Ingenium Don Quijotes,* pp. 97-99). It is perhaps well to observe that the narrators of the *Quixote* do employ the apostrophe at times free of parodistic intent and as a vehicle of sententious commentary (see II, 668), while at times literary parody is accompanied by serious thematic assertions (see II, 853).

[40] In fact Cervantes is here very close to mannerism, and, if the translator's comment questioning the value of the purely ornamental were lacking, we would have to admit that De Lollis' view of the *Persiles* as a manneristic work is valid in reference to this passage.

force against his playful opponent who dominates Book II. Again we observe the brief, parenthetical comment appearing frequently to justify and clarify the author's inclusion of an element and to recall the generic principles underlying the epic in prose. For example the narrator describes the departure of the ships of Arnaldo and Periandro from the Isle of the Hermits: "Borne by the same wind, the ships sailed away in different directions, *for this is one of those apparent mysteries of the art of navigation.*"[41] The inserted comment calls our attention to a marvelous occurrence and legitimizes it by reminding us of its scientific explanation. As a damsel comes tumbling to the ground from a high tower and is saved from death by the braking effect of her billowing skirts, the narrator justifies the wondrous event as "a thing quite possible without being a miracle."[42] In observing the coincidence of the marriage of Ysabela, the birth of her niece, and the death of her uncle, the narrator points out that there is a marvelous within normal human experience: "So strange are the events of this life: at the same moment some are christened, others married, and others buried."[43] The narrator interrupts the history of Ysabela to remark that "the story itself stirred up wonder."[44]

Of much more interest than the way in which literary concerns continue to color the narrator's brief remarks in Book III is the way in which his extended digressions, which throughout Book II deal primarily with ethical and courtly matters, suddenly concentrate on literature and the literary reality of the *Persiles.*[45] These

[41] "En esto, yuan las naues, con vn mismo viento, por diferentes caminos, *que estes es vno de los que parecen misterios en el arte de la nauegacion*" (II, 7). The italics are mine.

[42] "... cosa possible, sin ser milagro" (II, 141).

[43] "... quan estraños son los sucessos desta vida: vnos a vn mismo punto se bautizan, otros se casan, y otros se entierran" (II, 199).

[44] "... la historia misma se trae consigo la admiracion" (II, 192).

[45] This shift in the narrator's commentary parallels the full emergence of the same theme in the imaginary world of the prose epic. In Lisbon Periandro commissions a famous artist to paint "todos los mas principales casos de su historia" (II, 13). The inclusion of a pictorial display in heroic literature is a literary convention as old as the *Iliad* and is perfectly in keeping with Cervantes' aspirations in his prose epic. Moreover, the author utilizes the description of the painter's product to recapitulate in great detail the events of the first two books of his narrative. However, what is striking in the introduction of the convention in the *Persiles* is the literary consciousness of the protagonist, who like Don

commentaries generally have a bearing on a literary problem either illustrated in or raised by the surrounding context. In them we discover both the conservative, classical voice and the playful, self-deprecating voice asserting themselves. By far the most complex of these literary discourses is the introduction of the episode of the counterfeit captives, where both voices can be heard, and the conflict between them breaks out at closest quarters. As was pointed out above, the episode was conceived in illustration of the art of constructing properly a *fábula*, i.e., a verisimilar plot, in which the artist must skillfully mingle the historical and the invented to capture the belief of the audience. The students fail in this task, for they fail to observe certain fundamental precepts concerning the verisimilar. Although Cervantes and his playful narrator cannot resist turning about to ridicule the pedantic application of these precepts, it would appear that the classicist voice is dominant in the introductory excursus, as it affirms all the major principles underlying the *Persiles*: the pleasure of variety, the travel narrative as a literary medium of variety, the artistic value of the complex disposition of the narrative, the difference between history and fiction, and the dependence of the latter on verisimilitude for its success.

If the literarily conservative narrator appears to offer principles which are then illustrated dramatically in the interlude of the counterfeit captives, in one of his two other major appearances in the third book[46] he reflects on a problem raised by the following episodes. His commentary is basically an expansion of a type of brief remark which we have already examined, as it seeks to justify the

---

Quixote seems to be aware of his reality as a character in a work of art and creates his creator. In Ocaña the wanderers discuss the appropriateness of the canvas to depict such lofty events (II, 98-99). Moreover, the magistrate's allusion to this canvas refers by imaginative suggestion the literary implications of the episode of the counterfeit captives to the "properly constructed *fábula*" of the lives of the protagonists. In Badajoz the pilgrims meet a poet who offers to write a comedy based on their adventures but finds himself perplexed by Ginés de Pasamonte's problem as to where life ends and art begins (II, 18-19).

[46] The other major digression concerns poetry and the poet (II, 17-19). Its content and tone are classical, as it affirms the lofty mission of poetry to delight and teach and forms the prelude for one of Cervantes' classicist critiques of the contemporary theater. As such, it can be attributed to the conservative voice of Cervantes' discursive narrator. Nevertheless, it does not reflect directly on the aesthetic principles underlying the *Persiles*.

277

inclusion of an element which threatens to conflict with the generic principles on which the epic in prose is founded. However, whereas the narrator's parenthetical remarks are by and large concerned with problems surrounding the legitimate marvelous, here the issue is decorum.

In a series of escapades which include robbery, *loco amor*, murder, imprisonment, and the composition of a grotesque letter mingling stylistic ingenuity and vulgar matter, the muleteer Bartolome brings the discordant notes of the picaresque romance into the idealized world of the *Persiles*. The appearance of the muleteer is prefaced by a digression on the legitimacy of "low" subject matter in literature. Proceeding from the widely acknowledged equation of poetry and painting, the narrator observes that just as a painter includes "weeds and furze" (*hieruas y retamas*) in his paintings, the writer of *historia*[47] and poetry can employ "humble things" in his creation. He concludes: "This truth is revealed by Bartolome, the baggage-master of the peregrine and wonderful squadron, who at times will speak and be heard in our history."[48]

It should be observed that even in this theoretical justification of the inclusion of "low" matter, Cervantes betrays his independence of the critical movement to which he would pay homage throughout the *Persiles*. His phrase "poetry at times distinguishes itself by singing of humble things"[49] does in fact recall a principle acknowledged by contemporary theorists. The frequently cited example of such poetry was the bucolic of Virgil and the specific example most often invoked was the description of the bees in his *Georgics*. Nevertheless, theorists were in agreement in referring to this type of poetry as pertaining to an inferior literary order and in distinguish-

---

[47] I think it would be false to interpret *historia* in this context in terms of the equivocation which Cervantes exploits throughout the *Quixote* and on four occasions (I, 153; II, 100; II, 154; II, 174) in the *Persiles*. Here the narrator is employing the terms as do Periandro and Mauricio in Book II, all the other storytellers in the work, the theorist Carvallo, and nearly all Spanish writers of the sixteenth century. The term refers to an extended fictional narrative (i.e., with no allusiveness to the crucial distinction between poetry and history which preoccupied Aristotelian theorists).

[48] "Esta verdad nos la muestra bien Bartolome, bagagero del esquadron peregrino; el tal, tal vez habla y es escuchado en nuestra historia" (II, 139).

[49] ". . . la poesia, tal vez se realça cantando cosas humildes" (II, 139).

ing it from epic poetry, the genre to which the *Persiles* would be-long.[50] One of the repeated criticisms leveled at Ariosto by the "ancients" was his constant breach of decorum in introducing the "low" into a heroic context.[51] We should recall how Cide Hamete Benengeli facetiously submits to the classicists' theories of decorum by deleting some chapters concerning the friendship of Rocinante and Sancho's ass.

I do not believe that the narrator's theorizing here represents the type of parodistic misapplication of the Aristotelian criteria which Cide Hamete Benengeli employs as he answers his readers' objec-tions to his narrative procedures. The literary principles, although misapplied, are presented as a valid justification for the presence of the muleteer. I think that the digression must be interpreted as an indication of Cervantes' lingering preoccupation with his literary aspirations in writing the prose epic as well as the continuing un-easiness that marks his processes of artistic selectivity.

The Playful Voice: the Assertion of Artistic Freedom

THE UNDERTONE OF SELF-CRITICISM: BOOK I

Throughout Book I Cervantes' literary awareness would appear to be untroubled by the problems surrounding the value of his

[50] Tasso asserts that a poet can indeed "paint" (*dipingere*) *fiori e ucelletti* and praises Virgil's description of the bees, but adds that he must not exhaust his art on such insignificant things (*Del poema eroico*, pp. 193-195). Cervantes may be appropriating a passage from El Pinciano's *Philosophía antigua poética* and using it for his own purposes. In discussing the problem of whether a poetic imitation must of necessity be of a human action, Fadrique evokes the familiar poetry-painting analogy: "Dicho auemos que el poema es imitación en lenguaje, y *qual el pintor de heruajes es pintor como el de figuras, ni más ni menos el poeta que pinta* y descriue las otras cosas, es también poeta como el que imita afectos, acciones y costumbres humanas" (I, 264). The discussions of both El Pinciano and Tasso have nothing to do with the problem of the appropriateness of "low" characters in the lofty genre. El Pinciano admits that poetry can depict such characters (e.g., "los pastores," "los viandantes, pescadores, hortelanos, segadores, leñadores, y los demás"), but like most classicists finds such poetry to be of an order (e.g., the eclogue) inferior to that of the epic (see III, 244-245). Tasso is even more specific on the question: "Sdegni ancora il nostro poeta tutte le cose basse, tutte le populari, tutte le disoneste . . . e se pur alcuna volta riceve i pastori, i caprari, i porcari e l'altre sì fatte persone, deve aver riguardo non solo al decoro della persona, ma a quello del poema, e mostrarli come si mostrano ne'palazzi reali e nelle solennità e nelle pompe" (pp. 112-113).
[51] See Weinberg, pp. 1041, 1050.

artistic endeavor which come into the foreground in Periandro's recitation of Book II. The tone of his narrator's brief remarks concerning the appropriateness of subject matter is uniformly justificatory. Moreover, his participating storytellers are quick to recognize the validity of the Aristotelian demands of unity and credibility. However, just as the early critical exchanges between a storyteller and an audience contain the potential literary drama which actually unfolds in Periandro's narration, the initial commentary of the narrative voice contains the germs for a revolutionary development of that voice. They are visible when the brief comments suggest an uneasiness with stylizations in language and when the tone of justification modulates into a tone of evasion. Such comments can accompany a figure commonly used in colloquial discourse ("In this way, stumbling and scrambling, *as is commonly said*, they reached the shore")[52] or a figure dictated by the conventions of the lofty genre (i.e., the marvelous in language):

> The consideration that he was a man would pierce his soul with the hard lance of jealousy, whose point dares to penetrate the diamond of sharpest cut: *I mean to say that jealousy breaks through all security and prudence*, although the enamored heart be armed with both.[53]

> A great light came running toward them, just like a comet, or, *to put it better, a flaming vapor which travels through the air*.[54]

In these cases attention is deliberately drawn to the artificiality of figurative language, i.e., its removal from the reality to which it corresponds. By such statements, the artist succeeds in reducing his responsibility for the inclusion of what probably caused him some literary discomfort. One step further in the movement from justifi-

---

[52] "Desta manera, cayendo y leuantando, *como dezirse suele*, llegaron a la marina" (I, 28). The italics are mine.

[53] ". . . le traspassara el alma con la dura lança de los zelos, cuya punta se atreue a entrar por las del mas agudo diamante: *quiero dezir que los zelos rompen toda seguridad y recato*, aunque del se armen los pechos enamorados" (I, 14-15). The italics are mine.

[54] ". . . hazia ellos venia corriendo vna gran luz, bien assi como cometa, o, *por mejor dezir, exalacion que por el ayre camina*" (I, 28). The italics are mine. The appended statement underscores the artificiality of the figure by introducing a "better" simile, in which the analogy underlying its terms is more thorough.

cation to evasion will bring the narrator to literary parody, which will enable him to preserve and enjoy such stylizations through distortion. This step occurs at the conclusion of Book I, as the rising undertone of self-criticism embodies itself momentarily in the figure of a fictitious author who must bear the abuse of a rhetorically conscious editor, and, following the disappearance of the fictitious author, expresses itself freely in the parodistic comments of the new discursive narrator.

THE ASCENDANCE OF PARODY: BOOK II

In view of the breakdown of the classical narrator at the end of Book I and the direct confrontation of literary values in Periandro's recitation, it is not surprising that we discover in Book II an increase in the narrator's parenthetical remarks revealing the author's discomfort with his artistic medium. Many of these continue in the same vein simply expressing Cervantes' awareness of the artificiality of various literary figures: "Zenotia, who drank the winds, *as they say*, imagining how to avenge herself"; "time raced, as *it is wont to do*; the night flew"; "after the fear subsided a little in the resurrected ones, *who can be called that* (the term "resurrected ones" [*los resucitados*] is used in antithesis to the "living" [*los viuos*], and the whole context is allusive to the biblical account of the delivery of Jonah from the depths of Leviathan); ". . . and made into a knot, *or, to put it better*, a ball of yarn, they let themselves roll."[55]

However, in many of the literary comments of Book II we observe the narrator moving toward the position of full detachment and control which parody provides. He no longer retreats from responsibility as he uses literary conventions, but rather, by ridiculing those conventions, he asserts his freedom to stand above all conventional

---

[55] ". . . la Zenotia, que beuia, *como dizen*, los vientos imaginando cómo vengarse" (I, 222). "Corrio el tiempo *como suele*; volo la noche" (I, 302). ". . . despues que passò algun tanto el pauor en los resucitados, *que assi pueden llamarse*" (I, 162). ". . . y hechos vn ñudo, o, *por mejor dezir*, vn ouillo, se dexaron calar" (I, 156). The italics are mine. It is certain that the phrase *por mejor decir* like the phrases *como se ha dicho* and *quiero decir* was one of Cervantes favorite storyteller's mannerisms and does not necessarily indicate a self-consciousness about artificiality in his use of language. See for example I, 213, where it indicates simply the storyteller's desire for the correct word to convey the most precise meaning. It is always the context which determines the expressive value of a linguistic form, which is always in itself no more than a series of possibilities.

restraints, as the supreme literary craftsman who can laugh at his own creation. In effect the narrator of the *Persiles* is following the pattern of nearly all Cervantes' participating narrators. He is doing what Periandro does in his self-conscious recourse to the epic simile of the sheep and the wolves (see above), what Don Quixote does in the introduction of the toothpick into the underworld banquet of the Knight of the Lake, and what the counterfeit captives do in observing that the ships of their narration are affected by the size of the canvas depicting them. Through unexpected shifts of perspective, all narrators humorously remind their audiences that the pleasurable world of art is a great "hoax" and that its existence depends completely on the will of the poet and the courtesy of the audience.

The brief, parenthetical remark underscoring the artificiality of language functions in a parodistic context in King Arnaldo's rhetorical discourse on the restoration of Renato's honor. He exhorts the hermit to enjoy the treasure of honor in the company of "the peerless Eusebia, the ivy of your wall, the elm tree of your ivy, the mirror of your delight, and the example of goodness and thankfulness." The narrator follows with: "All the others, *though in different words*, offered them the same felicitation."[56] On another occasion we hear more clearly the self-deprecating voice of Cide Hamete Benengeli replacing the sober tone of the original authorial voice of the *Persiles*, as the narrator emphasizes the distance between reality and a figure of speech by a ridiculously literal interpretation: "He would gladly give half his life, if lives could be divided, not to have written that letter."[57]

The parodistic impulse in the narrator of the *Persiles* is most irrepressible in scenes of marked literary derivation and high pathos. As Sinforosa, who together with her father forms a double reincar-

[56] ". . . la sin par Eusebia, yedra de vuestro muro, olmo de vuestra yedra, espejo de vuestro gusto, y exemplo de bondad y agradecimiento" (I, 319). "Este mismo parabien, *aunque con palabras diferentes*, les dieron todos" (I, 319). The italics are mine.

[57] ". . . diera el por no auerle escrito la mitad de la vida, si es que las vidas pueden partirse" (I, 204). Compare: "Admirado quedó el canónigo de los concertados disparates que don Quijote había dicho, si disparates sufren concierto" (I, 1; the qualifying phrase, to be sure, did not appear in the first edition of the *Quixote*, and its authenticity is a matter of doubt among modern editors).

nation of Dido in this northern adaptation of the influential episode of the *Aeneid*, gazes from the tower at the departing ships of the hero, she declaims the familiar despairing plea in the grand style of oratory. After comparing her to her literary ancestors, the narrator introduces her speech with the curious statement: "She uttered these arguments or others that are similar."[58] The rescue of the wanderers from the capsized ship is another scene of melodrama and humorous deflation. Here we observe peripeteia and recognition, as the shipwrecked, who have held their death to be certain, are miraculously saved and, on reviving, discover themselves to be in the arms of their lost companions. Above we observed that in a scene of recognition in Book I the conservative narrator enters to call attention to the marvelous effect of anagnorisis in accordance with the literary theory of the neo-Aristotelians. In the present scene all possibilities for the marvelous are exploited: the change of fortune which accompanies recognition, the spectacular involvement of many characters, the nature of the events leading up to the scene (the violent storm and the unusual shipwreck), the despair of the travelers, and the imaginative association, through metaphor and myth, of the events with the Bible and an archetypal theme of romance literature—the ritual death of the hero and his resurrection and deliverance from the forces of evil.

Instead of intervening to emphasize the effect and the legitimacy of these marvelous occurrences, the narrator appears to sound the discordant note of literary humor. The description of the initial rescue operations is embellished by the attribution of characteris-

---

[58] "... dixo estas o otras semejantes razones" (I, 289). So strong is the parodistic impulse of Cervantes at this occasion that he allows it to shape the conversation of a character. Thus we observe the process carried out within the dialogue itself, as a character suddenly reveals the stylistic self-consciousness which we detect in the voice of the narrator. Following her outburst of despair in the tower, Sinforosa indulges in some declamatory self-deception: "¿No te parece que no camina tanto? ¡Ay, Dios! ¿Si se aura arrepentido? ¡Ay, Dios, si la remora de mi voluntad le detiene el nauio!" Her sober sister Policarpa cuts short her exclamation, cautioning her on the danger of self-deception, and echoes her rhetoric, curiously allowing literary considerations to color her words at this moment of potential tragedy: "El nauio buela, sin que le detenga la remora de tu voluntad, como tu dizes, sino que le impele el viento de tus muchos suspiros" (I, 290). The *Persiles* is full of what Vossler and Spitzer have called "die Literarisierung des Lebens." In this passage the complexity of the process equals that observable in two dialogues of Lope's *Dorotea* (see ed. E. Morby [Valencia, 1958], pp. 87-88 and 89-91).

tics of a living organism to the ship as it drifts on its side ("womb," "vomit," "parturition"). Accompanying allusions to the possibility of "reborn" human beings issuing from its stomach strengthen the evocation of the demonic sea monster, the biblical Leviathan, and the cluster of imaginative associations that surround the myth: Satan, Christ, Jonah, sin, the fall, suffering (*trabajos*), regeneration, the sea as the earthly world and the haunt of evil, and the apostles as fishermen.[59] Following these details of what we might call an "inflating" description, Cervantes proceeds to describe the grisly task of the rescuers as they examine the pile of cadavers in the ship, listening for heartbeats and separating the "dead who were truly dead" from the "living who appeared to be dead." Their task is the occasion for the introduction of a new metaphor "prey" to refer to the objects which they are seeking. The transformation of the cadavers into "prey," the gesture of the rescuers extending their arms through the hole in the side of the ship, and the marine setting lead to the introduction of the analogy of the fisherman, as the narrator offers one of his many generalizations of Book II about aspects of human life: "Each one pulled his prey out, and some, while thinking that they were pulling out live bodies, pulled out dead ones; *for fishermen are not always lucky.*"[60]

What we observe here is an unexpected subordination of the development of the entire scene to the dialectics of verbal association. The metaphor *pressa* generates the metaphor *pescador*. Although it may be argued that the metaphor is a coherent element in the mythic pattern visible in the background of the scene (i.e., rebirth-fisherman-apostle), the absurdly incongruous *sententia* which the metaphor *fisherman* in turn generates reveals that an inappropriate literary logic has gained control over the movement of the passage. Its effect is reductive, and the context of marvelous occurrences and mythical overtones dissolves in humor.

The rhythm of inflation and deflation continues as Cervantes invests his description of the recognition with a strong dramatic effect through the use of vivid detail and a long sentence constructed in a

---

[59] See Northrop Frye, *Anatomy of Criticism* (Princeton, 1957), pp. 189-192.

[60] ". . . cada vno sacò su pressa, y algunos, pensando sacar viuos, sacauan muertos: *que no todas vezes los pescadores son dichosos*" (I, 161). The italics are mine.

series of parallel independent clauses, each introduced by a verb in the preterite tense.[61] However, the final term of the climactic series contains an incongruous preservation of syntactic parallelism, unwarranted by the reality of the situation at hand:

> They washed their faces, rubbed their eyes, stretched their arms, and gazed about them, as one who awakens from a deep sleep. Auristela found herself in the arms of Arnaldo, Transila, in those of Clodio, Ricla and Constanza, in those of Rutilio, *Antonio the father and Antonio the son, in those of nobody,* because they came out alone, as did Mauricio.

As in the case of the fisherman metaphor, here style suddenly is accorded an autonomy which is manifestly ridiculous, and the movement toward climax abruptly collapses.[62] If these rhetorical incongruities diminish any serious effect which the scene of peripeteia and recognition may have, Auristela's inappropriate inquiry about her rival Sinforosa at the culminating moment of epic anagnorisis and mythic "rebirth" brings to completion the parodistic reduction of both traditional literary high moments.

THE HUMOROUS EXAMINATION OF THE GENERIC PRINCIPLES: BOOK III

In the final two books of the *Persiles* Cervantes' major instrument of parody—the brief, reductive remark of his narrator—occasionally reappears, following closely the pattern which we observe earlier

---

[61] Here we observe the dynamic *"veni-vidi-vici* style," which Hatzfeld has studied in Cervantes' writings. Hatzfeld uses the term to refer to passages in which "die Häufung von Satzgliedern oder Kurzsätzen nicht Seelenzustände in dynamische Wallungen auflöst, wie bei den unter 'Häufung' erwähnten Beispielen, sondern wo die gehäuften Kurzsätze einen hastig gedrängten Bericht geben, dem in Anbetracht der Fülle seines Inhalts tatsächlich die dynamische Kraft innewohnt (genau wie bei dem berühmten Cäsarwort), die dem Gedanken fast zu enge Form zu sprengen." For numerous examples of this stylistic technique, see *"Don Quijote" als Wortkunstwerk*, pp. 205-210.

[62] ". . . limpiaronse los rostros, fregaronse los ojos, estiraron los braços, y, como quien despierta de vn pesado sueño, miraron a todas partes, y hallóse Auristela en los braços de Arnaldo, Transila en los de Clodio, Ricla y Constança en los de Rutilio, *Antonio el padre y Antonio el hijo en los de ninguno,* porque se salio por si mismo, y lo mismo hizo Mauricio" (I, 161). The italics are mine.

The reductive technique is basically the same as that which we observed in the episode of the archetypal horse. There the grotesque subordination of life to an abstract literary principle corresponds to the present subordination of life to the exigencies of rhetoric.

in the work. For example, in the phrase "the ships were breaking, *so to speak*, not transparent glass, but rather blue glass,"[63] we hear the evasive tones which mark some of the narrator's comments as early as Book I. In the brief "so to speak" the narrator acknowledges the extreme artificiality of the figure of speech (the antithesis *claro-azul* heightens the audacity of the *conceptismo* of *romper cristal* ["to sail"] calling attention to the deviation from the normal in *romper* [i.e., to what "to break glass" usually means]), and, by sharing the potential objection of the reader to its extravagance, he withdraws from it to a safe distance, absolving himself from responsibility for its use. Similarly, in describing the persecuted Feliciana's refuge in a hollow tree, the narrator resorts to a fanciful metaphor, "the oak was pregnant," and must immediately add parenthetically "let us say it that way."[64]

At times such comments are tinged with the same parodistic coloring which appears throughout Book II. Like Sinforosa's lament at the departure of her beloved, Ruperta's monologue on revenge is an elaborately constructed piece of oratory. In introducing both declamations, the narrator uses a phrase ("[she uttered] these arguments or others that are similar"),[65] which, in calling attention to the formulaic character of their words, destroys any illusion of reality in the statements of emotions. Just as the narrator mocks the style of Arnaldo's discourse (see above), he ridicules the hyperbolic language of a bystander in Rome who compares the beautiful Auristela with Venus, suggesting that she has returned to pay homage to the memory of her beloved Aeneas: "Amidst these praises, as hyperbolic as unnecessary, the lovely band passes forward."[66] Such reductive remarks are, however, few in number in comparison with those of Book II which is unquestionably the high point of literary parody in the *Persiles*.

In Book III the literarily nongeneric narrator chooses a new direction for his commentary. His criticism turns from conventions

---

[63] ". . . yuan [las naues] rompiendo, *como digo*, no claros cristales, sino azules" (II, 7). The italics are mine.

[64] "Preñada estaua la enzina—digamoslo assi—" (II, 27).

[65] ". . . estas o otras semejantes razones" (II, 164). See also I, 289.

[66] "Con estas alabanças, tan hiperboles como no necessarias, passa adelante el gallardo esquadron" (II, 224).

of a specific nature, i.e., stylizations in language, structural devices, and traditional themes which appear in the text of the *Persiles*, toward the basic principles which underlie its composition. The formal shift in the conservative voice from the brief, justificatory remark to the justificatory digression parallels replacement of the brief, reductive remark by the narrator's extended commentaries. They, in turn, use equivocations couched in aesthetic terminology to assert humorously his independence of the Aristotelian literary dogma. It is in this book that the narrator of the *Persiles* finally assumes the shape of Cide Hamete Benengeli as a playful and articulate literary theorist.

Like the digressions of the conservative voice, the literary commentaries of the opposing voice reflect on problems either raised by or illustrated in the surrounding context. It should be recalled how the two voices are locked in conflict in the preface to the episode of the counterfeit captives. The nongeneric narrator successfully introduces into the passage Cide Hamete Benengeli's favorite literary equivocation, that based on the double meaning of the term *historia*, and nearly brings about the collapse of the classicist narrator's weighty arguments concerning the construction of the Aristotelian verisimilar plot. Although the latter prevails in this case, on two other occasions, his adversary is allowed the final word concerning problems of aesthetic theory.

The somber story of Ruperta, the beautiful widow who dresses in black and bears her husband's skull and bloodstained sword on a pilgrimage of revenge, is associated with the familiar literary problem of belief and its corollary, that of the marvelous vs. the verisimilar. Compelled by the desire to see "some strange marvel," the protagonists eagerly inspect the funereal trappings of the widow's room. In disappointment at the "low level" of this *maravilla* Periandro complains, and Ruperta's servant insists that he return to view the widow contemplating her grisly relics: "If you will return hither at the hour I have named . . . you will have something which will cause you to marvel."[67] The entire episode is introduced by a discursive comment by the narrator concerning Cervantes' favorite literary problem. Truth, the subject of the historian, is often

---

[67] "Si volueis a la hora que digo . . . tendreis de que marauillaros" (II, 158).

287

stranger than fiction, the fabrication of the poet: "If the imagination had the power to bring its boldest creations into being, it still could not match the strange things that come to pass in this world."[68] In their implausibility the truths of history can escape being judged apocryphal only if they are recorded with *juramentos*, which evidently means authoritative documentation. Without such documentation their credibility depends on the "good credit of him who recounts them." The narrator concludes with his personal opinion: "I say that it would be better not to relate them," citing an old Castillian *copla*, which offers a concise statement of the restrictions which the contemporary Aristotelian's interpretation of verisimilitude placed on the creative powers of the poet:

> Las cosas de admiracion
> no las digas ni las cuentes;
> que no saben todas gentes
> cómo son.[69] (II, 154)

The initial literary humor arising from this digression is based on the pretense of the narrator that what is obviously a fictional text (the *Persiles*) is history (here according to the Aristotelian definition of the term) and his feigned preoccupation with the problem of credibility which historical events present him who would record them. The humor is compounded as the narrative voice abruptly assumes a new form, reversing itself to speak from the vantage point of the poet and to affirm the principle of verisimilitude[70] and

---

[68] "Cosas y casos suceden en el mundo, que, si la imaginacion, antes de suceder, pudiera hazer que assi sucedieran, no acertara a traçarlos" (II, 154).

[69] "Neither tell nor recount marvelous occurrences; for not everybody knows about them." Compare Cascales' reasoning on the way in which poets should use history: ". . . algunas cosas suceden tan monstruosamente, que narradas ante quien no las ha visto, son dificultosisimas de creer. Y donde huviere esta dificultad en las cosas, aunque realmente haya sucedido, se debe quitar, o a lo menos esforzarla con fortisimas razones" (*Tablas poéticas*, p. 137).

[70] Adding to the humor of this elusive passage is the formulation of the controversial doctrine of classical derivation in the form of the popular *copla*, a humor not unlike that in the attribution of Aristotelian terminology to the monkey of Master Pedro. Cervantes' source for the *copla* was probably Antonio de Torquemada's *Jardín de flores curiosas*, echoes of which can often be heard when Cervantes deals with the problem of belief. The interlocutors cite a version which in nearly all details is repeated by Cervantes, and attribute it to the Marqués de

submit to the limitations which it demands, apparently deciding to omit in his narrative the historical event which is so incredible. As if this metamorphosis were not enough, the protean narrator abruptly returns to the form of the historian, proceeding to disregard his own principle and to do justice to the "true historical event," in this case the episode of Ruperta. In its marvelous aspects, repeatedly underscored by the playful narrator, this episode is anything but an historical occurrence and would be one of the "marvelous things" which the narrator, in the form of poet, would not allow in a fictional context: "Neither tell nor recount them."

The quandary of the narrator in his role as historian, "doing justice" to the historical event which in his role as poet he knows should be deleted for the sake of verisimilitude, recalls the plight of Cide Hamete as he decided rather to run the risk of being called a liar than to fail in his historian's responsibility to record truth. Both narrators turn serious principles of contemporary literary theory into an elaborate joke, and, in doing so, underscore their freedom from any restraint on their creative powers.

The episode of Soldino's cave is the only other case in which the narrator of the *Persiles* allows himself such liberties in the introduction of aesthetic theory. In its literary dimension the scene is particularly similar to those of Periandro's narration. Like the garden paradise and the marvelous horse, Soldino's cave is presented as an archetypal theme of imaginative literature, which is to represent the problematic aesthetic category of the marvelous and the freedom of the creative imagination from the restrictions demanded by contemporary theories of verisimilitude. In selecting the cave for these purposes, Cervantes once again chooses one of the most ancient and persistent topics of world literature. From Gilgamesh's underworld search for the plant of immortality to the knight Luzman's journey to the cave of the prophetess Cuma in the work of one of Cervantes' immediate predecessors,[71] the theme of the hero's descent

---

Santillana (p. 11). For the popularity of the *copla* in sixteenth-century writings, see Marcel Bataillon, "Gutiérrez de Santa Clara, escritor mexicano," *Nueva Revista de Filología Hispánica*, XV (1961), esp. pp. 407-408.

[71] Jerónimo de Contreras, *Selva de aventuras*, ed. B.A.E., III, 498-499. Literary historiography has designated this work as one of the linear precursors of the

to a mysterious lower region had never ceased to appeal to the creative artist. Its impact on Cervantes' imagination is attested by the episodes of the Cave of Montesinos, the Knight of the Lake, and Soldino's cave.

Moreover, like the archetypal garden and horse, the mysterious cave as a topic of imaginative literature had been assimilated in the literary theorizing of the Renaissance critical movement. In his observations on the epic poet's art of describing particular places, Tasso recommends the cave, emphasizing its possibilities for the marvelous, mystery, and allegory. Curiously he refers to the treatise of the neo-Platonic philosopher Porphyrius, who interpreted Homer's description of the cave near Ithaca (*Odyssey*, XIII) as an allegorical representation of the Platonic cosmology: "The cave is suitable for many allegories, like the cave of Plato, a figure of the world, and that of Homer, about which Porphyrius wrote a small but erudite treatise; and this can also have its occult meaning and its marvelous mysteries."[72]

It is important to observe the cumulative weight of literary tradition which Cervantes willfully imposes upon the episode of Soldino's cave. As in the case of the garden paradise and the perilous leap the description forms a richly interwoven texture of literary reminiscence. The descent to the underworld and emergence into a *locus amoenus* of pleasant fields, streams, trees, and fruits evoke a familiar pattern of the otherworld journey of romance, which we have observed in the two underworld scenes of *Don Quixote*. Soldino's subterranean prophecy of historical events of the sixteenth century, punctuated by an exclamation of compassion at the vision of the transfixed body of Sebastian of Portugal, recalls the pathos of Anchises' words forecasting the bloody wars of Rome in the most influential classical model of the underworld journey (*Aeneid*, VI). The figure of Soldino recalls not only the ancient Anchises and

---

Persiles (see Menéndez y Pelayo, *Orígenes de la novela*, II, 83-88; Ludwig Pfandl, "Cervantes und der Spanische Renaissance-Roman," *Jahrbuch für Philologie*, I [1925], 373-392).

[72] ". . . la spelunca riceve molte allegorie, come l'antro di Platone figurato per lo mondo, e quello d'Omero, del qual Porfirio compose un picciolo ma dotto libretto; e questo ancora può aver la sua occulta significazione e i suoi meravigliosi misteri" (*Del poema eroico*, p. 171).

the sorcerers of medieval romance, but also their contemporary descendants, who have replaced the infernal powers of their medieval ancestors with the scientific lore of the Renaissance. Like Tasso's old man of Ascalona, who dwells in a deep cave and has mastered the powers of nature and the movements of the heavens ("I contemplate the other unfathomed mysteries of nature and the various movements of the stars"),[73] Soldino has attained his powers not through an infernal connection but rather by the study of the heavenly bodies and mathematics ("I have pursued the study of mathematics, and I have contemplated the course of the stars and the movement of the sun and the moon").[74] In order to sound another note of literary resonance in this orchestration of literary motifs, Cervantes transforms the archetypal sorcerer into the world-weary courtier, who has fled the turmoil, the pomp, and the anxieties of the life at the palace to embrace the tranquility of the contemplative life. It is again an ancient literary theme, reinvigorated throughout the sixteenth century in the many reworkings of the Horatian *beatus ille*, in Guevara's extraordinarily popular *Menosprecio de la corte y alabanza del aldea*,[75] and in two of the generic precursors of the *Persiles*, Contreras' *Selva de aventuras* and Lope's *Peregrino en su patria*, as well as in Tasso's *Gerusalemme liberata*.[76] The fusion of orthodox religious elements and this contemplative ideal, which we observe in Soldino's profession of faith, was common in contemporary literary reworkings of the old theme.

In describing his retreat, Soldino employs the adverb *aquí* ten times in an accelerating rhythm which rises to its peak in the sentence: "*here* I am master of myself, *here* I hold my soul in the palm of my hand, and *here* I direct my thoughts and desires on the straight path to heaven."[77] In the anaphoric repetition of the adverb highlighting the enumeration of paradise features, we observe a

[73] ". . . e gli altri arcani di natura ignoti/ contemplo, e delle stelle i vari moti" (*Gerusalemme liberata*, p. 478).

[74] ". . . he dado fin al estudio de las matematicas, he contemplado el curso de las estrellas y el mouimiento del sol y de la luna" (II, 175).

[75] See Karl Vossler, *Introducción a la literatura española del Siglo de Oro*, Colección Austral (Mexico, 1961), pp. 112-113.

[76] See Contreras, pp. 492-523; Lope, pp. 425-427; Tasso, pp. 217-221.

[77] ". . . aqui soy yo señor de mi mismo, aqui tengo mi alma en mi palma, y aqui por via recta encamino mis pensamientos y mis desseos al cielo" (II, 175). The italics are mine.

traditional stylistic pattern of otherworld descriptions, the *"hic-ivi-là-aqui-topos,"* which Leo Spitzer has studied in its origins in Boethius' *De consolatione philosophiae* and in its florescence in Renaissance lyric poetry of Platonic-Christian otherworldliness.[78]

Appearing at this point, the literary mosaic which this scene represents should not be interpreted as one more piece of evidence in an indictment of the empty mannerism of Cervantes' final work. Once again, and perhaps for the last time, Cervantes is returning to that subject which preoccupies him throughout his career as creative artist—the trial of literature. Like Periandro and Don Quixote as they confronted their respective antagonists, Mauricio and the Canon of Toledo, the narrator of the *Persiles* is calling forth the power of a deep tradition of imaginative literature to meet the challenge of the neo-Aristotelian critical movement and its mimetic ideal in art. The narrator's intrusion supplies the frame of literary reference, posing and resolving the critical problem associated with the archetypal marvelous cave. For the first time since the beginning of Book II Cervantes exploits the functional possibilities of an editor's removal from a preexistent historical text:

> On another occasion it has been said *that all actions which are not verisimilar or provable are to be recounted in histories,* because if one does not give them proper accreditation, they lose

---

[78] "The Poetic Treatment of a Platonic-Christian Theme," *Romanische Literaturstudien* (Tübingen, 1959), pp. 130-159.

We should observe one more of the concentric waves of literary association which emanate from this simple scene. In view of the evident impact of Tasso's *Discorsi* on Cervantes and the *Persiles*, it is worth speculating on the double entrance of Soldino's cave and the cryptic utterance of the sage which concludes the scene: "Y por agora no mas, sino vamonos arriba; daremos sustento a los cuerpos, como aqui abaxo le hemos dado a las almas" (II, 177). As I have pointed out above, in recommending the use of marvelous caves, Tasso mentions the tract of Porphyrius. Porphyrius' imaginative allegorical analysis is inspired by Homer's description of the cave near the haven of Phorcys, where the Phaeacians leave the sleeping Odysseus: "Two doors there are to the cave, one toward the North Wind, by which men go down, but that toward the South Wind is sacred, nor do men enter thereby; it is the way of the immortals" (*Odyssey*, XIII; see Loeb Classical Library edition, tr. A. T. Murray [London, 1931], II, 11). The upper and lower entrances of Soldino's cave as well as the explicit association of the upper entrance with mortality and the flesh and the region surrounding the lower entrance with immortality and the soul suggest the possibility that Cervantes was through imaginative suggestion summoning forth the prestige of the *Odyssey* in this, his final defense of imaginative literature.

their value. *But it is incumbent on the historian only to tell the truth,* whether or not it appears to be true. *With this maxim in mind, the historian who wrote this history says that Soldino...*[79]

Like the passage prefixed to the Ruperta episode the observation associates the episode immediately following with the problem of verisimilitude. The narrator begins with the statement of a commonplace of contemporary literary theory—that the implausible contingencies that mark historical events are subjects for the historian and not the poet. Indeed if they are to be remembered and accepted as true, they must have the certification of the historian. By implication the assertion recalls the familiar Aristotelian distinction between historical writing and poetry, which always must eschew the implausible.[80] The narrator proceeds to acknowledge the incredibility of the forthcoming episode, as his observation abruptly turns into a justification for its inclusion. The justification hinges on the familiar hoax that the *Persiles* is history in the Aristotelian sense, a pretense aided by the equivocation in the term *historia* in its contemporary usage. However, the hoax is immediately evident, and the weighty Aristotelian theorizing that initiates the excursus collapses in a context of humor. What we observe here is once again the ingenious modification of the Ariostean disclaimer of responsibility developed by Cide Hamete Benengeli, who facetiously maintains the patent absurdity that his *historia* is the Aristotelian history as opposed to poetry and that consequently he must be true to his task as a historian to include only truth, even if in its occasional inverisimilitude it would not be allowed in a

[79] "Otra vez se ha dicho que todas las *acciones no verissimeles ni prouables se han de contar en las historias,* porque si no se les da credito, pierden de su valor; *pero al historiador no le conuiene mas de dezir la verdad,* parezcalo o no lo parezca. *Con esta maxima, pues, el que escriuio esta historia,* dize que Soldino . . ." (II, 174). The italics are mine.

[80] If, as I suspect, a *no* has been omitted before *se han de contar* in the printing, this distinction would be even more sharply drawn. The first *historia* would in fact mean *historia fingida,* i.e., fiction, and the first half of the sentence would describe the restrictions on the poet. If his fiction is implausible, the reader loses faith in its illusion of reality and does not accept it. The second half of the sentence describes the obligation of the historian to recount truth, which is occasionally implausible. Here *historiador* and *historia* refer clearly to the task of historiography.

poetic context and would render its transcriber liable to the accusation of being a liar. The refined literary humor arising from the
inclusion of the marvelous archetype, following the humorous play
with the aesthetic problem associated with it, reveals once again
Cervantes' independence of those very principles upon which he
founded the *Persiles* as well as his specific rejection of the contemporary doctrine of verisimilitude.[81]

THE TRIUMPH OF THE PLAYFUL NARRATOR

In style and tone the narrator's intrusions in the episodes of
Ruperta's revenge and Soldino's cave are examples of a new narrative technique emerging in Book III and marking the completion
of the metamorphosis of the sober, classical figure of Book I into
the familiar figure which we have observed in Cervantes' various
surrogates of the creating artist, Cide Hamete Benengeli, Periandro,
Master Pedro, and the counterfeit captives. In both episodes the
commentary refers to events contained in the work and presents
the transparent hoax that the author is not in control of his narration, that he is relying on the truths of history or a historical text
to justify his inclusion of subject matter which he as author considers inappropriate in his text. The effect of such statements of
helplessness is to emphasize the absolute control of the author over
both his work and his reader. In Book III such tricks appear frequently, as the narrator reminds us repeatedly of his presence as
creator and manipulator of his literary world in a series of self-

---

[81] Once again it is illuminating to contrast Cervantes' use of topics of the marvelous to mock the empirically-minded audience, i.e., the Renaissance Aristotelian, with
Tasso's insecurity with such topics, an insecurity deriving from his subservience to
the neo-Aristotelian theory. While Tasso could recommend the cave as a vehicle of
the legitimate marvelous (see above), he was very uncomfortable about the questionable verisimilitude of the topic in practice and took some pains to justify his
inclusion of the episode of the Old Man of Ascalona. Indeed Cervantes' narrator's
absurd pretense of being loyal to a historical text could be read as a parody of the
humorless Tasso's justification of his episode by pointing to the appearance of such
caves in medieval historical chronicles: ". . . sono ben io risoluto di rimuovere tutti
que' miracoli che possono offendere gli animi de' scrupolosi; ma fra questi miracoli
non numero l'abitazion sua sotterranea, perc' oltra che chiara è l'allegoria, c' altro
non è abitar sotto terra che il contemplar le cose che ivi si generano; *qual miracolo
è questo così grande? Ed io ho letto ne l'istorie gotice, novamente, cosa che a
questa mia invenzion s'assomiglia*: dico cosa naturale" (*Le lettere*, I, 197). The
italics are mine.

effacing poses reminiscent of the techniques of Ariosto and his various other descendants in the work of Cervantes.[82]

The narrator humorously asserts such control in commenting on the fall of Claricia. Shortly after having assured us that the fall is a "thing quite possible without being a miracle," he recalls the incident "of the miraculous flight of his [Domicio's] wife, *more to be wondered at than believed.*"[83] One of the most effective hoaxes of this type occurs at a moment of high excitement in the wanderings of the characters. As they journey through France, the pilgrims are suddenly swept into a whirlwind of adventures including the miraculous fall of a woman from a high tower, Periandro's struggle with a madman, the hero's apparently fatal fall, the arrival of a party of French ladies, the attack by a band of robbers attempting to abduct Feliz Flora, the felling of their chieftain by the arrow of Antonio, and the seemingly fatal blow sustained by the latter. The swift narration of the adventures leading to the scene of carnage, in which the cadavers of four characters—two protagonists and two antagonists—strew the earth, is abruptly interrupted at the moment of potential tragedy. The narrator unexpectedly appears and, assuming the pose of a member of an audience, produces a jarring change of perspective from which the events of his narrative are viewed:

> Up to this point in this battle, we have heard few sword blows, few martial instruments have sounded; the wail which the living are wont to make for the dead has not shattered the air;

[82] We have observed how Periandro employs the Ariostean narrative techniques not only in his discursive comments but also in his abrupt fragmentations of his narrative and suggestion that he is controlled by the events of his narration and that they continue even as he turns from them. At one point in Book II the narrator of the *Persiles* reveals his manipulation of his text in the same way: "Dexemos escriuiendo a Periandro y vamos a oyr lo que dize Sinforosa a Auristela" (I, 193). Similarly the two cases of humorous commentary on the fictitious author that begin the second book as well as the pose of helplessness before the marvelous bird, which "forces" the narrator to describe it, in Book I are early appearances of the technique, which is fully developed in Books III and IV.

[83] ". . . cosa possible, sin ser milagro" (II, 141). ". . . del buelo milagroso de su muger, *mas para ser admirado que creydo*" (II, 152). The italics are mine.

the tongues have kept their laments stifled in bitter silence; only a few cries are heard, muffled amid hoarse moanings.[84]

The narrator is suddenly reminding us that what we are witnessing is fiction and not fact, curiously measuring the scene by what we all know to be the fictional archetype of such a scene and stressing its nonarchetypal character. Even as he does so he playfully withdraws from responsibility for the creation of the scene to contemplate it from the vantage point of what might be termed a literarily conscious audience, which for all its critical awareness is nonetheless the captive of the author who has chosen to be nongeneric. The pose of complicity with the reader is basically the same as one of those practiced by Cide Hamete Benengeli, generally with parodistic intentions at the expense of a specific literary audience, that of the Aristotelians, on questions of probability. In this case no such parody is involved. The narrator is simply using a shock technique to remind the reader of the fictionality of his world as well as his control of that world and those who would contemplate it. The impact of the shift in perspective which marks this authorial intrusion is in part achieved through the abrupt shift from verbs in the preterite and imperfect tense in the narration of the series of events to verbs in the present and present perfect in the narrator's commentary. In effect the temporal removal of the world of fiction is replaced suddenly and briefly by temporal immediacy that marks the apprehension of the world of fiction from the vantage point of reality. The resumption of the narrative witnesses the immediate return to the preterite.[85]

On another occasion the narrator "submits" to the demands of

---

[84] "Hasta aqui, de esta batalla, pocos golpes de espada hemos oido, pocos instrumentos belicos han sonado; el sentimiento que por los muertos suelen hazer los viuos, no ha salido a romper los ayres; las lenguas, en amargo silencio tienen depositadas sus quexas; sólo algunos ayes entre roncos gemidos andan embueltos . . ." (II, 145).

[85] The narrator employs a traditional device of the epic poet, the sudden shift into the historical present tense, but in his context the technique curiously has an effect far different from its conventional one. Rather than bringing the events of the narrative into the foreground of the reader's view, the historical present here situates them in a deeper perspective; the commentary dramatizes the act of reading rather than the epic events, reminding the reader of his position as contemplator of a literary work that is unlike other literary works.

one of his characters: "They reached her, and they discovered her figure to be such, that it obliges us to describe it."[86] Similarly a pretense of equality with a character, who is consequently independent of his control, produces the illusion of his appearance in the story as a fictional character. As such, he offers advice to the avenging widow Ruperta: "Execute your wrath . . . but take care, O beautiful Ruperta, if you please, not to look at this beautiful Cupid," and upbraids the wanton Hipolyta: "O Hipolyta, good only for this! If, among all the pictures you possess, you had one of your good conduct and would leave Periandro in his good conduct. . . ."[87] On still another occasion the narrator suddenly appears amid his group of pilgrims counseling two of them to take time off to enjoy the therapeutic experience of weeping while another relates to the remainder of the group the story of her life. The narrator includes himself in the audience: "Let Auristela weep some more, let Constanza moan a bit more, and let both shut their ears to all consolation while the beautiful Claricia relates to us the cause of the madness of Domicio her husband."[88] In introducing the rhetorical monologue on revenge of Ruperta, the narrator observes that she has locked herself in her room and adds in a pose of helplessness and bewilderment: "I do not know how it came to be known that she had spoken alone these arguments or others that are similar."[89] Similarly he can feign ignorance as to the feelings of one of his characters: "He left Auristela, I do not know whether I should say repentant, but I do know that she remained pensive and confused."[90] In describing the baleful Ruperta, the narrator presents the elaborate literary hoax that his uncontrollable feelings

[86] "Llegaron a ella, y hallaron ser de tal talle, que nos obliga a descriuirle" (II, 59).
[87] ". . . executa tu ira . . . pero mira, ¡o hermosa Ruperta!, si quieres, que no mires a esse hermoso Cupido . . ." (II, 166). "¡O Hipolyta, sólo buena por esto! Si entre tantos retratos que tienes, tuuieras vno de tu buen trato, y dexaras en el suyo a Periandro . . ." (II, 249).
[88] "Llore, pues, algun tanto mas Auristela, gima algun espacio mas Constança, y cierren entrambas los oidos a toda consolacion, en tanto que la hermosa Claricia nos cuenta la causa de la locura de Domicio, su esposo" (II, 148).
[89] ". . . no se cómo se supo que auia hablado a solas estas o otras semejantes razones" (II, 164).
[90] ". . . dexò a Auristela, no se si diga arrepentida, pero se que quedò pensatiua y confusa" (II, 270).

in contemplating woman's capacity for cruelty prevents his continuing the account of Ruperta's plan:

> What enormous cruelties will not seem to her like the gentlest deeds? But no more, for what one could say in this affair is so much, that it will be better to leave it as it is, because words to do it justice cannot be found.[91]

What marks all these passages, the narrator's disclaimers of control, his assertion of being dependent on his characters, his bewilderment at the disclosure of the thoughts of a character in solitude, his entry into the fictional world as character, and his uncontrollable emotions before the actions of his characters, is a tone of helplessness and self-deprecation, which in its obvious artificiality reinforces the effect of the author's absolute control over both his text and his reader.[92]

CONCLUSION

The instability which marks the poses of the narrator of the *Persiles* is far more complex than the coherent evasiveness of Cide Hamete Benengeli. The literary badinage of the Moor, his editor, and his translator—their assertions, reversals, self-contradictions, and jokes on the reader—are all individual notes in the uniform tone of literary parody sounding throughout the world of *Don Quixote*. The commentary of the narrator of the *Persiles*, which is heard usually in the voice of an intruding *yo* and occasionally in a dramatic dialogue between a fictitious author and an editor-translator, observes no such consistent pattern. The first and most striking inconsistency concerns Cervantes' conception of the role of his narrator and the range of his commentary. As Durling has pointed out, a characteristic of Renaissance epic was "the tendency to combine conventions of ancient epic (which involved an abstract,

---

[91] "¿Que inormes crueldades no le parecen blandas y pacificas? No mas, porque lo que en este caso se podia dezir es tanto, que será mejor dexarlo en su punto, pues no se han de hallar palabras con que encarecerlo" (II, 165). The emphasis on the actual staying of the creative hand of the poet in excitement clearly distinguishes this type of remark from the traditional expression of diffidence of the epic poet, which we observed in the commentary of the classically drawn singer of the first book.

[92] We are once again confronted with an influence on Cervantes' narrative style which cannot be exaggerated—that of Ariosto. See Durling, pp. 112-123.

transcendent, or superpersonal 'I' as Narrator) with a strong assertion of a more discursively established, concrete identity for the Poet."
This characteristic is observable in the *Persiles*; yet what is evident is
an unsatisfactory assimilation of the two tendencies. It is clear that
throughout Book I Cervantes is complying with the Aristotelian
restrictions on the range of authorial commentary and following
Tasso, who in theory and example had successfully resurrected the
classical ideal of epic narration. Whereas the dedicated Aristotelian
Tasso could successfully construct and constrain his narrator in accordance with the Homeric and Virgilian models, Cervantes could
not avoid that combination made by most of his contemporaries.
At the beginning of Book II his classically conceived narrator, who
enters Book I rarely and in his most extended appearances in the
garb of the traditional singer, abruptly changes form. From that
moment until the end of the work he appears as the more personal,
discursive, and occasionally self-deprecating narrator whose descent
Durling has traced from the ancient satirical works of such poets
as Horace and Ovid through the medieval romances to its most
influential Renaissance development in the narrator of Ariosto.[93]

Perhaps symptomatic of Cervantes' increasing dissatisfaction with
the classical conception of and limitation on the narrative voice is
the nature of the comment by which his narrator breaks forth from
the classical mold. It is an utterance of self-deprecation of the
Ariostean type, which in addition to liberating the narrator, jarring-
ly disrupts the sober tone of the epic work with a discordant note
of humor. After this unexpected breakdown of his originally conceived role, the narrator appropriates for himself a central place
in the work, and his widely ranging comments assume an extremely personal quality. His reflections on the characters and events
offer opinions of a moralizing, satirical, and philosophical temper
on a wide variety of topics—from problems associated with love
and courtship, to the dishonesty of bureaucrats, and to such fundamental transcendental issues of the romance as the mutability of
the earthly world and the permanence of eternity.

The simple inconsistency which we observe in the shifting conception of the role of the narrator is compounded further by an

[93] Durling, p. 10.

instability which characterizes the personal utterances released following his emergence as a dominant voice in the work. It is observable specifically in his comments on the theme which appears in the *Persiles* simultaneously with the narrator's liberation—the fictional quality of the work itself. In general we can distinguish in these comments, all of which reveal Cervantes' ceaseless preoccupation with the problematic reality of his work, two divergent tendencies, which indicate that the author viewed his creation with conflictive attitudes. We can associate the two fundamental directions of these comments conveniently with the names of the Canon of Toledo and Cide Hamete Benengeli. On the one hand the narrator constantly recalls both his literary ambitions to write the Renaissance prose epic, modeled on Heliodorus, and the aesthetic principles associated with this ambition. Here his reflections on his selective processes in including phenomena in his narration modulate between a neutral explanatory tone and an uneasy justificatory tone. They can appear as brief, perhaps unconscious, parenthetical remarks—e.g., translating a bold metaphor into normal language, emphasizing the interest value of a description of a strange bird, or pointing out that the braking effect of a falling woman's skirts is not an implausibility. Or they can expand into extended digressions—e.g., on the obligation of a poet to compose an interesting plot without sacrificing verisimilitude, on the theoretical problem of the "low" subject matter in poetry, or on the appropriateness of a seemingly nongeneric element in the text. Occasionally, however, this aesthetically conservative voice generates a critical response, and we discern the mocking, self-deprecating tones of Cide Hamete Benengeli sounding a plea for artistic freedom and undermining the aesthetic foundations on which the prose epic is based. Here too we discover both the brief, perhaps unconscious reflection— e.g., those mocking the artificiality of lofty or figurative language or the exhausted literary conventions of the improbable peripeteia and anagnorisis—and the extended discursive comment. Both use equivocations couched in aesthetic terminology and literary humor to assert the narrator's disregard for limitations which aesthetic theory would impose upon his creative powers. Consistent with his turn from submission to the generic principles to affirmation of complete freedom in the final two books of the *Persiles* is the narrator's constant reminder to the reader that he is in control both of his fictional world and the reader's response to it through a series of self-effacing poses, hoaxes in which he mischievously feigns help-lessness to prevent what occurs in his imaginary world from oc-curring as it does.

PART FOUR:

THE CERVANTINE FIGURE OF THE POET

Impostor or God?

CHAPTER IX

The Cervantine Figure of the Poet:
Impostor or God?

IN THE microscopic examination of the complex of scenes in the *Quixote* and the *Persiles* in which the creating author confronts a critical audience, I hope to have shown an unbroken continuity in theme and structure. In all of these scenes the principle of authorial freedom is opposed to artistic restrictions which the great critical movement of the sixteenth century had formulated. The ensuing dramatic interplay is in each case comic, and in each case the comedy functions at the expense of the spokesmen for the classical aesthetic. Enough has been said of the particular aesthetic principles which form the substance for these interchanges and the ambiguity which the dramatic scenes bring to the *Persiles*, which was originally conceived in terms of the classical principles. It remains for us to redirect our attention from the classical aesthetic, which is always overcome, to the triumphant figure who continuously asserts his independence of it.

The Renaissance classicists' views of the poet and the poetic mission were founded on Strabo's oft-repeated phrase that the "excellence of a poet is inseparably associated with the excellence of the man himself, and it is impossible for one to become a good poet unless he has previously become a good man,"[1] on the high civilizing function which Horace attributes to poetry and the poet, on the Platonic notion of the poet as *vates*, an instrument of divine revelation, and on the neo-Platonic belief that the poet's creative powers are analogous to those of divinity. Contemplating human experience in relation to a set of rational principles, the classicists saw in the poet a conveyor of norms. He is preeminently a man of society and a spokesman for its conventional values, the values of the house and the city. For them the prototype of the poet is to be found in the mythic civilizers, Orpheus and Amphion, who, according to Horace, built the Theban wall and labored to "circumscribe men's rights" and to "build rampired towns, engrave their

[1] *The Geography of Strabo*, I, 63.

laws on wood/ And knit the bonds of social brotherhood."[2] The classicists' iconological conception of poetry was well suited to their view of the poet—the young maiden whose sweetness and beauty attracts all men, the *dotti* and the *rozzi*, and who is attended by moral and natural philosophy.[3]

Cervantes' various surrogate poets have little in common with the inspired figures who haunt the groves and springs of Parnassus. Nearly all of them are tainted with criminality; they glory not in the act of edification but rather in the act of deception; any supernatural connections which they may have are infernal; and their abode is not the city, but some underworld kingdom which is opposed to all conventional values. The contrast can be so sharply drawn that one is tempted to invoke Goethe's distinction between classical and romantic—*das Gesunde* vs. *das Kranke*. The problem is then why does Cervantes surround his poets with such "negative" attributes. Is it simply a question of negation; do the figures represent a parodistic inversion of the classical figure? Or is the "negative" in fact transvaluated into the "positive"; does it reflect a major function which Cervantes associates with the artistic undertaking? Two of the minor works are illuminating, for they deal directly with these questions. In *La Gitanilla* and *Pedro de Urdemalas* the figure of the poet, whom we glimpse only occasionally in the *Quixote* and the *Persiles*, assumes a central role, and his destiny as poet never ceases to be a part of the essential thematic substance on which the works are founded. Taken together these two works present the full biography, the apprenticeship and triumph, of the Cervantine figure of the poet.

THE POET AS AN OUTSIDER: *LA GITANILLA*

In Master Pedro we observe the figure of the poet moving back and forth across the border which separates society from a realm in which disorder, criminality, and demonic forces prevail and his redemption in his artistry. The situation of the artist beyond the pale of society is equally apparent in Cervantes' conception of the figures of the counterfeit captives, whose livelihood depends on

---

[2] See *Ars Poetica*, ll. 391-399. I cite Howes' translation, *The Art of Poetry*, ed. Albert S. Cook (Boston, 1892), p. 29.

[3] See Cesare Ripa, *Iconologia* (Siena, 1613), pp. 157-158.

deception, and the figure of Cide Hamete Benengeli, who descends from the race of liars, is on intimate terms with the devil, and takes delight in sophistry and the disregard for conventional distinctions. As we remember, it is Cide Hamete Benengeli who can swear like a Christian and get away with it, as it were, both transcending the geographical and racial distinctions on which the classicists' formulations of decorum are founded and dissociating himself from anything which is easily definable.

Perhaps Cervantes' most dramatic presentation of the artist's necessity of nourishing his creative powers in areas which conventional society has forbidden to its members lies in the *Gitanilla*, in the shadowy figure of Clemente, who appears and disappears like a will-o'-the-wisp in the world of this novella.[4] The role of this figure is most mysterious because he provides virtually the only discordant note in a comedy dramatizing the redemption of society in its entirety and celebrating Christian marriage as an image of universal order. In its structural workings and themes, *La Gitanilla*

[4] Both Harri Meier and Joaquín Casalduero have observed the ambiguity which surrounds the function of this figure. Their interpretations are based on situating the page within the central relationship between Preciosa and Juan-Andres. His presence provides a factor which complicates this relationship, reviving the jealousy which Juan must overcome to purify his love and for the only time in the novella revealing Preciosa in a moment of weakness in her faith in Juan. The difficulty in this interpretation arises from Cervantes' clear suggestion that Preciosa and the page are drawn to each other by a very deep bond. Casalduero concludes that the author's ambiguity is intentional and reveals his awareness of complicated dimensions of love, which cannot find expression through the media which social institutions provide for the expression of love (see *Sentido y forma de Las novelas ejemplares* [Madrid, 1962], p. 64). Harri Meier admits the difficulty of an interpretation emphasizing psychological plausibility and motivation, offering somewhat tentatively a conclusion not unlike that of Casalduero and at the same time allowing for the possibility of an artistic flaw: "Liebt Clemente die Preciosa? Ist Preciosa von Clemente angetan oder gar durch seine Anwesenheit beunruhigt? Hier tut sich uns ein Rätsel auf . . . es gibt nur die beiden Möglichkeiten, entweder anzunehmen, der Dichter habe uns gerade in diesen Zweifel bringen, die Undurchsichtigkeit des Lebens für den Beschauer noch mit in sein episches Werk hineinnehmen wollen, oder in diesem Motiv eine unnütze oder zum mindesten unausgearbeitete Komplikation der Handlung zu sehen" ("Personenhandlung und Geschehen in Cervantes' *Gitanilla*," *Romanische Forschungen*, LI [1937], 125-186; see esp. pp. 157-158). I suggest that the role of Clemente may be clarified by an interpretation emphasizing the symbolic nature of the work rather than its psychological plausibility and by viewing Clemente as the focus of a major thematic component of the work rather than as a secondary figure with a complicating role in the love intrigue at the center of the narration.

can be seen as a prelude to Cervantes' much more complexly orchestrated final work, *Persiles y Sigismunda*. Both move from the dissolution of an imperfect society to the rebirth and reintegration of that society around a pair of heroes who are united in the sacramental rite of marriage after journeying through "other," nonsocial worlds and suffering various trials. In both cases Heliodorus' work is the probable literary source for what is in reality one of the omnipresent situations of comedy, for which Cervantes' fondness is attested not only by these two works, but also with minor variations by *Pedro de Urdemalas, La ilustre fregona, La española inglesa,* and the tale of the *Cautivo* as well. A beautiful girl, whose parentage is either unknown or mysteriously complicated (viz., Zoraida), is held in bondage or is borne about the world on a path of sufferings by a mysterious destiny, which ultimately clarifies her parentage and in so doing elevates her and her society to a superior level of being.

In Cervantes' reworkings of the traditional literary pattern, recognition and the reintegration of society generally occur in the city or the court, symbols of the Spanish social-religious order, and the trials generally take the form of a quest from a city to a demonic wilderness (the sea, the Gypsy world, Algiers) and back to the city or court. Generally the persecuted heroine is a representative of the city and in her suffering a symbol of some momentary disorder which afflicts the world of the city and which disappears following her restoration. *La Gitanilla* follows the familiar pattern— from Madrid to the world of the Gypsies and a return to Murcia. Murcia provides the setting for the final, most difficult trial of Juan-Andres, the moment of potential tragedy in the traditional prison scene, and the traditional type of anagnorisis, in which we feel the presence of the miracle-working hand of Providence, as the ubiquitous jewels turn up as proof of the heroine's identity. In Murcia, Preciosa, whose chastity is linked with divine powers, suddenly appears as a member of the social order. Together with her lover Juan-Andres, she can now return to benefit society with the example of a lofty love, whose purity and fertility are sanctified in the sacramental rite of Christian marriage.

In the *Gitanilla* Cervantes stands in the tradition of comedy, and it is evident that he is holding to the classical pattern in which, in Aristotle's words, "those who, in the piece, are the deadliest enemies—like Orestes and Aegisthus—quit the stage as friends at the close and no one slays or is slain."[5] There is a place for nearly everyone in the harmonious society that emerges around the hero and heroine at Murcia. It never occurs to Don Fernando de Azevedo that punishment may be in order for the old Gypsy who confesses to having kidnapped his daughter fifteen years before. Even the villainous Juana Carducha, whose attempted seduction of Andres touches off the series of events that nearly costs him his life, is merely humiliated and almost immediately pardoned. The peculiar way in which Cervantes redeems her reveals dramatically his desire for a harmonious conclusion to his work. The traditional ending of the story is found not in the final but rather in the penultimate paragraph. In the familiar, dynamic *veni-vidi-vici* series of preterites Cervantes rapidly describes the reunion of the family of the hero, the wedding, and the immortalization of the young heroes in the poetry of their contemporaries. However, the author has forgotten one element which lingers as a reminder of the underworld which has been overcome:

> I forgot to say that the enamored damsel of the inn informed the officers of the law that the charge of theft against Andres the Gypsy was not true, and she acknowledged her love and her crime. On her no penalty was inflicted, because in the joy at finding the couple betrothed, *vengeance was buried and clemency came back to life.*[6]

So intent is Cervantes on maintaining the mood of comedy that he adds this paragraph after the conventional ending in order to include the antagonist of the heroes in their redeemed world. Indeed the final antithesis—vengeance *buried*, mercy *resurrected*—imaginatively associates the destiny of the sinful Carducha with that of

---

[5] *Poetics*, p. 49.

[6] "Oluidauaseme de dezir como la enamorada mesonera descubrio a la justicia no ser verdad lo del hurto de Andres el gitano y confesó su amor y su culpa, a quien no respondio pena alguna, porque, en la alegria del hallazgo de los desposados *se enterro la vengança y resucitó la clemencia*" (*La Gitanilla, Novelas exemplares*, ed. R. Schevill and A. Bonilla [Madrid, 1922], I, 131; the following page references are to this text). The italics are mine.

the protagonists as it implicates her in the ritualistic celebration of death and rebirth which lies behind the plot of the *Gitanilla*.[7]

Cervantes' evident concern for the redemption of la Carducha in his comedy is all the more significant as it throws into sharp relief the destiny of a character who remains excluded from the festive society of the city—the poet Clemente. Cervantes carefully draws attention to the contrast between the fate of Clemente and that of the others in a statement abruptly terminating a series which utilizes antitheses and the familiar dynamic style of the Spanish preterite to celebrate the triumphant transformations of the redeemed parties following Don Juan's release from prison. It should be observed how the rhythmical movement toward climax suddenly collapses in the syntactic complication that accompanies the introduction of the element of uncertainty.

> Don Juan put on the traveling clothes that the Gypsy had brought there. His imprisonment and iron chains turned to liberty and chains of gold, and the sadness of the imprisoned Gypsies into joy, since they were released on bail the next day. The uncle of the dead man accepted the promise of two thou-

[7] Images of death-rebirth and sterility-fertility (particularly in the first two poems) are important in maintaining a cosmic frame of reference in *La Gitanilla*. Cervantes' work forms a good illustration of the following observation of Northrop Frye on comedy: "The tendency of comedy is to include as many people as possible in its final society: the blocking characters are more often reconciled or converted than simply repudiated. Comedy often includes a scapegoat ritual of expulsion which gets rid of some irreconcilable character, but exposure and disgrace make for pathos, or even tragedy" (*Anatomy of Criticism*, p. 165). Not only are Carducha and the Gypsy kidnapper included in the festivities that conclude the work, but Cervantes is also careful to reconcile the soldier whose slaying is part of Andres' final trial by mentioning that his uncle was given ten thousand ducats to secure his pardon of the hero. Cervantes may be using as his source for the episode of Carducha an oral account of an innkeeper's daughter's attempted seduction of an unsympathetic pilgrim on the road to Santiago, as Bataillon suggests ("La dénonciation mensongère dans La Gitanilla," *Bulletin Hispanique*, LII [1950] 274-276), or a literary tradition (e.g., Demeta's treatment of Gnemon in Heliodorus' *Aethiopica* or the Joseph-Potiphar legend in the Bible). However, Cervantes' redemption of the temptress is a departure from these particular versions, in which she is severely punished (or, in the case of Joseph, merely forgotten) and reveals the harmonious vision that informs his creation of the novella. Cervantes' interest in such a scene of temptation and triumphant chastity is attested by its appearance on three occasions in the *Persiles* (Rosamunda-Antonio, Zenotia-Antonio, and Hipolyta-Periandro). For the frequency of the scene in literary tradition, see Hellmuth Petriconi, "Die verschmähte Astarte," *Romanistisches Jahrbuch*, XIII (1962), 149-185.

sand ducats which was made him, provided he abandon the accusation and pardon Don Juan, who, not forgetting his comrade Clemente, had him sought for, but he was not to be found, nor was anything known of him until four days after, when some information came that he had embarked in one of two Genoese galleys that lay in the port of Cartagena and had already sailed.[8]

Clemente alone is untouched by the forces of convergence centering on Murcia, and we may assume from his state as a fugitive from the law, from his initiation into the ways of the Gypsies, and from his destination that he is traveling the path of many illustrious rogues of the age,[9] submerging in a world of disorder and deception which he has come to know among the Gypsies.

As has been often noted, one of the major themes of the *Gitanilla* is poetry.[10] The development of this theme hinges on the relationship between the poet Clemente and the heroine Preciosa, who in this context is a symbol of poetry. The Gypsy maiden's close relationship to poetry is evident in the first paragraphs of the story, in the words "Preciosa came forth rich in carols, folksongs, *seguidillas*, sarabands, and other verses."[11] On one occasion she boasts of her powers of fantasy and on another offers to tell one of her admirers "more fortunes and adventures than are contained in a book of chivalry."[12] Moreover, the world of the Gypsies, in which she is raised and educated, is associated directly with the powers of the poetic imagination. As the Gypsy elder celebrates the abundance of

---

[8] "Vistiose don Iuan los vestidos de camino, que alli auia traydo la gitana; boluieronse las prisiones y cadenas de hierro en libertad y cadenas de oro: la tristeza de los gitanos presos, en alegria, pues otro dia los dieron en fiado. Recibio el tio del muerto la promessa de dos mil ducados, que le hizieron, porque baxasse de la querella y perdonasse a don Iuan, el qual, no oluidandose de su camarada Clemente, le hizo buscar, pero no le hallaron, ni supieron del, hasta que desde alli a quatro dias tuuo nueuas ciertas, que se auia embarcado en vna de dos galeras de Genoua, que estauan en el puerto de Cartagena, y ya se auian partido" (p. 129).

[9] Earlier in the novella Genoa is associated with dishonesty (p. 62).

[10] See Casalduero, *Sentido y forma de Las novelas ejemplares*, p. 58; Karl-Ludwig Selig, "Concerning the Structure of Cervantes' *La Gitanilla*," *Romanistisches Jahrbuch*, XIII (1962), 273-276.

[11] "Salio Preciosa rica de villanzicos, de coplas, seguidillas, y çarabandas, y de otros versos" (p. 32).

[12] ". . . mas venturas y auenturas que las que tiene vn libro de cauallerias" (p. 53).

the natural world, which sustains his society, he speaks of the Gypsies' powers of imagination to transform the destructive forces of nature: "For us the inclemencies of the weather are breezes, the snow refreshment, the rain baths, the thunder music, and the lightning torches."[13] Later in the sermon the Gypsy returns to the aesthetic powers of his fellows, asserting that they observe in the beauties of the natural landscapes what others seek in Flemish paintings and self-consciously employing conventional poetic language to describe their enjoyment in witnessing the dawn.

> We see how Aurora withdraws and locks up the stars of heaven, and how she issues forth with her companion the Dawn, refreshing the air, cooling the waters and moistening the earth, and immediately after her the sun *gilding the mountain tops,* as the other poet said, *and rippling the forests.*[14]

On two occasions Preciosa's function as symbol of poetry is skillfully blended with her function as the embodiment of moral perfection. Her defense of chastity is based on a compelling inversion of the traditional *carpe-diem* motif of lyric poetry: "The flower of virginity is one that, were it possible, should not permit itself to be offended even in thought. When the rose is cut from the rose-bush, with what rapidity and facility does it wither! This one handles it, that one scents it, another plucks off its leaves, and finally among rough hands it is picked to pieces."[15] Here we observe both an elaborate metaphor of vegetable sterility and fertility (there are several such elaborations), which links the plot of the *Gitanilla* to a cosmic process, and an example of Preciosa's skill at *die Literarisierung des Lebens.* In the climactic poetic dialogue of Juan-Andres and Clemente, Cervantes again fuses the two symbolic func-

---

[13] "Para nosotros, las inclemencias del cielo son oreos, refrigerio las nieues, baños la lluuia, musicas los truenos, y hachas los relampagos" (p. 79).

[14] ". . . vemos como arrincona y barre la aurora las estrellas del cielo, y como ella sale con su compañera el alua, alegrando el ayre, enfriando el agua y humedeciendo la tierra, y luego, tras ellas, el sol *dorando cumbres,* como dixo el otro poeta, *y rizando montes*" (p. 80).

[15] "Flor es la de la virginidad que, a ser possible, aun con la imaginacion no auia de dexar ofenderse. Cortada la rosa del rosal, ¡con qué breuedad y facilidad se marchita! Este la toca, aquel la huele, el otro la deshoja, y, finalmente, entre las manos rusticas se deshaze" (pp. 56-57).

tions of Preciosa. The maiden appears both as the siren of the Platonic tradition ("the siren who enchants and soothes those who are most prepared"),[16] whose music, as the "ultimate image" of the celestial harmony, can remind the most pure and aspiring minds of the true god,[17] and as the divine Muse. The association of the nine muses with Plato's sirens is an ancient tradition which enjoyed a revival in Renaissance neo-Platonism.[18] The sphere of the fixed stars, to which Clemente and Juan assign Preciosa ("It would be fitting and just to lift her fame to the eighth sphere"),[19] is the abode of Urania, the muse of cosmic knowledge and astronomy and the muse traditionally invoked by the epic poet.[20]

The most important association of Preciosa and poetry is made by Clemente as he offers the traditional emblematic view of poetry as a beautiful young maiden dwelling amid flowers, trees, and fountains. In his description he employs adjectives which recall the classical view of literature—*honesta, discreta, retirada*—and claims that the maiden "delights and instructs" whomever she meets. The young poet underscores the link between this figure and Preciosa by asserting that maiden poetry is *vna joya preciosissima* ("a most precious gem" [p. 63; see also pp. 43, 47]).

It is easy to follow the usual practice of isolating Clemente's statement on literature and various others like it in Cervantes' writings in order to make a case for the conventionality of the author's view of poetry. However, in the *Gitanilla* the emblem is subordinated to a broader context, within which it acquires an ambivalent character. As a symbol of poetry, Preciosa represents a significant modification of the traditional figure. In her mastery of the arts of dissimulation and her worldliness, which she attributes to the counsels of the mentor of all Gypsies, the devil, she is anything but *retirada*, and the fallen world in which she boldly moves is far

[16] ". . . la sirena que encanta/ y adormece a los mas apercebidos" (p. 108).
[17] Proclus, *Platonica Theologia*, VII, 36; see James Hutton, "Some English Poems in Praise of Music," *English Miscellany*, II (1951), 1-63, esp. pp. 1-28 and pp. 48-49; see also E.M.W. Tillyard, *The Elizabethan World Picture*, Vintage Books, (New York, nd), pp. 48-50.
[18] See Hutton, pp. 13, 24-25.
[19] "Que le lleuara hasta la octaua esfera/ fuera decente y justo" (p. 108).
[20] See Martianus Capella, *De nuptiis philologiae et Mercurii et de septem artibus liberalibus* (Frankfurt, 1836), pp. 69-70.

different from the *locus amoenus* surrounding maiden poetry. These "dark" attributes of Preciosa are crucial in Cervantes' treatment of the theme of poetry in the *Gitanilla*. Their significance will become clear if we examine his development of the Clemente-Preciosa relationship.

Prior to his nocturnal entry into the Gypsy camp and his encounter with Juan, the page Clemente is a nameless figure whose two fleeting appearances in the work are veiled in ambiguity. As Preciosa dances and sings in the streets of Madrid, the young man approaches her, offers her a *romance*, promises to continue giving her poems, and disappears. As Preciosa prepares to sing the *romance*, much to her astonishment she discovers a gold coin wrapped in the paper on which it is written and remarks: "it is more of a miracle for a poet to give me a crown than for me to receive it."[21] The poem contains a celebration of Preciosa's beauty and the miracle represented by its appearance in the humble world of the Gypsies as well as a confession of love.

The second meeting of Preciosa and the page is only slightly longer than the first, but it deepens the thematic texture of the work, introducing poetry as a major theme and surrounding the figure of the page with an aura of an unfulfilled destiny. After insisting that the young man swear to tell the truth, Preciosa asks him whether he is a poet. The latter replies that very few are worthy of the title of poet and that he is not among them: "I am not a poet, but only one addicted to poetry."[22] He proceeds to exalt poetry, employing the well-known emblem of the beautiful young maiden and affirming the high moral mission of the poet. Preciosa again insists that a poet must be poor and recalls the gold coin which he had given her before to substantiate his statement that he is in fact not a real poet but only an amateur:

That gold crown which you gave me wrapped up in your verses did cause me to marvel. But now that I know that you are not a poet, but only addicted to poetry, it is possible that you may be rich, although I doubt it, because that part of your nature which impels you to write verses is likely to drain away

[21] ". . . es mas milagro darme a mi vn poeta vn escudo, que yo recibirle" (p. 43).
[22] ". . . yo no lo soy, sino vn aficionado a la poesia" (p. 63).

whatever property you may have, for there is no poet, so it is said, who knows how to keep the property he has, or to gain that which he does not have.[23]

The page readily admits that he is not a poet and offers the maiden again a poem and a gold coin, requesting that she accept them without worrying about whether or not he is a poet. Preciosa accepts the poem and refuses the coin, insisting: "I like you as a poet, and not as a giver; and in this we shall have a friendship which may last."[24] Here a bond is sealed between the maiden and the young man, who willingly accepts the demand that he be poor of necessity and the assumption that only in such a condition will he be the poet that she desires ("Since it is so . . . Preciosa, that you desire that I should be constrained to be poor. . .").[25] He vanishes in the streets of Madrid and will return only after having obeyed her command.

Several of the ambiguous details concerning Clemente appear in a clearer light when viewed in terms of his relation to Preciosa as a symbol of poetry. The fact that he does not have a name, his youth, his profession of page, and the emphasis on his being not a poet but an *aficionado*, all suggest the state of apprenticeship. It is well to note how Cervantes employs several details to underscore the honesty of the youth in the encounter with the Gypsy maiden. At first he swears that he will tell her the truth even if it were to cost him his life. He proceeds to offer his classical theory of poetry, stressing the edifying value of literature and the lofty moral qualities of the maiden who represents poetry. Following this he contrasts his good intentions in his offer of an *escudo* to the maiden with the well-known usury of the Genoese bankers. Indeed his ingenuousness contrasts sharply with the worldliness which Preciosa has already revealed on more than one occasion, in her sharp re-

[23] ". . . causome marauilla aquel escudo de oro que me distes entre vuestros versos embuelto; mas agora que se que no soys poeta, sino aficionado de la poesia, podria ser que fuessedes rico, aunque lo dudo, a causa que por aquella parte que os toca de hazer coplas, se ha de desaguar quanta hazienda tuuieredes, que no ay poeta, segun dizen, que sepa conseruar la hazienda que tiene, ni grangear la que no tiene" (p. 64).
[24] ". . . por poeta le quiero, y no por dadiuoso, y desta manera tendremos amistad que dure" (p. 65).
[25] "Pues assi es . . . que quieres, Preciosa, que yo sea pobre por fuerça . . ." (p. 65).

joinders to her admirers and in her mastery of dissimulation. More-over, the affirmation that few deserve the title of poet, the identification of the object of the poet with a beautiful maiden, Preciosa's statement that she wants his devotion in poetry and not in wealth, and the page's apparent willingness to suffer or "be poor" as his beloved demands point toward the mission of the young man to pass from his apprenticeship to the higher state of poet. The initiation of the page demands his entrance into the world of the Gypsies, which is associated not only with the imagination but also with thieving, lying, and demonic forces. Here he must explore the "darker side" of the poet's destiny.[26]

In the structural arrangement of the novella the pact between poetry and the aspiring poet is of great significance. It follows immediately the pact between Preciosa and the still unnamed young hero of the story, who, attracted by her irresistible beauty, has declared himself willing to abandon his station at the pinnacle of society, to deceive his family, and to shirk his duty as a Spaniard in order to win his beloved by living for two years as a Gypsy. Thus the two young men are borne as doubles on parallel quests, following the object of their desires into a strange world beyond the outer limits of society.[27] As both undergo a process of development from youth to maturity, it falls on one to represent symbolically the fallen social order, restoring its lost perfection by suffering and redeeming from a lower world the maiden whom it has exiled. It

[26] The shifting symbolic value of the Gypsy world is all-important in the workings of the novella. Here I am concerned with its functions which are relevant to the theme of poetry—i.e., as a realm associated with the freedom of the imagination and as a demonic lower world in which Clemente must break with the conventions of society in order to become a poet. The infernal associations of the Gypsy world are sustained by such traditional images as the hammer and tongs, the garrote, the voracious bird of prey, and by many statements of characters and the discursive narrator (e.g., "Muger buena antes angel que gitana" [p. 119]). The asocial character of this world is most clearly stated by the Gypsy elder: ". . . viuimos por nuestra industria y pico, y sin entremeternos con el antiguo refran *yglesia o mar o casa real*, tenemos lo que queremos" (p. 80). However, it should be pointed out that the Gypsy world occasionally functions as an "otherworld" paradise, by which contemporary society is measured and condemned. This symbolic value is important in the early part of the work, which depicts society in an imperfect state.

[27] Preciosa's words underscore the parallelism in the destinies of the two heroes most forcefully: ". . . como auia don Ioanes en el mundo y que se mudauan en Andreses, assi podia auer don Sanchos que se mudassen en otros nombres" (105).

falls on the other to enter that lower world, a protean world of deception and shifting appearances,[28] and undergo the experience and sufferings which the poetic mission demands. While following his immersion in the lower world, the one hero moves in his quest ever upward toward a reestablished social order within the enclosed space of the city and the court, his double must follow his destiny ever downward, falling away from society through worlds of criminality and deceit to disappear as a fugitive somewhere in the open expanses of the sea that separates Spain from Italy.

The next appearance of the page in the novella marks the point at which the trajectories of the male protagonists intersect in their respective quests. One night, as Juan-Andres, Preciosa, and the Gypsies lie encamped in Estremadura, Clemente emerges from the darkness, pursued by the dogs of the Gypsies. He is dressed in an unseemly white garb, which Juan describes as that of a miller and which turns out to be that of a friar's servant. The uncertainty surrounding the clothing of the young man is meaningful, for it associates him immediately with the process of shape-changing which has been presented as the trademark of the Gypsy world.

The conversation of the following morning reveals that Clemente has been involved in an incident of violence which cost the life of two men and that he is now a fugitive from the law hoping to make his escape to Italy in his disguise. Thus we observe the youthful page, whose honesty and innocence are highlighted in his two previous appearances, suddenly transformed into the familiar disguised wanderer of picaresque literature represented most forcefully in Cervantes' works by Master Pedro and Pedro de Urdemalas. The page's transformation is the first stage of the initiation which Preciosa, as the symbol of poetry, has demanded. His change of clothes parallels that of the other hero in the ceremonies ritualizing his metamorphosis into a Gypsy.

The path that Clemente is to follow in his passage to a state of higher knowledge is revealed dramatically at the beginning of the

[28] The Gypsy world in the *Gitanilla* is introduced by a scene which associates it with mutability. Its inhabitants greet Juan with the suggestion that they "transform" his mule and sell it, boasting that in two hours they can change the appearance of the creature to the extent that neither his master nor his mother will be able to recognize it.

conversation with his double, who offers him the wisdom that he has hitherto lacked. At first the page wishes to avoid a disclosure of his condition as a fugitive and attempts to make up a lie that would convincingly explain his mysterious nocturnal arrival. Juan, who has become the leader of the troupe of Gypsies, catches him quickly in the lie, and, instead of proceeding immediately to ascertain the truth, offers the young man some advice on the correct way of lying.

> I do not care to know who you are, what is your name, nor whither you are going, but observe that, *if it suits you to lie on this journey of yours, lie with more appearance of truth. . . . Friend, rise up and learn to lie and go with good fortune.*[29]

Within the context of the page's quest, his evolution from apprenticeship to the profession of poet, adumbrated in the scene of his previous appearance, the paratactical exhortation of the final sentence acquires a ceremonial character. The relationship between this command and the poetic destiny as conceived by Cervantes may be difficult for the modern reader to discern. However, if we remember the deep tradition associating poetry and lying, and the uneasy concern of literary theorists of the epoch with defining a proper way for the poet to use lies, the allusiveness of the dramatic interchange will be clear. Indeed Juan's words, "Lie with more appearance of truth," for the seventeenth-century reader could not fail to recall Aristotle's statement that poets lie with the appearance of truth, a statement that was repeated in nearly every document of literary theory of the age, including the piece offered by the Canon of Toledo ("The more the lie resembles the truth, the better it is").[30] It is well to recall the various scenes which we have examined above

[29] "Yo no quiero saber quien soys, cómo os llamais o adónde vays, pero aduiertoos que *si os conuiene mentir en este vuestro viaje, mintays con mas apariencia de verdad. . . . Amigo, leuantaos y aprended a mentir, y andad enorabuena*" (p. 95). The italics are mine.
[30] ". . . tanto la mentira es mejor cuanto más parece verdadera" (*Don Quijote*, I, 482). It is worth noting that on another occasion Juan offers the young intruder advice on how to solicit help from the Gypsies, concluding: ". . . con darles algo de lo que lleuays, facilitareys con ellos otros impossibles mayores" (p. 101). The canon uses "facilitar impossibles" to describe the poet's process of lying skillfully, i.e., with verisimilitude (I, 482).

Impostor or God?

in following the appearances of the figure of the poet in Cervantes' work, for in each the problem of lying is central to the dramatic interplay, which often involves, as does that of the present, "catching someone in the lie." Master Pedro, the counterfeit captives, Sancho in the Clavileño episode, and Cide Hamete Benengeli on several occasions must contend with critical audiences who would question the truth of their statements. What is important to note here is that the page undergoes an initiation, which in several details—the change of clothes, the willing entry into the world of the Gypsies, and the acquisition of a name or rebaptism within this world—parallels that of the protagonist Juan-Andres Cavallero, and that his initiation, which begins the process of his evolution from page to poet, begins with the commandment that he learn to do what had been impossible for him before—to lie, or, seen in the context of Cervantes' various figures of the artist, to master and manipulate illusion.

After participating in the poetic dialogue celebrating the Gypsy maiden, Clemente disappears from the world of the protagonists. Excluded from the comic society that forms amid festivities in Murcia, excluded from the ritual of reclothing, which restores the abandoned cross of Santiago to his double, he is doomed to remain in his disguises, to continue his journey in the world of darkness which the others have renounced. He is not yet ready to enter the city, the symbol of the conventional values and wisdom by which humanity orders its experience. Apparently his quest as poet has only begun.

THE TRIUMPH OF PROTEUS: *PEDRO DE URDEMALAS*

In attempting to trace the features of Cervantes' figure of the poet, I think it useful at this point to recall the vocabulary to which my analyses consistently turned in dealing with the style of the various triumphant narrators in the dramatic confrontations of creating author and critical audience—irony, equivocation, ambiguity, evasion, elusiveness, mystification, reversal, metamorphosis, disguise, fluidity, change of perspective. To use a spatial analogy we might say that this is the vocabulary of the broken line, of the unenclosed, or of the formless. In temporal terms we could describe

319

it as the vocabulary of mutability, of endless movement, or of rest-lessness. The vocabulary of the imagination offers another expression, which I have often had occasion to use and which in human terms offers perhaps the best summary of the complex of ideas and techniques surrounding the figures of Cervantes' narrators—*protean*. The appropriateness of the word in this context goes beyond its descriptive value, for on an important occasion in his writing Cervantes turns to the very myth from which our word etymologically descends to celebrate in cosmic terms his most triumphant surrogate artist.[31]

If the *Gitanilla* describes the departure of the poet from the city and the beginning of his voyage of initiation through the asocial world of the *pícaro, Pedro de Urdemalas* presents the triumphant completion of his journey. In his transformation from the ingenuous Clemente into Pedro de Urdemalas, the poet not only has passed from youth to maturity and profited from the experience of journeys which have taken him at least as far as the Indies, but also has assimilated the vast corpus of wiles and wisdom of the legendary hero of Spanish folklore whose name he bears. The parallels which can be drawn between Cervantes' figure of Proteus and the figures who outwit the academic audiences in the scenes analyzed above are unmistakable. Like Don Quixote in his narration of the events of the underworld encounter with Montesinos, like Cide Hamete Benengeli, a magician who descends from a race of liars, like the counterfeit captives in their fictitious biography, like Periandro in

---

[31] As Jean Rousset has pointed out, the myth of Proteus was very popular in the seventeenth century. The Baroque imagination was fascinated with the mutability of the sublunary world and turned to such myths as Circe and Proteus ("l'homme multiforme dans un monde en métamorphose" [*L'Age baroque*, p. 22]) to recreate the spectacle of the world in flux in the *ballet de cour*. Cervantes was not alone in associating the poet with Proteus. Desmarets sees the artist as a manipulator of illusions, metamorphoses, and spectacles and compares him to the mythical sea god (ibid., p. 78). Similarly one of the masters of Italian *conceptismo*, Francesco Fulvio Frugoni, describes his style in the following words: "Spiegai la stessa verità con divise diverse, per farla meglio intendere con varie sembianze. Mi son ingegnato di proteizzare (mi si condoni la novità del vocabolo) con la diversificatura dell'Eleganza" (cited by Calcaterra, *Il parnaso in rivolta*, p. 134). These views of the Proteus myth should be contrasted with the Renaissance interpretation of the myth in an ethical context (i.e., for Conti, Proteus is the model of prudence and the golden mean [*Mythologiae* (Geneva, 1651), pp. 838-840]). The Renaissance figure of the poet is of course Orpheus.

Impostor or God?

his play with Mauricio, Pedro de Urdemalas is a master in lies and deception. Of all Cervantes' narrators, however, it is Master Pedro-Ginés de Pasamonte whom he most closely resembles. In these two figures the affinities of the poet's powers with those of the impostor and his close relationship to darkness and disorder are most clearly drawn by Cervantes. The origins of both Pedros lie somewhere in the mysterious underworld of criminality which finds literary expression in the picaresque romance. Pedro de Urdemalas is an outcast from society from birth:

> Yo soy hijo de la piedra
> que padre no conoci:
> desdicha de las mayores
> Que a vn hombre pueden venir.
> No se dónde me criaron.[32]

A mysterious destiny bears him on a life of wandering from his unknown place of birth to the distant Indies and to the cities of southern Spain. The *mozo de muchos amos* ("servant of many masters"), he passes rapidly from one to another enjoying the tutelage of such familiar figures in picaresque fiction as the blind man, the cardsharper, the pickpocket, and the ruffian soldier. All that Pedro reveals about his life is implicit in Ginés de Pasamonte's assertion that his biography will replace that of *Lazarillo de Tormes* as the best example of the picaresque genre (*Don Quijote*, I, 208). We hear about or observe both Pedro's and Ginés' capacities to commit the crimes typical of the *pícaro*—the theft of Sancho's ass, the trickery with the monkey, the swindling of the widow, and the robbery of the peasant.

There are other details suggesting that Cervantes conceived these two figures as doubles, and it is these details which link them imaginatively to the creative artist. Both characters have a mysterious power to change shape. Many of Ginés' forms are simply suggested in the analogy which he draws between his life and that of the

[32] "I am a child of the orphanage, one who knew no father, which is one of the greatest misfortunes that can befall a man. I do not know where I was raised." *Pedro de Vrdemalas, Comedias y entremeses*, ed. R. Schevill and A. Bonilla (Madrid, 1918), III, 139. The following page references are to this edition.

pícaro. However, we actually see him appearing first in the garb of the enchained rogue, then in that of a Gypsy, and finally in that of the Italian puppeteer, Master Pedro. The transformations of Pedro de Urdemalas are multiple. He appears on stage as a farmer's servant, as a blind man, as a Gypsy, as a hermit, and as a student.[33] Both figures are linked with dark, supernatural forces. Ginés–Master Pedro's powers of hindsight are attributed to the workings of the devil ("He has the devil within his body"),[34] and provoke a lengthy discussion between Don Quixote and Sancho concerning the difference between the demonic powers of the charlatan and the uses and abuses of the valid science of *astrología judicaria*. Pedro de Urdemalas claims that had he remained in the tutelage of his blind master longer, he would know more than the popular wizard of Arthurian romance, Merlin.[35] One of the details most suggestive of the link between Ginés and Pedro in Cervantes' imagination is the association of both with Ariosto's figure of Brunello, the wily

[33] Changing shape or appearance is of course a process traditionally associated with the "darker side" of poetry (lie, deceit, play, the asocial), from Plato's description of the slippery rhapsode Ion as Proteus to John Keats' "What shocks the virtuous philosopher delights the camelion Poet." Even the classicists of the Renaissance, who generally strove to eliminate the dark side of poetry, could see the rhetorical aspect of poetry in terms of appearance-changing. Giraldi for example claims that the poet must study all fields of knowledge and be like a chameleon, "atto a ricevere ogni colore che gli si appresenti" (*De' romanzi*, p. 214). Like Pedro, Periandro enjoys shape-changing: "Veysme aqui, señores que me estays escuchando, hecho pescador y casamentero rico con mi querida hermana, y pobre sin ella, robado de salteadores, y subido al grado de capitan contra ellos: que las vueltas de mi fortuna no tienen vn punto donde paren, ni terminos que las encierren" (I, 251-252).

[34] ". . . tiene el diablo en el cuerpo" (*Don Quijote*, II, 723).

[35] To be recalled are the traditions associating imaginative literature and the pleasures of the marvelous with diabolical forces and the "poetic" act with lying (see above, Chapter I). The Gypsy world of *La Gitanilla* with its infernal and poetic connections reveals perfectly the close relationship between the act of the magician and the poet according to Cervantes. On affirming the poet's godlike power over his characters, the epic hero Periandro associates poetry with astrology (". . . segun lo hallo yo en mi astrologia" [II, 72]). The traditional kinship of poet and magician is implicitly acknowledged by Tasso in his careful distinction between the poet and the sophist. Both are manipulators of appearances and creators of images; however, the poet's images correspond to a preexistent reality (he "deceives" with the appearance of truth) and appeal to the intellective faculties, while the sophist's images are of nonexistent realities and appeal to the lower faculty of the fantasy. The poet's act is similar to that of the mystic theologian (e.g., Orpheus), while the sophist's act bears analogy to that of the magician (". . . l'arte de' sofisti, che non è dottrina, ma inganno d'apparenzia e arte simile a quella de' prestigitatori" [*Del poema eroico*, pp. 87-90]).

Impostor or God?

Moorish enchanter who performs the incredible feat of stealing the mount of Sacripante from beneath its sleeping master. In describing the theft of Sancho's ass, Cide Hamete writes that Ginés employed "the cunning method which Brunello used when he got Sacripante's steed from between his legs at the siege of Albraca."[36] As Pedro enters the stage disguised as a hermit in preparation for his deception of the widow, the Gypsy Maldonado cannot restrain his astonishment and admiration:

> Brunelo, el grande embaydor,
> ante ti retire el passo.
> Con tan grande industria mides
> lo que tu ingenio trabaja,
> que te ha de dar la ventaja,
> fraudador de los ardides.[37]

Both Pedro and Ginés are endowed with a gift for languages. The latter "had put on Gypsy garb, and he knew how to speak the Gypsy language, as well as many others, as if they were his native languages."[38] The former, referred to on one occasion as "a Demosthenes in his ability to speak," boasts:

> ¡Valgame Dios, que de trages
> he mudado, y que de oficios
> que de varios exercicios.
> que de exquisitos lenguages![39]

These powers of language[40] point toward the redemption of these

[36] ". . . la traza y modo que usó Brunelo cuando, estando Sacripante sobre Albraca, le sacó el caballo de entre las piernas" (*Don Quijote*, II, 738).

[37] "Brunello, the great impostor, must step aside for you. With so much ingenuity do you measure whatever your genius shapes that he must admit your superiority, O trickster of such cunning devices" (pp. 179-180).

[38] ". . . se había puesto en traje de gitano, cuya lengua, y otras muchas, sabía hablar, como si fueran naturales suyas" (I, 309).

[39] "Good heavens! What costumes I have changed! What various trades and professions and what exquisite languages!" (p. 211).

[40] It should be recalled that Cervantes associates both Master Pedro's assistant at the puppet show and Periandro during his narration with the contemporary emblem depicting Hercules as the symbol of eloquence. Similarly powers over language are humorously associated with the counterfeit captives in their feigned history: "vno dellos . . . con voz clara y en todo estremo esperta lengua" (II, 101); "Admirado estaua Periandro y todos los mas de los circunstantes . . . de la velocidad con

323

figures, who hover so precariously at the brink of the fallen world of the *pícaro*. For in Cervantes' work language is both an image of the impalpable world of human experience, which is ever falling away from a central order toward perspectivistic fragmentation, and an instrument of order in the hand of the creating artist. Cervantes' preoccupation with linguistic fragmentation is observable both in the instability of proper names throughout his writings[41] and in his portrayal of the breakdown of human society into units, each with its own linguistic distinction. (We have only to recall Don Quixote's bewilderment before the language of the galley slaves, the necessity for initiating Rinconete and Cortadillo into the mysteries of the *hampa*'s argot, Preciosa's *ceceo*, Don Quixote's and Sancho's verbal misunderstandings which point to their respective experiential milieus, and Cervantes' deliberate introduction of the "linguistic barrier" between nations everywhere in the *Persiles*—the significance of the phenomenon here points beyond literary precedent, namely, Heliodorus, and the literary theories on verisimilitude of Tasso.)[42] Language everywhere reflects the diversity of the sublunary universe, but at the same time language is the medium by which the artist can create from this diversity a coherent order. It is the *divino don de la habla* in the words of another of Cervantes' many rhetorically conscious narrators, the dog Berganza, whose quest through a world of festivity and deceit is rewarded with this divine power for one night.[43]

Cervantes does not delay in emphasizing Pedro de Urdemalas' comprehension of the importance of perspective in human experience and his transcendence of linguistic fragmentation. In the opening scene the shepherd Clemente seeks his advice in his unsuccessful

---

que hablaua" (II, 107); "Por dios—dixo el segundo alcalde—, que este mancebo ha hablado bien, aunque ha hablado mucho" (II, 108).

[41] See Leo Spitzer, "Linguistic Perspectivism in the *Don Quijote*," in *Linguistics and Literary History* (Princeton, 1948; paper, 1967), pp. 41-85.

[42] It should be pointed out that the "linguistic difference" can at times have a moral significance: The language of the Turks and Moors is opposed to Spanish (i.e., *hablar cristiano*) and is a demonic attribute in the story of the *Cautivo*. The *ceceo* of the Gypsies, Cervantes assures us, is the product of art and not nature; it is a perversion of nature. The jargon of the *hampa* is similarly a sign of its perversion of values. The thunderous, unintelligible language of the barbarians in the *Persiles* is symbolic of their diabolic character.

[43] *Coloquio de los perros*, ed. cit., p. 213.

courtship of Clemencia. In his response Pedro reveals that human beings view love in a variety of ways and that their differing attitudes are reflected in different styles or levels of language.

> *Ped.* ¿Han llegado tus desseos
> a mas que dulces floreos,
> o has tocado en el lugar
> donde amor suele fundar
> el centro de sus empleos?
> *Cle.* Pues sabes que soy pastor,
> entona mas baxo el punto,
> habla con menos primor.
> *Ped.* Que si eres, te pregunto,
> Amadis o Galaor.
> *Cle.* No soy sino Anton Clemente,
> y andas, Pedro, impertinente
> en hablar por tal camino.
> *Ped.* Pan por pan, vino por vino,
> se ha de hablar con esta gente.
> ¿Haste visto con Clemencia
> a solas o en parte escura,
> donde ella te dio licencia
> de alguna desemboltura
> que encargasse la conciencia?[44]

In this masterpiece of stylistic gradation we observe three ways of asking the same question in descending degrees of literary refinement, from the metaphorical fineries of those initiated to conventional love lyrics, to the topical allusions familiar to the broad reading public, to the most literal level of communication—*pan por pan*. The styles reflect three distinct attitudes toward the erotic, ranging from an aesthetic exaltation reminiscent of the courtly love

[44] "*Ped.*: Have your longings achieved but sweet trilling flourishes, or have you played upon that place where love is wont to fix the center of his uses? *Cle.*: But you know I am a shepherd. Pitch the tone of your speech lower, speak with less high-strung charm. *Ped.*: Are you, I ask, Amadis or Galaor? *Cle.*: I am Anton Clemente and no other, and you, Pedro, speaking thus, walk the road of impertinence. *Ped.*: You have to call bread bread, wine wine, when you talk with these folk. Have you ever been with Clemencia alone or in some dark place where she gave you leave to take liberties that would weigh upon your conscience?" (p. 119).

tradition to an austere moralism characteristic of traditional Christianity, and including in the middle range a humorous tolerance of what is admittedly a sin.

On another occasion Pedro's consciousness of perspectivism and linguistic problems is contrasted with the indifference of the world around him. The rhythm pattern of the *romance* form of one of his speeches forces him to pronounce *mártir* with an accent on the final syllable. He employs the following line to offer a correction, as it were, emerging from the work of art to confront it from the perspective of a critical member of the audience: "mártir, digo, Maldonado." Maldonado's reply not only underscores the *Verfremdungseffekt* but also reveals his indifference to the literary problem and his ignorance of the momentary change of perspective.

> En esso, ¿que me va a mi?
> Pronunciad como os de gusto,
> pues que no hablays latin.[45]

In addition to the control of language there is another important quality of the artist shared by Pedro de Urdemalas and Ginés de Pasamonte—namely a richness of the fantasy and a desire to bring the world of the imagination and that of everyday life into contact. We have observed how Master Pedro offers the spectacle of his magical *retablo* to give pleasure to Don Quixote and the other guests of the inn and how he defends its imaginary world from the quibblings of the neo-Aristotelians, who would insist that art yield to the demands of empirical reality. Pedro de Urdemalas continually associates himself with the fantasy (e.g., "My fantasy embraces everything; it would be master of the entire world"), and undertakes the mission of providing the world with the pleasures of the imagination. From the opening line of the play ("De tu ingenio, Pedro amigo" [p. 118]), attention is drawn to Pedro's *ingenio*. Behind Cervantes' association of this term with Pedro and all his other surrogate poets[46] is a deep literary tradition, originating in

---

[45] "In such matters, what difference does it make to me? Pronounce as you please, as long as you do not speak Latin" (p. 141).

[46] Ginés de Pasamonte–Master Pedro (I, 209), Periandro (I, 264), the counterfeit captives (II, 107), and, of course, *el ingenioso hidalgo*, Don Quixote. Recent studies have dealt with the aberrant *ingenio* of Don Quixote, approaching it as a clinical phenomenon and explaining the psychological verisimilitude of the hero's madness

classical antiquity and culminating in the Baroque poetics of Emanuele Tesauro and Baltasar Gracián. From Quintilian to Tesauro *ingenium* was used to describe the inventive faculty of the poet, the faculty which functions through flashes of creative insight rather than the use of reason, and which takes delight in producing new and startling creations.[47] This literary implication of *ingenio* is perhaps most clearly presented in the magistrate's words of admiration for Pedro: ". . . vn moço que se me fue,/ de ingenio agudo y sotil,/ de tronchos de coles se/ que hiziera inuenciones mil."[48]

Cervantes' juxtaposition of Pedro to the magistrate, the embodiment of reason, law, and the social order, and the latter's recognition that Pedro is more prudent than a priest or a doctor (p. 125) represent a symbolic victory of the imagination in the world of practicality. Here the powers of the fantasy are such that it can in fact turn the world of practicality upside down, re-creating it according to its own desires. For the sentences which Pedro supplies the mayor to solve his juridical dilemmas are acclaimed not for their wisdom, but rather for their aesthetic value. They will give the world the pleasures of the marvelous and variety.

> Yo os metere en la capilla
> dos docenas de sentencias
> que al mundo den marauilla,
> todas con sus diferencias,
> ciuiles, o de renzilla.[49]

---

in relation to the contemporary physiological-psychological theories as set forth in Huarte de San Juan's *Examen de ingenios* (see above). While these studies are of unquestionable value and have illuminated much that had remained obscure until this century, the psychological implications of the term *ingenio* should not blind us to its significance in literary and oratorical tradition.

[47] See Friedrich, *Epochen der Italienischen Lyrik*, pp. 604, 628-636; Ezio Raimondi, "Ingegno e metafora nella poetica del Tesauro," *Letteratura barocca* (Florence, 1961), pp. 1-32. While it is evident that Cervantes' narrators do not represent the aesthetic goals of stupefying an audience through dazzling metaphor and creating an entirely fantastic poetic world through bold combinations of incongruous realities, both encompassed by Tesauro's theory of *ingegno*, they do, nevertheless, represent the liberation of the artist's inventive powers and the allowance for his working in the realm of the imagination.

[48] ". . . a servant left me, one whose creative faculty was so quick and subtle that he would make a thousand inventions out of the stalks of cabbages" (p. 161).

[49] "I shall put in your bonnet two dozen sentences, that will cause the world to marvel, ranging from civil to quarrelsome matters" (pp. 125-126).

The Cervantine Figure of the Poet

In all of his writings there is perhaps no clearer statement of the importance which Cervantes attaches to the spirit of play in the poetic undertaking.[50] In planning the dances with which Belica and the Gypsies will entertain the king and the queen, the talented Pedro returns to the theme of giving the world pleasure:

> ...mi Belilla
> con su donayre y sus ojos,
> os quitará mil enojos,
> dandoos gusto y marauilla.[51]

It is in the relationship between Belica and Pedro that the transformation of the *pícaro* into the triumphant figure of the artist is most evident. Indeed without the thread of Belica's ascent the work would be little more than a chaotic series of episodes centering on Pedro's picaresque affinities. A mysterious bond unites the roguish figure with the beautiful Christian girl, who, as an illegitimate child of the queen's brother, had been abandoned to the Gypsies in her infancy. Pedro has heard a prophecy of the famous magician Malgesi that he will one day be king, friar, and pope. Although he doubts that such absurdities can come to pass, he allows himself to believe in them ("Still I find in myself a mysterious inclination to strive to be everything which I heard").[52] In Belica's first appearance in the play she is associated with a similar absurd wish: she has

[50] "Play, we said, lies outside the reasonableness of practical life; has nothing to do with necessity or utility, or duty, or truth" (J. Huizinga, *Homo Ludens* [London, 1949], p. 158). To the extent that *utility*, *duty*, and *truth* are fundamental concepts in the classicist's view of art, *play* can never have a dominant role in the classical aesthetic. In view of the importance which Cervantes' surrogate poets attach to pleasure and play in art and their apparent indifference to the canon's *prodesse*, it is worth recalling Cervantes' judgment of *Don Quixote* in his late work, *Viage del Parnaso* (pp. 54-55):

> Yo he dado en *Don Quixote* passatiempo
> al pecho melancolico y mohino,
> en qualquiera sazon, en todo tiempo.

To be sure, it can be said that the conception of the *Persiles* represents a turn toward the *prodesse* on the part of the author, but we have already pointed out how Cervantes cannot successfully silence the artistic voice represented by Pedro de Urdemalas and his other artist-showmen in his final work.

[51] "... with her grace and her charming eyes my Belilla will unburden you of a thousand vexations, bringing you pleasure and causing you to marvel" (p. 187).

[52] "... todavia veo en mi/ vn no se que que me inclina/ a ser todo lo que oi" (p. 144).

328

just dreamt that she is a countess and an intimate of the king. Scolded by her companion Ynes for entertaining such thoughts ("Flee from such fantasies"—"Huye dessas fantasias" [p. 155]), she persists like Pedro in believing the impossible, expecting the hand of destiny to direct her ascent from the Gypsy world to the palace, and counters: "Let me follow my star" ("dexame seguir mi estrella" [p. 154]). Only Pedro understands her hopes and treats them with sympathy. She begs him not to mock her, saying: "From afar a hope reveals itself to me, and in it I discover a certain light which guides and bears me to the fortune which I desire."[53] Pedro's answer, which closes the first act, points toward the fairy-tale dream of the child: "When one beholds such rare beauty as yours, one can expect that it will be matched by good fortune" ("De tu rara hermosura/ se puede esperar ventura/ que la yguale" [p. 160]).

From this moment on Pedro begins to preside over the fulfillment of Belica's wish, which will parallel the fulfillment of his own. In the second act he defends her from the abuse with which the world of common sense treats her desires. Identifying himself with the dreaming maiden, he affirms the value of the imagination in life and celebrates his own powers of imagination in cosmic terms:

> *Mal.* veo que esta gitanilla,
> quanto su estado la humilla,
> tanto mas leuanta el buelo,
> y aspira a tocar el cielo
> con locura y marauilla
>
> *Ped.* Dexala, que muy bien haze,
> y no la estimes en menos
> por esso: que a mi me aplaze
> que con soberuios barrenos
> sus maquinas suba y trace.
> Yo tambien, que soy vn leño,
> principe y papa me sueño,
> emperador y monarca,

[53] ". . . de lexos se me muestra/ vna esperança en quien veo/ cierta luz tal, que me adiestra/ y lleua al bien que desseo."

The Cervantine Figure of the Poet

y aun mi fantasia abarca
de todo el mundo a ser dueño.[54]

Pedro employs the money which he has gained by defrauding the widow to make Belica's wish come true. The swindle itself is another of the triumphs of the imagination which fill the career of the charlatan. He uses his inventive powers to conjure forth a vision of the sister's sufferings in Purgatory and, like Master Pedro's assistant, captures the belief of his audience in his fictions. As if the reminiscences of Dante were not enough to suggest Pedro's affinities with the poet (the sister is suffering in a sepulcher covered by a bronze plate and calls to the wayfarer: "Si es que te lastima/ el dolor que aqui te llora,/ tu que vas al mundo agora,/ a mi hermana y a mi prima/ diras que en su voluntad/ està el salir destas nieblas/ a la inmensa claridad"),[55] he begins his speech with an invocation of memory to aid him in achieving accreditation of his lie:

> Memoria, no desfallezcas,
> ni por algun acidente
> silencio a la lengua ofrezcas;
>
> . . . .
>
> en los semblantes me muda
> que con aquesta viuda
> me acrediten, hasta tanto
> que la dexen con espanto
> contenta, pero desnuda.[56]

[54] "*Mal.*: I see that this little Gypsy girl, the more her station humbles her, the higher she attempts to soar and the more she aspires to reach the heavens with marvelous madness. *Ped.*: Leave her in peace; she is doing very well. Do not hold her in less esteem because of this. It pleases me that she devises and sets up her projects with haughtiness and vanity. I too, who am a dullard, dream of being prince and pope, emperor and monarch, and *my fantasy even aspires to embrace everything; it would be master of the entire world*" (p. 173). The italics are mine. Pedro's words recall those of another of Cervantes' surrogate poets, Cide Hamete Benengeli, who boasts that he has "habilidad, suficiencia, y entendimiento para tratar del universo todo" (II, 849).

[55] "If by chance the suffering which is weeping here before you moves you to pity, you who will now return to the world, you will tell my sister and my cousin that it is in their power to bring me out of these shadows and into the immense clarity" (pp. 196-197).

[56] "Memory, do not weaken, nor by some accident bring silence to my tongue;

Impostor or God?

Memory is of course the mother of the Muses and is traditionally invoked by the epic poet (e.g., Dante, *Inferno*, II; Tasso, *Gerusalemme liberata*, I). All this makes for a delightful interlude of literary parody, strengthening at the same time the association of Pedro, swindling, and poetry.

Pedro is aware of the power of Belica's beauty and grace and devotes his criminal profits to her adornment ("Quanto este dinero alcança, se ha de gastar in la dança/ y en tu [Belica] adorno, porque quiero/ que por galas ni dinero/ no malogres tu esperança").[57] All proceeds in accordance with his highest hopes: the king cannot resist the maiden's attractions; the jewels that had been placed in her swaddling clothes turn up as the traditional vehicle of anagnorisis; and the old courtier Marcelo reveals to the bewildered queen the maiden's illustrious parentage.

At this moment of climax, in which Belica finds herself elevated from the station of a lowly Gypsy to that of a princess, Pedro de Urdemalas appears alone on the stage in his greatest triumph. In his soliloquy he appears as an incarnation of the endless mutability of the sublunary world, conceived not in the perspective of Christian asceticism (the popular *vanitas* motif), but rather viewed as a grand spectacle in God's universal comedy. The aesthetic implications of the vision are drawn as Pedro explains the pleasure that the contemplation of endless variety affords:

> Dizen que la variacion
> haze a la naturaleza
> colma de gusto y belleza
> y està muy puesto en razon.
> Vn manjar a la contina
> enfada, y vn solo objeto
> a los ojos del discreto
> da disgusto y amohina.
> Vn solo vestido cansa.

... vary my features and expression in such a way that they accredit me with this widow and leave her in a contented fright, but stripped of everything" (p. 194).

[57] "Whatever the money amounts to, it is to be spent on the dances and on your [Belica's] adornment, because I do not want you to fail to realize your hope for want of fine dress or money" (p. 199).

The Cervantine Figure of the Poet

> En fin, con la variedad
> se muda la voluntad,
> y el espiritu descansa.[58]

He proceeds to associate himself with the principle of variety and here invokes the myth of Proteus to celebrate his participation in the plenitude of the sublunary universe:

> Bien logrado yre del mundo
> quando Dios me lleue del,
> pues podre dezir que en el
> vn Proteo fuy segundo.[59]

He concludes the soliloquy by embracing his destiny to be borne about the world according to God's unknowable designs:

> Si ha de estar siempre nuestra alma
> en continuo mouimiento,
> Dios me arroje ya a las partes
> donde mas fuere seruido.[60]

Pedro's explanation of the effect of variety on the will and the soul ("con la variedad/ se muda la voluntad,/ y el espiritu des-

---

[58] "It is said that variation makes nature an inexhaustible source of pleasure and beauty, and it is well said. One fine food served continuously becomes annoying, and a single object displeases and vexes the eyes of the fastidious man. A single dress is tiresome. In short, with variety desire can move about and the spirit rests" (pp. 210-211).
To appreciate the aesthetic implications of the soliloquy, we should recall that the analogy between the work of art and a banquet was common in the poetics of the time. It appears in the *Persiles* on at least two occasions (II, 72, 100). Pedro's speech recalls Cide Hamete's plea for variety and his assertion that writing of a *solo sujeto* is unbearable (II, 848).

[59] "Well fulfilled shall I leave this world when God takes me from it, for I shall be able to say that in it I was a second Proteus." Viewed within the literary tradition of comedy, Pedro in his role as manipulator of the comic action is an *eiron* figure, a descendant of the tricky slave of Plautus. In the first episode of the play Pedro's role is very traditional, as he arranges the marriage of Clemente and Clemencia by outwitting the maiden's father and overcoming his opposition to the union. In his disguising and shape-changing he resembles other contemporary developments of the traditional figure, the vice of the morality plays and Shakespeare's Ariel. As Frye points out such traditional figures embody the spirit of comedy itself. (See *Anatomy of Criticism*, pp. 175-176.)

[60] "If our souls are to be ever in continuous movement, may God cast me wherever I might serve Him best."

cansa"), as well as his allusion to the movements of the soul, is significant as it surrounds the aesthetic implications of the speech and the "darker side" of the artist's mission and all that it entails (lying, deception, disguise, play) with Christian overtones. As Augustine repeatedly reminds us, in the earthly life our souls are ever in motion, seeking that repose which they can find only in God.[61] Cervantes emphasizes here that the repose of the soul is dependent on its experiencing and assimilating (*mudarse*, "to change" and and "to reclothe," as in an initiation) the variety of the earthly world. I do not think that the Christian implications are strong enough to warrant the conclusion that Cervantes sees the artist fulfilling a function within the Christian teleology or usurping the powers of the priest. I rather think that, by appropriating the language of divinity, he suggests that the artist as Proteus is a type of god of a fallen kingdom, who offers his creations to his subjects as spectacles of the variety, flux, and illusion which form the fabric of that kingdom and which the Christian soul must experience on its earthly journey.

Following Belica's success, Pedro fulfills his own wish by becoming an actor. The transformation is solemnized in both cases by rebaptism; Belica becomes Isabel; Pedro becomes Nicolas de Rios. He will henceforth be a *quimera*, gaining fame throughout the world as he represents man in all his variety in the universal comedy. His words to Belica underscore the parallelism in their destinies:

> Tu presuncion y la mia
> han llegado a conclusion:
> la mia sóla en ficcion,
> la tuya como deuia.
>
> . . . .
>
> Yo, farsante, sere rey
> quando le aya en la comedia,

[61] See for example "In Thy Gift we rest; there we enjoy Thee. Our rest is our place. . . . When out of order, they are restless; restored to order, they are at rest" (*The Confessions*, tr. E. B. Pusey, Everyman's Library [London, 1926], p. 315). The idea is very important in Cervantes' conception of the *Persiles*; it recurs in one variation or another throughout the work (see I, 100-101; II, 5; II, 268; II, 290).

y, tu, oyente, ya eres media
reyna por valor y ley.[62]

Here we observe the point of intersection between the realms of
the imagination and the real, between the stage, on which Pedro
enjoys the fulfillment of his dreams, and the world of the audience,
in which Belica suddenly finds herself reclothed in the garb of a
princess. For both figures, the impossible has been realized, and who
is to say whether the triumph of the maiden is any more real than
that of the rogue, whether the law is any more valid a guarantor
of reality than the imagination? For Pedro is gifted with the divine
knowledge that the measure of reality in this world of mutability
resides in the perspective of the onlooker, and that, as one moves
away from the surface of the teeming phenomena, all outlines and
distinctions tend to dissolve, and one approaches the vantage point
of divinity.

The brief, farcical episode which immediately follows his invocation of the myth of Proteus is a dramatic presentation of Pedro's
mastery of the art of the variable perspective. He attempts to persuade a witless peasant to offer him his chickens as a gesture of
charity and to take pleasure in their transformation into venerated
relics:

Andad con Dios y dexaldas,
y desde lexos miraldas,
como a reliquias honraldas,
para el culto dedicaldas,
bucolico, y adoraldas.[63]

Significantly the peasant is bewildered by Pedro's language and
immediately reveals his inability to overstride the limits of his
single perspective and see *desde lexos*. For him chickens represent
labor and wealth: "Como me las pague, haga/ altar o reliquias

[62] "Your bold presumption and mine have reached their conclusions: mine only
in fiction, yours, as it should be . . . I, an actor, shall be king whenever there is one
in the comedy, and you, a spectator, are already half a queen by law and merit" (p.
223).
[63] "Take your leave, and leave them here; contemplate them from afar; honor
them as relics; dedicate them for the bucolic cult and adore them" (p. 212).

dellas,/ o lo que mas satisfaga a su gusto."[64] It is indeed the distance which Pedro retains in contemplating the occurrences of this world which links him to God. From beyond the circle of the moon chickens can be relics of a charitable act, the bucolic offspring of a poet's fantasy, or dollars and cents. It makes little difference. Similarly the distinction between the fictional ascent of Pedro and the real one of Belica vanishes; for, seen from that distant point, the whole world becomes a theater and Pedro's kingdom, a play within a larger play. As Don Quixote reminds Sancho, "There is no comparison which presents to us more truly what we are and what we ought to be than the play and the players. Now, tell me, have not you seen a play acted with kings, emperors and popes, knights, ladies, and various other personages? . . . and, when the play is over, and they have taken off their dresses, all the actors are equal."[65]

If death strips off all the masks and reduces their wearers to their fundamental moral reality, life nevertheless remains with all its "superficial" distinctions. Insofar as it concerns the role of the artist, it can be said that Cervantes turns the old theater topic inside out, focusing on the gaiety of the disguises and the masks rather than on the somber director, reminding man how he lives rather than how he should prepare to die. Indeed the work of art itself must come to be an image of that colorful lack of finality that marks human ex-

---

[64] "As long as you pay me for them, make of them an altar or relics or whatever pleases you." It is once again well to observe the extent to which this small scene of farce, which appears to be one of the least relevant episodes of an episodic drama, falls within the literary tradition of comedy. The peasant is one of the conventional forms of the "refuser of festivity, the killjoy who tries to stop the fun, or, like Malvolio, locks up the food and drink instead of dispensing it" (Frye, *Anatomy of Criticism*, p. 176). In "locking up his chickens," and seeing only dollars and cents, where Pedro sees a variety, Cervantes' peasant provides a foil for the wit of Pedro as well as an embodiment of the practical, and as such a marker of the range beyond which the mood of festivity cannot pass. Within the context of Cervantes' play, however, the apotheosis of Pedro achieves the destruction of this marker. In the introduction of the problem of perspectives and the implications which the the problem has concerning the artist's function, the scene departs from tradition and points toward the peculiarly Cervantine.

[65] ". . . ninguna comparación hay que más al vivo nos represente lo que somos y lo que habemos de ser como la comedia y los comediantes. Si no, dime: ¿no has visto tú representar alguna comedia adonde se introducen reyes, emperadores y pontífices, caballeros, damas y otros diversos personajes? . . . y acabada la comedia y desnudándose de los vestidos della, quedan todos los recitantes iguales" (II, 617).

perience. Like everything else it too is an illusion, and part of its impact depends on its reminding the audience of its illusory quality. This is why all Cervantes' surrogate artists insist on letting the audience observe them as they put on and take off their masks. In effect they all, like Pedro, stride toward the footlights and say, "This I did because I, like you, am in a play, and, as we all know, the play must not be taken too seriously."[66]

The comparison of Master Pedro and Pedro de Urdemalas yields a final insight into what takes place in Cervantes' play. Master Pedro's success in transforming the imaginary into the real brings catastrophic consequences for his professional career and leads to the reestablishment of a rigid boundary between reality and fiction. In the aftermath of Don Quixote's onslaught, the King of Zaragoza is viewed as a headless *papier-mâché* figure valued at four and one-half *reales*. In becoming prince, pope, and emperor, Pedro de Urdemalas not only gains the kingdom which Master Pedro has lost ("Not half an hour ago, indeed not half a minute ago, I was the master of kings and emperors, my stables were full"),[67] but also succeeds in destroying the boundary between the world and the stage. Fiction and reality momentarily hang in counterpoise, and neither seems to have the greater claim on truth. However, while Pedro presides over the metamorphosis of a Gypsy maiden into a

---

[66] In his *El retablo de las maravillas* Cervantes presents the triumph of another of his artist-showmen, Chanfalla. In addition to its satirical commentary on human weaknesses and social preoccupations of seventeenth-century Spaniards, in addition to its brilliant theatricality and comedy of situation and character, the little farce contains a clear statement of some of Cervantes' basic views of the artistic undertaking: the writer presents truth through the manipulation of illusion. Desire and fear are at the center of the audience's apprehension of a work of art, and the artist often addresses himself to such emotions. And finally, by reminding the audience of the fictional character of his work, the writer both increases the impact of its meaning and reminds the audience of the illusory quality of life itself. In surely one of the most ingeniously contrived *Verfremdungseffekte* in literature, Chanfalla brings the Jewish temptress Herodias onto the stage after announcing that nobody of Jewish ancestry can see the participants of his spectacle, who of course do not exist. One of the more alert members of the audience perceives the violation of logic and asks: "Pero si ésta es judía, ¿cómo ve estas maravillas?" Chanfalla mischievously replies: "Todas las reglas tienen excepción, señor alcalde" (*Obras completas*, p. 584).

[67] "No ha media hora, ni aun un mediano momento, que me vi señor de reyes y de emperadores, llenas mis caballerizas . . ." (II, 735).

princess, a judge requests his marvelous sentences, and a king forgets the affairs of state to follow his dances. One could say that the stage has absorbed the audience, that, in terms of the traditional metaphor, the world has become the mirror of the stage.

CONCLUSION

Classicism, Truth, and the Novel

THE AMBIVALENCE marking Cervantes' engagement with neo-Aristotelian literary theory may remain ultimately irreducible and be taken as another vindication of that useful catch-phrase of Cervantine criticism, the "two Cervantes." It is indeed tempting to add to the various traditional dualities—the romantic-realist of Menéndez Pelayo, the reactionary-progressive of De Lollis, the sincere hypocrite of Ortega and Castro, and the "Cervantes der Urerlebnisse–Cervantes der Bildungserlebnisse" of Hatzfeld—that of a Cervantes pro-Aristotle and a Cervantes contra-Aristotle. In fact such a distinction would confirm Hatzfeld's view: if Cervantes was attracted to classical theories because of their cultural prestige, this would be an "inauthentic" *Bildungserlebnis*, as opposed to the "authentic" *Urerlebnisse* responsible for his critique of those very theories.

The disadvantage of such a scheme is not primarily its implicit value judgment—the "good" vs. the "bad" Cervantes—but rather its suggested dissociation of Cervantes' great creative achievement—*Don Quixote*—from his critical thinking. There is, I think, in Cervantes' movement toward Aristotle something far more profound than his admiration for such figures as Tasso, Virgil, and Heliodorus and his disappointment over the success of Lope's non-classical drama. Both Cervantes and the neo-Aristotelians shared a belief that art must deal responsibly with truth and that conventional popular literature had failed to meet this responsibility. Against the common enemy, literary genres which cast human experience in the molds of the wish-fulfillment dream, disregard the limitations which reason discovers everywhere in experience, and in effect decline to make a meaningful statement about reality, Cervantes could join with the classicists in a united front.

However, at some point Cervantes realized that, lurking behind the central critical issue of Renaissance literary theorizing—the necessity of truth in literature—was a problem far more bewildering—the nature of truth itself. Like his greatest contemporaries he knew that neither of the traditional sources of truth, faith and

339

reason, was entirely adequate as a source of order in the variegated and intractable province of human experience. If experience mocks the order demanded by our dreams and embodied in the idealizing literary genres, it is no less cruel with all systems which our rational faculties can create. While never questioning the order of faith, Cervantes is continually turning experience back both on reason and desire to show their limitations. The inadequacy of Don Quixote's simple concept of justice is revealed in his encounter with people for whom such a system will not suffice. In the humanist cousin's conversation with Sancho Panza, the limits of the great Renaissance faith in knowledge and books as the ultimate source of wisdom suddenly come into sharp relief. At the same time, when Sancho reveals his ignorance of grammar and the goatherds gape in bewilderment at Don Quixote's speech about the Golden Age, the Renaissance faith in man's natural wisdom appears to be inadequate. The contradictory experience of various lovers in Cervantes' works gives the lie to all his spokesmen for conventional codes of courtship and love, who freely offer their wisdom concerning the great foundation of social order—marriage. And the judicial dilemmas which governor Sancho faces, and his personal, arbitrary manner of resolving them, dramatically reveal the limitations of perhaps the most elaborate system by which society deals with the variety of situations possible in experience, its codes of laws.

What is true? What is false? Cervantes' works are full of characters who are preoccupied with truth—the sober merchants of Toledo, who refuse to accept as true Don Quixote's description of Dulcinea without the proof of a picture; Sancho, who is concerned to show Don Alvaro Tarfe the important differences between the "true" Sancho and the "false" Sancho of Avellaneda; the humanist cousin, who seeks documentation and authority for the most ridiculous facts imaginable; Don Quixote as he employs an impeccable syllogism to prove that Sancho could not have ridden Clavileño through the region of fire; Cide Hamete as he playfully maintains that the incident of the Cave of Montesinos is apocryphal; the narrator of the *Persiles* as he discusses the "truth" of the Ruperta episode; the dogs Cipión and Berganza, who are not certain that their experiences are not a dream; and the bewildered Campuzano as he is prepared to "jurar con juramento que obligue, y aun fuerce, a que lo crea la misma incredulidad" that his "coloquio" is true. One has the feeling that all these seekers of truth are no more successful than those four tormented rationalists whose gigantic efforts to find the philosopher's stone, to square the circle, to write the perfect poem, and to cure the economic ills of Spain have led them no farther than Cervantes' most colorful microcosm of this world of desire and frustration—the sweat house in Valladolid.

If experience inevitably bursts through all boundaries erected by reason, it is because the human being himself is a protean creature, a complex agglomerate of desires and fears, beliefs, attitudes, and values, all of which are continually in flux as they collide and interact with one another and with the forces of their environment. As Don Quixote reminds Sancho, fear can make the eyes see many things ("turbar los sentidos y hacer que las cosas no parezcan lo que son"). The way in which desire can loosen a person's grasp on reality is illustrated in nearly every major character drawn by Cervantes, from the deluded Don Quixote to the cynical Teresa Panza. The classical example of Cervantes' perspectivism is of course the barber's basin, which can represent "un real de a ocho como un maravedí" for Sancho, a necessary tool of the trade for its owner, a warrior's helmet for Don Quixote, and in the hands of the artist an instrument functioning in the statement of a sad truth about existence. As Zoraida reminds her father, the act of a human being can appear at the same time necessary and just to one person and unspeakably cruel to another. To a mind uneducated in the evils that go along with the human condition, society's hand of justice may seem barbarously harsh. Throughout the *Quixote* the opposition between *ser* and *parecer* continues to confront the reader, and it would seem that below the circle of the moon *parecer* is the far more relevant verb.

This is not to say that Cervantes attempts to undermine religion, conventional morality, and the established order of the state. A Catholic and a patriot, a man who defended Christendom in what he called the greatest event of history and who spent years in the prisons of the infidel, Cervantes knew that there are certain truths and certain values beyond question and that, when man prepares to die, he dare not "take the other life in jest" (*burlarse con la otra vida*). Moreover, he was aware that in the eye of God all the complexity of human experience, all the variety and disproportion which delight Pedro de Urdemalas, vanishes. As the priest tells the despairing sinner Doña Ana in *El rufián dichoso*:

> Es Dios un bien infinito
> Y, a respeto de quien es,
> Cuanto imaginas y ves
> viene a ser punto finito.[1]

Cervantes would probably not press the argument with his various spokesmen for faith and reason, who claim that the safest way to deal with experience is to stay at home—Sansón Carrasco, Pero Pérez, the ecclesiastic at the duke's palace, the Castilian on the street of Barcelona, the niece and the housekeeper, Diego de la Llana, Inés, who counsels Belica to stay in her kitchen, and Auristela, who, fearful of the perils of the return journey to Tile, tells Periandro that it is safer to take the shortest route to heaven and decides to enter a convent. Midway between the extremes of the ascetic's self-denial and the fantasist's self-indulgence, between the cloister and the open road, stands Cervantes' embodiment of faith and reason, Diego de Miranda, the Caballero del Verde Gabán, and despite Cide Hamete Benengeli's lack of interest in his house, which he compares to a Carthusian monastery, this Christian gentleman speaks so persuasively that more than one critic has accepted his defense of reason, moderation, charity, and the house, as coming from Cervantes' heart.

Although the spokesmen for the house and the social-religious order which it represents usually triumph in his works, it is clear that Cervantes believed that man will always spend much of his life beyond those convenient walls and that life is truly interesting because he does so. In his greatest work, Cervantes does not bring the uncertainties of the earthly life under the rule of the certainties of the life everlasting. On the contrary, he gives full play to all those elements of humanity that must be ignored as somehow trivial

---

[1] God is an infinite Good, and beside Him, all that you can imagine and see amounts to a finite point.

or irrelevant when life is reduced to the conceptual scheme provided by law and religion. In other works, notably in the *Persiles*, a type of "divine comedy," Cervantes is prepared for such a reduction; in the *Quixote*, he is not.

Cervantes' relativism has been masterfully explored by such writers as Ortega, Castro, Casalduero, and Spitzer, and their conclusions scarcely need any repeating here. However, his dialogue with classicism and his ultimately anticlassical stance must be seen in the fundamental context which they have illuminated. It is not simply that the *sic-et-non* characteristic of his critique of experience generates an argument for both sides of the specific literary controversies—i.e., reason-emotion, edification-pleasure, *culto-vulgo*, the verisimilar-the marvelous, unity-variety, Tasso-Ariosto. Nor is it simply that classicism is the greatest system which the Renaissance created in aesthetics, but like all systems subject to grave limitations when confronted by real experience. It is rather that classicism, in asking the right questions about the artistic undertaking, was, like Cervantes' classicist *par excellence*, the Canon of Toledo, somewhat shortsighted in looking for the answers. Underlying its edifice were certain fundamental assumptions which it never called into question—that the universe is indeed well-ordered, that human reality can be reduced to a finite number of abstractions, that man's ethical life can be guided by unambiguous principles, and that, through reason, the mind can comprehend and communicate the universal order. Coupled with such faith in reason and truth was its distrust of the "lower" faculties and all art which indulged the fantasy and the emotions. Classicism's institutionalization of abstractions as the subject of the artist brought with it an impoverishment of his domain, and its strictures of theory were in a sense as menacing as those imposed by the paradigms of romance literature.

The principles of decorum, verisimilitude, unity, and exemplarity were convenient guideposts for creative activity, but the area which they circumscribed was very narrow. Beyond such limits the vast province which Montaigne had called "experience" lay excluded from artistic exploitation—the fluid interplay between real human beings as well as the inner realm of subjectivity, the blend of imagination and reality which makes every man an individual world. Cervantes chose to make experience the subject of his art, and he was acutely conscious of the revolutionary character of such an undertaking. Aware of the strength of his greatest adversary, he had to respond to Aristotle. If it is undeniably true that the modern novel is born in the critique of literary unreality, it is no less true that a critique of literary theory had to sanction that process. Cervantes remains a greater novelist than theorist, and his creative response to literary problems, greater than his theoretical response. However, he is not the mediocre theorist which critical opinion has consistently portrayed, perhaps relying too heavily on Cervantes' own self-deprecating description of himself: "el ingenio lego."

Throughout the *Quixote*, and oddly enough in the "classical" *Persiles*, we observe a process which we could describe as the birth struggle of the modern novel, a drama of disengagement as the new literary form breaks free from the strictures which ages had created. Cervantes applies his familiar methods of dealing with experiential phenomena and reductive systems, confronting the classical dogma with both experience and rational argument. Sancho Panza exasperates the classicist translator by speaking in a way in which, according to the classical doctrines of decorum, peasants cannot speak. Similarly a knight recounts what is obviously a falsehood, in spite of the bewildered historian's principle that knights do not lie. When Don Quixote objects to the "countless beatings" which the historian included and points out that Aeneas was not quite the hero which Virgil describes in the *Aeneid*, Cervantes is not only smiling at a madman but also commenting ironically on the limitations of such concepts as poetic truth, verisimilitude, and exemplarity. When Periandro's account of a dream of paradise enthralls the ladies and infuriates the scientist-classicist Mauricio, Cervantes is reminding us that human beings do in fact spend much time dreaming and that "verisimilar-historical" truth may be less interesting, less human, than subjective truth.

At the same time Cervantes employs reason to undermine the rational system. Herein lies the significance of the Tasso-Ariosto controversy and the various debates which I have traced through Cervantes' writings, as well as the series of comic techniques which he turns on the spokesmen for classical dogmas—the grotesque distortion of their principles, the burlesque of their syllogistic technique of argumentation, and their various self-contradictions. Although Cervantes appropriates specific arguments from classicists who defended the *romanzi*, he does not share their purpose of reconciling Ariosto and Aristotle any more than he shares Ariosto's intention of depicting for the reader the most distant reaches of the fantasy. He uses their arguments to turn reason back on reason and because Ariosto was for him the great exemplar of artistic freedom.

Moreover, classicism's exclusion of the peculiar actualities of experience from the work of art was closely connected with its inadequate notion of the process of aesthetic apprehension. Blinded by their rationalism and their faith that truth is easily apprehensible, the neo-Aristotelians attempted to push the concept of verisimilitude as far as possible in the direction of literal truth, failing to realize that aesthetic belief is of an order completely different from that of empirical belief. Obsessed by the notion that art must capture the belief of its audience and haunted by the implausibilities of the romances of chivalry, they imposed on the artist the obligation of reduplicating an external reality, which then became the sanction of his creation.

Throughout his works Cervantes addresses himself to the Renaissance interpretation of mimesis, ridiculing those who would tether the artist to the stake of factualism and type. Perhaps his clearest statement of the inadequacy of their view can be found in the *Colloquy of the Dogs*, in the opposition between the classical poet, who destroys his play because the director cannot supply the actors with the purple robes necessary for the illusion of reality, and the transcriber of the *Colloquy*, who questions the plausibility of his narration but allows it to survive. At the conclusion of his tale the ensign is embarrassed by its doubtful veracity (normally dogs do not speak) and recalls the reservations which he has made earlier. His companion, the licentiate, disposes of the issue with a tone of finality:

> "Ensign, sir, let us not return to that dispute. I follow the art and invention of the *Colloquy*, and that is enough. Let us now

Conclusion

go to the Espolón to refresh our *physical eyes,* as I have already
refreshed *those of my mind.*"[2]

The physical eye vs. the mind's eye; empirical reality vs. aesthetic
reality; the Renaissance Aristotle, we might add, vs. the true
Aristotle. Like Ariosto, Cervantes knew that artistic reality is illusion, and, living through the neo-Aristotelian movement, he knew
that all its efforts to bring the validating standards of empirical
reality to artistic reality are idle. Art never pretends to be anything
but illusion, and burdening it with such a pretense is in fact en-
dangering its expressive power.

In this context, it is easy to see that Cervantes' hostility to rationalism, factualism, and the presumption of the seeker of truth and
his rejection of literalism in the artistic undertaking are but two sides
of the same coin. When in the opening sentence of his masterpiece
he writes "un lugar de la Mancha de cuyo nombre no quiero acor-
darme," he is not only countering the romance beginning with its
precise lineages and geographies, but he is also reminding the reader
of the illusory quality of the work of art. At the same time he refuses
to yield responsibility for *Don Quixote* to an external reality. It is
the man Cervantes who is speaking, and his utterances need no
divine, scriptural, historical, or empirical authorization. When, in
the following pages, he adds that there is considerable disagreement
concerning the real name of Don Quixote and the location of his
first adventure, he is saying both that truth is elusive and that those
who demand an illusion of truth in a literary work are ignorant of
the fundamental nature of art. Even after the discovery of the
definitive historical manuscript of Cide Hamete Benengeli, who
of course is a member of a lying race, the intentional imprecision
surrounding the history of Don Quixote continues. Did the knight
lie or dream about the events of the Cave of Montesinos? Did
Sancho really say such things to his wife? Was it a beech tree or a
cork tree? We are always aware that we are at three removes from
truth (editor, translator, historian), and occasionally, when one
character reports the narration of another character, truth recedes

[2] "—Señor Alférez, no volvamos más a esa disputa. Yo alcanzo el artificio del
Coloquio y la invención, y basta. Vámonos al Espolón a recrear los *ojos del cuerpo,*
pues ya he recreado *los del entendimiento*" (p. 340). The italics are mine.

346

one or two steps farther away from our vantage point. In Part II the characters occasionally comment on the way in which the author treated them in Part I, and we experience the dizzy feeling of being lost somewhere at the margins of fiction and reality. It would seem that Cervantes is addressing us as if we shared the arrogance of the various seekers of truth whose failures are visible in his works. He mocks us if we accept his narration as truth even as he reminds us: Beware lest you commit the sin of Don Quixote and embrace too tightly the illusion which I am offering you. The work of art becomes a Janus-like image of truth, as it gazes inward toward the flow of experience which it depicts and outward toward the reader, compelling him to engage with the work in an experience analogous to that of its characters as they deal with problems of perception and judgment.[3]

Untouched by the deceptions which victimize reader and characters, the artist reigns serenely alone in the colorful world of experience. Like Pedro de Urdemalas he always looks from afar, but his seat is never so distant as Parnassus' sunny slopes or the austere peak of Zion. It is in this fallen world of humanity—somewhere and everywhere. He knows no home nor will he confine himself within the walls of any city. His favorite haunt is the open road, the symbol of his absolute freedom and the symbol of the limitless variety of man. Along this road he has journeyed through the world mastering its shifting perspectives, its infinite distinctions, and its blend of reality and illusion. With the hasty completion of the *Persiles* Cervantes' journey comes to an end, and, appropriately, in his immortal valediction he describes himself abandoning the open road to enter the gates of Madrid, coming home to die within that order which is everywhere celebrated in his final work. But it is the Cervantes of the open road who continues to speak to us. Always reminding us of the poverty of conventional schemes of order, of

[3] When we observe Don Quixote and Sancho standing "outside of" a book (as they "read," or rather comment on, Part I and the "future" Part II), yet "inside of" a book (the real Part II, which we have in our hands), must we not momentarily ask ourselves whether we too, like the characters who read, might not be in another book? Trapped briefly by the analogy, we feel most poignantly the power of a great theme of Cervantes: the fictional quality of experience. Illusion, madness, books, life itself—all are of a single fabric.

Conclusion

the disproportion of all proportion, he is also telling us that man is rich in his folly and his disorder. As he breathes life into the figures who populate his literary world and leaves them to their own devices to achieve greatness or failure, we behold in his act of creation a double act of faith—faith in humanity and faith in himself.

Bibliography

Primary Sources

Amadís de Gaula. Ed. B.A.E., XL.

Amyot, Jacques. Prologue [to his translation], *L'Histoire aethiopique de Heliodorus*. Paris, 1547.

Apuleius, Lucius. *Lucio Apuleyo del Asno de Oro*. Tr. D. López de Cortegana. Ed. N.B.A.E., XXI.

Ariosto, Ludovico. *Orlando Furioso*. Ed. S. Debenedetti and C. Segre. Bologna, 1960.

Aristotle. *Aristotle's Theory of Poetry and Fine Art*. Ed. and tr. S. H. Butcher. London, 1898.

Augustine. *De Civitate Dei*. Ed. J.E.C. Welldon. 2 vols. London, 1924.

————. *The Confessions of St. Augustine*. Tr. E. B. Pusey. Everyman's Library. London, 1926.

Balbuena, Bernardo de. Prologue to *El Bernardo*. Ed. B.A.E., XVII.

Campanella, Tommaso. *Poetica*. Ed. L. Firpo. Rome, 1944.

Capella, Martianus. *De nuptiis philologiae et Mercurii et de septem artibus liberalibus*. Frankfurt am Main, 1836.

Capellanus, Andreas. *The Art of Courtly Love*. Tr. J. J. Parry. New York, 1941.

Cartari, Vincenzo. *Imagini delli dei de gl'antichi*. Ed. W. Koschatzky. Graz, 1963.

Carvallo, Luis Alfonso de. *Cisne de Apolo*. Ed. A. Porqueras Mayo. 2 vols. Madrid, 1958.

Cascales, Francisco. *Tablas poéticas*. Ed. A. de Sancha. Madrid, 1779.

Castelvetro, Lodovico. *Poetica d'Aristotele vvlgarizzata*. Basel, 1576.

Cervantes Saavedra, Miguel de. *Comedias y entremeses*. Ed. R. Schevill and A. Bonilla. 6 vols. Madrid, 1915-1922.

————. *Don Quijote de la Mancha*. Ed. M. de Riquer. 2 vols. Barcelona, 1958.

————. *El ingenioso hidalgo Don Quijote de la Mancha*. Ed. D. Clemencín. 8 vols. Madrid, 1894.

————. *El ingenioso hidalgo Don Quijote de la Mancha*. Ed. F. Rodríguez Marín. 8 vols. Madrid, 1911-1913.

————. *La Galatea*. Ed. J. B. Avalle-Arce. 2 vols. Madrid, 1961.

————. *Novelas ejemplares*. Ed. F. Rodríguez Marín. 2 vols. Madrid, 1914, 1917.

————. *Novelas exemplares*. Ed. R. Schevill and A. Bonilla. 3 vols. Madrid, 1922-1925.

————. *Obras completas*. Ed. A. Valbuena Prat. Madrid, 1956.

————. *Persiles y Sigismunda*. Ed. R. Schevill and A. Bonilla. 2 vols. Madrid, 1914.

————. *Viage del Parnaso*. Ed. R. Schevill and A. Bonilla. Madrid, 1922.

Bibliography

Cicero. *Disputationes Tusculanae.* Loeb Classical Library. Cambridge, Mass., 1950.

Conti, Natale. *Mythologiae.* Geneva, 1651.

Contreras, Jerónimo de. *Selva de aventuras.* Ed. B.A.E., III.

Covarrubias, Sebastián de. *Tesoro de la lengua castellana o española.* Ed. M. de Riquer. Barcelona, 1943.

Galilei, Galileo. *Scritti letterari.* Ed. A. Chiari. Florence, 1943.

Giraldi Cintio, Giovambattista. *Scritti estetici* (includes *De' romanzi; Delle comedie; Delle tragedie*). Ed. G. Antimaco. Milan, 1864.

Góngora, Luis de. *Obras completas.* Ed. A. Marasso. Buenos Aires, 1955.

Gracián, Baltasar. *Agudeza y arte de ingenio, Obras completas.* Ed. A. del Hoyo. Madrid, 1960.

––––––. *El criticón.* Ed. M. Romera-Navarro. 3 vols. Philadelphia, 1938-1940.

Granada, Fray Luis de. *Del símbolo de la fe.* Ed. B.A.E., VI.

Hebreo, León. *Diálogos de amor.* Tr. Garcilaso Inga de la Vega. Ed. E. Juliá Martínez. 2 vols. Madrid, 1949.

Heliodorus. *Historia etiópica de los amores de Teágenes y Cariclea.* Tr. F. de Mena. Ed. F. López Estrada. Madrid, 1954.

Homer. *Odyssey.* Loeb Classical Library. 2 vols. London, 1931.

Horace. *The Works of Horace.* Ed. A. J. MacLeane. Cambridge, Mass., 1856.

Huarte de San Juan, Juan. *Examen de ingenios.* Ed. B.A.E., LXV.

Huet, Pierre-Daniel. *Traité de l'origine des romans.* Ed. A. Kok. Amsterdam, 1942.

La Noue, François de. *Discovrs politiqves, et militaires.* n. p., 1612.

Longus. *Daphnis and Chloe.* Ed. Loeb Classical Library. New York, 1924.

López Pinciano, Alonso [El Pinciano]. *Philosophía antigua poética.* Ed. A. Carballo Picazo. 3 vols. Madrid, 1953.

Marino, Giovanni Battista. *L'Adone.* Venice, 1626.

Martínez de Toledo, Alfonso. *El Arcipreste de Talavera.* Ed. L. B. Simpson. Berkeley, 1939.

Minturno, Antonio Sebastiano. *L'arte poetica.* Venice, 1564.

Montaigne. *Les Essais.* Ed. M. Rat. 3 vols. Paris, 1958.

Núñez de Reinoso, Alonso. *Historia de los amores de Clareo y Florisea y de los trabajos de Isea.* Ed. B.A.E., III.

Petrarca, Francesco. *I trionfi.* Ed. E. Chiorboli. Bari, 1930.

Pigna, Giovanni Battista. *I romanzi.* Venice, 1554.

Plato. *Ion. Plato Selections.* Ed. R. Demos. New York, 1955.

Plato. *Republic.* Ed. F. M. Cornford. New York, 1956.

Porphyrius. *Select Works.* Tr. T. Taylor. London, 1823.

Ripa, Cesare. *Iconologia.* Siena, 1613.

Sannazaro, Jacopo. *Arcadia.* Ed. M. Scherillo. Turin, 1888.

Scaliger, Julius Caesar. *Poetices libri septem.* Facsim. edition of 1561 edition of Lyon by August Buck. Stuttgart-Bad Cannstatt, 1964.

Bibliography

Sidney, Philip. *An Apologie for Poetrie*, in G. G. Smith's *Elizabethan Critical Essays*, Vol. I. Oxford, 1904.

Spenser, Edmund. *The Poetical Works of Edmund Spenser*. Ed. F. J. Child. 5 vols. Boston, 1855.

Strabo. *The Geography of Strabo*. Loeb Classical Library. 8 vols. London, New York, 1917-1932.

Tasso, Torquato. *Discorsi dell'arte poetica e del poema eroico*. Ed. L. Poma. Bari, 1964.

——. *Gerusalemme liberata, Opere*, Vol. III. Ed. B. Maier. Milan, 1963.

——. *Le lettere di Torquato Tasso*. Ed. C. Guasti. 5 vols. Florence, 1853-1855.

——. *Rinaldo*. Ed. L. Bonfigli. Bari, 1936.

Tatius, Achilles. *Clitophon and Leucippe*. Loeb Classical Library. London, 1917.

Torquemada, Antonio de. *Jardín de flores curiosas*. Ed. A. de Amezúa. Madrid, 1943.

Trissino, Giovanni Giorgio. *Tutte le opere*. 2 vols. Verona, 1729.

Valdés, Juan de. *Diálogo de la lengua*. Ed J. Montesinos. Clásicos Castellanos, no. 96. Madrid, 1964.

Vauquelin de la Fresnaye, Jean. *L'Art poétique*. Ed. G. Pellissier. Paris, 1885.

Vega Carpio, Lope de. *El peregrino en su patria, Obras sueltas*, Vol. V. Madrid, 1776.

——. *Jerusalén conquistada*. Ed. J. de Entrambasaguas. 3 vols. Madrid, 1951-1954.

Virgil. *The Aeneid*. Tr. W. F. Jackson Knight. Penguin Books. London, 1956.

Vives, Juan Luis. *Obras completas*. Tr. L. Riber. 2 vols. Madrid, 1947-1948.

——. *De institutione feminae christianae. Opera omnia*, Vol. IV. Valencia, 1783.

Secondary Sources

Abrams, M. H. "Belief and the Suspension of Disbelief," *Literature and Belief. English Institute Essays, 1957*. Ed. M. H. Abrams. New York, 1958.

——. *The Mirror and the Lamp*. Norton Library, N102. New York, 1958.

Arco y Garay, Ricardo del. "Estética cervantina en el 'Persiles,'" *Revista de Ideas Estéticas*, VI (1948), 167-173.

Asensio, Eugenio. *Itinerario del entremés*. Madrid, 1965.

Atkinson, William C. "Cervantes, El Pinciano and the 'Novelas ejemplares,'" *Hispanic Review*, XVI (1948), 189-208.

——. "The Enigma of the Persiles," *Bulletin of Spanish Studies*, XXIV (1947), 242-253.

——. "Miguel de Cervantes," *Fortnightly Review* (November, 1947), 371-378.

Bibliography

Auerbach, Erich. *Mimesis*. Tr. W. Trask. Anchor Books, A107. New York, 1957.

Avalle-Arce, J. B. *Deslindes cervantinos*. Madrid, 1961.

———. *La novela pastoril española*. Madrid, 1959.

Azorín [José Martínez Ruiz]. *Al margen de los clásicos*. Madrid, 1921.

Babelon, Jean. "Cervantes y lo maravilloso nórdico," *Cuadernos de Insula*, I (1947), 117-130.

Báig Baños, Aurelio. "Sobre el Persiles y Sigismunda," *Revista Castellana*. Valladolid. V (1919), 61-64, 138-142, 188-189.

Banal, Luisa. *L'ultimo romanzo di Miguel de Cervantes*. Florence, 1923.

Barto, P. S. "The Subterranean Grail Paradise of Cervantes," *PMLA*, XXXVIII (1923), 401-411.

Bataillon, Marcel. "Cervantès et le 'marriage chrétien,'" *Bulletin Hispanique*, XLIX (1947), 129-144.

———. *Erasmo y España*. Tr. A. Alatorre. 2 vols. Mexico, 1950.

———. "Gutiérrez de Santa Clara, escritor mexicano," *Nueva Revista de Filología Hispánica*, XV (1961), 405-440.

———. "La Dénonciation mensongère dans La Gitanilla," *Bulletin Hispanique*, LII (1950), 274-276.

Bell, Aubrey. *Cervantes*. Norman, Oklahoma, 1947.

Beltrán y Rózpide, Ricardo. "La pericia geográfica de Cervantes demostrada con la historia de los Trabajos de Persiles y Sigismunda," *Boletín de la Real Sociedad Geográfica*, LXIV (1923), 270-293.

Benardete, M. J. and Flores, A. *Cervantes across the Centuries*. New York, 1947.

Boehlich, Walter. "Heliodorus Christianus: Cervantes und der Byzantinische Roman," *Freundesgabe für Ernst Robert Curtius*. Bern, 1956.

Boje, Christian. *Über den altfranzösischen Roman von Beuve de Hamtone. Beihefte zur Zeitschrift für Romanische Philologie*, 19. Heft. Halle, 1909.

Bonilla, Adolfo. *Cervantes y su obra*. Madrid, 1916.

Booth, Wayne C. *The Rhetoric of Fiction*. Chicago, 1965.

———. "The Self-Conscious Narrator in Comic Fiction before *Tristram Shandy*," *PMLA*, LXVII (1952), 163-185.

Borinski, Karl. *Die Antike in Poetik und Kunsttheorie*. 2 vols. Leipzig, 1914, 1924.

Brinkschulte, Eduard. *Julius Caesar Scaligers Kunsttheoretische Anschauungen und deren Hauptquellen, Renaissance und Philosophie*, No. 10. Bonn, 1914.

Brüggemann, Werner. *Cervantes und die Figur des Don Quijote in Kunstanschauung und Dichtung der Deutschen Romantik*. Münster, 1958.

Buck, August. Introduction to his edition of J. C. Scaliger's *Poetices libri septem*. Stuttgart-Bad Cannstatt, 1964.

———. *Italienische Dichtungslehren vom Mittelalter bis zum Ausgang der*

Bibliography

Renaissance. Beihefte zur Zeitschrift für Romanische Philologie, 94. Heft. Tübingen, 1952.

Bush, Douglas. *Prefaces to Renaissance Literature.* The Norton Library, N261. New York, 1965.

Butcher, S. H. *Aristotle's Theory of Poetry and Fine Art.* London, 1898.

Calcaterra, Carlo. *Il parnaso in rivolta.* Bologna, 1961.

Canavaggio, Jean-François. "Alonso López Pinciano y la estética literaria de Cervantes en el 'Quijote,'" *Anales Cervantinos*, VII (1958), 13-107.

Casalduero, Joaquín. *Sentido y forma de las novelas ejemplares.* Madrid, 1962.

———. *Sentido y forma de "Los trabajos de Persiles y Sigismvnda."* Buenos Aires, 1947.

———. *Sentido y forma del Quijote.* Madrid, 1949.

———. *Sentido y forma del teatro de Cervantes.* Madrid, 1951.

Cassirer, Ernst. *The Individual and the Cosmos in Renaissance Philosophy.* Tr. M. Domandi. Harper Torchbooks, TB1097. New York, 1964.

Castro, Américo. "Cide Hamete Benengeli: el cómo y el por qué," *Mundo Nuevo* (Feb., 1967), 5-9.

———. *El pensamiento de Cervantes.* Madrid, 1925.

———. *Hacia Cervantes.* Madrid, 1967.

———. "La comedia clásica," in A. del Río and M. J. Benardete's *El concepto contemporáneo de España.* New York, 1962.

———. "Noruega, símbolo de la oscuridad," *Revista de Filología Española*, VI (1919), 184-186.

Charlton, H. B. *Castelvetro's Theory of Poetry.* Manchester, 1913.

Chevalier, Maxime. *L'Arioste en Espagne.* Bordeaux, 1966.

Cotarelo y Valledor, Armando. *El teatro de Cervantes.* Madrid, 1915.

Croce, Benedetto. Review of J. Casalduero's *Sentido y forma de "Los trabajos de Persiles y Sigismvnda,"* *Quaderni della Critica*, XII (1948), 71-78.

Curtius, Ernst Robert. "Zur Literarästhetik des Mittelalters I.," *Zeitschrift für Romanische Philologie*, LVIII (1938), 1-50.

———. *Europäische Literatur und Lateinisches Mittelalter.* Bern, 1948.

De Lollis, Cesare. *Cervantes reazionario.* Rome, 1924.

Deutsch, Helene. "Don Quijote und Donquijotismus," *Almanach der Psychoanalyse* (1935), 151-160.

Dilthey, Wilhelm. *Weltanschauung und Analyse des Menschen seit Renaissance und Reformation, Gesammelte Schriften*, Vol. II. Leipzig, 1914.

Dunlop, John C. *History of Prose Fiction.* 2 vols. London, 1896.

Durán, Manuel. *La ambigüedad en el Quijote.* Xalapa, Mexico, 1960.

Durling, Robert M. *The Figure of the Poet in Renaissance Epic.* Cambridge, Mass., 1965.

Endt, Johann. "Der Gebrauch der Apostrophe bei den lateinischen Epikern," *Wiener Studien*, XXVII (1905), 106-129.

Bibliography

Entrambasaguas y Peña, Joaquín de. *Lope de Vega y los preceptistas aristotélicos.* Madrid, 1932.

Entwistle, William. *Cervantes.* Oxford, 1940.

——. Review of Casalduero's *Sentido y forma de "Los trabajos de Persiles y Sigismvnda," Modern Language Review,* XLIII (1948), 426-429.

Farinelli, Arturo. "El último sueño de Cervantes," *Ensayos y discursos de crítica literaria hispano-europea,* Vol. I. Rome, 1925.

——. *Italia e Spagna.* 2 vols. Turin, 1929.

Fernández Gómez, Carlos. *Vocabulario de Cervantes.* Madrid, 1962.

Fitzmaurice-Kelly, James. *Miguel de Cervantes Saavedra.* Oxford, 1913.

Friedman, Norman. "Point of View in Fiction," *PMLA,* LXX (1955), 1160-1184.

Friedrich, Hugo. *Epochen der Italienischen Lyrik.* Frankfurt, 1964.

Friedrich, Klaus. "Eine Theorie des 'Roman nouveau,' 1683," *Romanistisches Jahrbuch,* XIV (1963), 105-132.

Fritz, Kurt von. "Entstehung und Inhalt des Neunten Kapitels von Aristoteles 'Poetik,'" *Antike und moderne Tragödie.* Berlin, 1962.

Frye, Northrop. *Anatomy of Criticism.* Princeton, 1957.

Fucilla, J. G. "The Cave of Montesinos," *Italica,* XXIX (1952), 170-173.

Gerhardt, Mia. *Don Quijote: la vie et les livres.* Amsterdam, 1955.

——. *La Pastorale.* Assen, 1950.

Giamatti, A. Bartlett. *The Earthly Paradise and the Renaissance Epic.* Princeton, 1966.

Gillet, Joseph. "Clavileño: su fuente directa y sus orígenes primitivos," *Anales Cervantinos,* VI (1957), 251-255.

——. "The Autonomous Character in Spanish and European Literature," *Hispanic Review,* XXIV (1956), 179-190.

Gmelin, Hermann. "Das Prinzip der Imitatio in den romanischen Literaturen der Renaissance," *Romanische Forschungen,* XLVI (1932), 83-360.

Godoy Alcántara, José. *Historia crítica de los falsos cronicones.* Madrid, 1868.

Green, Otis H. "El 'ingenioso' hidalgo," *Hispanic Review,* XXV (1957), 175-193.

——. *Spain and the Western Tradition.* 4 vols. Madison, Wisconsin, 1963-1966.

Greene, Thomas. *The Descent from Heaven: a Study in Epic Continuity.* New Haven, 1963.

Grismer, Raymond L. *Cervantes: a Bibliography.* 2 vols. New York, 1946 and Minneapolis, 1963.

Grube, G.M.A. *The Greek and Roman Critics.* Toronto, 1965.

Gudemann, A. *Aristoteles peri poietikes.* Berlin, 1934.

Guerrieri Crocetti, C. *G. B. Giraldi ed il pensiero critico del sec. XVI.* Milan, 1932.

Bibliography

Haley, George. "The Narrator in Don Quijote: Maese Pedro's Puppet Show," *Modern Language Notes*, LXXX (1965), 145-165.

Hamburger, Käte. "Don Quijote und die Struktur des Epischen Humors," *Festgabe für Eduard Berend*. Weimar, 1959.

Hathaway, Baxter. *The Age of Criticism: the Late Renaissance in Italy*. Ithaca, New York, 1962.

Hatzfeld, Helmut. *"Don Quijote" als Wortkunstwerk*. Leipzig, 1927.

———. *Estudios sobre el Barroco*. Various translators. Madrid, 1964.

———. "Three National Deformations of Aristotle: Tesauro, Gracián, Boileau," *Studi Secenteschi*, II (1961), 3-21.

Hazard, Paul. *Don Quichotte de Cervantès*. Paris, 1949.

Hefti, Victor. *Zur Erzählungstechnik in Heliodors Aethiopica*. Vienna, 1950.

Heinze, Richard. *Virgils Epische Technik*. Leipzig, 1908.

Herrick, Marvin T. *The Fusion of Horatian and Aristotelian Literary Criticism, 1531-1555, Illinois Studies in Language and Literature*, Vol. XXXII. Urbana, 1946.

Hibbard, Laura A. "Jacques de Vitry and Boeve de Haumtone," *Modern Language Notes*, XXXIV (1919), 408-411.

Highet, Gilbert. *The Classical Tradition*. Oxford, 1949.

Huizinga, John. *Homo Ludens*. London, 1949.

Hutton, James. "Some English Poems in Praise of Music," *English Miscellany*, II (1951), 1-63.

Kaiser, Walter. *Praisers of Folly*. Cambridge, Mass., 1963.

Keyes, C. W. "The Structure of Heliodorus' 'Aethiopica,'" *Studies in Philology*, XIX (1922), 42-51.

Krauss, Werner. "Die Kritik des Siglo de Oro am Ritter- und Schäferroman," *Gesammelte Aufsätze*. Frankfurt, 1949.

———. *Miguel de Cervantes: Leben und Werk*. Neuwied, 1966.

———. "Novela-Novella-Roman," *Gesammelte Aufsätze*. Frankfurt, 1949.

———. "Zur Bedeutungsgeschichte von 'romanesque' im 17. Jahrhundert," *Gesammelte Aufsätze*. Frankfurt, 1949.

Kristeller, Paul Oskar. *Renaissance Thought*. Harper Torchbooks, TB1048. New York, 1961.

Kruse, Margot. "Cervantes und Ariost," *Romanistisches Jahrbuch*, XII (1961), 248-264.

Lapesa, Rafael. "En torno a La española inglesa y El Persiles," *Homenaje a Cervantes*, Vol. II, Valencia, 1950.

Larsen, Karl. "Cervantes' Vorstellungen vom Norden," *Studien zur vergleichenden Literaturgeschichte*, V (1905), 273-296.

Leo, Ulrich, *Torquato Tasso: Studien zur Vorgeschichte des Secentismo*. Bern, 1951.

Levin, Harry. "Contexts of the Classical," *Contexts of Criticism*. Atheneum 29. New York, 1963.

Bibliography

Levin, Harry. "The Example of Cervantes," *Contexts of Criticism*. Atheneum 29. New York, 1963.

Lida de Malkiel, María Rosa. "Dos huellas del Esplandián en el *Quijote* y el *Persiles*," *Romance Philology*, IX (1955), 156-162.

Llorens, Vicente. "Don Quixote and the Decline of the Spanish *Hidalgo*." Lecture delivered at Fordham University, April 23, 1968 (to be published by Fordham University).

————. "Historia y ficción en el *Quijote*," *Literatura, historia, política*. Madrid, 1967.

————. "La intención del *Quijote*," *Literatura, historia, política*. Madrid, 1967.

López Estrada, Francisco. *Estudio crítico de La Galatea*. La Laguna de Tenerife, 1948.

————. "La novela de Feliciana y Rosanio en el *Persiles* o los extremosos amores de la Extremadura," *Anales Cervantinos*, VI (1957), 333-356.

————. Prologue to his edition of Heliodorus' *Historia etiópica*. Madrid, 1954.

Lorck, E. *Die "Erlebte Rede": Eine Sprachliche Untersuchung*. Heidelberg, 1921.

Lovejoy, A. O. "Nature as an Aesthetic Norm," in *Essays in the History of Ideas*. Baltimore, 1948.

———— and G. Boas. *Primitivism and Related Ideas in Antiquity*. Baltimore, 1935.

Lubac, André. "La France et les français dans le 'Persiles,' " *Anales Cervantinos*, I (1951), 111-130.

Madariaga, Salvador de. *Guía del lector del "Quijote."* Madrid, 1926.

Maldonado de Guevara, F. "Del 'Ingenium' de Cervantes al de Gracián," *Anales Cervantinos*, VI (1957), 97-111.

Marasso, Arturo. *Cervantes: la invención del Quijote*. Buenos Aires, 1954.

Maravall, José Antonio. *El humanismo de las armas en Don Quijote*. Madrid, 1948.

Meier, Harri. "Personenhandlung und Geschehen in Cervantes' *Gitanilla*," *Romanische Forschungen*, LI (1937), 125-186.

————. "Zur Entwicklung der europäischen Quijote-Deutung," *Romanische Forschungen*, LIV (1940), 227-264.

Menéndez y Pelayo, Marcelino, "Cultura literaria de Miguel de Cervantes y elaboración del 'Quijote,' " *Discursos*. Ed. J. M. Cossío. Madrid, 1956.

————. *Historia de las ideas estéticas en España*. 5 vols. Madrid, 1940.

————. *Orígenes de la novela, Obras completas*, Vols. XIII-XVI. Santander, 1943.

Montgomery, Robert L. "Allegory and the Incredible Fable," *PMLA*, LXXXI (1966), 45-55.

Bibliography

Novo, Pedro de y F. Chicarro. *Bosquejo para una edición crítica de "Los trabajos de Persiles y Sigismunda."* Madrid, 1928.

Oeftering, Michael. *Heliodor und seine Bedeutung für die Literatur, Litterarhistorische Forschungen*, Vol. XVIII. Berlin, 1901.

Olmedo, Félix. *El Amadís y el Quijote* (contains an essay on *Persiles y Sigismunda*). Madrid, 1947.

Ortega y Gasset, José. *Meditaciones del Quijote.* Madrid: Revista de Occidente, 1958.

Oviedo y Valdés, Gonzalo Fernández de. *Historia general y natural de las Indias.* Ed. J. Amador de los Ríos. 14 vols. Asunción del Paraguay, 1944-1945.

Panofsky, Erwin. *Idea: ein Beitrag zur Begriffsgeschichte der älteren Kunsttheorie.* Berlin, 1960.

Parker, A. A. "'Don Quixote' and the Relativity of Truth," *The Dublin Review*, No. 441 (Autumn, 1947), 28-37.

Patch, Howard R. *The Other World according to Descriptions in Medieval Literature.* Cambridge, Mass., 1950.

Paul, Jean [Johann Paul Richter]. *Vorschule der Aesthetik, Sämtliche Werke*, Vol. XI. Weimar, 1935.

Petriconi, Hellmuth. "Die Verlorenen Paradiese," *Romanistisches Jahrbuch*, X (1959), 167-199.

———. "Die verschmähte Astarte," *Romanistisches Jahrbuch*, XIII (1962), 149-185.

Pfandl, Ludwig. "Cervantes und der spanische Renaissance-Roman," *Jahrbuch für Philologie*, I (1925), 373-392.

———. "Die Zwischenspiele des Cervantes," *Neue Jahrbücher für Wissenschaft und Jugendbildung*, III (1927), 301-323.

Pierce, Frank. *La poesía épica del Siglo de Oro.* Tr. J. C. Cayol de Bethencourt. Madrid, 1961.

Predmore, Richard L. *The World of Don Quixote.* Cambridge, Mass., 1967.

Raimondi, Ezio. "Ingegno e metafora nella poetica del Tesauro," *Letteratura Barocca.* Florence, 1961.

Rajna, Pio. *Le fonti dell'Orlando Furioso.* Florence, 1900.

Randall, Dale B. *The Golden Tapestry: a Critical Survey of Non-chivalric Spanish Fiction in English Translation, 1543-1657.* Durham, North Carolina, 1963.

Reichenberger, Kurt. "Cervantes und die Literarischen Gattungen," *Germanisch Romanische Monatsschrift*, XIII (1963), 233-246.

Remos, Juan J. "Persiles," *Anales Cervantinos*, V (1955-1956), 159-182.

Riley, E. C. *Cervantes's Theory of the Novel.* Oxford, 1962.

Río, Angel del. "El equívoco del 'Quijote,'" *Hispanic Review*, XXVII (1959), 200-221.

Bibliography

Rivers, Elias. "The Pastoral Paradox of Natural Art," *Modern Language Notes*, LXXVII (1962), 130-144.

Robert, Marthe. *L'Ancien et le nouveau (De Don Quichotte à Franz Kafka)*. Paris, 1963.

Rohde, Erwin. *Der Griechische Roman und seine Vorläufer*. Leipzig, 1900.

Rousset, Jean. *La Littérature de l'âge baroque en France*. Paris, 1954.

Rubin, Louis. *The Teller in the Tale*. Seattle, 1967.

Rüegg, August. *Miguel de Cervantes und sein Don Quijote*. Bern, 1949.

Russo, Luigi. "La poetica di Aristotile e la coerenza degli interpreti del Rinascimento," *Problemi di metodo critico*. Bari, 1929.

Salillas, Rafael. *Un gran inspirador de Cervantes: el Doctor Huarte de San Juan y su Examen de ingenios*. Madrid, 1905.

Sánchez, Alberto. "El 'Persiles' como repertorio de moralidades," *Anales Cervantinos*, IV (1954), 199-223.

Sánchez Escribano, Federico. "Cervantes ante el problema aristotélico de la relación entre la fábula y los episodios," *Hispanófila*, No. 12 (1961), 33-37.

Savj-López, Paolo. *Cervantes*. Tr. A. Solalinde. Madrid, 1917.

Schevill, Rudolph. *Cervantes*. New York, 1919.

————. "Studies in Cervantes. I. 'Persiles y Sigismunda': Introduction," *Modern Philology*, IV (1906-1907), 1-24.

————. "Studies in Cervantes. I. 'Persiles y Sigismunda': The Question of Heliodorus," *Modern Philology*, IV (1906-1907), 677-704.

————. "Studies in Cervantes. 'Persiles y Sigismunda': III. Virgil's Aeneid," *Publications of Yale University*, XIII (1908), 475-548.

———— and Bonilla, Adolfo. Introduction to their edition of *Persiles y Sigismunda*. Madrid, 1914.

Schissel von Fleschenberg, Otmar. "Der byzantinische Garten: seine Darstellung im gleichzeitigen Romane," *Sitzungsberichte der Akademie der Wissenschaften in Wien*, CCXXI (1942), 1-69.

————. *Entwicklungsgeschichte des griechischen Romanes im Altertum*. Halle, 1913.

Schlegel, Friedrich. *Wissenschaft der europäischen Literatur, Kritische Ausgabe*, Vol. XI. Zürich, 1958.

Schürr, Friedrich. *Cervantes*. Essen, 1947.

Selig, Karl-Ludwig. "Concerning the Structure of Cervantes' *La Gitanilla*," *Romanistisches Jahrbuch*, XIII (1962), 273-276.

Seznec, Jean. *The Survival of the Pagan Gods*. Tr. B. Sessions. Harper Torchbooks, TB2004. New York, 1961.

Shepard, Sanford. *El Pinciano y las teorías literarias del Siglo de Oro*. Madrid, 1962.

Singleton, Mack. "El misterio del *Persiles*," *Realidad*, II (1947), 237-253.

358

Bibliography

Sletsjöe, Leif. "Cervantes, Torquemada y Olao Magno," *Anales Cervantinos*, VIII (1959-1960), 139-150.

Snodgrass El Saffar, Ruth. "The Function of the Fictional Narrator in *Don Quijote*," *Modern Language Notes*, LXXXIII (1968), 164-177.

Solerti, Angelo. *Vita di Torquato Tasso*. 3 vols. Rome, 1895.

Spingarn, Joel E. *Literary Criticism in the Renaissance*. Harbinger Books. New York, 1963.

Spitzer, Leo. *Classical and Christian Ideas of World Harmony*. Baltimore, 1963.

——. "Die Frage der Heuchelei des Cervantes," *Zeitschrift für Romanische Philologie*, LVI (1936), 138-178.

——. "La Norvège comme symbole de l'obscurité," *Revista de Filología Española*, IX (1922), 316-317.

——. "Linguistic Perspectivism in the *Don Quijote*," *Linguistics and Literary History*. Princeton, 1967.

——. "Note on the Poetic and the Empirical 'I' in Medieval Authors," *Traditio*, IV (1946), 414-422.

——. "On the Significance of *Don Quijote*," *Modern Language Notes*, LXXVII (1962), 113-129.

——. "The Poetic Treatment of a Platonic-Christian Theme," *Romanische Literaturstudien*. Tübingen, 1959.

Spoerri, Theophil. *Renaissance und Barock bei Ariost und Tasso*. Bern, 1922.

Stagg, Geoffrey. "El sabio Cide Hamete Venengeli," *Bulletin of Hispanic Studies*, XXXIII (1956), 218-225.

——. "Plagiarism in 'La Galatea,'" *Filologia Romanza*, VI (1959), 255-276.

Tayler, Edward W. *Nature and Art in Renaissance Literature*. New York, 1964.

Thomas, Henry. *Spanish and Portuguese Romances of Chivalry*. Cambridge, England, 1920.

Tigerstedt, E. N. "Observations on the Reception of the Aristotelian *Poetics* in the Latin West," *Studies in the Renaissance*, XV (1968), 7-24.

Tillyard, E.M.W. *The Elizabethan World Picture*. Vintage Books, V-162. New York, n.d.

Todemann, Friedrich. "Die erlebte Rede im Spanischen," *Romanische Forschungen*, XLIV (1930), 103-184.

Toffanin, Giuseppe. *La fine dell' umanesimo*. Turin, 1920.

Trueblood, Alan S. "Sobre la selección artística en el *Quijote*: '. . . lo que ha dejado de escribir,'" *Nueva Revista de Filología Hispánica*, X (1956), 44-50.

Vilanova, Antonio. "El peregrino andante en el *Persiles* de Cervantes," *Boletín de la Real Academia de Buenas Letras* (Barcelona), XXII (1949), 97-159.

Bibliography

Vilanova, Antonio. "Preceptistas de los siglos XVI y XVII," *Historia general de las literaturas hispánicas.* Ed. D. G. Díaz-Plaja. Vol. III. Barcelona, 1953.

Vossler, Karl. *Die Poesie der Einsamkeit in Spanien.* München, 1940.

————. *Introducción a la literatura española del Siglo de Oro.* Colección Austral. Mexico, 1961.

Walzel, Oskar. "Aristotelisches und Plotinisches bei Julius Cäsar Scaliger und Giordano Bruno," *Vom Geistesleben Alter und Neuer Zeit.* Leipzig, 1922.

Wardropper, Bruce W. "Cervantes' Theory of the Drama," *Modern Philology,* LII (1955), 217-221.

————. "*Don Quixote*: Story or History?", *Modern Philology,* LXIII (1965), 1-11.

Weinberg, Bernard. *A History of Literary Criticism in the Italian Renaissance.* 2 vols. Chicago, 1961.

Weinrich, Harald. *Das Ingenium Don Quijotes.* Münster, 1956.

Willis, Raymond S. "Sancho Panza: Prototype for the Modern Novel," *Hispanic Review,* XXXVII (1969), 207-227.

————. *The Phantom Chapters of the Quijote.* New York, 1953.

Wolff, Max Ludwig. *Geschichte der Romantheorie.* Nuremberg, 1915.

Wolff, Samuel. *The Greek Romances in Elizabethan Prose Fiction.* New York, 1912.

Zimic, Stanislav. "Cervantes, lector de Aquiles Tacio y de Alonso Núñez de Reinoso." Dissertation. Duke University, 1964.

Zonta, Giuseppe. "Rinascimento, aristotelismo e barocco," *Giornale Storico della Letteratura Italiana,* CIV (1934), 1-63, 185-240.

Index

Index

362

Index

Index

Index

theories of unity, 28, 29, 30, 43, 65, 117, 119, 120, 195, 198, 199, 202, 203, 204

Tatius, Achilles, 3, 19, 49, 67, 76, 77, 83, 217

Tayler, Edward W., 213, 218, 220, 235

Teresa of Avila, St., 13

Tesauro, Emanuele, 235, 249, 327

Thomas, Henry, 13, 18, 66

Tieck, Ludwig, 185

Tillyard, E.M.W., 313

Todemann, Friedrich, 260

Toffanin, Giuseppe, 4, 78, 106, 126, 136

Torquemada, Antonio de, 40, 138, 153, 271, 288

Trissino, Giovanni Giorgio, 27, 28, 44, 63; *L'Italia liberata dai goti*, 22, 23, 105, 117; *Le sei divisioni della poetica*, 23, 34, 42

Trueblood, Alan S., 155, 163

Turpin, 54, 80, 156

Unamuno, Miguel de, 7

Urania, 313

Urfé, Honoré d', 55

Valdés, Juan de, 19, 20, 21, 30, 44, 95

Valerius Flaccus, 67

Valla, Giorgio, 45

Vanegas de Busto, Alejo, 17, 92

Vauquelin de la Fresnaye, Jean, 69

Vega, Lope de, 249, 251; *La Dorotea*, 283; *Jerusalén conquistada*, 147, 239, 250; *El peregrino en su patria*, 96, 100, 102, 248, 291; *comedia*, 126, 150, 339

Velasco, Gregorio Hernández de, 200

Vergara, Francisco de, 49

Vida, Marco Girolamo, 76

Virgil, 12, 22, 28, 29, 62, 64, 72, 74, 76, 86, 118, 119, 184, 213, 217, 339; *Aeneid*, 11, 36, 67, 83, 87, 100, 137, 147, 181, 193, 194, 201, 208, 214, 215, 247, 268, 283, 290, 344; *Georgics*, 278, 279; narrative methods, 23, 32, 35, 66, 68, 75, 80, 99, 122, 123, 148, 175, 187, 198, 200, 227, 255, 258, 259, 261, 262, 273

Vitry, Jaques de, 246, 251

Vives, Juan Luis, 15, 16, 17, 44, 91, 95

Vossler, Karl, 283, 291

Wardropper, Bruce W., 126, 155, 156, 181

Warschewicski, Stanislaus, 49

Weinberg, Bernard, 24, 44, 47, 98, 103, 105, 113, 116, 117, 119, 123, 135, 228, 279

Weinrich, Harald, 127, 129, 275

Willis, Raymond S., 155

Wolff, Max Ludwig, 51

Zonta, Giuseppe, 47, 48

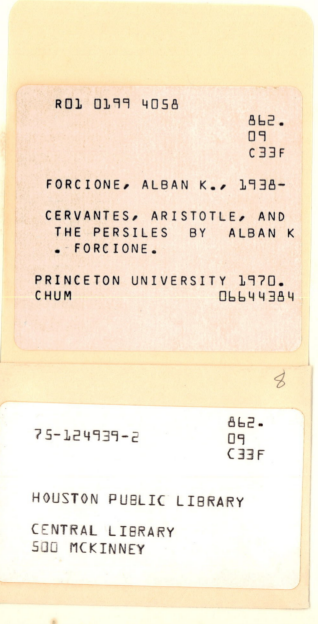